THE AMERICAN EMPIRE

Books by Amaury de Riencourt

THE AMERICAN EMPIRE

THE SOUL OF INDIA

THE SOUL OF CHINA

THE COMING CAESARS

ROOF OF THE WORLD

Amaury de Riencourt

THE AMERICAN EMPIRE

The Dial Press, Inc. New York, 1968

ACKNOWLEDGMENTS

Grateful acknowledgements are made for permission to use in this work material included in articles contributed by the author to *Orbis,* a quarterly journal published by the Foreign Policy Research Institute, and to *Life,* International Editions. Also, warm thanks are expressed to S.S. and M.A.H. for valued editorial assistance.

Contents

Introduction   vii

Chapter I   The Roots   3

II   The Suicide of Europe   32

III   Pearl Harbor: The Genesis of Empire   57

IV   Cold War: The Establishment of Empire   78

V   The Tools of Empire   96

VI   The Road to Suez   117

VII   Death and Transfiguration of the Commonwealth   139

VIII   Frontier Across the Pacific   161

IX   The Hawaiianization of the Orient   182

X   Latins, Guerillas, and Anarchists   202

XI   Race and Africa   233

XII   Empire and Nation-State: The Future of Europe   255

XIII   Economic Hegemony   280

XIV   The Great Condominium   310

Bibliography   339

Notes and References   343

Index   354

Introduction

Eleven years have gone by since the historical trends I described in *The Coming Caesars* appeared in print, and worldwide events during these years have brought them out in bold relief—the twin trend toward Executive predominance in Washington and toward the imperial extension of American influence throughout the world which, in turn, provokes the increasing concentration of ultimate power in the hands of the President of the United States.

The flow of history has moved fast and dramatically during this decade, and moved decisively in the direction outlined in that study of America's destiny in the light of world history. American presence has made itself felt all over the world with increasing weight. Militarily, the United States landed marines in Lebanon in 1958 and took a hand, under the Eisenhower Doctrine, in temporarily straightening things out in the Middle East; exerted a powerful and even decisive influence in the Congo when the withdrawal of Belgium's colonial administration plunged the heart of Africa into chaos; proceeded to occupy, if temporarily, the Dominican Republic in 1965 to ward off an alleged attempt at a Castroite revolution; and attempted to fasten its grip on Southeast Asia by engaging in large-scale warfare in Vietnam with all its side effects—American military protectorate over Thailand, the collapse of Communist influence in Indonesia, and so on. At a time when European Powers have set free almost all their overseas possessions and liquidated their military bases overseas, the United States not only retains its own imperial outposts from Panama to Okinawa (although acknowledging other nations' residual sovereignty) but is steadily extending its sphere of influence in many of Europe's former colonies.

Twenty-three years after the end of World War II, a quarter of a million American troops still garrison West Germany, fifty thousand are on guard in Korea, and well over half a million occupy South Vietnam and Thailand. America's Seventh Fleet actively promotes the extension of its Far Eastern empire, while its Sixth Fleet has become the main military force in the Mediterranean, far more important than all the European fleets combined. Other, less visible, forms of American influence are spreading increasingly tight networks around the globe—a vast intelligence, counterespionage and counterinsurgency apparatus, a Pentagon-directed authority over dozens of foreign military establishments, a developing financial and economic empire in foreign lands fueled to the tune of almost nine billion dollars a year, a relentless absorption of foreign talent through the worldwide brain drain—every item of this staggering American expansion being tightly welded to all the others to form one dynamic force in the process of establishing its imperium all over the non-Communist world.

This almost mechanical, partly unconscious expansion of worldwide interests and responsibilities has fostered in the 1960's a renewed flow of power into the White House, at the expense of the other branches of the American government. Toward the end of *The Coming Caesars,* it was pointed out that "wars are the main harbingers of Caesarism." [1] Events in the 1960's bear this out; and in November 1967, the United States Senate Foreign Relations Committee, in a unanimously approved resolution, stated emphatically that until Congress restores its limitations on Presidential powers, "the American people will be threatened with tyranny or disaster." [2] In a desperate effort, in the midst of the fierce Vietnam War which had mushroomed into an armed conflict of unforeseen dimensions, to cancel the blank check given President Lyndon Johnson with its 1964 Gulf of Tonkin Resolution, the Senate Foreign Relations Committee angrily rejected the idea that congressional war powers had become obsolete in an age of undeclared wars and pointedly accused the last four Presidents (President Eisenhower "a shade less than the others") of having "asserted unrestricted executive authority to commit the armed forces without the consent of Congress." The report even went so far as to accuse the Executive as having grasped its war powers by outright "usurpation" and claimed that the Gulf of Tonkin Resolution granted to President Johnson represented "the extreme point in the process of Constitutional erosion that began in the first years of the century." [3]

When the Senate Foreign Relations Committee's report was published, few bothered to read it and even fewer cared about the Constitutional issues raised in it. True enough, the *New York Times* commented upon it several times in its editorials. In its most notable paragraph, it had this to say about the report:

> Haunting second thoughts in Congress and the country about the Gulf of Tonkin resolution of 1964—under protection of which the administration has steadily expanded the American commitment in Vietnam—would alone justify searching debate. But the need is reinforced by enduring doubts about President Roosevelt's "shoot on sight" orders to the Atlantic Fleet prior to the formal American involvement in World War II; President Truman's commitment of American forces to war in Korea without even a request for congressional sanction, and the joint resolutions on Formosa, the Middle East and Cuba adopted on the initiative of Presidents Eisenhower and Kennedy. [4]

It is also true that, by breaking out of the narrow confines of the mere moment and reaching back to the troubled period ending in the outbreak of World War II, the Senate Foreign Relations Committee displayed a true and valuable sense of history. But, in its attempt to undo the harm done, it also overreached itself, as the same *New York Times* editorial pointed out; and it felt compelled to warn the distinguished Senators that:

> The hard fact is that a President today can maneuver the
> country into war without a declaration or resolution by the
> Congress, and the senators can devise no foolproof deterrent
> against this.[5]

It could have added that another hard fact is that, by and large,
public opinion has become indifferent to the Constitutional issues raised. Basically, it longs for leadership and follows it more
or less blindly whenever it asserts itself with sufficient demagogic
forcefulness—all the passionate controversies stimulated by the
Vietnam War notwithstanding. Public opinion cares mostly about
the staggering cost of the war, the racial riots in American
cities, inflation and taxes. The Constitutional issue of the eroded
division of powers and the rising Caesarian stature of the President are largely matters of indifference to the broad public.

The fact that Democratic Presidents were singled out as the
main culprits by a Democratic-dominated senatorial committee
was in itself significant, symbolizing another of those episodic
attempts on the part of Congress, without real public support, to
curb the growing powers gathering at the White House, regardless of the fact that the President belongs to the same party. This
attempt, besides temporarily disrupting the unity of the Democratic party, also exemplifies one of the main themes of *The
Coming Caesars*—the tight relationship between expanding democracy, growing imperialism, and rising Caesarism. In sponsoring this report on a unanimously approved resolution, Senator
Fulbright and his Democratic colleagues behaved more like
Republicans than Democrats—proving in the process that American lawmakers are so concerned by the evaporation of their
Constitutional powers and the rising threat of Caesarism that they
might be willing to sacrifice party unity in the slender hope of
recapturing their waning prerogatives.

The 1967 Senate Foreign Relations Committee's resolution,
designed to limit the President's power to commit the armed
forces to overseas combat without congressional sanction, is another belated effort to thwart the rising Caesarism of the Chief
Executive. Whatever its short-term effect, in the long run it is
bound to prove ineffective. The growing American empire is not
the result of short-term but of long-term historical trends, origi-

nating far back in time; and, in turn, the inevitable growth of this empire is bound to enhance the Caesarian stature of the Presidency at the expense of Congress. The historical meaning of the Gulf of Tonkin Resolution and of the United States Senate's belated effort to destroy its far-reaching implications, can therefore be read in the following sentence, written in *The Coming Caesars* years before this resolution could be dreamed of:

> The gradual convergence of historical trends joins ever closer together the unconscious longing for Caesarism and the external emergencies that bring it about.[6]

The following work is concerned essentially with the development of the American empire rather than the correlative development of Caesarism—a study of the United States' impact beyond its borders rather than a study of the slow metamorphosis of its political institutions. The parallel established in *The Coming Caesars* between the development of the Classical world and the development of the modern Western world provides the conceptual framework for this study of the rising American empire. In particular, the similarity of the ancient Greeks to the modern Europeans, and of the ancient Romans to the modern Americans, remains implicit throughout.

The main underlying thesis is that historical development is conditioned by long-term trends rather than a succession of unpredictable accidents and imponderables; and that, therefore, predetermination plays a far greater role than is usually recognized. The implication is that, in the unfolding of contemporary events, the margin of freedom allowed to statesmen is far smaller than is commonly thought. However unpleasant, not to say distasteful, the idea that we have very little freedom of choice, we must accept it because it alone explains in depth the seemingly irrational or paradoxical developments of history-in-the-making. There is, in this acceptance, something of the spirit of Greek tragedy which sits ill with the boundless optimism generated by our modern scientific outlook. But we are fortunate enough in having a rather extensive historical past and of being able to study it in our search for clues to the development of the contemporary world: wisely used—and after all, *gouverner c'est pré-*

voir—this perspective can assist us in determining the approximate margin of freedom at our disposal and the best course of action available under the circumstances. Willful disregard of this historical perspective can only justify the contention of those who claim that to ignore history is to be condemned to repeat it.

Equally implicit in this concept of historical predetermination is the correlative concept that the mainspring of historical motivations is only marginally conscious. Every important historical event can be interpreted in the light of the conscious motivations of its participants; but these will shed only a dim light on the whole historical trend of which this given event is but a small part. Since it is by now well established that all of us human beings, acting in our individual capacities, are strongly influenced by our obscure unconscious motivations, it is obvious that historical development, which is the total account of our collective development, must be similarly influenced. If this influence of the collective unconscious is taken into account, bright light is shed where hitherto there was only obscurity; apparently senseless events begin to make sense; profound, irresistible historical trends begin to appear in bold relief; intelligent, purposeful forecasting becomes possible and pointless controversies are muted; seemingly intractable problems become solvable and brick walls evaporate without our having to smash our heads against them. The shaping of a collective unconscious, mysterious as it may seem, is nevertheless amenable to analysis: the cultural, linguistic, ethnic, geographical, climatic, and historical elements that go into shaping the collective unconscious of well-defined human societies are all available for analysis; their impact on the collective psychology of a given society can be defined. It is the sum total of all the atavistic traits derived from these elements that conditions a human society's historical destiny.

From the fact that each civilization endowed with a specific culture has its own particular collective unconscious (as expressed in myths, legends, songs and poetry) in which all members share, springs the cyclical aspect of historical evolution; the unconscious bond between men of a common civilization has a life-course of its own: it is born, grows, decays and dies like any organism. This cyclical aspect (which *complements,* rather than supplants, the linear aspect) allows us to define the present moment in contemporary history as being roughly similar to, or "contemporaneous" with, that which saw, in the second and first centuries B.C., the leadership of the entire Classical world shift from the Hellenistic realms to Rome.[7] No single individual was responsible for it; no precise date can be given for this shift; it was a gradual development, taking place over a span of time covering several generations, finding its dramatic climax during the time of Julius Caesar and Augustus. Just as the major historical development in those days was the establishment of the Roman Empire, the major development of our time is the gradual and partly unconscious establishment of the American empire.

Since the distant days of Classical Rome, the words "empire" and "imperialism" have been used indiscriminately to cover all instances of relationship between different states involving the domination of inferior by superior power. In some cases, imperialism has been used exclusively in the economic and colonial sense—typically, imperialism of the Victorian era. An extreme application of this viewpoint is the Marxist interpretation given by Lenin, with its pre-World War I flavor, which focuses heavily on the economic aspect of imperialism, the "monopoly stage of capitalism." In deriding Karl Kautsky's own interpretation of the phenomenon, Lenin pointed out that in the capitalist world, *several* imperialisms coexisted and competed; and, quite prophetically, he foresaw that the era of several competing imperialisms could not last because of the inherent instability of the "colonial" structure. But, instead of foreseeing that the conflicting European imperialisms would eventually be replaced by one global, ecumenical American empire, he pinned his faith on the "scientifically" preordained, worldwide triumph of Communism—failing to see that the triumph of Communism in Russia and China would give new impetus to the atavistic imperialisms of the Russians and the Chinese. He himself lost no time, after coming to power, in retrieving Czarist Russia's own colonial imperialism in the Caucasus and Turkestan, while vigorously denying that he was doing just that; nor did Mao Tse-tung lose any time in retrieving the colonial imperialism applied by the former Sons of Heaven in Tibet, Sinkiang and Inner Mongolia.

If, instead of restricting our sights to the nineteenth and early twentieth centuries, we look at imperialism as it has manifested itself throughout history since the remote times of Egypt's great conquering Pharaoh Thutmose III and Babylon's equally great lawgiver Hammurabi, it becomes plain that economic impulses are only a marginal ingredient in its makeup. Something more is required—a "missionary" spirit, a will to power, a sense of universal responsibility, an idealistic longing for a united, lawful and ordered world, a striving toward ecumenism. The basic drive toward empire is a drive toward *world empire* which is lacking in imperialism of the "colonial" variety; or in a purely national, "racial" imperialism of the German National Socialist variety; or even in prewar Japanese imperialism, whatever the lip-service paid to it in the Tanaka Memorial. The basic drive toward world empire, in turn, springs from idealism, "the ordering of human society through unified dominion and common civilization." [8] This type of imperialism has very little in common with other, ephemeral "colonial" types because, unlike them, it implies a definite stage in the historical evolution of a civilization—the shift from the concept of the sovereign nation-state as the highest form of political organization (with or without its colonial appendages) to that of the world-wide imperium which encompasses all men who share a common culture and embodies their civilization in one universal political structure.

In former days, the "world" was only that portion of the earth that was visible to a given civilization—whether the valley of the Nile, Mesopotamia, the Mediterranean, India, China, or pre-Columbian Peru and Mexico. Nowadays, the world is the globe itself, an arena of conflict between the dominant civilization of the West and antagonistic non-Western civilizations attempting desperately to modernize themselves. Leaving aside the problem of the stresses born of such inter-civilization conflicts (the American impact on Asia, for instance) in order to restrict ourselves to the area covered by today's dominant civilization

(America and Europe), this epoch of imperialism in which we now find ourselves implies the ingathering of all societies and nations sharing a common culture (the North Atlantic community) into a *single dominion* under the auspices of the most powerful nation-state belonging to their cultural family. It is not due to the military conquests and political decisions of any one individual, but to the natural power of expansion of one specific, more efficiently organized, nation; its spiritual underpinning is an idea (Zeno's stoicism, in the case of Rome) whose devotees visualize a better world, unified, peaceful and always *more democratic;* it is essentially ecumenical and its establishment implies the creation—in fact or fancy—of a universal society free from wars and social conflicts under the overall rule of law.

We do not have to restrict our historical comparisons to the example of the Roman Empire—although the fact that our Western civilization has its roots in Greco-Roman culture makes this example more meaningful; other civilizations have reached the same imperial stage after going through similar sequences of development and, more astonishingly, all have tended toward the same democratic ideal rooted in some specific ideology—the equalitarian Buddhism of India's great Emperor Asoka, the democratic, antifeudal and authoritarian Legalism of China's first universal Emperor, Shih Huang-ti. But it was the cohesive strength of their nations that made possible the establishment of "universal" emperors (universal within the context of their respective civilizations); Asoka and Shih Huang-ti established the ecumenical empires, but it was the expansive power of their original nation-states, Magadha and Ch'in (and the lassitude of the other nation-states after generations of "world wars") that set the stage for their remarkable careers.[9]

Understood in this ecumenical sense, imperialism represents a definite stage in a given civilization's development—the natural goal toward which the evolution of increasingly democratic societies tends. Claudius Rutilius praised the Roman Empire "for having afforded to all peoples the equal protection of common citizenship and of a rational law. This empire would mean the end of all imperialism." [10] The ancient Greeks and the modern

Europeans were never able to reach this stage of imperialism and eventually forfeited all their "colonial" empires, prelude to their being themselves absorbed by their ecumenically minded cousins from overseas. It is not only in terms of size that Roman-American imperialism differs from the "colonial" Greco-European variety, but in terms of intrinsic nature. It emerges out of the Greco-European "colonialist" cocoon and, in its early stages, embodies the predominance of the part over the whole, of one nation over all other nations included in its imperial orbit; but, eventually, it sheds its colonialist mantle and evolves toward a *res publica,* a true "common wealth" in which all—imperialists and imperialized—have equal rights. Roman citizenship was eventually granted by Caracalla to all men dwelling within the borders of the empire—*cives vocavit quos domuit.* Today, as the unacknowledged American empire strives to find its shape and its limits, the same ecumenical dream is beginning to haunt the lands of Western civilization.

Seen in this light, the growth of an American empire is not a temporary aberration due to the nefarious activities of the last power-grabbing Presidents of the United States, as asserted in the 1967 Senate Foreign Relations Committee report; it becomes the logical outcome of centuries of historical development, and not merely of American historical developments but of worldwide trends. Congressional resolutions notwithstanding, the contemporary drift of events will not be halted or even deflected; it will proceed irresistibly and brush aside all those who refuse to see its depth in time and its magnitude in space. There may be times when, in the trough of the wave, the crest looming on the horizon may be invisible, and "normal" conditions may seem to have returned; but it can only be a temporary phenomenon, such as the isolationism that beset the United States during the interwar period. The broad direction in which the waves are rolling is clearly visible to those who keep an eye on history. The reluctance of all participants in the contemporary drama is understandable; not so the willful blindness of those who still refuse to acknowledge the existence of this imperial drift.

One can understand that the obligations of an officeholder

would compel Vice President Hubert Humphrey to state tremulously during a visit to Indonesia in November 1967: "We don't want any Pax Americana. We are not a Roman Empire. The United States can't remake the world." [11] But thoughtful historians and other intellectuals should see in such disclaimers the very proof that, reluctant as it may be, the empire-building process is well under way. And indeed, if one recalls that only a few months before, the same Vice President Humphrey had formulated the imperial "Johnson Doctrine" for Asia as ". . . a tremendous new opening here for realizing the dream of the Great Society in the great area of Asia, not just here at home," it becomes evident that Executive power in Washington was committing not just this generation but future generations of Americans to endless involvements in the affairs of that vast, alien continent, through the instrument of "a pledge to ourselves and to posterity to defeat aggression, to defeat social misery, to build viable, free political institutions, and to achieve peace"—as Hubert Humphrey expressed it. [12]

Every new President now aspires to have his historical monument—not in marble but in the form of some idealistic pronouncement: Franklin Roosevelt's Atlantic Charter, Truman's Doctrine, Eisenhower's Doctrine, and now Johnson's "Asian Doctrine," Caesarian pronouncements irrevocably committing the United States for generations to come. As Senator William Fulbright stated it, "All this must come as a big surprise to Senators who have not even been informed of these sweeping commitments, much less asked for their advice and consent . . ." [13] —this in reference to an Asian Doctrine which had been in President Johnson's mind for five years.

No more need be added about the close connection between rising Caesarian power in Washington and the relentless development of an American empire. The burden of the following work is the study of the evolution of the United States' imperial destiny as the Rome of the modern world—from its roots deep in the past, to the troubled present and the largely preordained future. Quite probably, the choice no longer lies between building or not building an American empire; the choice lies only between doing a good or a bad job of it: that seems to be all the margin of freedom left in the late 1960's. To paraphrase a remark made at the time of Franklin Roosevelt's attempt to pack the Supreme Court, the United States' leaders may not want to know where they are going, but they are on their way.

THE AMERICAN EMPIRE

☆ I ☆

The Roots

Empires come in all sizes, in time as well as space. Some are short-lived, others can last hundreds or thousands of years. Some are truly accidental, others the result of long-term historical developments with their roots deep in the past—and the deeper the roots, the more enduring the empire. The coming American empire which is developing in our time belongs to the latter category—the result of an immensely long process, a slow tidal wave originating far back in time, long before the American Revolution and the rise of the original Thirteen Colonies to independent nationhood.

The roots of all such historical developments are deeply embedded in the human heart and mind—in the emergence of a new personality, a new type of human being produced by a profound change in the cultural environment. Such a new man was the American Puritan—iron-hard, practical, sober fanatic dedicated to hard work and economic success. Being the strongest element in the emerging American society, he also became the most influential, and the ethical outlook of American society throughout the ages, along with its dry idealism and pragmatic approach, is essentially derived from the Pilgrim Fathers' initial impulse; so is its typical ruthlessness and its single-minded striving to reach a given goal. Strong enough to preserve human dignity and liberty, it was also strong enough to curb man's natural selfishness and subordinate it to the common good, to the welfare of society as a whole—whether it be a few thousand men in the early New England communities or the vast two hundred million American people of our time.

The specific quality of this new type of human being stamped its mark on American history from the beginning. Part and parcel of the expanding British Empire, the scattered colonies on the American coast inevitably became participants in the great imperial wars of the eighteenth century that pitted the British, French, and Spaniards against each other. They were not only passive participants but actively expansionist on their own. We find that in the early part of the century, while Massachusetts was begging the British Crown for assistance in order to conquer French Canada, South Carolina urged the Board of Trade in London to extend the borders of the colony all the way to the "Mischisipi" since most of the Canadian trade in furs and skins was bound to come down the great river. In fact, all through the three great colonial wars, the border colonies in the north and the south, Massachusetts and South Carolina, proved to be relentlessly imperialistic, far more so than the other colonies or the home government.

Successful imperialism requires power; and this, the American colonists knew how to accumulate. Between the Treaty of Utrecht (1713) and the fateful Peace of Paris (1763), the thirteen British colonies on the American continent grew in size, numbers, and wealth, uncomfortably ensconced between the much vaster but poor and thinly populated French territories. Their population swelled from 360,000 to over a million and a half, and the area of settlement trebled. True enough, London had no wish to see a new power develop overseas in competition with the home country, no wish to see American industry rival that of the United Kingdom (emigration of skilled artisans to the colonies with their tools was prohibited). There was subtle but constant political warfare between the colonists and the English in all matters pertaining to economics, finance, and taxation, with ultimate victory usually going to the determined colonists. However, there could be no parting of the ways so long as two other powerful empires threatened both the British and their American cousins; and, more often than not, the British relied largely on American militia to fight their wars against Spaniards and Frenchmen—as in the war of 1739 against Spain when Admiral Vernon attacked Cartagena with thousands of American volunteers from the Thirteen Colonies. This Anglo-Spanish conflict soon swelled into the War of the Austrian Succession, and in 1744 a New England army stormed the French fortress of Louisbourg—only to see it restored to France in exchange for Madras, in faraway India; demonstrating, in the process, that in the global scheme of British imperialism, the Thirteen Colonies were only a small part of the great British Empire-in-the-making, pieces of which could conveniently be bargained away without consulting the Americans. The fury of the New Englanders was only partly assuaged by the British assuming the entire financial burden of the expedition—and by their need of British protection against French imperialism.

The French were determined to hold and populate their immense but unsettled territories on the North American continent. Not only were the British unprepared to accept this; the American colonists themselves were even more determined to prevent it—and by the middle of the eighteenth century the Thirteen Colonies had become a power in their own right, with over twenty times the French population in Canada and the West. Willingly or not, London would have to go to war against the French, if only to satisfy the Americans. Virginians and New Englanders were in the van of the warmongers, and with the assistance of the imperialist lobby in London, American public opinion practically compelled the timid Duke of Newcastle to initiate a state of war with the French. There was peace between France and England in 1755—that is, everywhere except in America.

Soon enough, one thing leading to another, the old "French and Indian War" merged into another global conflict matching one coalition of European Powers against another. After some initial successes, the French began to feel the adverse military

aided

weight of large British forces bolstered by equally large American militias from the colonies: Colonel Dudley Bradstreet of Massachusetts and his New Englanders captured Fort Frontenac; George Washington's troops fought alongside General Forbes' army, captured Fort Duquesne (Pittsburgh); General Amherst captured Ticonderoga but never appeared near Quebec where he was supposed to assist England's General Wolfe—and it was Wolfe who, unassisted by the Americans, broke the power of France in Canada. Perhaps, this was a symbolic portent of things to come—the retention of Canada within the British Empire while the rest of the continent fell under the sway of the original Thirteen Colonies.

The collapse of French power in North America was only a prelude to the greater drama to come. The French had disappeared but the Indians remained as a constant threat to the welfare of the American colonists. In an aggressive mood, the great Indian confederacy of the Ohio Valley almost wiped out all the settlements in that part of the West and menaced the frontier. This time, however, it was the British redcoats who crushed it, rather than the colonists. Did this influence the Government in London when the time came to organize the vast new possessions that had been won from the French? At any rate, it can be asserted that the closing of the West to settlement by the colonists was one of the decisive moves which brought about the American Revolution. The Royal Proclamation of October 7, 1763, emphasized: "We do strictly forbid, on pain of our displeasure, all our loving subjects from making any purchases or settlements whatever in that region." [1] All the western land claims of the Thirteen Colonies were, *de facto,* wiped out at one stroke by London's decision: the "Proclamation Line" following the crest of the Alleghenies would, if respected, have restricted the Americans to the narrow coastal plain between the mountain range and the ocean. Although intended at first to be a provisional measure, to be withdrawn when the Indians were pacified, with large areas west of the line to be opened for orderly settlement, it eventually came to be a permanent boundary. London began to view the West as one vast reservation for Indians, to be run by an imperial Indian civil service for the ultimate benefit of an expanded fur trade. This change took place when Shelburne was forced out of office and replaced by Lord Hillsborough—"Let the savages enjoy their deserts in quiet . . . were they drove from their forests, the peltry trade would decrease," wrote General Gage to the Board of Trade.[2]

The prohibition of western settlement was never withdrawn. But the American backwoodsmen penetrated through the "Proclamation Line" as through a sieve. In a letter to the Colonial Secretary, Lord Dunmore, Governor of Virginia in 1772, wrote:

> I have learnt from experience that the established Authority of any government in America, and the policy of Government at home, are both insufficient to restrain the Americans; and that they do and will remove as their avidity and restlessness incite them. . . . They do not conceive that Government has any right to forbid their taking possession of a vast tract of country, either uninhabited, or which Serves only as a shelter to a few Scattered Tribes of Indians. Nor can they be easily brought to entertain any belief in the permanent obligation of Treaties made with those People, whom they consider, as but little removed from the brute Creation.[3]

Following his thoughts to their logical conclusion, Governor Dunmore then proceeded to lead the pioneers across the border in an expedition against the Shawnees, provoking a massive withdrawal of the Indians south of the Ohio. This did not please the authorities in London who reemphasized their determination to hold the line by ordering royal governors to grant no western land to settlers. They went even further: by the Quebec Act of June 22, 1774, the British annexed to the Province of Quebec all the territory north of the Ohio River, thus formally canceling, once and for all, the western claims of four colonies. The Americans promptly expressed their anger, and Thomas Jefferson, in his audacious *Summary View of the Rights of British America,* vigorously upheld the view that the Government in London had no right to dispose of western land. The colonies already had their own local imperial interests to look after, even though they clashed with Britain's worldwide imperialism.

That the American Revolution was brought about by multiple

other vexations needs no repeating. But there is no denying that the more or less conscious desire of the London Government to reestablish a balance of power in America by replacing a vanished French threat with an Indian one, was instrumental in triggering the revolt. Sensing the approaching danger, one noble British lord pointed out that "Awe of the French keeps our Colonys dependent upon the Mother Country" and more than one Englishman thought of handing Canada back to the French, for the mere purpose of keeping the American colonists in line.[4] But it was too late to do anything of the kind; all the British could do now was to attempt a buildup of Indian power under British protection. But what came to be known later as the "Old West," stretching from the widely scattered settlements of northern and western New England, through the Mohawk Valley, western and northern Pennsylvania, the Shenandoah Valley and western Virginia to the Piedmont in the Carolinas, was the home of almost a million rough inhabitants whose expansionist instincts were never far below the surface. Sturdy and democratic, this population was essentially imperialistic, far more so than the more settled and civilized communities in the East. Fiercely land-hungry, they firmly believed that all available land belonged to the white man by natural right. While they used the American Revolution to promote democratic and egalitarian reforms and to fight against the social evils from which they were suffering (underrepresentation in legislative assemblies, poor transportation, indebtedness to the more wealthy easterners), they blended these democratic ideals with an innate and relentless expansionism which has remained, ever since, a hallmark of the American temper throughout the ages and in all fields of human endeavor. This territorial expansionism was not entirely unreasonable: they suffered from constant border warfare with marauding Indian tribes against whom the eastern authorities provided next to no protection—while the easterners accused them often enough, and with some justification, of provoking the Indians. The 1764 raid of the "Paxton Boys," ending in the massacre of peaceful Christian Indians, symbolized this attitude as well as the sectional hatred that existed between East and West.

The American Revolution showed its true colors at the very

beginning. The extralegal Congress which gathered in Philadelphia in September 1774 promptly proclaimed the "Suffolk Resolves," which included, among other demands, the creation of a continental legislature which would have full control over Indians and western land grants. Beyond this, the Americans demanded nothing more than what later became known as "dominion" status—which was promptly refused by the London Government. Hostilities began quickly, followed by the proclamation of the Declaration of Independence. In no time, the French, backed up by Spain, took this opportunity to revenge themselves by assisting the American revolt against British authority.

In entering the war, the French and the Spaniards had far more in mind than the idealistic purpose of helping the American colonists achieve independence. The French minister at Philadelphia sought covertly to take the West away from the American colonists and give it to Spain. Having witnessed this intriguing piece of double-dealing, one of the main American negotiators, John Jay, soon came to the conclusion that France's Foreign Minister Vergennes was attempting to partition the West between England and Spain: in fact he was suggesting that Britain keep the whole West north of the Ohio, while Spain would get everything west of a border stretching from the northwest corner of Florida to the mouth of the Cumberland. As Benjamin Franklin stated it indignantly, this proposal indicated a determination "to coop us up within the Allegheny Mountains." [5] After all, why not? Then and there, the forthcoming United States could have remained cooped up between mountain and sea, becoming a peaceful Western Hemisphere, "Switzerland," leaving to others the occupation and settlement of the West. It was not a matter of right but of might, and the American colonists already had both the strength and the determination to wrest the West from its European owners as well as their Indian protégés; their inborn will-to-power was incompatible with a placid historical destiny. It was just not in their dynamic temper to become the peaceful Swiss of the Western Hemisphere; they left that destiny to the Uruguayans in South America.

John Jay and Benjamin Franklin promptly abandoned their erstwhile French ally and negotiated directly with London. The

Peace of Paris give them almost everything they could desire: a northern frontier along the St. Lawrence and the Great Lakes up to the Grand Portage on Lake Superior, and the West all the way up to the Mississippi—still leaving Spain in possession of all the immense territories west of the great river and south of the thirty-first parallel of latitude. The first phase of the great imperial drama had come to an end: the United States became independent and had full possession of a large slice of the West. Rather than agree with France and Spain in keeping the West out of American hands, the British quite naturally decided to overcome their bitterness and favor their "rebellious" American cousins.

The Americans lost no time in expanding into, and settling effectively, the Old West. Vermont was the first new commonwealth to emerge out of hitherto virgin territory; Kentucky and Tennessee followed in short order. The Alleghenies were washed away as a barrier to the swelling flood of American settlers pouring across the mountains; as for the Indians, they were either wiped out, cooped up in reservations, or pushed back into the depths of the West, beyond the Mississippi. Streaming out of North Carolina and Virginia and pouring through the Cumberland Gap, or marching out of Maryland and Pennsylvania up to the headwaters of the Potomac and crossing the Alleghenies and down into the Ohio Valley, an irresistible flood of settlers began to inundate the West. This invasion was spontaneous and intensely individualistic, unassisted by state, church, or military protection. Those of the original Thirteen States who claimed large slices of the West were persuaded to surrender these claims to the Federal Government: it was then decided to carve out of this western pool sixteen new states, to be eventually admitted on a basis of equality with the original Thirteen—a novel formula for growth which betrayed the instinctive political genius of the American leaders of the day, and which found its historical formulation in the Ordinance of 1787. The venerable theory according to which colonies were founded for the benefit of the mother country, the doctrine according to which they were to remain subordinated, was thrown aside; a new form of expansionism was substituted, one which provided for *organic* growth, for the birth of new living social cells to be grafted onto the main body politic, of which they became part and parcel. From that time on, and with the temporary exception of the Philippines, American expansion shed the "colonial" coloration typical of European-style expansion; territorial acquisitions and possessions were not mere garments worn for the benefit of the mother country but became part of the flesh and blood of the United States.

But of what use was it to expand into the West if these new territories and states had no outlet for their trade? Only the Mississippi and the St. Lawrence could provide it. One step toward expansion automatically entailed another; the main goal of American policy during that period became the possession of the two gates controlling the commercial outlets of the entire West and shutting off the Americans from further westward advance —New Orleans and Montreal, the two locks on the two main waterways of the continent, respectively in the hands of the Spaniards and the British. Obviously, Spain viewed the new American federation with a jaundiced eye, in spite of its temporary alliance during the War of Independence. With great foresight, Charles III's Prime Minister Florida Blanca wanted to halt the floodlike western migration; he saw clearly that the growing strength of the American Republic threatened to overwhelm Spain's large but almost empty possessions. In alliance with the Creek, Choctaw, and Chickasaw Indians, who opted for a virtual Spanish protectorate (although dwelling on United States territory), the Spaniards proceeded to strangle the southern outlet of the American West. Armed by the Spaniards, the Creeks and Cherokees repeatedly attacked American settlements on the Cumberland and Tennessee rivers—who retaliated with as much ferocity as the Indians themselves displayed in their raids. Refusing to hand Natchez back to the United States, to whom it had been attributed by the British, and in firm possession of New Orleans, the Spaniards had full control of the lower Mississippi and bottled up the West. Moreover, many western settlers, willing to listen to Spanish advice, were tempted to secede from the United States in exchange for free navigation on the great river. In fact, most Europeans in those days expected the Trans-

Appalachian West to break away from the original Thirteen States. Quite clearly, either the United States made up its mind to secure the great riverway and control its southern gate (New Orleans), or it would have to forfeit any hope of territorial greatness.

Shortly after throwing back a hostile confederation of Indian tribes armed by the British governor of Lower Canada, and securing by treaty with the Indians a large slice of the Northwest Territory, the United States proceeded to wrest from the weakening Spaniards the right to navigate the lower Mississippi on behalf of its western settlers. But now, the problem was no longer with Spain. In the aftermath of the French Revolution, the ruling Directoire in Paris sought to recoup all the losses France had suffered in the Western Hemisphere by persuading Spain to hand Florida and Louisiana over to the French, and by persuading the French Canadians in Quebec to rise against the British and form an independent Canadian republic. This contemplated nutcracker scheme was a new and deadly threat to the young American Republic. While French persuasion came to nought in Canada, Spain agreed to retrocede the immense territory of Louisiana to France in the secret Treaty of San Ildefonso (1800). With New Orleans as a base, Napoleon hoped to create a vast and powerful French empire on the North American continent, thus not only thwarting any hope of the United States for further extension, but also endangering the shaky allegiance of the new western states to the Union—so true it is that wherever and whenever expansion ceases, centrifugal forces take over and disintegration threatens. When Jefferson heard of the treaty in 1801, he stated without ambiguity: "The day that France takes possession of New Orleans, . . . we must marry ourselves to the British fleet and nation. . . ." [6]

Fortunately for the Americans, France, embroiled in a disastrous expedition to Santo Domingo, found it impossible to take effective possession of New Orleans. Anticipating a resumption of the war against England, Napoleon promptly made up his mind to sell the whole of Louisiana to the United States before the British seized it by force of arms. Jefferson moved fast and decisively, and concluded in 1803 the greatest financial bargain in history, doubling the size of his already large country at one stroke, pushing the western border of the United States all the way from the Mississippi to the Rocky Mountains . . . for a mere sixty million francs, which was only half of what he had been willing to pay for only a part of it!

But Louisiana was not enough, or rather Jefferson felt that he had been cheated on the matter of borders, believing that these should have included both Texas and West Florida. For a while, not much could be done about the matter; but in 1810, while there were two Spanish governments and the Spanish Empire was giving signs of collapse, the settlers dwelling in that part of West Florida which bordered the Mississippi "voted" themselves into the United States and found themselves incorporated by Presidential proclamation: within two years, their territory became the State of Louisiana. Meantime, considerably aggravated by the behavior of the British in Canada, Congress declared war against Great Britain in June 1812.

The basic reason for this war was not the multiple vexations inflicted upon American seamen by an England locked in a desperate struggle against its deadly Napoleonic enemy, but the desire of the United States frontiersmen for more land—which could be had only at the expense of the British and the Indians. For reasons of practical necessity, the pioneer farmer of those days was essentially a woodsman, who needed wood for fuel, building and fencing. He could not settle in the treeless plains of the Middle or Far West, refused to move into the prairies of Illinois and fight powerful Indian tribes; he would rather fight the Indians living in the woods of Indiana or the fertile and empty regions of Upper Canada which were in British hands. In addition, the Americans were alarmed at the efforts made by the great Tecumseh to regenerate the Indians, and firmly believed that his organization of a great Indian confederacy threatened the western settlers. There was widespread suspicion throughout the West that the British were behind Tecumseh, in fact that they were behind every defensive move made by the Indians for sheer survival in front of the endless inflow of American pioneers. Governor Harrison of Indiana Territory lost no time in attacking

Tecumseh's Indians and crushed them at Tippecanoe. But war between British and Americans had become inevitable, and the Indian conflict was a mere cover for the Americans' desire to conquer and absorb Canada.

A wave of enthusiasm swept through the United States, fueled by talk of its destiny to expand as far as the North Pole—even though many voices were raised against the shamefulness of attacking the British cousins at a time when they were locked in a decisive struggle with Napoleon. But the prospect of easy loot was too much for most Americans who felt that the balance of power favored them: by then, they numbered over seven million, as against a mere five hundred thousand inhabitants in Canada, most of them French. Even so, the United States' military establishment was in poor shape and no match for the British-Canadian forces, strongly backed by Tecumseh's Indian confederacy. Furthermore, the young Union was not very cohesive, as yet; the British had high hopes that the reluctant New Englanders would secede and either join Canada or form a separate Union of their own. When peace finally came with the signing of the Treaty of Ghent, the Americans had not won a single one of their goals; Canada had refused to let itself fall into the United States' lap, largely because of the loyalty of the French Canadians to the British Crown and their fear of the Americans' power of absorption. In fact, the fledgling United States itself was fortunate in being able to preserve its own fragile unity, which remained at stake until the Civil War decided the matter, once and for all.

The war over, settlers began flowing into the Trans-Appalachian West again, raising its population in a decade from one to over two million; General Andrew Jackson invaded Spanish Florida, severely punished the Seminole Indians in 1818, and hauled down the Spanish flag in St. Marks. Although he was forced to surrender his conquest, the Spanish Cabinet in Madrid read the handwriting on the wall: better sell Florida before it was seized by force of arms without any financial compensation. On February 22, 1819, Spain ceded Florida and all lands east of the Mississippi, as well as all its rights to the Oregon territory. And with that, the second phase of the United States' continental expansion came to an end.

The immense territories gained by the United States after In-dependence were no more virgin land than the Old West had been. They were still the home of numerous, and sometimes redoubtable Indian tribes; one way or the other, they had to be removed all the way to the Far West, beyond the Mississippi. Between 1829 and 1837, no less than ninety-four Indian treaties were signed, millions of acres acquired for settlement, and many thousands of Indians transported, willingly or not, to the Far West. Most of the time, the Indian tribes were too weak to resist and accepted their sad fate with typical stoicism. Occasionally there was trouble: the wanton massacre of Chief Black Hawk's tribesmen and their families by the Illinois militia, for instance. The Cherokees of Georgia were unfortunate enough to be found sitting on rich gold deposits; and in spite of the fact that they had settled down to "civilized" life, complete with permanent houses, good roads, book publishing in their own language, and a politi-cal constitution, they were forcibly removed westward in 1838. As for the Seminoles of Florida, they fought the United States Army tooth and nail for years; their chief Osceola was finally captured by treachery while bearing a flag of truce. Undaunted, the Seminoles pursued their fight until 1842, by which time, after an expenditure of twenty million dollars and at the cost of fifteen hundred men killed, they were practically exterminated. Soon enough, almost all the redskins had been removed to the Far West, and were separated from the settled West by a chain of military posts. In 1835, President Jackson pledged the United States to keep this barrier for all times—but within a bare twenty years, most of it was torn aside and the Indians pushed back further into the wilderness or dwindling reservations.

Columns of pioneers started pouring into the far West and Southwest—one along the Oregon Trail, another fanwise into Illinois and Iowa, and a third down into Texas, that is, Mexican territory. Some columns even branched off the Oregon Trail into Upper California over the passes of the Sierra Nevada, again penetrating into Mexican territory. A fourth column, consisting mostly of American traders, followed the Santa Fe trail into what became New Mexico. But it was in Texas that the first substantial settlement of English-speaking pioneers implanted itself within the borders of Mexico. By the 1819 Florida Treaty, the United States had formally given up all its claims to Texas— and no sooner had this been done than many American states- men began to voice their regrets, especially John Quincy Adams and Andrew Jackson. They did not have to worry; by the time Mexico's President Santa Anna woke up to the fact of Texas's peaceful occupation, it was too late. The Texas colonists threw off the Mexican yoke and applied for annexation to the United States. Washington's hesitation on account of the slavery issue was eventually brushed aside in 1845, but not soon enough to avoid awakening European appetites.

Ever since the Louisiana Purchase, a number of European statesmen had become alarmed by the sheer size of the United States in both territory and swelling population. Talleyrand, Canning, and Louis Bonaparte were determined to seize every available opportunity to establish, at some time or other, a bal- ance of power in North America—and at this stage, it could only be done by preventing further American expansion in the south and southwest. The temporary independence of the Lone Star Republic whetted their appetites: it was an ideal buffer state between the United States and Mexico, which Lord Aberdeen, the British Foreign Secretary, and the French Premier Guizot attempted to bolster through loans and diplomatic recognition. They both urged Mexico to recognize the independence of Texas, in exchange for full Franco-British guarantee of Mexico's fron- tiers against United States aggression. The Texans would have accepted the scheme, but Mexico would not hear of it. Once again, historical fate played into the hands of the United States. While Mexico stubbornly refused to grant independence to Texas, the United States elected James Polk as President in the midst of a powerful awakening of atavistic imperialism; it was then discovered and proclaimed that it was the "Manifest Destiny" of the United States to expand toward the west and south, that it was justified by the Anglo-Saxon genius for colonization and self-government. The Europeans refused to recognize any such Manifest Destiny and pursued their dream. Guizot kept insist- ing that "France has a lasting interest in the maintenance of independent states in America, and in the balance of forces

which exists in that part of the world" [7]—to which President
Polk angrily retorted: "Jealousy among the different sovereigns
of Europe . . . has caused them anxiously to desire the establishment of what they term the 'balance of power.' It cannot be
permitted to have any application on the North American continent, and especially the United States." [8] But by then, Texas was
only part of the problem, and California was fast becoming an
even more tempting prize.

The time finally came to fight it out with Mexico, regardless of
European reactions. Polk ordered American troops in Texas to
cross the Nueces River and occupy the whole left bank of the Rio
Grande. Cautiously, the Mexican Government refrained from
military action. But nothing could now stop Polk's pursuit of his
imperialistic design. Unscrupulously stating that Mexican troops
had invaded United States territory(whereas they had merely
attempted to reoccupy territory between the Rio Grande and the
Nueces which had never even been part of Texas), Polk pre-
vailed upon Congress to declare war. Hostilities were short and
to the point; American troops eventually reached Mexico City
itself and the American plenipotentiaries had to wait two months
before finding a Mexican government willing to negotiate away
half of its territory—since this is what it eventually had to give
up by the Treaty of Guadalupe Hidalgo: Texas along with its
new Rio Grande frontier, Upper California, and all the land in
between (New Mexico, Arizona, Utah and Nevada). Again,
great and cheap success only whetted the appetite of many
jingoist Americans who claimed that the *whole* of Mexico should
be absorbed by the United States—only to be coldly dismissed by
Polk who knew when to stop. From that time on, and apart from
minor border rectifications, the continental United States has
kept within the limits achieved after the Mexican War.

Except for Russia, its size dwarfed that of any European nation, however powerful—in fact was, and still is, larger than the
whole of Europe without Russia. Conscious of its enormous size,
dynamism, and power, the United States felt that it had a right to
look down on the Europeans with mild contempt, and rarely was
it expressed with such bluntness as in Secretary of State Daniel
Webster's reply in 1851 to Austrian protests at the American

rescue of the Hungarian revolutionist Kossuth: "The power of this republic at the present moment is spread over a region, one of the richest and most fertile of the globe, and of an extent in comparison with which the possessions of the House of Habsburg are but a patch on the earth's surface." [9] The haughty court circles in Vienna must have been slightly amazed at this arrogance, worthy of the Chinese Emperor Ch'ien Lung.

One would have thought that by the middle of the nineteenth century the United States could have looked forward to digesting its enormous acquisitions without casting a covetous eye beyond the seas. But, somehow, the European revolutions in 1848 seemed to arouse that blend of democratic idealism and imperialistic drive that the Americans have never lost. Prompted by the requests of local revolutionists, there was irresponsible but loud talk in 1848 of annexing both Ireland and Sicily. Senator Stephen A. Douglas stated emphatically but prematurely that "Europe is antiquated, decrepit, tottering on the verge of dissolution. It is a vast graveyard." [10] The expansionist ambitions of American leaders seemed to know no bounds. In 1848, again, James Polk offered to buy Cuba from Spain for a hundred million dollars, an offer which was contemptuously rejected by the Madrid Government. The United States had also become vitally interested in Central America because of its new Californian window on the Pacific; land communications across its vast western territories being rather difficult, it was imperative that secure sea communications be established between the east and west coasts; Central America's narrow waist could offer either an interoceanic canal or land for roads and railroads. The main obstacle was the active presence of British interests; and Lord Palmerston, England's new Foreign Minister, was in no mood to sympathize with the United States' self-proclaimed Manifest Destiny. But, once again, compromise saved both powers from head-on collision: the 1850 Clayton-Bulwer treaty settled all differences amicably, even though many latter-day Americans regarded it as an unnecessary surrender of United States' interests.

But bigger issues were looming, the biggest being the actual degree of cohesion of the enormous Union itself. The greatest

test of all was coming, and when the Civil War broke out, far-sighted European statesmen had a last hope of seeing the United States collapse into smaller, more manageable fragments. The fact that Lincoln pointed out that slavery was not the main issue, did not quite prevent the division of European opinion along class lines; but he insisted, time and again, that the basic issue was the preservation of the Union, the preservation of the giant's organic unity from the threat of being torn to pieces, limb by limb, by its own centrifugal forces. Quite naturally, in the England of 1861, the Union had few vocal upholders, and sympathy for the South was widespread. Did the British wishfully think that a breakup of the American colossus might end forever the United States' incipient imperial rivalry, and leave the British Empire as the dominant world power?

At any rate, it seems probable that European sympathies (in Britain and France, especially) were instrumental in encouraging the founders of the Confederacy to move ahead with their planned rebellion at the Montgomery Convention. The active encouragement given by the Americans to the numerous revolutionary movements in Europe was bound to antagonize the ruling classes of the Old World—encouragement for the Irish, the German liberals, the Hungarians and other oppressed nationalities in the Austrian Empire, including the Garibaldian Italians. Determined and united action on the part of the ruling Europeans might have swung the balance in the Western Hemisphere in favor of the Confederacy's breakaway and formal Secession; but, as usual, mutual distrust and jealousy between the Europeans effectively thwarted all unified policy. Nevertheless, they gave it a good try.

Although many voices were raised in Great Britain for intervention against the North, it was France's Napoleon III who took the most decisive step in the matter by sending an army to invade and occupy Mexico. Materializing the dream of Talleyrand, Canning, and Aberdeen, Louis Bonaparte was determined to establish, by force of arms if necessary, a balance of power in North America. Aligned with Napoleon III were Francis Joseph, Emperor of Austria, and Lord Palmerston, Queen Victoria's Prime Minister—all of them anxious to see the United States collapse into smaller parts, but not with the same degree of vehemence. Palmerston, for instance, was cautious and pragmatic; Louis Bonaparte was an unrealistic visionary who attempted to hustle Palmerston along in letter after letter: "There is no need for me to enlarge upon the common interest which we in Europe have in seeing Mexico pacified . . . if it were regenerated it would form an impassable barrier to the encroachments of North America," [12] he explained in one of his messages to the British Prime Minister. During the whole of 1862 and the early part of 1863, the possibility was great that several European Powers would grant diplomatic recognition to the Confederacy—implying automatically war with the Union, warned United States Secretary of State Seward.[13] This threat did not frighten off the Europeans. Lord Russell, British Foreign Secretary, prepared secretly for recognition, with Palmerston's discreet approval. Karl Marx, who then worked as the New York *Daily Tribune*'s correspondent in Britain, pointedly reminded his readers, in a short historical briefing, that it was Palmerston who, "after a severe struggle with his colleagues, dispatched three thousand men to Canada, an army ridiculous, if intended to cover a frontier of fifteen hundred miles, but a clever sleight-of-hand if the rebellion was to be cheered, and the union to be irritated. He, many weeks ago, urged Bonaparte to propose a joint armed intervention 'in the internecine struggle,' supported that project in the Cabinet council, and failed only in carrying it by the resistance of his colleagues. He and Bonaparte then resorted to the Mexican intervention as a *pis aller*." [14]

In the end, Palmerston was frustrated and the British were deterred from diplomatic recognition of the Confederacy by what was going to become a recurring American miracle in their chosen field of endeavor—economic productivity. The amazing speed with which the Union built and commissioned its navy (from 42 ships at the beginning of the Civil War to 300 in 1862 and over 650 at the end of the hostilities) paralyzed the will of the British leaders, in spite of the early Confederate victories on land. And Napoleon III was not bold enough to go ahead and recognize the South without the British—although bold enough to actually encourage Texas to secede from the Confederation in order to save something from the approaching collapse of the South and provide a buffer state for his Mexican satellite. But all his intrigues failed; and French opposition to his policy was growing by leaps and bounds—not only on humanitarian and anti-slavery grounds, but also feeding on the ever-present anglophobia of the French: "The unity and independence of America, that is to say the sole maritime power that counterpoises England, constitutes for all Europe the only guarantee of the liberty of the seas . . ." [15] claimed Edouard Laboulaye, one of France's leading public figures at the time.

It is worth noting, furthermore, that it was largely *western* Europeans that were longing for a breakup of the American colossus; the *eastern* Europeans, deprived of wide openings on the sea and jealous of the growing wealth and industrialization of the western part of their continent, were wholeheartedly on the side of the Union. That was the position of Prussia, before and during Bismarck's rise to power; more strangely still, it was the position of Czar Alexander II and of his foreign minister, Prince Gorchakov. Quite apart from the fact that the Germans were struggling for national unity and therefore sympathized with the Americans' efforts to preserve theirs, and also quite apart from the fact that Czar Alexander's emancipation of the Russian serfs seemed to parallel Lincoln's emancipation of the American slaves, there was the atavistic hostility of the eastern Europeans toward their more fortunate (geographically) western European neighbors. The same jealousy of American power that was evident in Spain, France, and Britain, was equally apparent in the east of the Continent toward the west.

With all that, it is clear that had the fate of the Civil War decided otherwise, Louis Bonaparte might have succeeded in materializing his dream. Slidell, the Southern agent in Paris, boldly asserted support for the French-backed Emperor Maximilian in Mexico. In his turn, Napoleon III suggested a peace conference in 1863, with the object of securing the independence of the South—a suggestion which was promptly rejected by Lincoln. In its endeavors, France was backed by Spain, and a Spanish historian summed up the problem neatly and wistfully: "A little audacity and France was assured of her possessions, England of Canada . . . ourselves of the treasures of our Antilles, and the future of the Spanish race. Mexico and the Southern States . . . were the two advanced redoubts which Europe in its own interest should have thrown up against the American colossus." [16] But it was not to be. Impressed by the Emancipation Proclamation, liberal and left-wing sentiment in Europe was shifting over to the Union and against the Confederacy. When, in the desperate year 1865, Confederate President Jefferson Davis offered Europe abolition of slavery in the South in exchange for diplomatic recognition, it was too late. The surrender of General Lee meant the reestablishment of the Union in its full extent, and Europe lost its last chance to establish any kind of balance of power across the Atlantic: the American colossus came out of the ordeal bruised but intact, and ripe for further growth and development.

The Union had been not only preserved but vastly strengthened. The original federal union was no longer federal but national and unitary in everything except its administrative apparatus: the federal image had been preserved, but that was all. The American giant's inner structure was more compact than it had ever been, and subsequent historical forces, along with industrialization and technological progress, were going to make it more compact still.

The restored Union first flexed its muscles by demanding, and obtaining that France give up all claims to Mexico, leaving Emperor Maximilian to his tragic fate in 1867. The same year, the United States purchased the enormous territory of Alaska from the Russians, for a little over seven million dollars. This purchase, soon dubbed "Seward's Folly," was made by Secretary of State Seward in anticipation of a merger between Canada and the United States, a fusion which was hoped for by many citizens of both countries. Anglophobe Czar Alexander II and his foreign minister Prince Gorchakov sold this immense territory in the hope of stirring up trouble between the two English-speaking Powers. But Britain cunningly granted self-government to the newborn Canadian federation, the very same year that Alaska was purchased. Other expansionary plans of the United States suffered the same fate as the abortive merger with Canada. The Senate rejected a treaty to buy the Danish West Indies; President Grant was very much interested in the acquisition of Santo Domingo: again, the Senate rejected the proposed treaty of annexation.

Meantime, internal colonization proceeded at an increasingly rapid tempo. In the space of one generation after the Civil War, the West's settled area increased 100 percent under an enormous flood of immigrants; thanks to technological improvements, the Great Plains were at last conquered and settled—the so-called Great American Desert passed away and became one of the granaries of the world. The Indians were ruthlessly suppressed: between 1850 and 1860, their numbers in California alone shrank from one hundred thousand to thirty-five thousand. From 1860 to 1887, the Indians of the Great Plains and the Rocky Mountains were relentlessly pursued and massacred—a sad tale of greed and corruption, of broken promises and violated treaties, driving the Indians to become and behave as outlaws in their own land. It was only with the Dawes Act of 1887 that the American Government faced up to its moral responsibilities and obligations. Eventually, parked within the confines of some two hundred reservations, the demoralized Indians began to disintegrate physically and spiritually, some being more fortunate in their ability to adjust to some extent to the strange white man's world erected on the land of their ancestors. And with the last battle of Wounded Knee Creek in 1890, the Frontier disappeared on the North American continent—but, to this day, its spirit has remained an integral part of the American ethos.

The passing of the old continental Frontier in 1890, synchronized with a staggering increase in America's industrialization and economic productivity, became the turning point in the United States' relations with the rest of the world. This was the era of worldwide European colonization on a grand scale, of a frantic search for new commercial markets and new sources of raw materials. In this fast-changing world, the United States' foreign policy revolved around two axes. The first was the Monroe Doctrine which excluded European attempts at new colonial ventures in the Western Hemisphere, and left the United States free to dominate it politically and economically. The second axis was American expansion across the Pacific.

Having turned its back on the Old World and acquired an immense window on the Pacific, it was only natural that the restless Americans would start looking across the enormous expanse of the world's largest ocean. As early as 1853, Washington had sent a powerful fleet under Commodore Matthew Perry's command to break Japan's traditional isolation; and the following year, the Treaty of Kanagawa opened Japan to the world. The Midway Islands, west of Hawaii, were annexed; and Hawaii, where American missionaries-turned-businessmen had overthrown the Polynesian monarchy, soon followed suit. In the space of two generations, the western Pacific became included in the American realm, prelude to the whole ocean becoming, in due course, an American *mare nostrum*. Commodore Perry himself stated the long-term goal of America's policy in the Pacific when he said: "It is self-evident that the course of coming events will ere long make it necessary for the United States to extend its jurisdiction beyond the limits of the western continent, and I assume the responsibility of urging the expediency of establishing a foothold in this quarter of the globe. . . ." [17] The ghostly outline of a new American Frontier across the Pacific was beginning to loom.

The first phase of American imperialism was now in full swing. Dormant for a generation after the Civil War, the spirit of "Manifest Destiny" began to stalk the land again. Having once served for the conquest of Texas and California, it was now dusted off and brought into service abroad, and its main conjurer was the brilliant Captain Alfred Thayer Mahan who, in his famous studies on the political implications of sea power, became the theoretician of the new American imperialism overseas. Caught by the spirit of colonial expansion so prevalent in those days, and fearful of being left behind in the race to fill the power vacuums still left on the globe, Senator Henry Cabot Lodge stated very plainly his, and many of his countrymen's, belief: "From the Rio Grande to the Arctic Ocean there should be but one flag and one country. . . . Small states are of the past, and have no future." [18] Here was no aspiration to world dominion, just an effort to "keep up with the Joneses" of colonial imperialism. How to put it into practice was another matter.

For a while, this new American imperialism was strictly defensive, being content to uphold the Monroe Doctrine in the Western Hemisphere. The celebrated fracas with Great Britain over the Guiana-Venezuela border prompted Secretary of State Olney to utter a shrill warning: "Today the United States is practically sovereign on this continent, and its fiat is law upon the subjects to which it confines its interposition. . . ." [19] The Latin Americans were not even consulted. But true enough, Britain had been perhaps a little too active in that part of the world—for instance, Palmerston's seizure of Belize (British Honduras), the British takeover of the Nicaraguan customs in 1895. A little twisting of the Lion's tail could do no harm, and would certainly sit well with millions of Irish immigrants. And already then, the time was past when the British Lion dared roar at the United States, in spite of the backing of a global but aging British Empire. The Salisbury Government swallowed its pride, being far too busy in other quarters.

Soon enough, however, an opportunity presented itself to switch from a purely defensive imperialism to an offensive one: the Cuban revolution of 1895. Long before, in words prophetic not only for the end of the nineteenth century but perhaps for the second half of the twentieth, John Quincy Adams had written: "In looking forward to the probable course of events, it is scarcely possible to resist the conviction that the annexation of Cuba to our Federal Republic will be indispensable to the continuance and integrity of the Union itself" [20]—the perennial fear that if the United States ceased expanding, it was threatened with disintegration. And on the eve of the Civil War, a Senate committee was bold enough to state that "the ultimate acquisition of Cuba may be considered a fixed purpose of the United States." [21]

The Cuban revolt against Spanish tyranny soon led to the Hispano-American War, backed in the United States by an enthusiastic public opinion. Pushed into the war by a popular demand whipped up by the Hearst Press, President McKinley reluctantly gave in and ordered United States armed forces into

Cuba and the Philippines. In ten weeks, the United States crushed and destroyed Spain's fleets and armies, and took over the remains of her once global empire. It was, in John Hay's words, a "splendid little war" [22] which left the United States in possession of Puerto Rico, the island of Guam, and the Philippines, and freed Cuba from Spanish domination.

The acquisition of an empire was all right, but of a *colonial* empire—that was an entirely different matter, which disturbed the consciences of many Americans who felt that it was a betrayal of the ideals that had presided at the foundation of the United States and the principles of the Declaration of Independence. Furthermore, the United States soon found itself saddled with a full-fledged Filipino revolt, which cost almost as many American lives as the whole Spanish War. The Americans ended by doing in the Philippines exactly what they had fought Spain for doing in Cuba; and the not unnatural result was a wave of anti-imperialist revulsion in the United States itself, in the course of which Mark Twain pointedly accused McKinley of "playing the European game" of colonial imperialism; [23] imitating the Europeans was not in the American style. Cuba remained under the rule of the United States Army until 1902 and was eventually evacuated in 1909, only to be taken over again by American marines in 1912, and again in 1917. American investments in Cuba rose from fifty million dollars on the eve of the Spanish War to about two billion dollars half a century later, making it an economic appendage of America rather than a formal colony. Puerto Rico, on the other hand, was slowly absorbed by the United States. An organic act of 1917 granted American citizenship to Puerto Ricans and semiautonomous government to the island.

The acquisition of the Philipppines—and also the fear that Japanese immigration would flood the islands, at a time when Japan itself was becoming a world power in its own right—finally moved McKinley to proclaim the formal annexation of Hawaii. A year after the annexation, in 1900, full American citizenship was granted to all its inhabitants. As for the Philippines, the American Government soon made it clear that it did not wish to annex them, but would prepare them for full independence; in that sense, the United States promptly shed the "colonialist" mantle which the Europeans wore so proudly and, they hoped, permanently. The reason for this was not so altruistic as it sounds, and was strongly motivated by economic factors. A few years after the American conquest of the Philippines, all its local products, including sugar, were admitted in the United States free of duty, hurting the local sugar producers, especially in Utah and Louisiana whose representatives in Congress became the foremost advocates of independence for the Far Eastern archipelago. American businessmen were disappointed by the lack of commercial and industrial opportunity in the islands; while American naval experts were of the opinion that the Philippines were indefensible in case of war with Japan—all of which left the United States' leaders with little incentive to retain such a useless and cumbersome colony. Accordingly, the Philippine Independence Act of 1934 set the archipelago on its road to independence, leaving the United States in charge of its military defense—in which state they were caught by Pearl Harbor and the Japanese invasion.

The *colonial* imperialism of the turn of the century was a superficial, ephemeral phenomenon. It was not part of the United States' historical destiny to ape the European Powers, and America's voluntary abandonment of the Philippines, long before the process of "decolonization" became worldwide, is symbolic of this reality. The true character of the United States' inevitable imperialism was to reveal itself later. Right then, America proclaimed the "Open Door" policy in regard to China while the rest of the world's Powers were tearing the prostrate body of the Middle Kingdom apart, casting upon China "looks of tiger-like voracity, hustling each other in their endeavors to be the first to seize upon our innermost territories," in the words of the Dowager Empress.[24] Of course, the United States' Open Door policy was not entirely altruistic either. The various Powers that were grabbing large hunks of Chinese territory were also threatening the Philippines' trading potential with China—and threatening Great Britain's long-established position in the Far East, which explains Britain's espousal of the United States' policy.

America's Open Door policy in China was not duplicated in

the Western Hemisphere; when some foreign project was deemed essential for the welfare of the United States, the American leaders did not let scruples stand in their way. Colombia's refusal to let the United States build an interoceanic canal across the isthmus of Panama provoked a violent reaction on the part of President Theodore Roosevelt against "Those contemptible little creatures in Bogotá," prompted him to "encourage" an anti-Colombian revolt in Panama while ordering the American Navy to prevent Colombia from crushing the revolt.[25] Within three days of its inception, Washington recognized Panama's rebel government, and twelve days later signed with it a treaty granting the United States a perpetual lease on the Canal Zone. While Colombia was hit over the head with Roosevelt's Big Stick, the rest of Latin America was put on notice that the United States would stand no nonsense when it came to important matters concerning its hegemony in the Western Hemisphere.

The Monroe Doctrine had squarely placed the entire hemisphere under virtual United States protectorate and Washington saw to it that no European intervention was allowed to challenge its supremacy in the area—courtesy of the British, of course, since the Royal Navy was still supreme throughout the world, and the American Navy had barely started its buildup. James Gerard, American Ambassador in Berlin before and during World War I, records that "certain at least of the German statesmen contemplated a *rapprochement* with Great Britain and a mutual spanking of America and its Monroe Doctrine by these two Great Powers. Later I was informed by a man high in the German Foreign Office that Germany had proposed to Great Britain a joint intervention in Mexico, an invasion which would have put an end forever to the Monroe Doctrine, of course to be followed by the forceful colonisation of Central and South America. I was told that Great Britain refused." [26] Indeed, by now, Britain had moved so close to the United States that she had given up all exercise of power in the Western Hemisphere— and was far more worried by the swift buildup of Germany's war fleet in the North Sea. As far as London was concerned, Washington had a free hand in the Western Hemisphere.

After the turn of the century, the United States began interfering in the affairs of many Caribbean and Central American republics. In 1904, President Roosevelt announced that "chronic wrong-doing or an impotence which results in a general loosening of the ties of civilized society may . . . require intervention by some civilized nation. . . ." [27] Those words were as good as deeds. In 1906, Roosevelt intervened forcibly in Cuba and put its internal affairs in order, warning, however, that "if elections become a farce and if the insurrectionary habit becomes confirmed . . . it is absolutely out of the question that the Island should remain independent; and the United States . . . would again have to intervene. . . ." [28] In 1905, Roosevelt intervened in Santo Domingo, and in hardly more than two years had put the affairs of that nation in good order. Shortly after, American marines landed in Nicaragua and ran the country for a while, negotiating a treaty leasing from that country the Gulf of Fonseca and the Great Corn and Little Corn islands which definitely curtailed Nicaragua's sovereignty to the extent of being indignantly denounced by the Central American Court of Justice. In 1914, the United States had to intervene in Haiti, then in full anarchy; and in 1915, American marines occupied the island and ran it until 1930. In 1916, President Woodrow Wilson started another military occupation of the Dominican Republic which lasted eight years.

All these displays of military power were prompted by American impatience at the lack of self-governing talent in the American tropics, not by colonial ambitions. On the basis of historical analytical comparisons, it has already been made clear elsewhere that the United States' coming imperialism was to be of the "Roman" and not the "Greek" type, to which, by reasons of geography and psychological disposition, the European Powers were restricted. Roman-type imperialism, in contrast to the Greek, is not of the "colonial" variety; it does not want to hold foreign nations in bondage for the benefit of the home country— in spite of temporary fits of economic imperialism. It is essentially ecumenical, in the political sense, and arises when a whole *civilization* and way of life is, or feels, threatened; it has definite idealistic undertones, is basically democratic (in contrast to the more aristocratic colonial type, as exemplified by the British

Empire), and looks forward to the eventual attainment of equality among all its citizens, conquerors and conquered alike . . . by which time it has ceased being an empire and has become a "common wealth," a true *res publica*. More than anything else, it is fundamentally reluctant, is compelled to step into power vacuums when it feels that its "way of life" is menaced.

At the turn of the century, the world situation was not remotely dangerous in that sense. Nowhere was there any visible threat to Western civilization as such. The United States' sole ambition in the world was to stay clear of foreign entanglements of any kind—its sporadic fits of jingoism being more the exuberance of great vitality and restlessness than the consuming greed which animated most European colonial ventures. There was still plenty to be done at home before the new lands and the new immigrants became an organic part of the United States. There was no standing army and no permanent bureaucracy—in contrast to the great "Hellenistic" kingdoms and empires of Europe. Although its growth throughout the nineteenth century had been staggering in its amplitude (its population increased from 5 to 76 million, its national wealth from 7 to 88 billion dollars), the United States was a *potential* Power of great magnitude, not an *actual* one. What actualized America's imperial potential was the suicide of Europe and the opening of worldwide power vacuums.

European Powers and smaller nations had become so embroiled in their petty quarrels that few European statesmen took the rising power of the United States into account. Following the failure of European intervention in the affairs of North America during the Civil War, they had almost given up hope of destroying the overseas giant whose influence was beginning to be felt in the Old World in many ways. Still, a few gave it a thought; a leading statesman of Austro-Hungary, Count Goluchowski, advocated drawing Russia into the Triple Alliance and forming a league of European Powers in order to preserve the continent against "trans-Oceanic" influences. But no one listened. And as early as the turn of the century, some of the British thinkers who felt in their bones the approaching hurricanes in which Europe's world ascendancy was going to be shipwrecked, consoled themselves with the thought that, after all, "it is England who, in Southern Asia, in Australia, in Africa and in America, has founded those parvenu powers which ruffle the complacency of Europe, and has called the New World into being which impairs the ascendancy of the Old." [29]

Not all citizens of the "parvenu powers" were blind to the irresistible trend of the times—and none was quite as farsighted as Walter Hines Page who had been appointed United States Ambassador to the Court of St. James's soon after Woodrow Wilson became President. In an astonishingly prophetic letter, dated October 25, 1913, almost a year before the outbreak of World War I, he wrote from London to the President:

> The future of the world belongs to us. A man needs to live here, with two economic eyes in his head, a very little time to become very sure of this. Everybody will see it presently. These English are spending their capital, and it is their capital that continues to give them their vast power. Now what are we going to do with the leadership of the world presently when it clearly falls into our hands? . . . The great economic tide of the century flows our way. *We* shall have the big world questions to decide presently. Then we shall need world policies. . . . We are in the international game—not in its Old World intrigues and burdens and sorrows and melancholy, but in the inevitable way to leadership and to cheerful mastery in the future; and everybody knows that we are in it but us. It is sheer blind habit that causes us to continue to try to think of ourselves as aloof.[30]

The American mastery in the future was not to be as cheerful as Walter Page thought—but, as he knew intuitively, it was pre-ordained; and, across the Channel, there were few farsighted men such as Goluchowski who could see it. For by now, in the dead eye of the storm, no one on the Continent cared enough to pay any attention to this cardinal fact. At Serajevo, a fuse was lighted in the Balkan powder keg and Europe exploded.

The Suicide of Europe

In 1914, Europe owned and controlled most of the world; the United States was still a marginal offshoot of Europe's worldwide expansion. Europe's colonial empires and overall economic power dominated the globe—colonial empires conquered and ruled for the benefit of the European Powers concerned; overall economic power which fueled even the economic expansion of the United States and Russia, although they were politically outside Europe's control.

By far the largest and most powerful, the pace-setting British Empire was a conglomerate of self-ruled dominions, outright colonies on every continent, and, set apart with a special status of its own, India, the brightest gem in Great Britain's imperial crown. *Primus inter pares,* the British Empire was, in fact, the only true *global* empire girding the world, global by virtue of the monetary lordship of the pound sterling and the unique trading position of the City of London, and global because the British Navy ruled all the waves of the oceans and enforced a worldwide *Pax Britannica;* Britain was all at once the banker and the policeman of the world, and a quarter of the human race was included within the borders of its empire. The only area on this planet where British hegemony was not in effect was the Continent—Europe, and its Russian extension. Even the Western Hemisphere, which the United States had come to dominate toward the latter part of the nineteenth century, depended on the British fleet for its security from external aggression. Without the Royal Navy to enforce it, the Monroe Doctrine was dead letter. And even though Britain's influence on the United States was merely financial, and limited at that, her economic lordship in other countries of the Western Hemisphere such as Canada and Argentina was supreme.

Britain's global empire ended on the shores of the narrow Channel isolating her home islands from the Continent. In Europe itself, Britain's main concern was to preserve the "balance of power" in such a way that the Continent could never fall under the sway of a single state; this balance had been preserved for a full hundred years, the time that had elapsed since the fall of Napoleon. Extremely convenient tensions had developed between the various Continental Powers—between the Austro-Hungarian Empire and Russia, between Germany and France—all of which kept the political situation more or less on an even keel and internal tensions strong enough to pevent a Continental coalition from ever overwhelming Britain.

But, quite unobstrusively, profound changes had been taking place in the actual power relationship between Britain and the most dynamic of Continental Powers: Germany, the youngest and boldest European state, a Prussianized Germany dreamed up and created by Bismarck in 1870, a Second Reich seeking its self-appointed place in the sun, its *lebensraum*. While Britain was aging, Germany was young and aggressive. Without realizing it, Britain was at the tail end of its imperial destiny, exhausted by the Boer War, its imperial swan song. Since 1870, it is true, its empire had grown tremendously in all quarters of the globe; British capital had been overflowing in ever-increasing amounts the narrow boundaries of Britain proper; the outward-bound stream of money seeking profitable investment had dragged British imperialism in its wake for political and military protection. But decay had already set in and British capitalism no longer had the dynamism required to compete against aggressive newcomers—more particularly, the fast-rising economic power of the hardworking Germans. One commercial defeat after another began to puncture Britain's economic and financial preeminence. Worse still, Germany's Kaiser Wilhelm had decided, at the turn of the century, to challenge Britain's naval supremacy and build a powerful fleet in the North Sea—besides having the most powerful army on the Continent.

Out of this basic conflict between an aging empire and a young, vigorous and ruthless would-be empire on the Continent, arose the great two-phase (1914–18, 1939–45) European civil war that was to destroy all Powers on the Continent as well as Britain's worldwide empire; and by stripping them all of their overseas possessions and impoverishing them, reduce them all to the rank of second- and third-class Powers—when it did not destroy them altogether. The Austro-Hungarian and Ottoman empires vanished into nought; once-powerful Germany, the only aspirant to Continental hegemony, was amputated of all its conquests and some of its richest provinces, and what was left was split into two hostile states; the whole Continent was cut in half, each half becoming a more or less thinly disguised protectorate of non-European Superpowers; and the British Empire became a ghost: the policeman of the world lost its club, and the banker, its capital. Unconsciously, the world began looking for imperial heirs to the global throne vacated by the Europeans.

Although neutral, the United States was directly and powerfully affected by the First World War now raging in Europe— and, in the early stages, determined to stay out of it; the affairs and troubles of the Old World were no concern of hers. While quite prepared to send military expeditions hither and thither for their own imperial aggrandizement in the Caribbean and the Pacific, the Americans saw no national benefit in becoming embroiled in European hostilities. Political isolationism, however, did not imply emotional neutrality; American opinion was, by and large, sympathetic to the cause of the Allies and hostile to the Teutonic Central Powers. Furthermore—and as later, in 1939–41—war in Europe pulled the United States out of a serious economic depression by compelling France and Britain to become clients able and anxious to gobble up enormous amounts of sundry American exports. Cecil Spring-Rice, the British Ambassador in Washington, pointed out in November 1915: "The brutal facts are that this country has been saved by the war and our demand from a great commercial crisis. . . . We have therefore the claims of their best customer and at the present moment our orders here are absolutely essential to their commercial prosperity." [1]

A year after the outbreak of the war, the economies of the United States, France, and Britain had become so intermingled that any brutal severance between them would have been disastrous for all concerned. But the intermingling, of course, was all to the advantage of the United States which, from being a debtor nation at the beginning of the hostilities, promptly became a creditor nation as foreign investors liquidated their securities in Wall Street and floated huge American loans. Europe's holdings of American securities totaled roughly five billion dollars in 1914—a figure so large that Wall Street financiers trembled at the idea of having to repurchase such an enormous quantity of stocks and bonds; but this was underestimating their enormous financial power, and the repurchase was made with the greatest of ease. Simultaneously, American money on loan began to pour into Europe: on the eve of the United States' entrance into the war in 1917, the Americans had already loaned one and a half billion dollars to the Allies, as against a mere twenty-seven million dollars to the Central Powers. When, three years later, the dust began to settle on the Continent, the United States had spent a grand total of twenty-five billion dollars for its participation in the war, in addition to lending over ten billion dollars to its European associates and repurchasing some five billion dollars' worth of European investments in America—an extraordinary financial feat, accomplished in less than five years. As an American financial writer put it a few years later: "To us it was an astounding self-revelation." [2]

Ostensibly, it was Germany's decision to engage in unrestricted submarine warfare and the dramatic sinking of the *Lusitania* that drew the United States into the war. In fact, and at a deeper level, it was plain that Britain's military struggle against

Germany's drive toward hegemony in Europe was also America's. A unified Europe under Germany's economico-military hegemony would be almost as much a permanent threat to the United States as it was to Great Britain; and if Britain had to go to war, the United States was immediately affected. The United States could never afford to let Britain go down to defeat—and in 1917, defeat was staring France and Britain in the face. By then, as the historical record shows, the Allies had reached the limit of their strength and were rapidly going downhill: Russia was disintegrating, the French army was torn apart by devastating mutinies, and in the spring Britain had only six weeks' supply of grain; the British Government had come to the conclusion that, under the circumstances, it would have to give up the struggle by November 1. With Germany triumphant on the Continent, the venerable balance of power was just about to be destroyed forever, consecrating Germany's hegemony in the Old World, the reduction of France to the status of a German satellite, and the drastic shrinking of Britain's geopolitical role to that of a small offshore island at the mercy of a mighty, united Europe under Prussian domination. The United States simply could not afford to see the old mother country placed in such a precarious position.

In his memoirs, James Gerard, American ambassador in Berlin at the time, shows quite clearly how vital Britain's defense was for the United States; and how it was Britain's own intervention in the war to preserve the traditional balance of power that, in turn, drew the United States into the European conflict in order to save Britain from defeat. After Kaiser Wilhelm, who had hoped in 1914 that Britain would remain aloof from the affairs of the Continent, had remarked despondently that the "British change the whole situation—an obstinate nation. They will keep up the war," Gerard himself remarked: "It was the entry of Great Britain into the war . . . which saved the world from the harsh domination of the conquest-hungry Prussians and therefore saved as well the two Americas and their protecting doctrine of President Monroe." [3] Gerard's theme was to become a recurrent one throughout the twentieth century—that Britain was America's advanced bastion across the Atlantic, that it should never be allowed to fall, but that it should be militarily assisted only when on the very brink of disaster and at the end of its tether.

Gerard illuminates as well Germany's profound misunderstanding of the real nature of the United States and of the remarkable success of its melting-pot policy which was making a compact nation out of immigrants from all over Europe. He once quotes Zimmermann, a high German official, as stating flatly: "The United States does not dare to do anything against Germany, because we have five hundred thousand German reservists in America, who will rise in arms against your Government if your Government should dare to take any action against Germany." [4] In fact, nothing surprised and disappointed the Germans so much as the relative indifference of their former compatriots in America whose descendants had been completely absorbed by the United States and had largely forgotten their European roots. But then, as Hermann Keyserling pointed out, "German soul and German spirit are such that they are even less capable of survival in the forms of Americanization than in those of an exaggerated Prussianization." [5] It is in this power of absorption, in this power of organic digestion which no European nation possesses, that the United States' capacity for growth and development resides—in fact, in its superb political and social metabolism.

In London, Gerard's counterpart, United States Ambassador Walter Hines Page, summed up in another of his remarkable letters to President Wilson his own view of the interaction between the Allies' plight and the fate of the United States. Dated March 5, 1917, it states:

> The inquiries which I have made here about financial conditions disclose an international situation which is most alarming to the financial and industrial outlook of the United States. . . . There is . . . a pressing danger that the Franco-American and Anglo-American exchange will be greatly disturbed; the inevitable consequence will be that orders by all the Allied Governments will be reduced to the lowest possible amount and that trans-Atlantic trade will practically come to an end. The result of such a stoppage will be a panic

in the United States. . . . The financial and commercial result will be almost as bad for the United States as for Europe. We shall soon reach this condition unless we take quick action to prevent it. . . . It is not improbable that the only way of maintaining our present preeminent trade position and averting a panic is by *declaring war on Germany* [author's emphasis].[6]

In other words, it had become clear that an Allied defeat would have been a disaster for the United States, already committed financially and economically to an Allied victory. Having committed itself that far, it now found itself compelled to go all the way and join the war against the Central Powers in order to save its substantial investment in the solvency of the Allies.

Given all the elements that went into the tragedy of the First World War, military participation by the United States was all but inevitable. Just as trade and financial commitments had drawn the European nations into colonial ventures they would never have thought about in other circumstances, America's financial and economic stake in Europe were irresistibly dragging the United States into the European conflict. Not only was this intervention inevitable; it was also decisive. As the Allies began to face their doom in 1917, the United States mobilized its manpower and economic resources with stupefying rapidity. While the German submarine fleet was sinking Allied shipping at the rate of half a million tons a month before the United States joined the war, new constructions started in American shipyards were soon going at twice the sinking rate, nullifying the German threat. Furthermore, the Allies were facing financial bankruptcy and were saved in the nick of time by massive American loans.

It was no easy task to accomplish all this and swing around an American public opinion hitherto devoted to isolationism. This swing from apathy and indifference to a positive hysteria was largely the work of propaganda. For the first time, the new technique of commercial advertising, adapted to political purposes, brought to bear with astonishing and even alarming success, the full weight of mass suggestion on a whole population reluctant to become militarily involved in the conflict. The most extreme legislation (1917's Espionage Act and 1918's Sedition Act), now fully supported by public opinion, enabled the American Government to arrest fifteen hundred people for disloyalty; witch-hunting of a type prefiguring Senator Joseph McCarthy's thirty years later gripped the whole nation.

Meantime, the tide of military events was going from bad to worse for the Allies. The newly installed Soviet Government pulled Russia out of the war, releasing hundreds of thousands of battle-hardened German troops who were rushed to the Western Front; the Italian army collapsed at Caporetto, compelling the Allies to detach badly needed troops to plug the hole before the Austrians had time to flood the plains of northern Italy. The Germans were close to complete victory and knew it—but, with incredible speed, almost two million American soldiers landed in France in 1917 and 1918, restoring the numerical balance and turning the tide of war, psychologically as much as militarily.

It is legitimate, at this point, to ponder the following questions, academic as they may seem: Was the United States intervention in World War I inevitable? Was it decisive? And, if so, what would have happened if it had not taken place at all? Given its expansionist nature, there was only scant chance that the United States could keep out of the war if only because, by supplying the Allies with the economic and financial means to prosecute the war, the United States was already altering the balance of power between the warring states; this being insufficient to prevent the probable collapse of the Allies in 1917, military involvement was bound to follow, inasmuch as the victory of the Allies had become vital to the eventual solvency of the United States' new debtors. In the eyes of history, if not those of historical mythology, military incidents between America and Germany only triggered a ready-made fuse. Only a clear-cut Allied victory could have avoided America's military involvement.

Of the fact that American intervention made all the difference between victory and defeat for France and Britain, there is hardly any doubt. After the United States declared war on Germany, Field Marshal Hindenburg, the worried Commander-in-chief of the German army, asked rhetorically: "Would she [America] appear in time to snatch the victor's laurels from our brow?" [7] She did, and on the fact that this intervention decisively altered the preordained course of the war, we have the vital testimony of both Erich Ludendorff, Quartermaster General of the German army, and France's Marshal Foch, Commander-in-chief of the Allied armies. Expatiating at length on the amazement and alarm of the German High Command at the speed with which huge numbers of American troops were shipped over to Europe, Ludendorff stated without ambiguity: "Thereby, America became the decisive factor." [8] Marshal Foch was no less emphatic in his testimony as to the decisive nature of this intervention from overseas: he repeatedly emphasized in his memoirs that both the French and the British were exhausted, and fought on mostly in the hope of prompt and massive American support, stressing time and again that American manpower was required "immediately." [9] In fact, the decisiveness of this assistance was such that Germany's first peace feelers were communicated to President Wilson through the Swiss Government, in the vain hope of making him an arbiter between the Allies and the Central Powers, rather than a cobelligerent of the Allies.

If the United States was thus the decisive element in the picture, it implies that she disrupted what would have been the normal outcome of the war without overseas involvement— German victory, France reduced to the minor position of a German satellite and Britain considerably weakened, and both constantly at the mercy of Germany's unchallengeable military might. Both Austria-Hungary and the Ottoman Empire would have been saved, along with their hegemony in Eastern Europe and the Near East. On the other hand, no social revolutions would have taken place in Europe at that time, while the victorious German Empire would have destroyed the Soviet regime in Russia, probably establishing some kind of protectorate over the Ukraine. A new balance of power would have been established —but on a global scale this time. It would have been transferred from the shrinking continent of Europe, where it had been maintained for the benefit of Britain, to the whole world where it would have become established between the United States, potential master of the oceans, and Germany, full master on the European Continent.

Just as clearly, Germany's defeat, and indirectly the collapse of the Austro-Hungarian Empire into small fragments, triggered social revolutions all over Central and Eastern Europe, transformed the Kaiser's brutal but civilized and efficient empire into a still-powerful but wounded country, racked by revolution and financial chaos, and eventually metamorphosed into Hitler's barbaric realm. Just as surely, it saved Soviet power in Russia from annihilation by destroying the only Power that had both the will and the power to extinguish Marxism-Leninism. Most of the seeds of the worldwide developments of the century were sown in 1917 when the United States entered the war.

Having won the war, the United States promptly proceeded to lose the peace. Woodrow Wilson was determined to control the peace negotiations, which not only was likely to antagonize his allies but lost all justification when congressional elections in the United States indirectly repudiated his leadership. His idealistic Fourteen Points never had a chance of being accepted, nor would they, if accepted, have spared the world a resumption of hostilities and another round of warfare. They were not geared to the concrete political reality of the times. Nor did the creation of the League of Nations endear him further to an already hostile Congress. When the time came to ratify the Treaty of Versailles, Wilson had collapsed and the Treaty was defeated in the Senate. In 1920, the Presidential elections gave a majority of the vote to his Republican opponent and, for the last time, the American people turned back to an outdated isolationism—outdated because, having already powerfully interfered in European affairs and temporarily upset the new balance of power that would have been established without its intervention, the United States then refused to accept the new balance of power that would have been established if the British, and especially the French, had been allowed to dictate the peace terms as they saw fit. Anthony Eden recalls in his memoirs that ". . . after the war, the French aim had been to guarantee their country's security by the separation of the Rhineland provinces from the rest of Germany. The French government were persuaded to abandon that position by means of an arrangement which comprised a fifteen years' occupation of the zone itself, its permanent demilitarisation and, most important of all, a guarantee of security from ourselves and the United States. That guarantee was never forthcoming. The United States failed to ratify and, since our ratification was dependent upon theirs, the guarantee came to nothing." [10]

But even the British and the French were at loggerheads, the British being atavistically suspicious of French attempts at establishing their "hegemony" on the Continent by splitting up Germany into several separate states. In this postwar attempt, it seems, the French had the full support of a relatively unknown Oberbürgermeister of Cologne named Konrad Adenauer who attempted to sell the idea to the British. But Lloyd George and the rest of the British Cabinet, distrusting the aims of Foch and Clemenceau, shuddered at the thought of a Rhenish-Westphalian republic under French protectorate, and refused point blank to endorse this scheme.[11]

If anything, the paralyzing antagonism between the British and the French should have convinced the Americans that they could not afford to retreat into isolationism, lest all the benefits won by the Allied victories be lost in a subsequent conflict. Furthermore, political isolationism was an even greater blunder owing to the fact that it could no longer imply economic and financial isolationism. The United States had emerged from the war with a vastly stronger economy and a far more powerful financial structure. From a debtor nation, she had become creditor to the tune of over ten billion dollars (seven billion dollars in war loans and three billion in peace loans). Before the outbreak of the war, American private investments abroad totaled three billion dollars; fifteen years later, they had risen to fourteen billion. These figures imply that the United States now had a big stake to protect abroad, and in particular in Europe, which made nonsense of political isolationism and led to constant American intervention in the economic and financial affairs of Europe.

In addition, the collection of the war debts proved to be a major problem, mixed up as it was with a multitude of interconnected debts between all the Allies, and with the ticklish problem of reparations owed by the Germans to the Allies. Inter-

Allied bitterness mounted rapidly as the outraged European accused "(U)ncle (S)hylock" across the ocean of a lack of generosity. Since most of the money borrowed had been spent in the United States, the Allies felt that it was part of that country's contribution to the common war; they complained that since Germany felt unable to meet its payments for reparations, her victims should not be held accountable for American loans; they also stated that the American tariff policy made it impossible for the European nations to pay back their debts through increased trade. The disastrously prohibitive Fordney-McCumber tariff of 1922 established the highest rates in American history and made it difficult for European goods to compete in the United States. Needless to say, European nations retaliated in kind, hurting American exports and putting a crimp on world trade. But this was not enough yet. In 1930, the Hawley-Smoot Tariff Act raised rates all down the line, compelling twenty-five countries to establish retaliatory tariffs and depresssing American trade still further. Soon enough, the Great Depression took over and swept the world.

Little time was required after the end of the war before some wise and thoughtful Europeans woke up to the fact that they were no longer sole masters of the world—even those who, like the British and the French, had increased their colonial holdings in Africa and the Middle East. In a significantly titled book, *Qui sera le Maître—Europe ou Amérique?*, a noted French writer, Lucien Romier, set out in 1927 to explore the new relationship between the Old and the New World. Starting from the premise that Europe and America now jointly dominated the world (Soviet Russia was then a poorly developed outcast), he went on to point out that America had, for the first time, become emancipated from European tutelage and had become a completely distinct entity in its own right. He further pointed out that overpopulation in Europe had produced the vast emigration that had given birth to its American rival, but that what was left of overpopulation had driven Europe to the fratricidal World War, weakening it in relation to the more cohesive United States where immense space and unlimited opportunity had given it a remarkable degree of social stability. No such immensity existed in Europe where overpopulation had become the root cause of bitter national and social conflicts; the structure of European society itself was being challenged from within—whereas the United States, focusing on the twin ideas of service and profit, enjoyed both social flexibility and political stability. His thesis: in the age of the revolt of the masses, to which the United States had already become fully adapted, Europe had to find a new formula for survival.[12]

Counting its blessings, Romier then emphasized that Europe had preserved its creative genius; how to keep on preserving it while entering an age of mass civilization, was the problem he attempted to solve. The United States of Europe, as suggested by many Germans? He rejected it for reasons which have kept their validity half a century later: Europe cannot give up its fragmentation because, in denying its historical background, every one of its component nations would deny its own consciousness and would destroy its own vitality.[13] He believed that international initiative still belonged to the old (i.e., European) nations because the vast spaces of the new nations, offshoots of the Old World (United States, Canada, Australia, Argentina, Brazil), precluded their becoming vitally interested in the rest of the world: they had no political life worthy of the name because they did not need politics—whereas Europe did, precisely because of the relative smallness of its nation-states, the multiplicity of its international boundaries and frictions, and its complex social conflicts. But if Europe persisted in its *economic* balkanization, it would prove unable to catch up with America. Having stated that it would prove impossible to overcome Europe's political fragmentation into many separate nation-states, he saw some hope in a subtle form of economic unification around international trusts and cartels. He added that European individualism was already condemned by history in favor of America's emphasis on *social* collective well-being. He ended by stating that it was too early yet to decide whether Europe or America would remain master of the world.

While Romier skirted the specifically political aspect of the situation, Edouard Herriot, one of the most influential statesmen of the interwar period in France, grappled directly with it. In his 1930 opus *The United States of Europe,* he squarely faced the problem. He started by quoting a study published in 1920 by a distinguished professor at the Sorbonne, under the suggestive title *The Decline of Europe.* It already stated plainly, right after the end of the First World War, that "European hegemony has been seriously checked" and that "from some points of view she has already come to appear like a colony of young America, her god-daughter." [14] Drawing inspiration from this rather somber statement, Herriot went on to make a thorough study of what he called the "rationalization" of a relatively small continent split up into thirty-eight states. In the process, he gives us a vivid picture of the debates of the 1920's in the Old World still bleeding from self-inflicted wounds.

The Pan-European idea was first presented officially by Aristide Briand, Prime Minister of France, on September 5, 1929, in a speech at the tenth general assembly of the League of Nations: "I think that between people constituting geographical groups, like the peoples of Europe, there should be some kind of federal bond." [15] The European reaction to this revolutionary proposal was, on the whole, favorable, especially in Germany, while shading all the way to frigid in Britain. Twenty-seven European states welcomed the proposal officially. Perhaps the most enlightened and prophetic reply came from Eduard Beneš, Czechoslovakia's Premier, who said without mincing words: "The only issue for us today is this: either we work to form a sort of union between European states and nations, as much from the moral point of view as from the economic and political . . . or else we shall always be living in danger of difficulties, conflicts and perpetual crisis, ending in wars and catastrophes in which European culture will be submerged." [16]

Toward the end of his work, Herriot endorsed the Briand Memorandum, stressing that this European organization "should destroy neither the national nor the international framework." In other words, Europe could probably form a loose federation, along with economic unity, but no more.[17] Any hope of matching the tight concentration of power in a federal government modeled after that of the United States, should be discarded.

All such speculations left the British cold, dedicated as they were to the outdated concept of a Continental balance of power. At all times, they were the leading opponents of any scheme put forth to unify the Old World. And when the Great Depression blew like a hurricane through the world, Britain, under the leadership of Stanley Baldwin, did not look to the Continent but to the Empire and Commonwealth; the British adopted important measures of imperial preference, leaving their European neighbors to their dismal economic fate. The Americans followed in Britain's footsteps, wanted no part of European unification, and voiced their suspicions of Briand's proposals, "seeing in them methods of excluding American economic interests for selfish European reasons." Instead of understanding that Briand's proposals aimed primarily at a *rapprochement* between France and Germany, the Americans saw them merely as evidence that "Europe was ganging up against America." [18]

The dramatic developments of the 1930's made short shrift of all the grandiose plans for European unity—leading directly to the gruesome attempt of Germany's Third Reich to impose it by force and for its own benefit, and in the process, to the destruction of Europe. With typically perverse *schadenfreude*, Hitler even confessed to Sumner Welles in 1940: "I believe that German might is such as to make the triumph of Germany inevitable but, if not, *we will all go down together* [author's italics]— whether that be for better or for worse." [19]

As a matter of fact, it was a German thinker, Max Weber, who had seen the real trend of the times. Writing as early as November 1918, he foresaw the rise of America to world supremacy to be "as inevitable as that of Rome in the ancient world after the Punic War"—because Europe could never become an organic unit.[20]

While European statesmen found it impossible to set up a modicum of federalism linking the numerous states of their balkanized continent, the intrusion of the United States in Europe's economic affairs complicated matters further. After having taken part in the war as an "associated" rather than an "allied" Power, and saved Britain and France from certain defeat, the Americans promptly decided to set Germany up on its feet again. While distrusting both the Allies and the former Central Powers, they, in fact, held the Old World's precarious balance of power in their inexperienced hands. Not strong or determined enough to impose their policy on the British and the French thirsting for revenge, yet too strong to let France apply her own consistent, if selfish and shortsighted, policy, the Americans ended by sowing the seeds of a new conflagration. Believing, along with John Maynard Keynes, that Europe could never be prosperous without a prosperous Germany, the Americans extended their financial generosity to Germany in large amounts, while denying their former European "associates" the compensation to which they were entitled—then blaming the latter for not repaying their debts to the United States. All told, the Americans loaned the staggering amount of two and a half billion dollars to Germany in the 1920's. The various schemes devised to make Germany solvent again (the Dawes Plan and the Young Plan) were contrived under American auspices and named after the American chairmen of their planning commissions. The more money they poured into Germany, the greater stake they had in its financial solvency and political stability, and the Germans knew it. But the Americans were merely throwing good money after bad. When the Great Depression began to sweep the world and compelled President Hoover to ask for a moratorium on war debts and reparations in order to save Germany from financial collapse, an American financial writer noted at the time, "Comment in Germany was brutal and a little exultant. The Americans were obliged to save Germany from bankruptcy in order to protect the two and one half billions or more they had already loaned to her. It was to save themselves they were saving her and saving Europe." [21]

In fact, the United States had seen, in the 1920's, a reformed and renovated Germany—an "Americanized" Germany—as the cornerstone of peace in Europe; there was a shadow of substance to this illusion. The ease and speed with which a substantial portion of the Germans "Americanized" themselves in the post-war era certainly misled many Americans. Hermann Keyserling wrote: "It is with real terror that I note the increasing idealization of the conditions existing in the United States on the part of Germany's 'spiritual leaders.' " [22] And he added: "Today Americanism is becoming, psychologically, the substitute for Prussian militarism." [23] But after stating his own recipe for the proper recovery of Germany's pre-imperial spirit, he warned prophetically: "If, in the next few decades at most, no restoration in this sense takes place, then Germany will inevitably evolve into a caricature of America; into a caricature, because that which is essentially colossal avoids becoming a caricature only when it finds a colossal form" [24]—an apt description of the future, post-Hitler Germany in the shape of Adenauer's Bundesrepublik. Meantime, Prussianism had remained very much alive in the background, unseen and undetected by the innocent, in the small but superbly trained and equipped Reichswehr under General von Seeckt's leadership, and in the unaltered social structure and ideals of Prussian society.

Thus was the recovery of Germany—a Germany still nursing the myth that its "temporary" defeat had been due to a stab in the back—sponsored and largely financed by the United States, whose financial role in postwar Europe was as decisive as its military role had been in the latter part of the war. Not that the Germans were even grateful for this massive American assistance. As stated at the time, ". . . every German has it in his heart that his country was beaten by America, not by the Allies. But for the vast weight of American resources, first as they were loaned to the Allies and then as they went directly into the war, German victory had been inevitable, according to destiny. American money thwarted that destiny. . . . It follows that they have no sense of debt on account of reparations. Simply, reparations are tribute. . . . How could they be expected to care very much about what happened to the money they borrowed? It was the money of their enemies." [25]

Germany's precarious recovery was shattered by the Great Depression, making the rise to power of extremists inevitable. Germany's "insolvency" had never extended to its tight-knit

Reichswehr; the spirit of Prussianism was now throwing off the mask it wore in the 1920's, and the splendid military instrument was at hand, to be used by the National Socialists as a hard nucleus around which to build a new war machine, backed by a powerful industrial establishment. A great deal of the money borrowed in the United States went directly into what was soon to become Germany's great war industry: "With American chemical science dimly in sight of its goal, which is to make this country independent of Germany's synthetic chemistry, American credit is loaned to the German Dye Trust, whereby its offensive powers, in trade or in war, are strengthened," complained an outraged American economist in the early 1930's.[26]

If we add that the Great Depression itself was largely the doing of the United States, it becomes clear that American policy in the interwar period was the decisive element in the world picture. Having become a creditor on international account rather than a debtor, the United States should have lowered its tariffs rather than raised them. Its surplus of exports over imports, which used to pay the interest on loans from Europe, persisted and had to be paid for by transfers of European gold to the United States—or private American loans to Europe. Rather than correct this fundamental imbalance, the United States had repeatedly raised its tariffs. Debts went into default, American exports fell sharply, accelerating the onsetting Depression. And so it went on, chain-reaction fashion, until the whole world's economic structure disintegrated into self-sufficient economic units geared to the war policies of the German and Japanese extremists which the Great Depression had helped raise to supreme power in their respective lands.

But rather than feel responsible for this alarming turn of events, many leading Americans began expressing annoyance at their never-ending involvements in the affairs of Europe—financial involvements which inevitably had political implications such as the strong pressure exerted from the United States for the overthrow of Britain's extravagant Labour Government; those were the days when the Federal Reserve Bank of New York was accused of "putting a pistol to Britain's head." Grappling with their own depression at home, the Americans began longing for a further retreat into isolationism rather than for a concerted international effort to cope with what had become an international calamity. A noted financial writer expressed in 1931 the complaint that "In less than ten years, finance had accomplished a fact the idea of which had been rejected by the American people for a century and a half, namely, the fact of foreign entanglement." [27]

The Americans proceeded to disentangle themselves as fast as they could. Franklin Roosevelt's new Administration intimated that from now on, isolationism was to become the United States' official policy, leaving the French and the British to face the German problem, now assuming the proportions of a Frankenstein monster, alone. Nothing could have made the rise to power of Hitler more inevitable than Roosevelt's first major foreign policy decision—the wrecking of the World Economic Conference, which might have staved off disaster if all Powers concerned had cooperated. But isolationism had now taken a firm grip on the American imagination and, fueled by the distress of the Depression, it grew by leaps and bounds in the early 1930's. It was all part of a pattern—rising tariff barriers, increasing emphasis on economic self-sufficiency, refusal to join the World Court. And behind the concrete decisions lay the pervasive sentiment that the United States was morally superior to the grasping and decadent nations of the Old World whose contamination had to be shunned if this moral superiority was to be preserved.

And yet, the repercussions of America's original involvement began to be felt with increasing intensity. Having repudiated the Treaty of Versailles and claimed that Germany had been unjustly victimized, American historians and political and financial leaders had effectively encouraged Germany's resurgence without noticing that under a superficial veneer of Americanization, Prussianism was gathering strength for another round. That this resurgence was not to their liking when it assumed the National Socialist form, in no way detracts from the United States' immense influence in shaping Europe's political evolution between the World Wars. Also, its abstention from the League of Nations made it impossible to give global validity to the latter's decisions; if economic sanctions were decreed (cutting off Italy's supply of oil during the Abyssinian War, for instance), there was no guarantee that Washington would abide by them. Every European crisis triggered the same dilemma—the United States refused to go along with the European democracies while condemning them morally for indecisiveness. Even by doing nothing beyond refusing to become committed, the United States acted as a negative agent which paralyzed the small amount of will power left in British and French statesmen.

When, on January 6, 1936, President Roosevelt stated that the United States would, in the future, remain neutral as far as European affairs were concerned, Hitler is reported to have said: "There has been no development during recent years more welcome than this." [28] Results followed promptly: two months later, violating the 1925 Locarno Treaty which Germany had signed of her own free will, Hitler sent the German army into the demilitarized zone of the Rhineland, quite confident that France, lacking any backing from Britain and the United States, would not have the nerve to put up a fight. And it was the same all over the world, even in the Far East where, after having raised a storm over the Japanese occupation of Manchuria in 1931, the United States refused to join Britain in common action against Japan's further imperial expansion at China's expense in the late 1930's.[29] Roosevelt was lucid enough to fear that Britain's position in the Far East was deteriorating to such an extent that "she might be compelled to withdraw from her position there and that as a consequence, the United States might some day have to deal, maybe, alone, with a greatly strengthened Japanese power across the Pacific Ocean." [30] But isolationist sentiment was too strong. As Anthony Eden put it, ". . . it was disappointing that we were not able to secure effective joint action, but there were reasons of internal United States policy for this. Suspicion was rife that British diplomacy had as its aim to entangle the United States in problems which were not properly its concern, and that we were trying to get that country to pull our chestnuts out of the fire." [31]

In late 1936, isolationist sentiment in the United States had reached its zenith; had it remained there, a new balance of power would have been gradually established throughout the world as a result of American inaction; and its erstwhile pupils and imitators, Germany and Japan, now in the totalitarian grip of their fanatical *grands simplificateurs,* would have established their empires, counterbalancing the growing might of Soviet Russia between them. But from this zenith, isolationist sentiment began to recede. And when, early in 1937, Washington displayed a greater interest in propping up France and Britain—to the extent of promising them ample supplies but not to the extent of actively participating in an eventual conflict—the inevitable result was bound to be a new round of European warfare in which, eventually, all Europeans would lose. Staunch isolationism on the part of the United States would have paralyzed the will of Britain and France to fight Germany; German hegemony in western Europe would have been achieved without firing a shot through a succession of "Munich" piecemeal surrenders; the temporary results of the First World War and the Versailles Treaty would have been undone without bloodshed. Alternatively, a straight alliance between America and the European democracies, backed by massive rearmament, would most likely have deterred German aggression altogether; there is plenty of evidence that the German General Staff, alarmed at the recklessness of Hitler's foreign policy, would then have had the courage to strike him down.

Instead of a straightforward, consistent American policy, the European democracies had to contend with vacillations, due to the swing of American public opinion's pendulum from a greater to a lesser degree of isolationist feeling. Already in the late 1930's, the vital decisions concerning the future of the world originated—spasmodically, unconsciously, and instinctively, it is true—in the United States, no longer in Europe. Caught between American moral judgments and promptings, and the unwillingness of the United States Government to do anything positive to assist Europe's democracies, France and Britain procrastinated and made war more certain: Germany's military occupation of the left bank of the Rhine in 1936, the Anschluss with Austria in 1938, the Sudetenland crisis and the Munich surrender late in the same year, the German invasion and occupation of Czechoslovakia early in 1939—fateful landmarks in a steady retreat in front of Hitler's swelling ambitions, accompanied by mounting anger and frustration in the Western democracies. Sooner or later, war had to break out, as it did in September 1939.

The steady approach of war in Europe has to be seen, in retrospect, in the light of internal conditions in the United States at the time. A decade after the onset of the Great Depression, its sequels were still quite visible. America was economically and socially sick, its enormous productive machinery still half paralyzed. Ten years of New Deal and considerable efforts had not cured the disease. In 1933, the gross national product was about a third of what it had been four years earlier. The physical volume of production did not reach the level of 1929 until 1937 —and then promptly slid down again; and until 1941, the dollar volume of production remained below that of 1929. Until 1940, only once (in 1937) did the average number of unemployed dip below eight million, and on the eve of the outbreak of the war in Europe, one worker out of five was unemployed. The economic and social fruits of isolationism were bitter. But then, as war fever began to mount in Europe, the moral indignation of the Americans at the outrages of the totalitarian regimes began to mount also. In a sense, American public opinion was more united in its anti-German stance in 1939 than it had been in 1914—although more determined than ever not to become embroiled again in the hostilities. But becoming embroiled in the military struggle was one thing, and becoming the "arsenal of the democracies" was another. There was so much slack in the American economy still reeling from the Depression, that plenty of guns could be supplied to the Allies without having to cut down on butter for the Americans.

During the "phony war" (September 1939–May 1940), the improvident British and French leaders had plenty of time to consider the dismal statistics: as against Germany's 190 divisions, the French could only pit 100 and the British 10, stated the French Premier Paul Reynaud.[32] No allies were in sight. The Czechoslovakian army no longer existed, any more than the state of Czechoslovakia itself; and the Polish army had been annihilated in a few weeks. There were no American divisions to plug the gap, this time; indeed, in May 1940, President Roosevelt assured Congress that the United States would not allow itself to be dragged into the war.[33] But while reemphasizing America's decision to maintain its official isolationist policy, Roosevelt had already begun to think in terms of another policy of what could be termed "protective imperialism."

On May 17, quite alarmed at the disasters inflicted upon the Anglo-French armies, he asked a startled Lord Lothian, British Ambassador in Washington, to convey to London his "desire to see His Majesty's Government place the fleet in the shelter of American ports." [34] The possible defeat and invasion of Britain was viewed in Washington as an unexpected catastrophe which could only be mitigated if and when the Royal Navy withdrew from European waters to come under American control. When, a few weeks later, the Royal Navy was ordered to destroy the French warships which had sought refuge in African harbors, it was not so much out of fear that the Germans might get control of them but as a spectacular undertaking designed to convince American public opinion that Britain meant business and intended to prosecute the war to the end—rather than surrender its own fleet to the United States and make peace with Germany. The irony of this fateful decision, which drew a curtain of blood between the two erstwhile European allies, can be appreciated to the full when one reads Prime Minister Churchill's reply to President Roosevelt after the latter's talk with Lord Lothian. After stating that his "administration" would never surrender, he added: "If members of the Present Administration were finished and others came in to parley amid the ruins, you must not be blind to the fact that the sole remaining bargaining counter with Germany would be the Fleet, and if this country was left by the United States to its fate no one would have the right to blame those then responsible if they made the best terms they could for the surviving inhabitants." [35]

An added irony is that Hitler, faithful to the thesis developed in *Mein Kampf,* had no intention whatsoever of destroying Britain, once France had been reduced to impotence. On May 24, 1940, at a meeting at his G.H.Q. in Charleville, and in front of an astounded audience, Hitler began to speak "with admiration of the British Empire, of the necessity for its existence and of the civilization that Britain had brought into the world. He compared the British Empire with the Catholic Church—saying they were both essential elements of stability in the world." And Liddel Hart records that he concluded by saying "that his aim was to make peace with Britain on a basis that she would regard as compatible with her honour to accept." [36]

As military matters went from bad to worse in Europe, President Roosevelt began to take a hand in those developments that appeared to be of vital concern to the United States. Reassured that Britain intended to fight on, he turned to France and especially the fate of the French fleet. In a message to his ambassador in Paris, he specified: ". . . if the worst comes to the worst, we regard the retention of the French fleet as a force in being as vital to the reconstitution of France and of the French colonies and to the ultimate control of the Atlantic and other oceans. . . . This means that the French fleet must not get caught bottled up in the Mediterranean." [37] In turn, faced with inevitable disaster, the French Premier Paul Reynaud sent an urgent message to Roosevelt on June 14, insisting that the "only chance of saving the French nation, the advance guard of the democracies, and hence of saving Britain, at whose side France will then be able to remain with her powerful fleet, lies in throwing the weight of American power into the balance this very day. . . . unless you can give France firmly to understand, in the hours ahead, that the United States will enter the war in the very near future, the destiny of the world will change . . ." [38] as it indeed did. The following day, President Roosevelt replied, expressing his profound sympathy and stating that "in conformity with its policy of non-recognition of the acquisitions of gains achieved by force of arms, the government of the United States will refuse to recognize the validity of any attempt of a nature to impair the independence of France." But he had to add: "I know that you will understand that these declarations imply no military commitments. Congress alone can undertake such engagements." [39] In the 1950's and 1960's, Congress was to wonder what had become of this Constitutional privilege.

News of the armistice between France and Germany was greeted by a burst of frantic activity in Washington—freezing all French property in the United States, congressional resolution forbidding any transfer of Western Hemisphere territories belonging to non-American Powers. Ten days later, again, Secretary of State Cordell Hull summoned both the French and British ambassadors in Washington, urging the former to avoid letting the French fleet fall into German hands and bluntly stating to the latter "that it was high time the British government placed the Royal Navy in the shelter of American ports." [40]

The outcome of all this agitation is now part of history: on July 3, the Royal Navy crippled the French fleet at Mers-el-Kebir but stayed in European waters and, along with the Royal Air Force, saved the British Isles from a negotiated peace with Germany—making it that much easier for the United States to prepare its eventual military return to the European Continent, four years later.

☆ III ☆

Pearl Harbor:
The Genesis of Empire

For all practical purposes, Britain became America's advanced bastion off the hostile shores of the Continent in June 1940. Having become *de facto* an American protectorate implied that the whole British Empire and Commonwealth came under the protective umbrella of the United States—and nowhere more so than in the Far East and Southeast Asia where the Japanese, pleasantly surprised by the dramatic events in distant Europe, were anxious to exploit the unparalleled weakening of European Powers to their own advantage.

Driven mainly by the fear of potential German and Japanese aggressions, the United States virtually took over Britain's possessions in the Western Hemisphere (in the form of long-term leases on a multitude of bases stretching from Newfoundland to the Caribbean, and to which the British themselves were refused access, ostensibly to ward off the danger of German attack), established a military protectorate over Canada with the August 17 Ogdensburg Agreement (which exluded British membership on the Joint Defense Board),[1] brought Greenland and Iceland into its military sphere of influence, and eventually concluded an agreement with the Portuguese Government concerning the Azores. Agreements were also painfully reached with most Latin American countries—painfully, because of the latter's endemic fear of *imperialismo yanqui;* indeed, the same fear put a crimp in the negotiations between Canada and the United States—"fear of alienation from Britain and of excessive dependence upon, or even annexation to, the United States." And the same apprehension animated the leaders of many West Indian islands, apprehension which was not put to rest by the outspoken desire of many American isolationists and jingoists (whose sentiments, while apparently contradictory, were in fact quite compatible), who clamored for outright annexation of these territories as well as of the French West Indies.[2] (Some even ventured to suggest a horse trade according to which these territories would be exchanged against a cancellation of all First World War debts.[3])

It is not only what took place that gives its particular significance to an historical era; it is also what might have taken place. What might have happened, for instance, had German policy been more active in the Atlantic and the Western Hemisphere instead of marching east and getting lost in the depths of Soviet Russia? Roosevelt was prepared to go to any lengths to protect the United States: to make full use of American armed forces to forestall Axis-inspired revolutions in Latin American nations, to undertake the preventive occupation of Dakar and parts of West Africa, if need be, as well as military occupation of the Azores if the Portuguese Government did not comply with American wishes—in short, to ensure the steady buildup of a protective empire on both sides of the Atlantic.

But the most important item remained the matter of the United States' assistance to Britain's war effort—the types of weapons to be produced, the financing of this assistance on a enormous scale, and so forth. Britain was displaying plenty of evidence that it could hold out militarily, if assisted from overseas; and no military bases on either side of the ocean were as valuable as Great Britain itself. Its preservation became the main object of American policy in the Atlantic; but from now on, the relationship between Washington and London became that of a suzerain and his vassal. In every respect, London had to bow to Washington's inflexible will. Painful as it was to British pride, the Americans decided to impose weapons of American design, in spite of the hardships this switch inflicted on the British armed forces. But beggars cannot be choosers; Britain was virtually out of dollars by the end of 1940, although it still owned substantial investments in the United States, which its Government was not inclined to liquidate. On the other hand, the Americans were determined to avoid loaning money to the British, after the painful defaulting on their First World War loans.

Here again, the Americans were implacable: the British were earnestly requested to state frankly their financial position: "Only if the British emptied their pockets, only if they gave the United States Government a complete statement of their resources, both in America and elsewhere, would the Congress and the people of the United States offer effective aid." [4] Rather harsh, considering the fact that the British were locked in a life-and-death struggle, to a great extent on the United States' behalf; but realistic. Secretary of the Treasury Morgenthau put it bluntly: "It gets down to the question of Mr. Churchill putting himself in Mr. Roosevelt's hands with complete confidence. Then it is up to Mr. Roosevelt to say what he will do." [4] Prime Minister Churchill surrendered and sent to President Roosevelt a detailed account of Britain's precarious position and dismal prospects. Concluding, he stated bitterly that he thought "it would be wrong if . . . Great Britain were to be divested of all saleable assets so that after victory was won with our blood, civilization saved, and time gained for the United States to be fully armed against all eventualities, we should be stripped to the bone." [5] But, as a result of this full disclosure, and with lightning speed, Franklin Roosevelt came up with his historic "Lend-Lease" decision. Having put itself entirely in the hands of the American leaders, Britain was saved *in extremis*.

There is little doubt that all the moves made, and decisions taken, by President Roosevelt edged the United States into the war. America was not sucked into the war but pushed into it by its own leaders with great and deliberate skill. The virtual embargo on trade with Japan, which promptly followed the Japaness implantation in French Indochina, made it certain "that Japan could not continue under such pressure for more than a few months"; [6] all the more so since the member nations of the British Commonwealth and the Dutch East Indies followed in the United States' footsteps. As Japan's Prime Minister Tojo stated it, "To adopt a policy of patience and perseverance under such impediment was tantamount to self-annihilation of our nation. Rather than await extinction, it were better to face death by breaking through the encircling ring and find a way for existence." [7] Similarly, the September decision to provide American armed escort for the protection of all convoys as far as Iceland, was bound to lead to hostile contact with the German navy. Gradually inched into the war by President Roosevelt's devious but single-minded policy, the American people began to wake up to the fact that, sooner or later, the American armed forces would be engaged in full-scale warfare simultaneously in the Pacific and the Atlantic, in Asia and in Europe. The isolationists could not halt the irresistible trend because their own fortress, Congress, was being increasingly bypassed by the White House's executive orders (the "Shoot on sight" order to the Atlantic fleet, for instance), which committed the United States beyond recall. As Senator Brooks put it, "you cannot shoot your way a little bit into war any more than you can go a little bit over Niagara Falls." [8]

The most important fact concerning American public opinion is that, whereas a great majority of the American people remained adamantly opposed to entering the war against Germany, there was, on the contrary, a strong sentiment in favor of war with Japan if the Empire of the Rising Sun did not knuckle under. Isolationism had always applied to Europe rather than the Far East in which many leading Americans were emotionally involved through their missionaries in China, and politically committed through their military retention of the Philippines. Also, and not far below the surface on the West Coast, there was a feeling of racial antagonism going all the way back to the harsh Exclusion Acts against Asian immigrants, and now focusing on the Japanese. This anti-Japanese sentiment grew steadily through 1941, and on November 14, Japanese Ambassador Nomura telegraphed Tokyo his acute analysis of the situation: "There are even now many arguments against war with Germany as opposed to internal questions, but there is not the slightest opposition to war in the Pacific. It is being thought more than ever that participation will be carried out through the Pacific area." [9]

Indeed, Roosevelt was so well aware of this favorable psychological disposition that he dreaded the thought of missing the coming war in the Pacific through miscalculation and searched for every conceivable way to provoke the Japanese into firing the first shot. Toward the end of 1941, it was quite plain to the American authorities in Washington that it was only a matter of time before the Japanese attacked—but where, when, and whom, remained an open question. If the Japanese attacked either the British in Malaya or the Dutch East Indies, the American Government felt fairly confident that the United States could declare war, even though the Japanese would not have assaulted the Americans directly. But American public opinion would remain reluctant and divided. Thus, on November 25, as noted in Secretary of War Stimson's diary, Roosevelt "raised the question of how to maneuver the Japanese into firing the first shot without too much danger to the United States." [10] Roosevelt even went so far in his search for a cheap *casus belli* that, on December 2, he ordered the Admiral in command of the Pacific Fleet to charter three small vessels under the American flag to be stationed in the path of the Japanese fleets sailing toward British Malaya and the Dutch East Indies. One incident would have been enough, another deliberately provoked "Lusitania" in the Far East. But preparations had had hardly time to get under way when the Japanese attacked Pearl Harbor, solving Roosevelt's problem for him.

When, on the morning of December 7, the Japanese bombed Pearl Harbor, they unlocked a Pandora's box for all concerned. Hundreds of years from now, when latter-day historians attempt to sift the evidence, they will see in Pearl Harbor a most fateful event—not because it precipitated the whole American nation into war across both the Pacific and the Atlantic (Hitler obliged by declaring war against the United States four days later), nor because it led straight to the destruction of the Japanese Empire and of the Third Reich, but because it released the bottled-up potential of America's protective imperialism on a global scale—a reluctant imperialism, this time, and therefore that much more effective and durable, an imperialism without talk of "Manifest Destiny," of superiority of the Anglo-Saxon race and of its right to rule the world and its "inferior" people—an ecumenical imperialism dedicated to the preservation of a "way of life." Pearl Harbor opened a new and dramatic era in American history, whose dynamic trend did not come to an end when the Second World War was concluded but went straight into the Cold War and beyond, and is still proceeding relentlessly, decades later. Just as everything of significance that happened in the third and second centuries B.C. points, from our late perspective, to the rise of the Roman Empire, everything that happened in the nineteenth and twentieth centuries will probably seem, to future historians, to point to the rise of the American empire as the most striking event of our time. This amounts to stating that the buildup of this empire is no "accident" but the inevitable result of long-term trends spanning several centuries.

To return to Pearl Harbor and its aftermath: The United States' internal situation in 1941 was vastly different from that of 1917. This time, America was fully prepared to go to war. As late as 1938, the United States' regular army ranked only eighteenth among the world's standing armies; but, starting in January of that year, and overcoming the strenuous opposition of isolationists of all hues, President Roosevelt struggled forcefully and successfully to build up America's military power. Thanks to Selective Service, the American forces now numbered over one and a half million men, with over a hundred thousand officers as well as facilities for training thirty thousand pilots a year. Industry had gradually switched over to armaments' manufacturing, while military bases were being built from Alaska and Greenland all the way down to the Caribbean. As for the fleet, ever since

Congress passed the "Two-Ocean Navy" bill in 1940, it had increased rapidly in size and had acquired valuable experience since mid-1941 in the Atlantic where it actually patrolled under wartime conditions. The whole American structure, both in its productive capacity and in its fighting capability, had been geared up since 1940, all its Depression-born economic slack taken up. Unemployment was virtually wiped out as six million workers were added to public and private payrolls. From 1939 to 1941, the index of industrial production rose from 109 to 169, roughly a 50 percent increase in a mere two years. This immense productive apparatus was now ready to switch instantly to full war production; all it needed was a Pearl Harbor to kick it up to a pitch of colossal efficiency.

All told, over fifteen million men and women served in the armed forces of the United States during World War II. Progress between the two World Wars had taken place, not only in terms of numbers, but in quality too: while only one tenth of the draftees of the first war had a high school education, almost half were high school graduates in the second war. They did not have to be rushed into battle more or less untrained as in 1917 and 1918; this time, they had had a breathing spell during the undeclared war which afforded them ample time for thorough preparation.

The greatest fallout of the war effort was undoubtedly technological. Nothing else could have given the United States the overwhelming military and technological supremacy that its early lead in the development of nuclear weapons eventually gave it. In a gigantic and top-secret operation enlisting many of the greatest scientific brains, both American and foreign, including the tight cooperation of countless universities and laboratories with the armed forces, the United States eventually produced the first successful nuclear weapon the world had ever seen, and retained the atomic monopoly for several crucial years after the war; and after Soviet Russia broke its monopoly, retained an unchallengeable lead in quantity and quality of nuclear weaponry down to this day. As Secretary of War Stimson put it, the atomic bomb "was the greatest achievement of the combined efforts of science, industry, labor and the military in history," [11] under the auspices of the Federal Government.

It is worth pondering for a while the deeper reasons for the United States' remarkable success in a scientific field in which most of the outstanding brains were actually European. The fact that most of the leading European physicists (Germany's Albert Einstein, Italy's Enrico Fermi, Denmark's Niels Bohr, Holland's Samuel Goudsmit, Austria's Victor Weisskopf, Hungary's Leo Szilard and Edward Teller, and countless others) were irresistibly drawn into the vortex of America's scientific and military power structure, is no more accidental than the fact that the few note-worthy physicists who remained in German-occupied Europe should have successfully struggled against, or escaped from, German power—Frédéric Joliot-Curie to become a pillar of the French resistance, Werner Heisenberg to slow down to a crawl the German progress in the development of nuclear weaponry, and Niels Bohr to escape from Denmark to America. The utter madness of Hitler's regime struck the overwhelming majority of physicists, both German and non-German, with horror. Even before war broke out in 1939, the tight-knit international fraternity of physicists, transcending parochial nationalist sentiment, was determined to prevent any kind of German hegemony in nuclear military power. Furthermore, Germany's National Socialist regime itself distrusted theoretical physicists and was mentally geared to technological progress only in the strictly utilitarian, engineering sense. Ideology is an enemy of science and the Third Reich became a victim of its own anti-Semitic activities. When, in the autumn of 1933, Albert Einstein left Berlin forever and transferred himself to the Institute for Advanced Studies at Princeton, Paul Langevin, one of the leading French scientists, is reported to have prophesied: "It's as important an event as would be the transfer of the Vatican from Rome to the New World. The Pope of physics has moved and the United States will now become the center of natural sciences." [12] The prophecy turned out to be deadly accurate.

The extraordinary perception that the lock guarding nature's innermost secret could be broken to unleash a new form of power of apocalyptic dimensions, came to a number of physicists in the late 1930's; the more terrifying idea of using it as a military weapon came to small groups of scientists in 1939—some in Germany, and others in the United States. One such group in America, all of whose members originated from Central Europe (Leo Szilard, Eugene Wigner, Edward Teller, and Victor Weisskopf), overcoming their inhibitions due to the fact that not one of them (except Wigner) had even been long enough in the United States to have taken out American citizenship, decided to draw the attention of the American Government to the military implications of the recent advances in theoretical physics. Spurred by recent news of German progress in nuclear research, they enlisted Albert Einstein's assistance—his fame and moral authority was bound to make the authorities in Washington sit up and listen. History knows few such dramatic ironies as Einstein, who had been hounded out of the Third Reich, actually pressuring the American Government into developing a nuclear weapon which, under other political circumstances, might have been developed in Europe by European brains and for the benefit of Europe's predominance in the world. But the brain drain from Europe to America had already started.

Years later, Einstein was to regret bitterly his role in the nuclear drama, and, along with many other scientists, to be tortured at the thought of his personal responsibility in the creation of the monstrous weapon. After the war, he confessed sorrowfully: "If I had known that the Germans would not succeed in constructing the atom bomb, I would never have lifted a finger." [13] But the thought that Hitler might one day have the monopoly of nuclear weaponry was too much for these scientists. However much they may have regretted later this handing over of unlimited military power to the United States, there is no doubt that at the time they saw it as a lesser evil.

It is of great historical significance that the nuclear physicists within Germany followed the dictates of their consciences in obstructing the development of atomic weapons while those who were elsewhere had no such qualms. It is the natural reward bestowed by historical destiny on those people who can simultaneously develop national power to the highest pitch of efficiency while, being fundamentally ethical, remaining committed to the preservation of individual freedom and the rule of law. Many years later, a German scientist explained this contrast in attitudes when he stated: "We were really no better morally or intellectually than our foreign colleagues. But by the time the war began we had already learned from the bitter experience of nearly seven years under Hitler that one had to treat the state and its executive organizations with suspicion and reserve. The citizens of totalitarian countries are rarely good patriots. But our colleagues elsewhere had at that time complete confidence in the decency and sense of justice of their governments." And he added: "I doubt, incidentally, whether exactly the same situation prevails in those countries today." [14] The truth of the matter is that there are no citizens in totalitarian countries, only rulers and ruled; individual initiative, being strongly discouraged by the overpowering authorities, is reduced to the minimum. There could be no equivalent in such countries to the disinterested and voluntary role of a well-known Wall Street banker, Alexander Sachs, who served, in his capacity as a free American citizen, as a transmission belt between Einstein and Roosevelt. Not only the Third Reich, but even Soviet Russia became a victim of its prevailing ideology and political tyranny when it jailed and tortured such noted physicists as Fritz Houtermans and Alexander Weissberg who had sought refuge in Russia from Nazi persecution. However, in a deliberate change of policy concerning scientists, the shrewd Russians, belatedly enlightened as to the crucial importance of technology in military matters, were to make up for it later on: the German National Socialists never did.

Only the United States had the means and foresight to harbor all the refugee scientists from Europe—going to the length of seeking them out and offering them top positions, even when they showed no signs of wanting to become refugees. In the summer of 1939, for instance, the chairman of the Physics Department at Columbia University offered a professorship to Werner Heisenberg to induce him to remain in America—in vain, for, although Heisenberg told him at the time that he was sure that Hitler was going to lose the war he was about to unleash, he did not want to desert Germany. It is actually possible, if not probable, that Heisenberg was more useful to the Anglo-American cause by braking nuclear progress inside Germany than working at furthering it in the United States.

At any rate, the main spur to frantic work on what was becoming the "Manhattan Project" was the overcoming of the Germans' presumed lead: "We were told day in and day out that it was our duty to catch up with the Germans," recalled a scientist later.[15] This, of course, soothed the uneasy consciences of many leading physicists. Nor was this atmosphere of frantic urgency in any way disturbed by the vital message, emanating from Houtermans and transmitted in 1941 by Professor Reiche who had just escaped from Germany, to the effect "that the German physicists had hitherto not been working at the production of the bomb and would continue to try, for as long as possible, to divert the minds of the German military authorities from such a possibility." [16] The news was promptly conveyed from Princeton to Washington by another immigrant physicist, Rudolf Ladenburg, but never reached the scientists engaged in the Manhattan Project, by now wrapped in all the cloaks of military security and secrecy, under the overlordship of the Military Policy Committee. By then, too, Winston Churchill had complied with Roosevelt's desire to concentrate all the work of both American and British research teams in the Western Hemisphere—Canada and the United States.

Later, toward the end of the war, a special intelligence organization, code-named "Alsos" and devoted exclusively to science and technology, followed immediately in the footsteps of the advancing American army, scouring all the liberated territories for scientists and evidence of technological progress, or the lack of it, in Germany. It was in liberated Strasbourg, still under the shelling of German guns firing across the Rhine, that they found out that German nuclear research, far from being ahead, was two years behind that of the Anglo-Americans; and that there were no factories yet for the production of uranium ($U235$) or plutonium ($PU239$). Further evidence of Heisenberg's crucial role in Germany's uranium project pointed to him as the main "military objective." Confident by now that Germany's potential nuclear power was nonexistent, "Alsos" turned its attention to preventing Heisenberg from falling into the hands of the French troops of General de Lattre—symbolic of the attitude of suspicion of the Americans toward their allies and of their determination to concentrate all the available sinews of technological power in American hands.[17] Gradually, with the rapid advance of Allied troops across German territory, a large booty of German scientists actually fell into the hands of the Americans (Otto Hahn, Nobel prizewinner Max von Laue, and eventually Werner Heisenberg himself), some to be flown back immediately to the United States (Werner von Braun and his team of rocket experts who, twelve years later, launched the first successful American space satellite). Needless to add, the Russians were not idle either, and kidnapped all the German scientists they could lay their hands on.

As it became apparent to all that the ostensible reason for the development of America's nuclear power had disappeared, many a scientist thought naïvely that the United States' Government would never make use of such a monstrous device against any other enemy. After Samuel Goudsmit had discovered in the papers of Carl Friedrich von Weizsacker that the Germans had not even come close to the development of an atom bomb, he went for a walk with an American major who acted as liaison officer between the War Department and the Alsos group, remarking as they went along: "Isn't wonderful that the Germans have no atom bomb? Now we won't have to use ours." But, to his profound dismay, the major replied: "Of course, you understand, Sam, that if we have such a weapon, we are going to use it." [18] It was not long before the international scientific community realized that it had handed the United States a revolutionary weapon of incalculable power which would be under Washington's, and not their, control. As the reports of the Alsos agents came in from the captured cities of Heidelberg, Celle, and Hamburg, where all the members of Germany's Uranium Society were taken into military custody, the scientists in the United States had quickly come to understand, in spite of the "top secret" nature of the news, that the Germans had no nuclear weapons of any kind. Many felt and reacted as Goudsmit had, and just as fruitlessly. Against the prospect of the war possibly ending before the bomb could be built and tested, General Groves, head of the Manhattan Project, pressured his scientists into greater and ever greater efforts.

A last attempt was made by Leo Szilard, who had originally triggered the development of the bomb, to put the monstrous genie back into the bottle from which he had conjured it, and prevent the Americans from using the devastating weapon on Japan, the sole remaining enemy. As he admitted later: "During 1943 and part of 1944 our greatest worry was the possibility that Germany would perfect an atomic bomb before the invasion of Europe. . . . In 1945, when we ceased worrying about what the Germans might do to us, we began to worry about what the government of the United States might do to other countries." [19] It was too late to worry, now: the bomb was just about to be released into the hands of power politics. Niels Bohr had interviews with Roosevelt and Churchill, and later reported that he had been treated as if he were a child; Leo Szilard, unable to reach President Truman after Roosevelt's death, had to settle for James Byrnes, future Secretary of State. One and all, the scientists were politely invited to return to their laboratories and drawing boards and leave politics to the politicians. The panel of scientific advisers appointed to guide the United States' Chief Executive were not called upon to advise *whether* the atom bomb should be used at all but *how* it should be used. The genie would not go back into the bottle.

Long before this came to pass, in the immediate aftermath of Pearl Harbor, it quickly became clear that the United States and its new associates had to face the most critical situation in the Pacific and Far East rather than in the Atlantic where Britain was holding out magnificently and, with Germany's main forces plunging into the remote vastness of Russia, in no immediate danger of being overrun. Japan's lightning offensive in the Pacific, its swift occupation of Malaya, Burma, the Dutch East

Indies, and the Philippines, its surprising military effectiveness and the equally stunning collapse of American, British, and Dutch power in Southeast Asia, everything conspired to make the situation look even more threatening than it actually was. Although official priority was given to the European theater of war, the military situation was reversed sooner in the Pacific— thanks in part to the American naval victory at Midway, and thanks in part to General MacArthur's bold leadership in Southeast Asia.

When Douglas MacArthur established his headquarters in Australia as American proconsul in the Southwest Pacific, he confronted a grave situation, made worse still by the Australians' plans for defense; panic-stricken, they had decided to abandon three-quarters of their continent and erect a last-ditch line of defense along the Darling River from Brisbane to Adelaide. At the other end of the world, their British cousins, hard-pressed themselves, could be of no assistance to their Commonwealth partners. Only the United States could be relied upon; only the United States ruled the waves of the South Pacific, no longer Brittania. From that fateful period in Australia's history dates its increasing reliance upon America and its gradual inclusion in the American sphere of influence. MacArthur's leadership, in itself, was instrumental in promoting this gradual shift of allegiance. With great courage and foresight, he rejected the Australian plan of defense and substituted one which set up its first line of defense a thousand miles to the north of the continent, along New Guinea's jungle-covered Owen Stanley range where almost impenetrable mountains could stop any large-scale Japanese penetration. In his *Reminiscences,* MacArthur stated that "this decision gave the Australians an exhilarating lift, and they prepared to support me with almost fanatical zeal." [20]

This zeal was necessary because American support and supplies were meager. MacArthur explains that "Australia's contribution throughout the war was of paramount importance. Less than a hundred thousand tons arrived from the United States during the critical final quarter of 1942." But, he continues, "Our ground and air forces in the Southwest Pacific Area were vastly more self-sufficient than those of any other theater of operation. Local produce and materials furnished 65 to 70 percent of the resources needed by them for the second half of 1942. To the adjacent South Pacific theater, I shipped a greater tonnage of supplies than the United States delivered to my own area. In general effect, therefore, the Southwest Pacific, far from being a drain on the United States, was self-sufficient." [21] Indeed, it was as if an autonomous, self-supporting portion of the United States itself had been detached and towed across the Pacific, to remain anchored in its southwest corner as bastion and staging area for a northward thrust against the Japanese Empire. A hundred and fifty years of British occupation and settlement of a virgin continent, built up into a completely Westernized and Anglicized replica of the mother country, became irretrievably included in the United States coming empire in the Pacific, as an increment to American, and no longer British, power. But for all its self-sufficiency, it still remains, however, that American military leadership and technical skills, along with some vital supplies, were needed to save Australia from invasion and destruction.

While the United States' forces were slowly reconquering the Pacific and grinding the Japanese Empire into dust, Washington did not forget that Europe came first in its order of priorities—first because it was geographically closer to America's center of gravity, first because it was the Old World from which most Americans' ancestors had come and where millions of near relatives still dwelt, and first also because it was the only other area in the world that could match in population figures, in human skills, and in industrial potential the United States itself. Americans took the eventual defeat of Japan as a matter of course; and, in a sense, so did the clear-sighted but despondent Japanese themselves who knew that, given enough time, America could crush them; not so the defeat of Germany whose huge and restless realm, at the height of its extension, included four hundred million human beings and stretched all the way from the Pyrenees to the Caucasus, from the North Pole to the Sahara. Adolf Hitler's domain seemed to be invasion-proof, and his armies, then sweeping victoriously through Russia, invincible;

his *Festung Europa* was the greatest and most extensive military fortress ever erected in history; his army, the most efficient military machine ever built.

The United States had hardly entered the war against Germany when the first step in its new role as unquestioned leader of the Allies was taken: the creation of a common command, the combined Chiefs of Staff, "the most complete unification of military effort ever achieved by two allied nations," in General Marshall's own words.[22] The Combined Chiefs of Staff operated under the joint direction of Roosevelt and Churchill—that is, mostly Roosevelt. For his own political reasons, the American President had promptly accepted the British priority on victory in Europe; a bold and clever decision since—and it is worth repeating—whereas all Americans were united in their desire to crush Japan, they were more divided by old national loyalties and by the feeling that their vital interests were not so much at stake in the Old World. Besides, Germany had inflicted upon the Americans no such stinging blow as Pearl Harbor. And again, subdued but real, there was an undercurrent of racial antagonism toward the Japanese that was lacking in their feelings toward the Germans. In a sense, the ultimate destruction of the Third Reich and the liberation of Western Europe was a by-product of the popular hostility felt in the United States toward the Far Eastern upstarts.

The most important development, however, was psychological —the swift metamorphosis of the isolationist sentiment into a more or less unconscious form of protective imperialism—suspicion of General de Gaulle because, as Anthony Eden put it, "They feared his dynamic personality," [23] hostility to any form of British hegemony in postwar Europe such as would naturally flow from Norway's Foreign Minister Trygve Lie's plan, according to which Western Europe's smaller states would have become virtually British satellites. But some of the smaller and weaker European states were not blind to the United States' potential imperialism. At the time of the discussions with Portugal about the use of the Azores, "The Portuguese were strongly pro-British, but they did not feel the same sympathy for the United States. They suspected that whereas we would withdraw at the end of the war, the Americans might prefer to stay," recalled Anthony Eden.[24] Looking at Washington's policy toward France, he stated further:

> So far as I have been able to piece together the various indications I have received, I would say that they [the United States Government] did not wish to see a strong central administration for the French Empire built up in Algiers. They would have preferred if possible to deal separately with each part of the French Empire. They dislike the growth of an independent spirit in any French administration anywhere and consider that any French authority with whom they deal should comply without question to their demands.[25]

The seeds of the French challenge to American leadership in the 1960's were sowed at that time. Looking toward the future, Eden uttered these fateful words, which must have haunted him when he became Prime Minister a decade later:

> In dealing with European problems of the future we are likely to have to work more closely with France even than with the United States, and while we should naturally concert our French policy so far as we can with Washington, there are limits beyond which we ought not to allow our policy to be governed by theirs.[26]

Anthony Eden applied this principle to the letter at the time of the Suez Crisis in 1956; the end result was disaster.

Winston Churchill, who was half American, felt a kinship with the United States which made it easier for him to comply wholeheartedly with President Roosevelt's wishes. That this was not always to the taste of his British colleagues is made glaringly evident in Anthony Eden's memoirs. An entry in his diary dated September 10, 1943, states bluntly:

> Roosevelt has had his way again and agreed to Moscow for the Foreign Secretaries' conference with alacrity. His determination not to agree to a London meeting for any purpose, which he says is for electoral reasons, is almost insulting considering the number of times we have been to Washington. I am most anxious for good relations with U.S. but I don't like subservience to them and I am sure that this only

lays up trouble for us in the future. We are giving the impression, which they are only too ready by nature to endorse, that militarily all the achievements are theirs. . . .[27]

To General de Gaulle, who complained about British dependence on American policy decisions,[28] and more specifically about the fact that no agreement had been reached on the civil administration of France in the post-liberation phase:

> Mr. Churchill declared that, if it came to the point, he would always side with the United States against France. I [Anthony Eden] did not like this pronouncement nor did Mr. Bevin, who said so in a booming aside.[29]

In his war memoirs, Charles de Gaulle relates that Churchill shouted at him: "Here is something you should know: whenever we have to choose between Europe and the high seas, we shall always choose the high seas. Whenever I have to choose between you and Roosevelt, I shall always choose Roosevelt." [30] Quite clearly, and over the objections of some of his colleagues in the Cabinet, Churchill deliberately turned his back on the Continent and chose a "partnership" with the United States which amounted to a thinly veilèd "satellization"; it was all in the logic of his wartime leadership. Eventually, de Gaulle left for Washington to plead his case and attempt to sell it to Roosevelt. As one historian described it two decades later:

> . . . de Gaulle had the American standpoint explained to him in Washington by Roosevelt himself. What it amounted to was that the postwar world would be ruled by a quadrumvirate composed of the United States, the Soviet Union, Great Britain and China, with a parliament of smaller countries— the future United Nations—acting as a chorus and giving a democratic look to the directorate of the "big four." Among the latter Washington then counted on having China on its side, so that the U.S.S.R. would be isolated and outmatched. For the rest, there would be American bases throughout the world, some of them on French soil. The coming peace would be an American peace, and the world would enter the American Century—all in the name of democracy, of course.[31]

That Roosevelt, for all his beliefs in democracy, was in fact an unconscious imperialist, there is hardly any doubt; as de Gaulle stated it, "Comme cela est humain, l'idéalisme y habille la volonté de puissance (How human it is that idealism cloaks the will to power)." [32] In Roosevelt, the striving for Caesarian authority within the United States was combined with a truly imperial view of America's destiny in the twentieth century. And from that historic interview, dates Charles de Gaulle's unshakable determination to fight the hegemony of the new Romans of the modern world.

But the British, under Churchill's guidance, acquired no such determination; quite the contrary. Time and again, they granted American requests without being able to make their own views on Europe and elsewhere prevail. The entry in Eden's diary dated July 1, 1944, notes: "Long telephone talk with W. [Churchill] about strategy: we have to give way to United States. Argentine: we have to give way to U.S. (by withdrawing our Ambassador). I wish that I could persuade W. to be more vigorous in support of my French thesis. We are in the right there and have a right to have our say and our way." [33] Time and time again, United States leaders imposed their views, wise or unwise, on their British partners, treating them effectively as satellites.

The fateful Yalta Conference paved the way for the rise of Soviet Russia's power to political and military supremacy over half of the European continent, eventually compelling the United States to organize its own Western bloc as a counterweight. It is not that the Russians underestimated the growing power of the United States at the time; they gave to it just as much consideration as to their own imperialistic proclivities. During the conference, recalled James Byrnes, "Stalin made a very interesting reference to his conception of the United States in world affairs. Whether the United States wished it or not, he said, we were a world power and would have to accept worldwide responsibilities. Without our intervention in the last two wars, Germany could not have been defeated. In fact, he added, the history of the last thirty years shows that the United States has more reason to be a world power than any other state . . ." [34]

encomiums which did not fall on deaf ears, even though Stalin was then in the process of making mincemeat of the naïve policy of his American allies.

The disastrous seeds that were sown at Yalta sprang from the ancestral outlook of the Americans on European affairs. Referring to Roosevelt's views, Eden states: "The President shared a widespread suspicion of the British Empire as it had once been and, despite his knowledge of world affairs, he was always anxious to make it plain to Stalin that the United States was not "ganging up" with Britain against Russia. The outcome of this was some confusion in Anglo-American relations which profited the Soviets." [35] And he added: "Roosevelt did not confine his dislike of colonialism to the British Empire alone, for it was a principle with him, not the less cherished for its possible advantages. He hoped that former colonial territories, once free of their masters, would become economically and politically dependent upon the United States, and had no fear that other powers might fill that role." [36] Sentiment was promptly transformed into action against the French and the Dutch in Southeast Asia. Clearly, all the seeds of the collapse of Europe's worldwide power and influence were, more or less consciously, sown by the Americans, and opened power vacuums which some of them were longing to fill.

The founding of the United Nations was partly designed to irretrievably embroil the Americans in world affairs and make it impossible for them to withdraw into a neo-isolationism at the last minute. For the same reason, the first United Nations Conference was to take place, with every participating nation's blessing, on United States soil. But over and beyond that, it quickly became plain that the endemic isolationism would only be put to sleep to the extent that the United States could dominate whatever international body it joined: the Americans would only join it wholeheartedly if they could make it their own. In the case of the emerging United Nations, indirect control of the enormous bloc of Latin American votes was bound to give the United States a predominant influence which the forthcoming Communist bloc could not effectively challenge.

The nuclear annihilation of Hiroshima and Nagasaki was viewed by many, especially the scientists, as barbarous and unnecessary. Certainly the awesome power suddenly unleashed in the Far East was responsible for bringing the war to an almost immediate conclusion, although there were many signs that the Japanese were getting ready to offer an honorable surrender before the atomic holocaust took place. However, it is clear, in the light of hindsight and in view of subsequent misgivings about Soviet Russia's attitude, that Hiroshima was meant just as much a warning to the Russians as an effort to subdue the Japanese. American policy immediately assumed a "new look," an increasing toughness which was displayed immediately when President Truman stated that Japan would not be divided into occupation zones, rejected the Russian request that Japanese troops surrender to the Russians in northern Hokkaido, and in fact refused the Russians permission to take part in the military occupation of Japan at all—and became bold enough to ask the Russians to hand over one of the Kurile islands for use as an American air base; the Russians were not sufficiently awed by America's new nuclear power to comply. But of the deep anxiety of the Russian leaders, there is no doubt; nor of their utter determination to equip themselves with the new and terrifying weapon as promptly as they could.

☆ IV ☆

Cold War:
The Establishment of Empire

In that glorious autumn of 1945, in the aftermath of victory in the Atlantic and the Pacific, it is rather strange that the Americans should have thought that the United Nations was the answer to the world's problems. They had distrusted the League of Nations, their own brainchild, to the point of refusing to join it; they had seen it founder in the 1920's and collapse in the 1930's. The reasons for this failure had become common knowledge; yet the United States chose to believe that all would be right with the world, now that the League of Nations' legitimate child was born, even though it retained most of its parent's defective features—as if this newborn baby could take care of the multitude of troubles springing from the war, just at the time when the hot war was turning into a cold one. This outlook was neatly summed up by Secretary of State Cordell Hull after the 1943 Moscow Conference and the decision to set up the United Nations: ". . . there will no longer be need for spheres of influence, for alliances, for balance of power, or any other of the special arrangements through which, in the unhappy past, the nations strove to safeguard their security or to promote their interests." [1]

The United States lost no time in acting out its mistaken belief. True enough, the old spirit of isolationism was now just about dead, even though Washington had carefully refrained from binding itself by any formal ties and commitments to any individual nation. Sole owner of nuclear power, for the time being, the United States felt confident that all other nations in the world, including Soviet Russia, would be suitably impressed and unwilling to risk challenging America's might and sense of justice. So it was that speedy demobilization under the nuclear shelter whittled down America's armed strength abroad to almost token dimensions within six months; by the end of 1945, the staggering number of six and a half million men had already been released from the armed forces—this being "one of the most expensive economies" which duly alarmed General Marshall and Admiral King.[2] President Truman's efforts to counteract this dangerous evaporation of military muscle by imposing Universal Military Training "for our future safety and for the peace and security of the world" aroused no enthusiasm in Congress.[3] The War Department, faced with a disastrous weakening of America's various armies of occupation, ordered a slowdown of demobilization, reaping for its pains the anger of a great part of America's public opinion and a wave of near mutinies in American garrisons abroad (Paris, Munich, Frankfurt, Manilla, Yokohama). By the summer of 1946, the United States' armed forces had melted from a peak strength of twelve million to hardly more than two million. Not even the official breakout of the Cold War and the Berlin Blockade of 1948 could halt this shrinking process which brought the American army down to a low of 600,000 men on the eve of the Korean War.

But the most pressing problem in the immediate postwar period was strictly economic: Europe was broke, disorganized, and hungry. Lend-Lease came to an end a few days after the end of the hostilities with Japan; the abruptness with which Washington, instinctively hostile to the new Labour Government in London, terminated Lend-Lease to Britain and effectively pulled the rug from under its feet, brought out in bold relief the precariousness of the United Kingdom's situation in spite of the fact that it was nominally one of the victorious "Big Three" Powers.[4] But the Americans had no intention of allowing the mortified British to collapse into insolvency and bankruptcy. Washington moved swiftly to set Britain back on its feet—writing off 25 billion dollars' worth of lend-lease aid, granting an immediate credit of 650 million dollars to tide the British over the transitional period, and in addition a line of credit of almost 5 billion dollars to be used over the following five years.

As usual, Congress grumbled: Britain had defaulted on her First World War debts; worse still, she was ruled by a profligate socialist government hostile to free enterprise, although, paradoxically, she remained imperialistic abroad, combining in one state all possible sins under the American sun; critics had it both ways: there was enough there to irritate both conservative and liberal Americans. In spite of this, President Truman won the day and Britain was temporarily saved. Salvaging the rest of the world after this breakthrough was no problem: about eleven billion dollars' worth of aid was granted to all other needy nations until the spring of 1947.

That Soviet Russia had no intention of abiding by the agreements concluded at Teheran, Dumbarton Oaks, and Yalta, had become painfully obvious to Washington insiders before the war was even over, although largely ignored by American public opinion. Shortly before his death, President Roosevelt had told James Byrnes that "he had grave misgivings about the future." [5] But it was too late now to undo the damage. Into the power vacuum created by Roosevelt's lack of foresight, the Russians poured all their remaining military and political strength. Eastern and Central Europe, now under the heel of the Soviet armies, had already become a lost cause, as far as Western influence was concerned. But that was not enough to satisfy Soviet greed. Stalin wanted to expand fast into all the available power vacuums, and the first area where he decided to challenge the West was the Middle East—Greece, Turkey, and Iran, the warm waters of the Mediterranean and Persian Gulf for which the landlocked Russians have thirsted since the eighteenth century. Kremlin policy included pressure on Turkey to hand over virtual

control of the Dardanelles and Bosporus and relinquish the eastern districts of Kars and Ardahan, continued Soviet occupation
of northern Iran fostering and protecting local Communist regimes in Azerbaijan and Kurdistan, and in July 1945, formal
encouragement (through its satellites in the Balkans) to the
Communist guerillas who were waging a ruthless civil war
against the legitimate Greek Government. Soviet imperialism
was on the move all over the Near and Middle East.

Simultaneously, in Europe and all over the European-
controlled world, a spontaneous disintegration had started; the
former European Powers, victor and vanquished alike, could no
longer cope with the rot that had set in at home as well as in their
colonial empires. The pace-setting British Empire was being
gradually emptied of its substance, its prestige shattered in the
Orient by its humiliating defeats at the hands of Japan in the
early part of the war; only swift and orderly liquidation of its
imperial responsibilities could save what was left of British face
in the Orient—and, one by one, the major pieces of the once-
great empire were set free: India, Pakistan, and Ceylon went off
in 1947, Burma in 1948. The Dutch were unable to reconquer
their immensely wealthy East Indies, thanks in large part to
American opposition; the French faced insurmountable hostility
in their former Indochinese possessions, which led them, in less
than ten years, to a disastrous collapse. Wherever a vacuum occurred between retreating European power and advancing communism, the United States was bound by historical compulsion
to step in. The tale of the immediate postwar era is the tale of this
gradual, involuntary, and reluctant involvement leading to the
Korean War and the Great Debate which marks a watershed in
the history of the United States—and consequently, in the history of the modern world.

It was utterly naïve to think that Europe's position in the world
could collapse without awakening and setting loose vast anti-
Western (and not merely anti-European) forces—most of them,
and the most effective, under Communist auspices; but also
many that were not, such as the flare-up of Arab nationalism and
Islamic fanaticism. What were presumed to be "nationalist" revolts in the non-Western world had nothing to do with national-

ism in the strict etymological sense; these were, broadly speaking, anti-Western revolts, rebellions against the disruptive impact of Western Civilization. Non-Western people were struggling to take advantage of the collapse of European colonialism in order to achieve two incompatible results: modernize themselves as fast as possible in order to acquire the sinews of modern industrial power—and revive their dying civilizations, submerged by the triumph of industrialization and of the Western culture of which it was an essential component. Whether Marxism-Leninism came into play in the process depended on local cultural elements rather than on the degree of their hostility to the West.

American illusions did not last long. Gradually, almost unobstrusively and as a matter of course, the United States began to pick up the broken pieces all over the world, north and south, east and west, getting involved in countless local civil wars and conflicts, rescuing Western Europe from the brink of chaos and communization, signing pacts and treaties of alliance so numerous and varied as to make up for having signed none between the American Revolution and the late 1940's. The tale had best been told in chronological order.

Greece was the first place where the simmering Cold War started getting hot before its existence was even acknowledged openly. As in so many other areas under German or Japanese occupation, some of the most effective underground and guerilla movements were organized and led by local Communists. Alone among all political parties, the Communist movement seemed able to instill religious fanaticism and devotion in its members, along with a truly military discipline and a complete mastery of the technique of revolutionary warfare. Powerless in a well-organized state, they became highly dangerous when the state organization collapsed in the aftermath of a foreign military invasion and the virtual destruction of its regular armed forces. In order to prosecute the war against implacable enemies, the Anglo-Americans often thought it convenient to assist and subsidize what they believed to be the most effective underground movements—which were almost invariably Communist-led. From

Italy and Yugoslavia to Malaya and Vietnam, the Westerners themselves sowed the seeds of potential trouble by building up their future enemies in order to shorten the struggle against Germans and Japanese; the result of this shortsighted policy became plain in Greece sooner than it did anywhere else.

In the Greeks' instance, the most powerful underground movement was the Communist-led ELAS, which quickly outstripped its right-wing rivals and soon received the major portion of the British supplies dropped behind German lines. Their remarkable efficiency, in propaganda as well as on the battlefield (when they chose to fight), gave the Communists a decisive edge on all their rivals, whom they strenuously sought to eliminate while fighting only lackadaisically against the occupying Germans and Italians—just enough to induce the British to send them ample supplies, but not enough to wear themselves out. When royalist Colonel Grivas (of latter-day Cyprus fame) formed his own right-wing underground, "X," the British at first declined to add it to their payroll or supply it with weapons.[6]

However, the time eventually came, as it had to, when it began to dawn on the British that it was their favorite protégés who were planning to turn against them as soon as the Germans faded from the scene. Having discovered that ELAS headquarters was always reluctant to embark on dangerous sabotage work against the Germans, the British liaison officers started dealing directly and successfully with local ELAS units, more forthright and patriotic men than their Machiavellian political leaders. This bypassing of the exclusively politically-minded ELAS headquarters strained relations between them; and, rather late, the British understood that the ELAS leadership was attempting to keep its armed forces intact for an eventual takeover of Greece. The British began warming up to the right-wing guerillas.

Greece was an exclusively British show. The United States refused to take part in any military expedition to liberate it; and when liberation took place, the British found themselves alone to cope with an extremely dangerous situation which was partly of their own making. Returned from exile, the Greek Government proved unable to reestablish its authority, compelling the British to take a hand in Greece's internal affairs and, in effect, assist the right-wing elements against ELAS, their erstwhile allies. British troops had come into Greece as a liberating force; they stayed on as an ever-present police force to prevent the country from being taken over by the Communists. Greece had now become one of the numerous—but at the time the most important—pawns in the international rivalry between Soviet imperialism and the West in disarray; in 1945, Greece became a client state of Britain, for as long as Britain had the military and financial strength to protect it. But Britain's financial strength was ebbing fast while the Greek Communists became bolder and openly challenged the right-wing Greek army to a guerilla-type warfare in which they had the full backing of the Communist states to the north—Albania, Yugoslavia, Bulgaria, and looming behind them, Soviet Russia.

By then, Moscow's open challenge to the West had at last been understood by American public opinion; the United Nations' impotence had also become quickly evident. And Winston Churchill, in speech after speech, warned that only a tight alliance between the British Commonwealth and the United States, binding all English-speaking nations together, could stop the otherwise inevitable progress of international communism, bolstered by Russian imperialism. Swiftly, the idea of a policy of containment began to take shape in Washington. The Russians' complete takeover of Eastern and Central Europe, the gradual disintegration of Western Europe's economic and social structures, considerably aggravated by the witheringly cold winter of 1946–47, everything conspired to strike the American leaders' imagination with the imminent danger of a wholesale collapse of the Old World into the wide-open arms of Soviet Russia.

Britain herself was one of the weakest links in a weak chain. Clearly, Britain's imperial role would have to be curtailed. The dramatic announcement of this fact came suddenly with the publication on February 21, 1947, of a White Paper entitled "The Economic Survey for 1947," which predicted a severe economic crisis in Britain, and as a consequence, her inability to honor any longer her worldwide commitments: the Treasury was empty, coal supplies were running low, unemployment rising, industrial plants closing down—a dismal picture for the mistress of the world's greatest and most venerable empire. Simultaneously, Britain's Foreign Secretary confidentially informed Washington that Britain would have to drop the Greek and Turkish burden on March 31, being unable to extend them aid of any kind beyond that date. Could the United States step in and take over?

March 1947 saw the beginning of that transfer of imperial power and responsibilities from the disintegrating British Empire to the United States, which is still going on, a generation later. On March 12, President Truman addressed a joint session of Congress; later, he was to define the plan he put forth as "the turning point in America's foreign policy which now declared that wherever aggression, direct or indirect, threatened the peace, the security of the United States was involved." [7] This became known as the Truman Doctrine, the foundation stone on which the United States' reluctant imperialism was going to be erected. The key word in the statement is "indirect." Direct aggression is easy to define, and although it might not always justify the open intervention of the United States, it could be partly warranted if Soviet Russia were to attack a weaker neighbor, or openly back an aggressor. Indirect aggression, however, is another matter, a matter of interpretation involving the forcible intrusion of American power in any number of local civil wars against the side that is aided and abetted by the bigger Communist Power—or Powers, since Red China has struck out on her own. More than anything else, indirect aggression and the struggle against it became the main catalyst of America's preordained imperialism.

Greece and Turkey being the first concrete instances of indirect aggression, President Truman asked for an appropriation of four hundred million dollars to assist their shaky governments and finance the various economic and military missions dispatched by the United States: "The free peoples of the world look to us for support in maintaining their freedoms. If we falter in our leadership, we may endanger the welfare of our own Nation." [8] This Roman-like attitude struck Winston Churchill as a "great event"—Winston Churchill who, half American himself, was to hail and encourage unconsciously this transfer of worldwide responsibilities from Britain to America. The Truman Doctrine enjoyed from the start bipartisan support in Congress, expressed by an overwhelming majority of three-to-one in its favor.

Greece and Turkey were saved, although the cost to Greece was a long-drawn-out guerilla war that lasted a number of years. The end came for the Greek Communist guerillas more quickly than actually expected, as an offshoot of Yugoslavia's breakaway from the international Communist fraternity. Excommunicated by the Cominform in June 1948, at odds with Russia's satellites in the Balkans and Eastern Europe, Marshall Tito's regime was saved from economic strangulation by America's assistance. But as a result of his "heresy," the Titoist leader of the Greek rebels, Markos Vafiades, was replaced by a docile "Cominform" Communist, Ioannis Ioannides (the "barber of Volos"). In retaliation, Yugoslavia closed its southern border and cut off the guerillas from most of their external supplies. A quick mopping up of the Vitsi and Grámmos mountains by the American-advised and -equipped Greek army was all that was required to put an end to communism's armed threat to Greece.

More serious even than in the Balkans, the situation in Western Europe had become dramatic during the drastic winter of 1947. All the loans and forms of aid extended by the United States since the war had been unable to prevent the gradual dislocation of the Continent's economy. Secretary of State Marshall, in his historic speech at Harvard on June 5, 1947, stated flatly that Europe could not pay the cost of feeding and housing its inhabitants, and would not be able to do so for years to come. Aid and charity were not enough; Europe had to be rebuilt from the ground up, and given the means to do so; what had been done since the war had been a mere palliative; what was now required was a cure—the Marshall Plan. The essence of the Marshall Plan was that it was not a dictation of the United States to Europe, but an invitation to the Europeans to join together in planning their mutual recovery and sending on their collective requests for economic assistance to Washington within the framework of a Continental program. Britain and France invited all the other European nations to attend, on July 12, the Conference on Economic Cooperation; sixteen free countries attended, but all Communist countries declined. Thus, the Marshall Plan, generously offered (with strings attached, of course) to Soviet Russia and her satellites who turned it down, became the major instrument for the recovery of Western Europe and major economic weapon in the emerging Cold War.

While the United States extended its financial assistance to Europe, there were plenty of voices raised against it—from the penny-pinching like Senator Taft ("Operation Rat Hole") to the left-wing proponents of appeasement at all costs such as Henry Wallace ("the Martial Plan") who warned that war would be the consequence. Yet again, American opposition largely evaporated when the Communists made their brutal seizure of power in Prague (February 1948); two months later, Congress approved by an overwhelming margin the Economic Cooperation Bill. Until 1951, when the Economic Cooperation Administration was superseded by the Mutual Security Agency as a result of the Korean War, the ECA extended over twelve billion dollars' worth of aid, which boosted Western Europe's industrial production some 40 percent. In the process, it so strengthened the social fabric and the political regimes in Western Europe as to make them immune to the danger of internal Communist takeovers (in France and Italy, mostly).

Military assistance in the Balkans and economic assistance in Western Europe were only a start. Within a week of signing the Greek-Turkish Aid Act, President Truman asked Congress to approve the transfer of American weapons and supplies to Latin American states, as well as the training of their military personnel; this request was to lead, a short while after, to the first treaty concluded by the United States since the American Revolution —the Rio Pact in 1947 (Treaty of Reciprocal Assistance), followed in 1948 by the Charter of the Organization of American States. Back in the Old World, the obvious threat from the East prompted the Western Europeans themselves to band together for mutual protection in the five-nation Treaty of Brussels. But

five bankrupt European nations with weak military establishments could hardly hope to fight successfully the formidable Soviet war machine; it desperately needed an American shield.

Breaking with a tradition as old as the United States itself,
Senator Vandenberg suggested a congressional resolution according to which the United States would formally join "by Constitutional process with such regional and other collective arrangements as are based on continuous and effective self-help
and mutual aid, and as affect its national security." [9] Gradually,
step by step, America's political leaders dragged a reluctant and
sometimes alarmed public opinion down the path that led
straight to the twelve-nation North Atlantic Treaty Organization.

The progressive crystallization of the situation in Europe
came to its full conclusion with the Berlin Blockade in 1948–49.
It followed hard on the heels of the 1947 merger of the American, British, and French zones of occupation in Germany and
the introduction of a new currency in the "Trizonia" thus
formed. The Berlin Blockade unified the West's response under
American leadership; as so often before and after, Soviet Russia's clumsy aggressions resulted in an increase in the West's fears
and stimulated the United States' increasingly extensive control
over the whole of Western Europe. Where the various weak European nations might have knuckled under Russian threats,
Washington was not to be intimidated and boldly took the lead
in resisting Soviet encroachments—and in so doing, was inevitably driven to encroach more and more on Western Europe's
pseudo independence.

Nothing could have been more impressive at the time than the
technical miracle of the Berlin airlift itself: over a quarter of a
million flights carrying well over two million tons into the be-
leaguered city in less than a year. Impressed by this technical
prowess at a time when the success of the Marshall Plan was
becoming obvious, and intimidated by the demonstration of
Western solidarity implied in the recent signing of the North
Atlantic Treaty, Soviet Russia began a slow retreat behind its
Iron Curtain and responded, in turn, to every Western consolida-
tion move by a countermove of its own. When, in 1949, the
Federal Republic of Germany came into being, Moscow an-

nounced the formation of its very own German Democratic Republic in its East Zone. The partition of Germany into two hostile states became an accomplished fact, and few sincere tears were shed over it, in spite of official lip service paid to the ideal of German reunification. As Andrei Vishinsky was reported to have said, addressing his Western colleagues with grim satisfaction: "You have your Germans and we have ours."

Thus, in the short time-span of two and a half years, the United States had overthrown most of the foreign policy principles it had stood for during the entire course of its history. The Truman Doctrine put an end to the principle of aloofness from European affairs; the Marshall Plan resulted in open and sometimes forceful intervention in other nations' internal affairs; and NATO buried forever the principle of avoiding entangling alliances of any kind. But, as noted previously, the key word was sounded when President Truman stated emphatically that the security of the United States was involved whenever *indirect* aggression took place. From now on, the United States was likely to become involved in countless wars overseas—civil wars, regular wars, guerilla wars, police actions, and endless series of conflicts which entail, *de facto,* the establishment of an American imperium over a large part of the world.

It was perhaps an effort on the part of Secretary of State Acheson to tone down the universal potentialities of the Truman Doctrine that, indirectly, triggered the next and most decisive catalyst of America's reluctant imperialism: the Korean War. Europe and the Balkans, on the one hand, Latin America on the other, had not been the sole concern of the United States' policy makers. Thanks to war and victory over Japan, United States armed forces were also spread all over the Far East. Having retrieved the Philippines and promptly granted them independence, saved Australia from invasion and destruction, and persuaded the Dutch to set their East Indies loose on the path to independence, the United States found itself in virtual control of all the former possessions of the Japanese Empire—including Japan itself. That the collapse of this empire was bound to create power vacuums that would have to be filled, sooner or later, does not seem to have occurred to American policy makers. While Douglas MacArthur ran occupied Japan as American proconsul and reconstructed its social and political fabric without tolerating any Soviet interference, various parts of its former empire were left to drift aimlessly.

No sooner had the United States eliminated its only rival across the Pacific, transforming the ocean into an American lake, than a far more deadly enemy established its authority in China—so promptly and suddenly did the Nationalist regime collapse that Washington did not know how to react. The Kuomintang sought refuge in Formosa, greatly embarrassing the American Government which had just barely avoided being dragged into the Chinese civil war and wanted to wash its hands of the whole mess. On January 12, 1950, Dean Acheson addressed the National Press Club in Washington, and what he had to say was quite remarkable. In effect, in his effort to set some artificial limits on the applicability of the Truman Doctrine, he stated without ambiguity that Formosa was outside the United States' "defense perimeter"; and, for good measure, he incautiously excluded South Korea too. Having drawn the limits of this defense perimeter from the Aleutians through Japan and the Ryukyu Islands down to the Philippines, he carelessly added, as if it were an open invitation to aggression: "So far as the military security of other areas in the Pacific is concerned, it must be clear that no person can guarantee these areas against military attack . . . it is a mistake, I think, in considering Pacific and Far Eastern problems to become obsessed with military considerations." [10] Within a few months, the United States found itself involved—in "other areas in the Pacific"—in its first major war since 1945.

American armed forces had been withdrawn from Korea two years before, and the Joint Chiefs of Staff had repeatedly stated that the United States would be unwilling to defend South Korea if it came under attack from the north. Not only was this statement an open invitation to Communist invasion, besides being an inaccurate forecast of America's instinctive reaction if such an invasion were to take place; it also truly reflected Washington's policy which was focused on an even greater distrust of its own allies and satellites than of its open, avowed foes. South Korea's four divisions were no army but a mere constabulary force with light weapons, lacking in artillery and tanks, without a navy or an air force—this extreme weakness being necessary, according to State Department spokesmen, to prevent the South Koreans from invading the Communist-controlled north. It is highly likely that had South Korea been granted an army to match that of North Korea, no Communist aggression would have taken place at all; and in view of the part played by the Korean War in reshaping America's foreign policy all over the world, it is difficult to escape the conclusion that weakness invites aggression, which in turn evokes unnecessary violence and over-response on the part of the heretofore weak. As MacArthur pointed out in his *Reminiscences,* referring to the Korean situation: "Now was the time to recognize what the history of the world has taught from the beginning of time: that timidity breeds conflict, and courage often prevents it." [11]

Almost overnight, acting by instinct rather than according to a well-thought-out plan, President Truman reversed Washington's whole policy in the Far East. Instructing MacArthur to use his navy and air force against the North Korean invaders, he also placed the Seventh Fleet under MacArthur's command and instructed him to isolate Formosa from the Chinese mainland—officially to prevent the Chinese Nationalists from attacking Red China, but in fact placing Formosa under American military protectorate. On June 30, fortunate in being able (through an oversight of the Russians at the Security Council) to enlist the United Nations under its banner, the United States decided to send American ground forces to assist the hard-pressed South Koreans and, in effect, also placing South Korea under its military protectorate. And a few weeks later, the United States' new Far Eastern policy was made explicit. Following MacArthur's quick visit to the Chinese island late in July, President Truman issued a public statement emphasizing that the "occupation of Formosa by communist forces would be a direct threat to the security of the Pacific area and to the United States forces performing their lawful and necessary functions in that area." [12] The

American "defense perimeter" had suddenly been stretched to include several areas involved in Asian civil wars, irretrievably involving the United States in every single one of them.

The Korean War became the main catalyst of American military involvement in the Far East and Southeast Asia. Not only that; it prompted the Americans to become more deeply involved all over the world, wherever they saw, rightly or wrongly, a threat of Communist penetration or subversion. Japan was allowed to rearm under American supervision and a peace treaty was signed with it in September 1951, which, besides consecrating the total loss of its former empire, also included the transfer to American control, under a United Nations trusteeship formula, of its strategically valuable island possessions in the Pacific, notably the vast archipelagoes of Micronesia; and retention by the American military of the Ryukyus. In quick order, a number of mutual defense treaties were arranged in 1951 between the United States and most island nations in the Far East and Southeast Asia—with Japan and the Philippines, and more especially the ANZUS pact with Australia and New Zealand, excluding Britain, now forever unable to come to the assistance of her Commonwealth partners on the other side of the globe. This established a virtual American protectorate over the whole chain of islands running from Hokkaido in northern Japan down to New Zealand's South Island. Everywhere, whenever needed, United States armed forces stationed in countless military bases, were ready to spring into action at a moment's notice.

These new commitments, along with those already entered upon in Europe, in the Balkans, and in Latin America, finally brought about the Great Debate in Washington. Uneasy at the speed with which their country was being tied down by this multiplicity of commitments and responsibilities, unable to grasp the fact that the disintegration of European power all over the world (thoughtlessly encouraged and assisted by Washington's own deeds) was creating power vacuums right and left, many Americans began to question the need for these commitments. One thing leading to another, the Korean War prompted President Truman to establish the United States' protectorate not only all over the maritime fringes of the Far East, but over Western Europe as well. When, in September 1950, he ordered substantial increases in the strength of American forces in Europe, many influential Americans were outraged. Had not Dean Acheson told the Senate Foreign Relations Committee in April 1949 that the United States would not be required to send additional troops to Europe?

Fighting a rearguard action, as he did most of his life, former President Hoover stated that the United States should confine itself to strengthening its own defenses and, by developing its own naval and air power, make the whole Western Hemisphere impregnable—a "Gibraltar of Western Civilization"—presumably abandoning the rest of the world to its fate. Senator Taft, alarmed at the growth of the President's Caesarian powers, challenged his right to commit in advance American troops to fight in NATO's multinational army. Everyone seemed oblivious of the fact that no country in the world was strong enough to drag the United States into a conflict against its will; that, in fact, it was the United States itself that was in full control of the destinies of those numerous nations that were tied to it by mutual treaties. In the last report, Washington could always do as it pleased. By looking at the world scene through the wrong end of the telescope, the isolationists doomed their last offensive from the start; by making short shrift of the immense weight of the historical past which was inexorably dragging the United States forward on the road to empire, they displayed a remarkable misunderstanding of the contemporary evidence.

The Senate Foreign Relations Committee and the Armed Services Committee held open hearings in February 1951; and the Great Debate concluded on April 4 of the same year when the Senate approved President Truman's appointment of General Eisenhower as Supreme Allied Commander in Europe—military proconsul of the Old World; it also confirmed the President's decision to send four additional American divisions to Europe; and eventually, as a sequel, both Germany and Italy, now firmly welded to the Western cause, were allowed to rearm as part of NATO. And thus, the Great Debate was lost by the diehard isolationists who never understood that the Second World War had made their views obsolete, that Pearl Harbor had set them on the road to empire—and was won by those who were bound to become unconscious imperialists, and when eventually conscious, reluctant.

Defeated on Capitol Hill, the isolationists continued the Great Debate in speeches and in the press. Not all were blind to the imperial overtones of America's multiplying involvements in the affairs of all and sundry. But they could no longer find a way out of their fast-accumulating commitments. America's top soldiers, Eisenhower and MacArthur, saw no other choice but armed resistance to Communist expansion in Europe and Asia. Senator Taft, in his *Foreign Policy for Americans,* could not help admitting that "I see no choice now except to rely on our armed forces and alliances." [13] Indeed, the trend was irresistible. Along with the steady growth of Executive power at the expense of Congress, the metamorphosis of America's position in the world brought to the fore the military establishment—which is never a self-liquidating establishment. Along with the growing network of alliances and foreign commitments and the transformation of the United States into the greatest military power on earth, the finely but tightly meshed network linking the United States' fast developing Pentagon, the foreign alliances which made it imperative that the Pentagon develop its power rapidly in order to give them real muscle, and the supremacy of the Executive as sole decision-maker in foreign policy, could no longer be broken. Business interests followed in the footsteps of the soldiers abroad, and were also attracted by a military establishment at home that was becoming, by far, the major business contractor. In other words, there was there a mechanical process whereby a self-generating cluster of power was in the process of taking over the direction of American foreign policy—and directing it straight onto the road of imperial expansion.

But the Great Debate never really came to an end. In the late 1960's, it is still going on. Revived by President Johnson's decision to intervene massively in Vietnam in 1965, by the temporary resurrection of French nationalism under Charles de Gaulle's inspiration, by the profound split between Soviet Russia and Red China, and by the loosening of Russia's control over its

East European satellites, the Great Debate is still raging but working with different material and a different set of circumstances. The unconscious heirs of the old isolationists now claim that the American empire was acquired "accidentally" as a result of the Cold War [14]—as if the Cold War itself was an "accident" rather than the inevitable, even if temporary, sequel to the two World Wars. The new isolationists further claim that this empire has been incapable of protecting America's true interests, that it is too burdensome, that it involves the United States in the affairs of countless nations, and that it has a nefarious effect on American society. They further argue that the loosening of the ties binding together the Communist countries and the Sino-Soviet breakup imply that there is no further reason why the United States should maintain its empire. Since there is no more Communist "bloc," they argue, why attempt to preserve a Western one? They see nationalism as superseding Communist imperialism and as being the most potent force in the world today; and claim that it should be encouraged and given free play.

The historical record of the postwar decades does not support their main contention, even though some of their arguments have partial validity. A closer look at this record, when seen in conjunction with the historical record of the remoter past, yields very different conclusions: the American empire is not accidental but was predetermined generations ago by the development and evolution of *Western society as a whole;* this growing empire has effectively protected not only the United States' interests but those of the entire Western world, of Western Civilization, in fact; it is not too burdensome in terms of either manpower or economic power, and is far easier and cheaper to maintain than it would be to dismantle it and create new power vacuums all over the world.

☆ **V** ☆

The Tools of Empire

In a few short years, in the late 1940's and early 1950's, the international commitments of the United States began to gird the world. All in all, the United States was driven to assume a *de facto* "protectorate" over more than forty nations covering some fifteen million square miles with populations amounting to over six hundred million human beings. And even such large "neutralist" nations as India could not be left unprotected in case of a threat of outright invasion by the Red Chinese; nor could Israel, whose creation was strongly supported by the United States, ever be abandoned to the tender mercies of a Soviet-backed Arab invasion. Alongside formal treaties of alliance and pledges of economic assistance, the United States entered into countless agreements involving the uses of bases and military assistance with other nations. Providing arms, giving military aid and advice, teaching hundreds of thousands of officers and men from dozens of foreign countries in its military training centers, the United States has been compelled, in fact, to become profoundly involved in the internal policies of all its "allies."

Thus starts the road to empire. The fact that the United States must be defended all over the world as far away as possible from its own shores, in Latin America, Europe, Asia, and Africa, implies the unlimited liability to go to war in any part of the world at the slightest provocation. In the process, the United States has gradually become a garrison state in which the military establishment controls the largest business undertaking in a country noteworthy for the already huge size of its business concerns. Maintaining a sizable lead over the Soviet Russians in ICBM's and in overall nuclear power, the United States' military leaders are now convinced that their main task is going to be to fight large and small brush-fire wars against subversion and insurgency, while maintaining the nation's present lead in nuclear weaponry.

Nor is the American military machine's influence and effectiveness limited to its own armed forces; it controls, in effect, the military establishments of scores of allied and "protected" states; to a greater or lesser degree, the armed forces of South Korea, Japan, Taiwan, the Philippines, South Vietnam, Laos, and Thailand are controlled by Washington; the military protection of Australia and New Zealand is almost entirely in the hands of the American Navy and Air Force, and their own forces are just as dependent on American training and equipment as are those of all the European nations (France excepted) bound by NATO's integrated alliance. The ties binding Latin American armed forces to the Pentagon make them into semiautonomous units of the United States' military apparatus.

Such pervasive influence is costly: from 1949 to the middle of 1966, for example, the United States Government sold to foreign nations over sixteen billion dollars' worth of arms and equipment, and gave away another thirty billion dollars' worth—a total exceeding by four billion dollars the amount of economic grants and loans handed out all over the world since the beginning of the Marshall Plan.[1] This enormous outlay has its advantages; besides helping, in a minor way, to keep a huge armaments' industry going at a greater rate than it would if limited strictly to supplying the American armed forces, it is also a convenient way of disposing of partly obsolete weaponry. But the chief advantage lies in binding to the Pentagon satellite military establishments in Latin America, the Far East, and Europe; and by doing this, not only strengthening American influence with the military of a given country, but eventually giving Washington the potential use of much less costly troops for service outside their own borders—the very effective South Koreans in Vietnam, for instance. Already in 1957, it was estimated that, whereas it cost a yearly average of seven thousand dollars to keep an American soldier overseas, it cost the Americans a mere hundred and twenty-five dollars to keep a Nationalist Chinese soldier on Taiwan during the same span of time.[2]

In addition to supplying weapons (which binds the recipient army to the extent that it depends on American spare parts), the United States trains thousands of foreign military personnel and generally instills in them a pro-American outlook—which the official American handbook on military assistance training points out clearly: "As a side effect, trainees from under-developed countries obtain a better appreciation of Western culture. Mutual understanding and communication are enhanced by English-language training. Field reports attest to the strong pro-Western orientation of foreign personnel who have received training under the Military Assistance Program, especially those who have received training in the United States."[3]

From all this, it is clear that the actual military power at Washington's disposal is far greater than the Pentagon's raw statistics would suggest.

This is an entirely new situation for the United States. Looking upon its permanent military apparatus with a deeply rooted suspicion, the American people dismantled its enormous power after every war with remarkable speed—only to have to resort to crash mobilization every time a new unwanted conflict crossed its doorstep. To a lesser extent than formerly, the same thing happened after the Korean War when the Eisenhower Administration put forth the Dulles doctrine of "massive retaliation." But how could this doctrine cope with the multidimensional "wars of national liberation" sponsored by the Communists throughout the world, in which economic sabotage, social upheavals, civil wars, political subversion, and guerilla warfare substitute for outright military aggression? It could not; and the United States' next Administration adopted, in the early 1960's, the far more costly, complicated, and politically significant "flexible response" policy.

In effect, this new policy was more in tune with the United States' vast network of varied commitments throughout the world; it implied the abandonment of the "fortress America" attitude which, alone, could justify massive retaliation. But it also implied a great increase in the American military apparatus, and an even greater increase in the United States' political involvement in the internal affairs of scores of allies and satellites. Fighting a multidimensional war on the military, social, and political levels, determined to crush Communist-inspired rebellions almost before they have had time to get started, the United States Government finds itself deeply concerned and compelled to influence the internal and local policies of half the world.

So that, while the nuclear stalemate with Soviet Russia has resulted in probable peace at the highest technological level for our time, the enormous potential for smaller international conflicts, civil wars, and guerilla wars now compels the United States to maintain an equally enormous military establishment on a permanent basis in order to deal with the countless brush fires that are sure to flare up repeatedly over a great part of the world. Having become the policeman of the non-Communist world, in addition to shielding it from outright Communist aggression, the United States finds itself saddled with a military apparatus the relative size of which has never been seen, *mutatis mutandis*, since Rome established its imperium over the civilized world.

The increasing role of the military in American society has to be seen in historical perspective. No country in the world has been less militaristic; none has been more reluctant to prepare for war ever since the Continental Congress stated in 1787: "Standing armies in time of Peace are inconsistent with the principles of republican governments, dangerous to the liberties of a free people and generally converted into a destructive engine for establishing despotism." [4] All of which is perfectly true; and even more prophetic, the accusation leveled in 1790 by Senator William Maclay of Pennsylvania against Secretary of War Knox who sought to increase the size of his puny thousand-man army:

"Give Knox his army and he will soon have a war on hand." [5] Given its present military establishment and the revolutionary temper of a large part of the world's population, the United States is sure to have at least one war, of the brush-fire variety, permanently on hand. Parkinson's Law decrees that "work expands so as to fill the time available for its completion." An extension of this law to the military world decrees that wars will always be produced in time to justify the existence of any military establishment.

This is not to suggest that objective reasons for the existence of a powerful American military apparatus do not exist; they do, and a correct reading of the trends of world history could have shown quite conclusively the historical inevitability of the sudden development of the Pentagon's power. The mutual destruction of Europe's Powers combined with the rise of Soviet Russia's military might to supremacy in Eurasia's heartland, the disintegration of the British Empire and the collapse of Europe's far-flung colonial empires in Asia and Africa, left a global vacuum that had to be filled by the only Western Power available to do so. Again, it was not the will or conscious desire on the part of American statesmen that dictated this development—although many took to it as cats to milk. In the interim between the drastic dismantling of United States military power in the late 1940's and its rapid buildup as a result of the Korean conflict, a subtle change had taken place: unlike World War I, the Second World War had vastly increased the prestige of the military in American society. As early as 1947, in the very midst of the virtual evaporation of the American army, the *New York Times'* military expert Hanson Baldwin had expressed a certain alarm at "the militarization of our government and of the American state of mind." [6] This timely warning, sounded three years before war broke out in Korea, could not alter the historical trend, which had been strongly confirmed by the events of the World War and the proconsular role played by America's military leaders—from General MacArthur's virtual assumption of the Japanese Emperor's authority in reshaping Japanese society in depth, to General Clay's proconsulate in Germany where he was not only carrying out Washington's policy but shaping it when, on his own initiative, he halted the dismantling of industrial plants earmarked for Soviet Russia, took a hand in the formation of political parties and elections against Washington's advice, committed the United States beyond recall to the maintenance of the West's position in Berlin after the Russians had destroyed the four-power government of Germany. In contrast, General Pershing, of World War I fame, was only the commander of an American expeditionary force under the overall command of a French marshal and with no proconsular role.

Having fought simultaneously in Europe and Asia, in deserts and jungles, island-hopping in the Pacific or moving millions of men across the European continent; having had to become familiar with the most abstruse notions of applied science and advanced technology, with the techniques of industrial production, with high-level diplomacy as well as with obscure intelligence-gathering, with psychological warfare and social upheavals, with the proconsular rule of defeated nations, the new American military quickly established its position as the most influential element in American society. Encompassing in its vast new establishment the most complete and up-to-date information in every field of knowledge—from nuclear physics to anthropological knowledge of the mountain tribes of Southeast Asia—the United States military has come to occupy a central position of decisive importance in the life of the world's most powerful country.

In his astonishing "Farewell Address" to the nation on January 17, 1961, President Eisenhower, a war hero himself and a symbol of this new stature, stunned the American people when he stated bluntly: "We can no longer risk emergency improvisation of national defense. We have been compelled to create a permanent armaments industry of vast proportions. Added to this, three and a half million men and women are directly engaged in the defense establishment. . . . Now this conjunction of an immense military establishment and a large arms industry is new in the American experience. The total influence—economic, political, even spiritual—is felt in every city, every State House, every office of the Federal Government. We recognize the imperative need for the development. Yet we must not fail to comprehend its grave implications. Our toil, resources and livelihood are all involved; so is the very structure of our society." [7]

Having described the revolutionary impact of this militarization, he then went on to advise: "In the councils of government, we must guard against the acquisition of unwarranted influence, whether sought or unsought, by the military-industrial complex. The potential for the disastrous rise of misplaced power exists and will persist." [8] Indeed, military and industrial forms of power are now closely intertwined and can hardly be separated. The immense power of America's military apparatus springs from its own society's accomplishments in the economic and financial realms, its dedication to relentless research, its managerial skill and its utter devotion to the ideal of bringing up its productive capacity to the highest pitch of efficiency—whatever the purpose to which it is applied. The same ideals which animate its economic life animate its military endeavors; they help one another, and technological breakthroughs in one field are immediately applied to the other, merging in one gigantic expansionary drive all the benefits of free enterprise's unlimited initiatives with the Federal Government's almost limitless resources.

Ever since the first atom bomb was built under military supervision, the American military have been acutely research-minded, more so than any other military establishment anywhere, save perhaps Russia. With a yearly budget of over six billion dollars, the Pentagon's contribution to the American industry's overall progress is staggering. While almost fifty thousand military men test and evaluate new weapons and equipment, about one hundred thousand civilians work in the Pentagon's research laboratories. But this is only a sideshow compared with the military work accomplished by private industry. In the process, however, the militarization of American industry is proceeding apace; not only has the Pentagon become, by far, the biggest and therefore most influential contractor; not only have the boards of directors of innumerable American companies engaged in defense work been hospitable in the extreme to retired generals and admirals; a large segment of this industry has come under military supervision through the increasing enforcement of its security regulations in countless plants working for the Defense Department, subjecting millions of workers to security clearance. This is not all. A great deal of the technological superiority enjoyed by American industry springs from the government-sponsored secret research carried out in many universities. In spite of the reluctance, and sometimes outright anger, of some scholars and students, it is only by participating in classified research that they can hope to remain on top of vital technological developments. In a sense, both the industrial and the academic worlds have been "satellized" by the Pentagon.

Occasional complaints are heard that the defense load is too heavy a burden to bear, complaints which rise in a steep crescendo whenever a large military operation is undertaken overseas. The figures disprove this contention, since the gross national product was approximately 260 billion dollars a year in 1951, whereas it had reached beyond 800 billion in 1968; translated in military expenditure, the Pentagon, at the Korean War peak in 1952–53, absorbed 13.4 percent of GNP, whereas from 1965 to 1967, during the much larger buildup for the Vietnam War, it had risen from 7.5 percent to only 9.5 percent. If anything, the relative economic and financial burden has decreased from the Korean to the Vietnam War. Furthermore, having become so completely meshed with the private sector of the economy, military spending now has a vital importance for the entire economic structure. In September 1967, the Labor Department Bureau of Labor Statistics reckoned that the buildup of the war in Vietnam had created a million additional jobs in the United States and that additional increases in military spending unrelated to the Vietnam War had created an additional two million. Further statistics from the same source illustrate the extent to which defense expenditures contribute to the economy: 22 percent of all electronic and electric technicians, 18 percent of all engineers and science technicians, and 14 percent of all draftsmen held defense jobs in 1967.

In spite of President Eisenhower's warning, the military-industrial complex has become increasingly powerful and has gradually acquired a vested interest in the development of the American empire, by force of arms or otherwise. In fact, Charles

Wilson, Eisenhower's Secretary of Defense, stated the case quite well when he claimed that "one of the serious things about this defense business is that so many Americans are getting a vested interest in it; properties, business, jobs, employment, votes, opportunities for promotion and advancement, bigger salaries for scientists and all that." [9] In other words, the very momentum of the machinery itself tends toward imperialism as a justification for its continued existence.

In December 1967, Senator William Fulbright noticed with alarm: "In general, industrialists, businessmen, workers, and politicians have joined together in a military-industrial complex—a complex which, for all the inadvertency of its creation and the innocent intentions of its participants, has none the less become a powerful new force for the perpetuation of foreign military commitments, for the introduction and expansion of expensive weapons systems, and, as a result, for the militarization of large segments of our national life." [10] He added that the universities, which might have provided a countervailing force, had now joined the "monolith" because of the irresistible appeal of money and influence. Deploring the trend whereby the Government, the economic leaders, and the universities had become adapted to the requirements of unending warfare, he wondered on the floor of the United States Senate whether America had to give up its traditional self-image of a creative democracy in exchange for that of a "traditional" world empire.

If the military has acquired such predominance in American life in our times, it is partly due to the deleterious effects of prewar isolationism. John J. McCloy pointed out: "The isolationism of the 1920–40 period had produced a vacuum of political objectives. The State Department did not have, indeed it was not encouraged to have, any political aims in the world. More thinking along political lines was being done and being asserted in the Munitions Building—this was before the era of the Pentagon—than in the old State Building." [11] From this deficiency of political objectives, the State Department never really recovered. Wartime conditions after Pearl Harbor further reduced its role and influence in what amounted to a thoroughly militarized nation headed by a President with almost dictatorial powers. The Secretary of State found himself barred from attending many meetings of great import in foreign affairs. In his memoirs, Cordell Hull, the wartime incumbent, made no bones about this steady downgrading of his department's role:

> Prior to Pearl Harbor I had been a member of the War Council . . . and I took part in its meetings. After Pearl Harbor I did not sit in on meetings concerned with military matters. This was because the President did not invite me to such meetings. I raised the question with him several times. It seemed manifest to me that, in numerous important instances, the Secretary of State should sit in on the President's war councils, particularly on those of a combined military and diplomatic nature, for it was obvious that scarcely any large-scale military operations could be undertaken that would not have diplomatic aspects. . . . The President did not take me with him to the Casablanca, Cairo or Teheran conferences, nor did I take part in his military discussions with Prime Minister Churchill in Washington, some of which had widespread diplomatic repercussions. . . . I learned from other sources than the President what had occurred at the Casablanca, Cairo and Teheran Conferences. . . . I was not told about the atomic bomb. . . .[12]

In other words, Secretary Hull and the State Department were shunted aside, bypassed even in matters of great importance in foreign affairs where many of the most crucial decisions were eventually made by the military in their new proconsular role. And what was left of the State Department after the war was demoralized and largely paralyzed by the McCarthy fracas of the early 1950's. Secretary of State John Foster Dulles' preeminent role in the 1950's had nothing to do with the State Department as such; he was primarily President Eisenhower's alter ego in the realm of foreign affairs, which he handled personally, flying all over the world from one capital to another, while making minimal use of the diplomatic personnel at his disposal.

While the foregoing explains both the supremacy of the military in foreign policy planning and the extreme weakness of America's conventional diplomacy, it also explains that some substitute had to be found for a deficient State Department. In any case, every country's conventional diplomacy came out of the Second World War badly damaged; the Cold War and its aftermath of revolutions and subversions had made it largely obsolete as a means of international information, communication, and influence. And while the supremacy of the military was accepted as almost inevitable in the postwar United States, no one wanted to hand over to it all the imperial tools that had been forged in the emergency of the Cold War.

One of the major fallouts of the surprise attack at Pearl Harbor, as was stated by the Hoover Commission in 1955, was the prompt recognition of the need for better intelligence. At Pearl Harbor, the United States finally lost its innocence dating back to the days after the First World War when Henry L. Stimson closed down the State Department's "Black Chamber" for deciphering, because "gentlemen don't read other people's mail." [13] British gentlemen did; but then, Britain was still running the world's largest empire. Now it was the United States' turn and American officials would have to start reading other people's mail.

Following the wartime OSS, a relatively small-scale cloak-and-dagger organization, it was deemed essential in the late 1940's to create a centralized organism for the collection of confidential information; and, as Allen Dulles insisted, one that would be headed by civilians and would not be "merely a co-ordinating agency for the military intelligence services." [14] He wanted a central espionage organization which would not be under the heel of the Pentagon but an autonomous organization in its own right, under the National Security Council. After having insisted that this organism should have nothing to do with policy-making and merely collect the facts on which others would base their policy, Allen Dulles did not press the point, and the National Security Act of 1947 included, among the specific duties of intelligence-gathering, a vague Section 102 which provided that it should also perform "other functions and duties" under the overall direction of the National Security Council. Indeed, Allen Dulles himself, in a memorandum submitted to Congress in 1947, demanded that the newborn Central Intelligence Agency "have exclusive jurisdiction to carry out secret intelligence operations." Years later, former President Truman was to lament the extension of the CIA's functions from intelligence-gathering to actual armed operations and claimed that "the last thing we needed was for the CIA to be seized upon as something akin to a subverting influence in the affairs of other people." [15] But, for all that, it was President Truman himself who, in 1951, established the Plans Division which was put in charge of the CIA's special operations.

Thus was born one of the United States' most powerful tools for its imperial mission, a dagger concealed behind the cloak of overt diplomacy—its worldwide network of secret intelligence agencies. This enormous apparatus is to conventional diplomacy what the submerged part of an iceberg is to its floating top above the waterline. Its core is the celebrated Central Intelligence Agency; its head, the Director of Central Intelligence, runs not only the CIA but presides over the entire intelligence community which includes nine other agencies dealing with State Department Affairs, Defense, Atomic Energy, the Federal Bureau of Investigation and, especially, the National Security Agency whose vast temple of cryptography, with its fourteen thousand top-flight employees, houses the greatest concentration of computers and communications brains in the world.

This entirely new institution in the United States is the inevitable result of its postwar leadership throughout the non-Communist world and of the Cold War in which it became engaged since the hot one came to an end in 1945. We can take it from the man who did more to shape its growth and development than any other, Allen W. Dulles, that its enormous importance and influence cannot be overestimated: "The National Security Act of 1947 has given Intelligence a more influential position in our government than intelligence enjoys in any other government in the world." [16]

Secretly employing over two hundred thousand men and women, enjoying a secret annual budget unofficially estimated at several billion dollars, it is, by and large, the most powerful secret organization in the world today. Established in the heart of most American embassies abroad, utilizing channels of communications and codes of its own, the CIA has drastically reduced the power and influence of the professional diplomats. Unlike the State Department, it was very effectively shielded from the McCarthy rampage, and put in a position where it could attract competent men and offer them salaries that were substantially higher than those prevailing in the diplomatic service.

Putting aside those instances where the CIA's cloak-and-dagger operations have erupted in a dismal explosion of unfavorable publicity, it is certain that an increasing number of covert operations are carried out with considerable success; past successes testify eloquently, although they were less publicized than the failures: the overthrow of Premier Mohammed Mossadegh in Iran (1953), the destruction of President Jacobo Arbenz Guzmán's pro-Communist regime in Guatemala (1954), salvaging the Congo from the brink of chaos in the early 1960's, and countless other operations, some large and some small, some successes and some failures, most of which we shall never hear about in our lifetime.

Here again, the typical American qualities of organizational ability, brutal efficiency, technical proficiency, and practical purposiveness come into play to such an extent that, today, not only is the intelligence apparatus of the United States the greatest network of its kind in the world in terms of numbers of operatives and budgetary size, but it is also becoming qualitatively excellent. It is obvious that it has become a precious tool for the extension of American influence throughout the world; it is also obvious that the dagger (secret operations) has become just as important as the cloak (counterespionage, intelligence-gathering and evaluation).

That this was not the purpose for which it was created, as former President Truman asserted, has little to do with the fact that it has become an immense apparatus with immense power; and that a great deal of its activity is not so much concerned with countering its main antagonists, Soviet Russia's KGB (Interior Ministry) and GRU (Military Intelligence), as with keeping the non-Communist world in line—in effect, increasing the United States' imperial control over its allies, satellites, and outright possessions. For instance, the CIA-engineered overthrow of the Laotian Government of Premier Phoui Saninikone on January 1, 1960, was largely a failure because its willing tool, General Phoumi Nosavan, had no support in the country; still, it was a remarkable, if dangerous, display of remote-control power, only lacking in better political engineering.

In the process of its development, the CIA has adopted most of the techniques of its main, and most successful, antagonist—Soviet Russia's own secret services which make maximum use of journalistic, commercial, and diplomatic cover. Experts estimate that over half of the Soviet diplomatic apparatus is drawn from the ranks of the KGB and GRU, and that a substantial portion of all Soviet journalists and commercial representatives belong to one secret organization or other. Nor should it be forgotten that they all have at their disposal, throughout the world, many members of the local Communist parties who are fanatically devoted to furthering the aims of the mother country of all "socialist" parties—an inestimable advantage which the United States does not possess abroad. In his *Papers,* Oleg Penkovsky quotes the following instance: "Ananyev, our officer in Paris, told me that the GRU and KGB have very close working relations with Communists. . . . It is true that if we approach an ordinary Frenchman and he realises that he is talking to Russians, he will immediately run and report the contact to the police. But French Communists, generally speaking, readily agree to work for us, asking only directions on how and what to do." [17] The same is true the world over.

Since it is difficult to fight an opponent without using his own best weapons, the Americans were quickly driven to duplicate, to a certain extent, the Soviet apparatus. Further reasons, derived mostly from the United States' own political structure, have compelled the American authorities to give the CIA a major role in multitudes of activities seemingly unrelated to intelligence-gathering and secret operations. One major reason is that the Executive, in its endless struggle to overcome or bypass the obstacles raised by Congress, has found it convenient over the years to use the only tool at its disposal which is not publicly

supervised or audited, for purposes for which it was not originally intended. In a country such as Soviet Russia where all
social organisms—labor unions, academic institutions, student
organizations, commercial and industrial firms—are part and
parcel of the state apparatus, there is no such need; and its intelligence and subversive activities have, at all times, the free and
discreet use of any such organisms. In a free society, the problem
is vastly more complex and requires an additional degree of
secrecy.

So it was that the news exploded in 1967 like a bombshell: the
CIA had been financing for years just about every American
institution working abroad and many more at home. The immense spider web covering the entire non-Communist world had
drawn into its fine mesh an extraordinary number of respectable
organizations—the Institute of International Labor Research,
headed by old-time Socialist leader Norman Thomas, Billy Graham's Spanish-American crusade, the Friends of India Committee, the International Food and Drink Workers Federation, the
National Council of Churches, the Harvard Law School, and
hundreds of others—universities and colleges, Churches, labor
unions, and legal organizations, American and foreign publications in Europe, Asia, and Africa. Some were assisted merely for
the purpose of enabling them to stand on their financial feet;
others, on the contrary, were practically managed by the CIA,
such as the National Student Association to whose budget it contributed up to 90 percent of the total amount, and many of
whose representatives abroad were in fact intelligence agents
rather than student representatives.

While the explosion of publicity compelled the American
Government to devise some other means of financing these institutions that were merely drawing money from the CIA without
necessarily being under its influence, it would be naïve to think
that America's secret services are going to interrupt a highly
effective and successful way of spreading American influence
throughout the world. Many instances of this effectiveness have
been revealed. For example, in 1962 and 1963, the American
Federation of State, County, and Municipal Employees had
turned its International Affairs Department over to the CIA to

be used as a base for strikes and subversive activities aimed at the overthrow of Premier Cheddi Jagan's proto-Communist regime in British Guiana—which was duly accomplished when pro-American Forbes Burnham took over as Premier in December 1964, thus avoiding turning what was renamed Guyana into a new Cuba.[18]

Everything is grist to their mill. Not only do they collect precious information, as they did after the war through the International Transport Federation's work among European dock workers, seamen, and train crews; they also work actively to influence and shape events as they did when they went to work in Italy and practically won the crucial 1948 election for the Christian Democrats, or when they actively supported the emergence of a third force in France and its foundation of the ill-fated Fourth Republic. A furor was raised when it was disclosed that Michigan State University had been used, from 1955 to 1959, as cover for CIA agents in South Vietnam who were working on a large-scale program of technical assistance to train the local police. [19] Often enough, the CIA assists enemies of the United States' allies, and by doing it secretly, avoids antagonizing those allies while keeping all its options open for the future and under-cutting Communist influence. Thousands of students fighting colonial regimes in Algeria, Mozambique, Angola, South Africa and Southwest Africa, and many others, were and are subsidized secretly.[20] In 1967, the Spanish authorities publicly accused the CIA of assisting unrest on Spanish university campuses in spite of the fact that anti-Communist Spain leases a number of valuable bases to the United States armed forces.[21] It was common knowledge in the 1950's that the American Federation of Labor's representative in North Africa was actively encouraging the buildup of anti-Communist labor unions and simultaneously striving to undermine French authority and influence in the area; it is only years later that the decisive role played by the CIA has come out in public. Strong links between the CIA and the merged American Federation of Labor–Congress of Industrial Organizations have been hinted at by a top official of the United Auto Workers union who claimed that it is "a lot bigger story" than that of the CIA's support for student groups.[22]

It is easy to imagine that, on top of its own gigantic resources and organization, the CIA also has at its disposal all the secret intelligence services of its allies and satellites. *Primus inter pares,* of course, is Britain's famed but drastically shrunken apparatus— MI 5 (external intelligence) and MI 6 (counterespionage), to many of whose multifarious activities the CIA became heir. No great effort of imagination is required to figure out that, while the CIA probably has its own intelligence network inside Red China, alongside the technological eyes provided by overflights and space satellites, a great deal of its information must be provided by the extensive Chinese network directed from Formosa; similar ties bind it to similar Japanese services. When, after the war, the CIA recruited one of Germany's master spies, Reinhard Gehlen, it was able to mount an all-German espionage structure of great effectiveness; and when the Gehlen organization was turned over to the West German Government in 1955, the CIA remained at the receiving end of the information provided by its numerous activities on both sides of the Iron Curtain. In other words, it is with the CIA as with the Pentagon: they have to be seen *in toto,* with all their external ramifications and satellites.

In 1963, Harry Truman complained again, "There is something about the way the CIA has been functioning that is casting a shadow over our historic positions, and I feel that we need to correct it." [23] Correct what? It would be the height of naïvety to think that the United States, inescapably saddled with a growing empire, can dispense not only with secret intelligence services but with outright cloak-and-dagger operations. Faced with uncompromising enemies, it has no choice. But the drift of events is such that a great deal of the CIA's work consists, in the process of struggling against Communist subversion, in keeping allies and satellites subservient to Washington's wishes. In the plainest sense of the term, it is a prime tool for the task of empire-building.

It is highly probable that the CIA gets a great deal of credit for influence it does not have and operations it has never undertaken. But is it entirely fanciful to imagine that it might have had a finger in the Indonesian pie when President Sukarno was overthrown by the 1965 military takeover? After all—and Sukarno was aware of it—the CIA had several times, notably in 1958, participated in attempts to overthrow him.[24] Would it be naïve to think that, when the overthrow was successfully carried out in 1965, wresting well over a hundred million people from the clutches of an impending Communist coup, the CIA had something to do with it? Or was it just spite that prompted former Congolese Premier Moïse Tshombe to accuse it of being responsible for his kidnapping to Algeria in 1967?[25] The motive was, of course, obvious: Washington was backing to the hilt Congolese President Mobutu and wanted to rid him of his only dangerous rival. Accusations fly right and left; few can ever be proved, but many are plausible.

After twenty years' experience, the machinery of the United States intelligence network is well oiled and has all the spare parts required to keep and even gain indirect and relatively discreet control of client states throughout the world. Its growing reputation is such that the merest rumor about it can actually influence the decisions of foreign statesmen and shape their policy. In 1965, for instance, a vast plot was uncovered in Cairo, presumably linking the powerful underground Muslim Brotherhood and the CIA in a joint effort to topple President Nasser. The Egyptian Premier was soon convinced that Washington had, at long last, lost patience with him and was determined to destroy his power. Washington's loss of patience was subsequently made increasingly plain when the Americans decided to curtail their economic assistance unless Cairo complied with American wishes—withdraw its troops from the Yemen and settle its quarrel with Saudi Arabia. Early in 1967, the worried Egyptians were beginning to feel the tightening of the screws and apprehended an approaching blow, without knowing where it would come from or when it would fall. When, on April 21, the Greek Government was overthrown by a military junta, the Egyptian apprehensions became certainties. The screws were being tightened further; Syria was presumed to be next on the list, and the general strike which had paralyzed Damascus a few days before this event was probably a warning of worse to come. Israel's own exasperation against the regime in Damascus and its open threat to destroy it confirmed the ruling Egyptians in their conviction that they had to stand by the Syrians or be struck down by the CIA. War became inevitable.[26]

While all this may sound fanciful as far as the factual development of events is concerned, it represents in schematic form the actual thought process of the leading Egyptians during the months preceding the lightning war between Israel and the Arabs in 1967. In other words, the mere threat, real or imaginary, of CIA underground action in the Middle East, and the actualization of the military coup in Greece, were enough to influence the overheated imagination of the Egyptian leaders in Cairo.

Another instance of this spreading fear of American cloak-and-dagger activity was printed on the front page of *Borba*, Yugoslavia's major newspaper. On October 31, 1967, it listed and simultaneously discounted rumors about the CIA's presumed activities in Yugoslavia—denying that it was responsible for the drop in the price of Scotch whiskey, for the burning of hundreds of Croatian factories mysteriously destroyed by fire, for the escape of a leading Nazi war criminal, and countless other phenomena.[27] Again, the all-pervasive influence attributed by Yugoslav public opinion to the American intelligence agency could be sufficiently infectious in the future to have a direct impact on Yugoslavia's policy decisions.

The lengthening shadow of the CIA over a large part of the world is beginning to make it look three times its actual size; and, in a sense, this mythmaking process can make its work easier, rather than more difficult, to perform.

Early in this century, Albert J. Beveridge, Senator from Indiana under Theodore Roosevelt, declared: "God . . . has made us the master organizers of the world to establish system where chaos reigns. . . . He has made us adepts in government that we may administer government among savage and senile people. . . . He has marked the American people as His chosen nation to finally lead in 'he regeneration of the world. This is the divine mission of America. . . . We will not renounce our part of the mission of the race, trustee under God, of the civilization of the world." [28] While his words may be dismissed as the rantings of a wordy senator, the missionary spirit persists—no longer preaching the word of Christ but the virtues of free speech and free enterprise, democracy and the rule of law. Spreading around the world and converting the modern heathen with all the energy and far more conviction than those of an automobile salesman, contemporary Americans, whether military or Peace Corpsmen, diplomats or CIA agents, businessmen, engineers or traveling Rotarians, are fanning out across the world and giving the Message. It might have been more peaceful and quiescent if this missionary spirit had not found a worthy antagonist in the Communist spirit with its own missionary outlook. The end result is not a willing but a reluctant imperialism because it is essentially a by-product of the clash between two contending missionary spirits attempting to fill power vacuums.

The fact that empire-building begins unconsciously and becomes reluctant as the builders begin to realize what they are doing is clearly demonstrated in history. Rome did not really want to build an empire but eventually found itself saddled with a rudimentary one after the First Punic War; from then on, in the process of discharging new responsibilities thus acquired, all it could do was to go on conquering and subduing and civilizing for the protection of its new wards, and learn to enjoy it. Britain never intended to conquer India; British penetration in India was, at first, a strictly commercial venture and the East India Company sternly warned its local representatives against becoming embroiled in local Indian politics; but embroiled they eventually had to become in order to fight off France's growing influence—and, one involvement leading to another, the British found themselves unwitting masters of an enormous oriental empire in India, which they then had to protect by securing all the entrances to the Indian Ocean and putting locks on them: so that a new string of possessions had to be added in South Arabia and the Persian Gulf, in South and East Africa, in Malaya and Singapore; similarly, all the continental approaches had to be secured, leading to armed expeditions to Afghanistan, Tibet, and Burma.

It is no different in our times. Just as the threat of Germany's imperialism prompted Washington to edge gradually into two world wars, the threat of Communist expansion has become the main catalyst of the United States' reluctant imperialism during the Cold War. The fragmentation of its power center, the disruption of its former monolithic structure into a polycentric movement divided against itself, has not blunted communism's missionary drive toward widespread expansion. Unfolding revolutionary warfare in Southeast Asia, Latin America, and Africa is bound to increase the already extensive American involvement in the political, social, and military life of countless nations—to the extent, at least, that the local national establishments find themselves unable to crush those rebellions without extensive American assistance.

The subtle point here is that strong interference on the part of the United States cannot help but promote further the very Communist action it is fighting—and, that, most of the time, communism will gradually monopolize and exploit the latent feeling of fear and hostility toward the United States that is swelling throughout the world. In other words, the truth and the tragedy of the matter is that the United States and a great many of the world's nations are trapped by historical necessity in a mechanical process of mutual involvement, leading the United States inexorably toward an extensive, if reluctant, imperialism.

☆ VI ☆

The Road to Suez

While the steady expansion of America's legal commitments was taking place on a global scale, the disintegration of Europe's colonial empires was going on relentlessly. But, somehow, this disintegration seemed to have an almost beneficent influence on political and social developments in the Old World. Europe had been set up on its feet economically by the Marshall Plan; militarily, by the setting up of NATO, with the addition of a substantial body of American troops and limited rearmament of the European nations involved; and politically, by the impotence of the local Communist parties.

As a highly industrialized continent, Western Europe could well do economically without most of its former colonies and spheres of influence throughout the world. Two areas, however, are geopolitically vital to Europe, to the extent that the Continent aims at military and economic independence from the United States: North Africa, which covers its Mediterranean underbelly, and the Middle East where the Suez Canal gives it a direct maritime link with the Orient, and whence springs oil, the vital fuel that is the lifeblood of its vast industries—in other words, the entire Arab world, from Casablanca to the Persian Gulf.

In spite of Britain's military withdrawal from Egypt proper to the Canal Zone in the late 1940's, European control or influence was still paramount in that part of the world. The Suez Canal was run by an Anglo-French company; and both the French and the British owned a major slice of the oil wells and pipelines of the Middle East. Their stake in that part of the world meant more to Europe, in economic, political, and military terms, than all the colonial territories they were giving up in other parts of the world. Deprived at home of many of the natural resources that bless the huge territory of the United States, they partly made up for this deficiency by exerting a great deal of control over this non-European piece of valuable real estate. Without it, Europe was bound to sink lower still in the scale of international power, fall even more decisively into the sphere of America's military protection, and be, economically, thrown at the mercy of American handouts. Sooner or later, this fatal development was bound to occur—and occur it did, dramatically, in 1956.

In terms of internal politics, the Middle East has always been explosive—mostly because the Arab temper is at all times volatile and because geography has so fragmented the area that, in spite of a common language and culture, any kind of political unification has been out of the question. Into this already explosive situation, an additional element of combustion had been injected in the shape of a large-scale Jewish immigration to Palestine, culminating in the setting up of the new state of Israel in 1948. Although the British had encouraged Jewish immigration after World War I, their worried Arab subjects and protégés had compelled them to curtail it before World War II broke out, in spite of an increased need for it during the Nazi holocaust.

As in so many other areas, the British lost control of the situation during the Second World War. In 1942, the American-dominated World Zionist Organization made it clearly known that it wanted an end to the immigration restrictions, along with a Jewish state and army. In 1944, the United States Congress, for domestic electoral reasons, began to display a great deal of interest in the idea of a Jewish state; and so did the United States' two major political parties, along with a strong endorsement from President Roosevelt.

Encouraged, the Palestinian Jews began a campaign of terrorism against both the Arabs and the British—who were thus expected to cope alone with a difficult situation, made twice as difficult by the declarations of American political leaders who had no responsibility in the administration of the territory. Shortly after the Potsdam Conference in 1945, President Truman asked Britain's Prime Minister Attlee to allow a hundred thousand Jewish immigrants into Palestine; Attlee accepted at once, provided his weakened country was allowed to give up its Palestinian mandate to a United Nations trusteeship, and also provided an Anglo-American Committee of Inquiry was appointed to study the problem: in effect, he quite naturally invited the United States to share in the responsibility of policy-making in Palestine. President Truman refused point-blank and restated his proposal to admit forthwith a hundred thousand Jews, regardless of consequences. In this way, naïvely hoping to placate the Arabs in whose oil resources they had a considerable stake and whose friendship they wanted to retain, while pleasing the Zionists who pulled a great deal of electoral weight at home, the American leaders added a great deal to the British burden without wanting to share in any responsibility.

Britain could no longer carry the load, having already dropped the Greco-Turkish burden in America's lap. As the White Paper of February 1947 made clear, the British were determined to unload as much of their global responsibilities as they could; and since the American lap was not available, they shifted the problem of Palestine onto the shoulders of the United Nations the same month. Deeds followed words, and on May 15, 1948, the British pulled out their last troops and gave up the Mandate. President Truman had at first accepted a United Nations resolution to divide Palestine into a Jewish and an Arab state; then, on March 19, 1948, announced that he had changed his mind and advocated a temporary United Nations trusteeship. This irresolution increased the chaos and bloodshed in Palestine, but did not prevent the United States from extending immediately *de facto* recognition to the newborn state of Israel as soon as its birth was proclaimed on May 14.

War broke out immediately between Arabs and Israelis. The most remarkable feature of these hostilities was not the surprising defeat of the Arab armies nor the flight of one million Palestinian Arabs out of Israel; it was the fact that this Middle East situation became involved in the United States' approaching elections and that both Republicans and Democrats, courting Jewish votes, indicated their marked preference for an Israeli victory— made largely possible by the vast amounts of American money flowing into Zionist organizations. In a sense, therefore, Israel was a natural child of the United States which could never be totally disowned, however bitter the Arabs might be about it. But the child might prove rebellious at times; American military planners in Washington foresaw that easy military victories over the Arabs might tempt the Israelis to break the U.N. July 1949 armistice agreement and overrun the rest of Palestine. In order to ward off this danger, Washington persuaded France and Britain in May 1950 to join the United States in a Tripartite Declaration under which the three Powers guaranteed the terms of the United Nations armistice. But the temptation remained, and Israel's yielding to it six years later was one of the important elements in the Suez Crisis.

The collapse of Europe's power and influence in the Middle East began in 1951 when Iran's Prime Minister Mohammed Mossadegh abruptly nationalized the Anglo-Iranian's extensive oil properties, including Abadan's giant refinery. Those were the days when two-thirds of its production filled nine-tenths of Britain's oil requirements. Negotiations leading nowhere, Britain's Labour Government, behaving out of necessity in true old imperial fashion, spoke of taking "severe measures." When Mossadegh ordered British technicians out of Abadan because their presence there had become "redundant," British Prime Minister Attlee sent an urgent message to President Truman, warning him that either the British stayed, using military force if necessary, or the entire Western position in the Moslem world would be in danger. Harry Truman vetoed the use of force. A few hours later, the Iranian army took over Abadan and expelled the British. As *Newsweek* editors put it, "This new sort of Dunkirk sent sweeping across Britain a stinging sense of national humiliation—plus a tendency to blame the United States for failing to support military intervention." [1]

An appeal to the United Nation's Security Council led nowhere either. And while Washington's State Department genuinely tried to assist Britain in its diplomatic struggle, there was no doubt that Britain's privileged position in Iran had received a blow from which it would never recover. Mohammed Mossadegh was eventually overthrown in 1953 by the aforementioned CIA-engineered coup, and the new Iranian Government of General Zahedi quickly proceeded to reopen negotiations. But all the while, during Mossadegh's tenure and even after, it seems clear that Washington was eager to substitute for the departing British rather than express its solidarity with them—sending American technicians to Abadan along with some machinery in order to restart operations, for instance. To this, Anthony Eden ". . . said at once that I must emphasize in the strongest possible terms the deplorable effect on Anglo-American relations which the presence of Americans working in stolen British property would cause." [2] Then, right after Mossadegh's fall from power, according to Eden, "reports reached the Foreign Office that the State Department had been holding meetings with the American oil companies. At these, it was alleged, the State Department pressed for the formation of an all-American company to buy out the Anglo-Iranian. This idea was not to the liking of the American oil companies. The Foreign Office rightly expressed its concern that the State Department should apparently be discussing with these companies plans which were so different from the joint proposals we had agreed upon." [3] But then, who had overthrown Mossadegh? The CIA.

While the final settlement did not follow the lines of a complete American takeover of the former Anglo-Iranian oil empire, it gave American interests a solid participation in an international consortium: 40 percent divided between Gulf Oil, Standard Oil of New Jersey, Standard Oil of California, Socony Mobil, and the Texas Company—leaving the former Anglo-Iranian with another 40 percent. Thus, the Mossadegh episode ended in a clear-cut American victory, giving American economic interests a substantial position in an area that had hitherto been an exclusive British preserve. It also left the Iranians with a victory of sorts, in the sense that their nationalization had been fully accepted by all concerned. Britain's monopoly in Iranian oil had come to an end, and so had her political influence.

An immediate by-product of the Iranian fracas was Egypt's abrupt attempt to expel the British from their huge half-billion-dollar base at Suez. Mustafa Nahas Pasha, Egypt's Premier, failed in his purpose, however. Unlike Iran's Mossadegh, he had to face a tight Anglo-American alliance concerning the Suez base, which allowed the British to ignore his decrees and refuse to leave.

The overthrow of King Farouk in the summer of 1952 by a group of army officers and the emergence of Gamal Abdel Nasser as their leader altered the whole situation, injecting a revolutionary element in a straightforward nationalist attempt to expel British power. Nasser's fanatical desire to lead Arab nationalism toward the path of reunification of the Middle East, and to destroy Israel in the process, was bound to collide with Britain's military presence at Suez. Coincidentally, Britain was growing steadily weaker and soon found it difficult to hold on to the great Canal base; financial costs and Egyptian pressure finally drove the London Government to promise Nasser in 1954 that British troops would evacuate their great Suez base by the spring of 1956.

Alarmed by the possibility of Soviet penetration in the Arab Middle East as a result of the disintegration of Britain's imperial position, the United States began to take a hand in the political and military strengthening of the pro-Western Arab leadership—without becoming too openly committed itself: setting up the Middle East Treaty Organization, then the defensive Baghdad Pact in 1955. None of this was to the liking of Egypt, which turned increasingly to Soviet Russia for economic and military assistance. The Baghdad Pact had little military value; but it did allow Britain to keep a few bases and watch her Iraqui oil holdings. It could be debated, however, whether it needlessly antagonized Egypt and whether it promoted that very Soviet penetration in the Arab world that it was designed to prevent.

In 1955, the Egyptian Government announced to the world that it intended to build the largest dam and hydroelectric power station ever built at Aswan, eight hundred miles up the Nile from Cairo, athwart the great life-giving river. The estimated cost was well over a billion dollars, which could not be met by Egypt's meager resources. In December of the same year, both the United States and Great Britain announced that each would provide some financial and technical assistance which, in turn, would allow the World Bank to make its own contribution. Such Western kindness was not altogether altruistic; Britain and America both hoped to block further Soviet penetration in Egypt —a slightly naïve idea, since it was the very beginning of that penetration that induced them to make the offer in the first place.

Nasser's balancing act between East and West having proved remarkably successful so far, he saw no reason to discontinue it; and, probably in the hope of extracting more financial concessions from the Westerners, he then proceeded to multiply his friendly gestures toward the Communist Powers and stepped up the terrorist Fedayeen raids against Israel. He badly miscalculated. Far from being softened up, crusty Secretary of State Dulles decided to delay the granting of the loan. Exasperated, the Egyptians then presented him with what amounted to an ultimatum in June 1956: if the Western Powers did not underwrite the dam, the Soviet Union would. In July, Dulles replied by slamming the door in Nasser's face and stating that it would not be "feasible in present circumstances" to extend a loan; Britain meekly followed suit.

Although informed beforehand of Washington's decision, London had not been consulted "and so had no prior opportunity for criticism or comment." [4] The decision was fundamentally an American one, which automatically committed the World Bank to follow suit and almost automatically compelled the British to go along even though they had had no share in the decision-making. As Anthony Eden stated later: "We were sorry that the matter was carried through so abruptly, because it gave our two countries no chance to concert either timing or methods, though these were quite as important as the substance." [5] In fact, a little more tact in the matter might have softened the blow to Nasser; the decision might have been postponed or announced less brutally, rather than, in Nasser's own words, with such an utter "disregard for the principles of international relations." [6]

It would have been, and was, foolish to expect that Nasser would suffer this stinging blow to his prestige without seeking revenge. It was the United States Secretary of State who slammed the door in his face without consulting his European partner. And it was France and Britain who were vulnerable through their financial stakes in the Universal Suez Maritime Company—which Nasser promptly nationalized in retaliation for the rebuke administered by the United States against which he was powerless because the Americans had no economic or financial stake in the country. No postwar crisis has displayed so glaringly the fact that whenever the American colossus moves in the world's china shop, it is mostly European china that gets broken—or rather got broken, since Europe has now very little china left.

It was no coincidence that Nasser nationalized the Suez Company on July 26, 1956, almost immediately after the British pulled their last troops out of the Suez base in June, in fulfillment of their 1954 pledge. In fact, it seems incredible that, in view of the increasingly tense relations between Egypt and the Western Powers, the evacuation of the base was not postponed—since it was that very evacuation that made Nasser's nationalization an effective takeover rather than an ineffective proclamation of intention. It also seems strange that before Dulles' brutal announcement and Nasser's predictable countermove, no Western policy adviser seems to have given a thought to the fact that this countermove was almost sure to come now that the last British soldier had left the Canal Zone.

What made the situation infinitely more dramatic than at Abadan in the days of Mossadegh, was that Britain and the rest of Western Europe's oil reserves on hand totaled hardly more than a month's supply. As Eden summarized the situation "The continuing supply of fuel, which was a vital source of power in the economy of Britain, was now subject to Colonel Nasser's whim." [7] Indeed, in 1955, half of the 140 million tons of oil produced in the Middle East came through the Canal, and another 40 came through the pipelines streaking the territories of other Arab states—Saudi Arabia, Iraq, Syria, and Lebanon. Western Europe's enormous industrial machinery could come to a grinding halt at the mere command of a small Middle Eastern chief of state! If this could be allowed to happen, Europe had indeed fallen low on the scale of international power. Addressing Commonwealth diplomats at the time, Selwyn Lloyd admitted regretfully: "It was a mistake to give up the Palestine Mandate for the sake of creating Israel. It was a mistake too to withdraw from the Suez Canal Zone. On both occasions we submitted to strong American pressure, and ever since we have striven hard to arrive at a common Anglo-American policy without success. We have to look after ourselves now." [8] The threat implied in the last sentence was going to shape up as the decisive power confrontation between Europe at bay and the United States.

The wonder is not that the two European Powers eventually took military action, but that they took it so belatedly. One reason was sheer military inability to quickly mount an expeditionary force of sufficient size to regain control of the Canal. However, Prime Minister Eden did inform President Eisenhower that Britain and France might eventually have to use force—to which the American President replied that the United States would not participate in any act of aggression; Secretary of State Dulles, author of most of the trouble in the first place, added brusquely that Great Britain should not try "to shoot its way through the Canal." Thus forewarned that Washington would not look upon a European military expedition with favor, the British and the French decided to keep their own counsel and prepare discreetly for an eventual armed intervention.

The American Secretary of State then put forward a complicated scheme according to which the Canal would be placed under the authority of an international board and its freedom of navigation to all nations would be guaranteed. Nasser rejected this scheme out of hand. On September 6, Anthony Eden wrote a long letter to President Eisenhower, in which he attempted to convince the President that military action might have to be taken, and which concluded thus: "If our assessment is correct, and if the only alternative is to allow Nasser's plans quietly to develop until this country and all Western Europe are held to ransom by Egypt acting at Russia's behest, it seems to us that our duty is plain. We have many times led Europe in the fight for freedom. It would be an ignoble end to our long history if we accepted to perish by degrees." [9] Yet, perish by degrees they did.

A military action might, in fact, have proved quite unnecessary; the mere credible threat of one would have probably been enough. And, time and again, when the Europeans attempted to intimidate Nasser with the prospect of military intervention in order to avoid one, some official or other in Washington quickly proclaimed the United States' determination to find a peaceful solution—determination which almost invariably leads to armed conflict. For instance, Australia's Prime Minister Menzies, speaking in Cairo on behalf of the Europeans, warned Nasser of forceful action and felt sure that Nasser had been duly impressed —only to be completely undercut the next day when President Eisenhower made another statement about his determination to find a peaceful solution. At another time, it was John Foster Dulles who declared that the Canal was not of primary importance to the United States! [10] Indeed, no; but what about their European allies?

The work of intimidation of Nasser carried out by the Europeans was thwarted at every turn by American statements reassuring to the Egyptian leader, making him more determined and uncompromising than ever. Secretary of State Dulles then put forth the "Users' Club" scheme, which was duly accepted by the Europeans, only to discover that the United States would do nothing to enforce this American project and that each nation was free to act as it pleased: "The whole purpose of the Users' Club had been, by a display of unity in association with the United States, to avoid having recourse to force. American torpedoing of their own plan on the first day of its launching left no alternative but to use force or acquiesce in Nasser's triumph." [11] Anthony Eden later recalled, and continued, with appropriate indignation: "Yet here was the spokesman of the United States saying that each nation must decide for itself and expressing himself as unable to recall what the spokesman of a principal ally had said. Such cynicism toward allies destroys true partnership. It leaves only the choice of parting, or a master and vassal relationship in foreign policy." [12]

The master and vassal pattern of relationship was going to develop soon enough. Unencumbered by Great Britain's moral qualms and desire to remain on good terms with the United States, the French had taken a practical view of the matter by sending arms and supplies to Israel, while working discreetly with the British on the buildup of an Anglo-French military expedition to the Middle East. Events now began to unfold with increasing rapidity, the only predictable factor being the approaching Presidential elections in the United States. Believing, mistakenly, that the need to court Jewish votes would compel President Eisenhower to refrain from condemning their planned attack on Egypt, the Israelis began to prepare themselves for their military campaign in the Sinai; the Hungarian revolution, which was then tying up Soviet Russia's troops in Central Europe, clinched the matter and determined the timing for them. On October 29, Israel launched its lightning four-day campaign across the Sinai Peninsula and destroyed the Egyptian army.

Had this stunning blow been left to resound throughout the Arab world without any further intervention from any quarter, it is quite likely that the apparent desire of the French and the British would have been promptly fulfilled. Nasser's prestige and power would have been largely destroyed, and he might well have collapsed in ridicule. He had been in power for only a few years and it was only recently that he had been able to destroy the far greater popularity of his predecessor, General Naguib. Whereas, by the time the next Arab-Israeli conflict broke out in June 1967, he had truly become the indispensable popular leader of Egypt—thirteen years in power had made him the father of his country—in 1956, he was still a new, untried leader whose hold on the imagination of the Egyptian masses was precarious. Under the circumstances, he could never have retrieved the prestige and authority required for his dictatorial office and, in all likelihood, would have had to give way to a more responsible leader of the old prerevolutionary school, who might have come to terms with the West—an Egyptian "Zahedi." However, this was not to be.

It was not to be for the simple reason that the Suez Crisis was one between Egypt and Israel on only one level; and one between the Franco-British allies and Egypt on only another. On the real historical level, the Suez crisis had finally become a crisis between the United States and the leading Western Europeans. For the last time, European nations attempted to behave as big Powers in their own right, and demonstrate in action their independence of the United States. The British and the French attacked Egypt and occupied Suez, not for the hypocritical reason put forth at the time—that they were intervening to separate Israelis and Egyptians and bring peace to the area—nor merely for the more obvious reason that they wanted to reestablish their military and economic influence in the Arab world, but mainly to retrieve their former independence from America, which was fast slipping. True enough, the British wanted to regain control of the vital hinge between three continents through which flowed most of the oil that was the lifeblood of Europe's industrial complex. The French wanted to strike an indirect blow against the elusive Algerian guerillas they could not pin down in Algeria itself. Both wanted to restore their vanishing prestige in the Arab world. But more than anything, and quite unconsciously, they now wanted to prove to Washington that they had not yet become anyone's vassals.

Harold Macmillan was quite correct in stating that if the British did not react to Nasser's challenge, Great Britain would become a new Netherlands. And when, in August, the French Parliament, by a crushing majority of 422 votes to 150 (all Communists), voted full powers to the Government to use force if need be, a French commentator summed up the situation by stating that "the French bourgeoisie thus freed itself from the American tutelage to which it had been subject . . . since 1946." [13] In all fairness to the Americans, they were largely unconscious or unaware of this element of hidden struggle between Europe and America. Still mentally wrapped in the traditional anticolonial mythology, many thought only of putting down a last attempt of the Europeans at gunboat diplomacy. Completely misreading the true significance of the events, Vice President Richard Nixon even went so far as to claim that Dulles' attitude toward Europe constituted "a new declaration of independence." [14]

So it was that, quite effectively, Washington decided to show the world that the Europeans had indeed become vassals in everything but the name. The General Assembly of the United Nations met on the morning of November 2. As Anthony Eden stated it later, "It was not Soviet Russia, or any Arab state, but the Government of the United States which took the lead in the Assembly against Israel, France, and Britain." [15] The American Delegation introduced a resolution urging all members engaged in hostilities in the Middle East to cease fire immediately. The American resolution did not suggest any concrete step to solve the problems of the Middle East on a long-term basis nor did it attempt to use this opportunity, which would not recur again without a new round of warfare, to put an end once and for all to the endemic hostility between Arab and Israeli. The Americans did not try to strike while the iron was hot because they did not know how they wanted it shaped. All they instinctively knew was that they wanted to crush the Franco-British show of independence, once and for all.

Sensibly, Canada refused to join the United States in a mere condemnation and suggested instead the setting up of a United Nations police force. Eden recalls bitterly: "Had the United States been willing to play a part as balanced as Canada's the course of history must have been different, but this was not to be. The Assembly was in a mood to punish. The hunt was up after Israel and the 'colonial' powers." [16]

There could be no doubt as to the issue. Condemned in the Assembly by 64 votes to 5, humiliated by the United States' sharp rebuke, Britain and France agreed to a cease-fire on November 6, followed shortly after by Israel. When, in the interim, the British and the French urged the Security Council to debate the unfolding Hungarian tragedy, "the United States representative was reluctant and voiced his suspicion that we were urging the Hungarian situation in order to divert attention from Suez" [17]—which was exactly Britain's and France's intention. But the United States Government would not be diverted from its primary purpose: to break the will of its European allies: "The United States Government appeared in no hurry to move. Their attitude provided a damaging contrast to the alacrity they were showing in arraigning the French and ourselves." [18] Being temporarily allied with Soviet Russia did not bother the authorities in Washington—even the fact that, encouraged by the United States Government attitude, Soviet agents were busy whipping up Egyptian crowds in Port Said and increasing their activities in the rest of Egypt, while Soviet military supplies were pouring into the country.

The French and the British had not only miscalculated politically. They had not only mismanaged their military campaign to the extent of making it almost ineffective through lack of speed; they also seemed to have completely overlooked the economic and financial consequences. Prime Minister Eden states: "A more formidable threat than Marshall Bulganin's confronted us. A run on the pound, at a speed which threatened disaster to our whole economic position, had developed in the world's financial markets. . . . The position was made immediately critical by speculation against sterling, largely in the American market or on American account." [19] In November alone, British dollar reserves fell almost 15 percent. The game was up.

In complying with American wishes on November 6, the British had thought that the Americans would prove more amenable to their suggestions for a lasting settlement of the Middle Eastern problem. They were wrong: "I did not foresee then," stated Eden, "that the United States government would harden against us on almost every point and become harsher after the cease-fire than before." [20] Indeed, success inspires admiration and failure contempt. Failure to proceed with their military operations was second only to the Franco-British mistake in starting them at all. As Robert Murphy claims in his *Diplomat Among Warriors,* "to the amazement of many Americans, including myself, when the operation seemed about to achieve its goal, Prime Minister Eden decided to quit short of the objective." [21] But the final touch of irony was put by Dulles when he asked Selwyn Lloyd, who had come to see him in the hospital after the fracas was over: "Why did you stop?" [22]

All efforts on the part of the British and French Premiers to be allowed to come to Washington and confer with President Eisenhower were strongly discouraged; the Europeans first had to give up their occupation of a small part of the Canal Zone, without even the compensation of a United Nations' military force to replace their garrison in Port Said. Furthermore, the French and the British wanted to get on right away with the task of clearing the Canal, in which the Egyptians had sunk thirty-two ships—in fact, they were frantic to get on with it "all the more so because the United States showed no sign of readiness to assist France and Britain with oil supplies from the Western Hemisphere." [23] But the United States held firm and refused to cooperate until the Europeans had evacuated Port Said. Eden even claims that Washington's "only reaction to reports of Russian infiltrations in the Middle East was to press us to remove our forces more quickly." [24]

President Eisenhower postponed indefinitely the consultations which the European Premiers were seeking, did not receive Britain's Foreign Secretary nor Australia's Foreign Minister when they came to Washington. Eden wrote: "The United States Administration seemed to be dominated at this time by one thought only, to harry their allies." [25] And harry them out of Port Said they did, before the year was out. The Europeans could no longer hold on. Their currencies were under strong attack, they were not allowed to clear the Canal of its sunken ships, and they were, sooner or later, going to run out of oil: "The Secretary of the Treasury, Mr. Humphrey, telephoned to Mr. Butler and made it clear that the United States would not extend help or support to Britain until after a definite statement of withdrawal had been made." [26]

The drama was coming to an end. The French and the British gave in and started their withdrawal; the Americans then came forth with financial assistance to shore up the weakening pound and supplied Europe with Western Hemisphere oil through the following winter and spring. Never again could any European

Power or combination of Powers challenge the paramount authority of Washington. In no part of the world would they be allowed to have more than moral influence—except at the specific request of the United States, when it was found convenient to maintain British military presence in Singapore and the Persian Gulf, for instance. The venerable Entente Cordiale between Britain and France collapsed, now that Britain had been reduced, as Harold Macmillan had feared, to being a "new Netherlands" under American protectorate. Ultimately, French rule was doomed in Algeria, and in the agonizing process of attempting to cope with the Algerian rebellion, Charles de Gaulle came to power, to implement a new anti-American policy—a predictable dividend at the end of the road to Suez.

Meantime, Egypt remained sole mistress of the Suez Canal, until the new round of warfare in June 1967. The Canal was not cleared of its sunken hulks by Anglo-French teams as the Europeans had hoped but by a United Nations salvage operation headed by the American Lieutenant General Raymond A. Wheeler. From then on, Egypt ran the Canal with cool efficiency. From 1956 to 1966, the number of ships passing through rose from a little more than fourteen thousand to over twenty thousand; both tonnage and revenues more than doubled; the Canal was widened by eighty feet and deepened to accept drafts of thirty-eight instead of thirty-five feet.

Breaking Europe's attempt to recapture control of the Middle East was not enough. Sooner or later, the United States itself had to display its power and determination in the area—not alone but suitably accompanied, in a subordinate position, by one of the European Powers whose grip on Port Said had been loosened in 1956. The collapse of the European position in the Middle East was bound to create another of those power vacuums; and into this vacuum, Gamal Abdel Nasser naïvely thought that he could move without running into American opposition. Soviet Russia had, of course, increased its military assistance to Egypt, hoping to step into the vacuum behind Nasser. At the same time, Nasser, who only a short time ago had been about to collapse in ridicule, had now become a hero to the Arab masses everywhere.

The Franco-British aggression had given him his alibi. He became the outspoken leader of Arab nationalism from Algeria to Aden, and steadily undermined the moderate, pro-Western regimes that had seen the collapse of European influence with deep misgivings. But the Americans themselves lost no time in making their intentions plain to the people of the Middle East.

The last European troops had scarcely left Port Said forever when, on January 5, 1957, the President proclaimed the Eisenhower Doctrine—a bold declaration of virtual American protectorate over the whole area— a modern "Monroe Doctrine" for the Middle East. More specifically, it stated that "military assistance should be extended to any countries that sought such help" and, further, that such assistance could well "include the employment of armed forces of the United States to secure and protect the territorial integrity and political independence of such nations, requesting such aid, against overt armed aggression from any country controlled by International Communism." [27] Here was the United States further committed, by Presidential fiat, to eventual military action in a part of the world that had been left, until now, to the tender care of the Europeans. President Eisenhower did admit that it entailed new military risks, but did not see how these new commitments could be avoided.

The Eisenhower Doctrine was soon formalized when it became implemented by an American ambassador appointed for the specific purpose of applying it. In no time, the Arab nations divided and placed themselves on either side of the Doctrine— Syria and Egypt to the left from where they denounced it as a new form of imperialism, Lebanon noncommittal in the middle, Jordan, Iraq, and Saudi Arabia to the right, in favor of it; approval entailed precious economic assistance from the United States in addition to some form of military protection. This military protection was made tangible by the presence of the United States' powerful Sixth Fleet whose massive firepower was no puny little firecracker like that of the Anglo-French expedition to Suez.

The net result of all this was to speed up an inevitable showdown between the United States and its antagonists—left-wing Arabs, backed by Soviet Russia. In the spring of 1957, King

Hussein's wobbly throne was saved by an immediate grant of ten million dollars; Nasser's hope of linking up geographically with Syria was dashed. Nasser moved ahead anyway and, early in 1958, proclaimed the brith of the United Arab Republic welding Egypt and Syria—and, to a lesser degree, Yemen—into one confederate state. A few months later, a revolution in Baghdad overthrew the pro-Western regime of King Faisal and Premier Nuri es-Said, costing them their lives, and putting in power a strongly left-wing nationalist regime under the leadership of General Abdel Karim Kassem. Repercussions in Jordan and Lebanon were immediate. Weak and internally divided, their rulers applied right away for American help in the name of the Eisenhower Doctrine. Now, the testing time had come.

The fact that the "United Nations observers on the spot denied that there was subversive activity by Nasser in either country" [28] did not deter the American leaders. Washington did not hesitate to send thousand of marines via the Sixth Fleet onto the beaches of Lebanon where a civil war (not even an external aggression) was in progress, quickly reinforced by thousands of American troops flown in from West Germany. And two days later, dutifully subservient, Anthony Eden's successor as British Prime Minister, Harold Macmillan, sent British paratroopers to safeguard King Hussein's throne. Iraq they abandoned to its revolutionary fate. The world's neutralists protested loudly but could do nothing. And Soviet Russia, although protesting with verbal violence, was put on notice that henceforth it would no longer be dealing in the Middle East with pusillanimous Europeans but with determined Americans. The crisis eventually fizzled out; the two regimes in Lebanon and Jordan having been saved by the Anglo-Americans and tempers having cooled, the Western nations felt free to withdraw their troops in October. From now on, the West spoke with one voice in the Middle East, and that voice was Washington's.

No permanent solution had been found for the problems of the Middle East, and none is likely to be found for a long time because, quite apart from the complexity of the local issues, it has become a prime area of the global confrontation between American and Russian imperialisms. It is not so much a matter of halting the penetration of *Communist* influence since Marxism-Leninism as an ideology has little appeal for the Moslems in general, and the Moslem Arabs in particular. Most of the time, Nasser has kept his few Egyptian Communists under lock and key, even at the height of his flirting with Moscow. It is not fear of Communist infiltration, as such, but fear of *Russian* imperialism, divorced from its Marxist component, that induces the Americans to become involved in an area it is determined to defend against Russian encroachments.

Therefore, while Nasser came closer to Soviet Russia and announced in December 1958 that the Russians had offered to underwrite at least part of the Aswan Dam, the United States bolstered the Baghdad Pact, now shorn of Iraq, by identifying itself officially with its purposes and by increasing its military assistance to its member nations—Turkey, Iran, and Pakistan; the former Baghdad Pact became the Central Treaty Organization (CENTO), in August 1959. However, the United States refused to become a full member and remained content to let Britain, now a safe and obedient satellite, act as proxy for Washington.

But the festering sore was still there. Arab-Israeli tension remained as fierce as ever, symbolizing on the local level the worldwide Soviet-American tension. With the stepped-up military assistance provided by Moscow to its Arab friends, Egypt and Syria, a new round of local warfare was inevitable. The crushing defeat inflicted by Israel on the combined military forces of the Arab world in June 1967 was widely interpreted as a defeat for Soviet Russia and an indirect victory for the United States. In the global scheme of things, Israel has largely become the more or less willing instrument used by Washington in its attempt to expel Russian influence from the entire Arab world and establish in Arab lands sound, businesslike types of administration on the pattern of Indonesia's post-Sukarno regime.

As was to be expected, this new round of warfare in 1967 virtually completed the disintegration of Britain's imperial power. The long closing of the Suez Canal, costing Britain some six hundred million dollars a year in higher shipping costs, the massive withdrawals of Arab money from London and overall trouble between Britain and most of the Arab world, finally broke the back of the pound sterling. Devaluation of the pound in November 1967 was followed two months later, as it was bound to, by the announcement that Britain's imperial role east of Suez was over. On January 16, 1968, Prime Minister Harold Wilson declared that the withdrawal of all British forces east of Suez would be considerably speeded up; withdrawal from Southeast Asia where it would not only give up its protection of Singapore and Malaysia, but cut off its last military link with Australia and New Zealand, now forever included in the American sphere of influence; withdrawal from the Persian Gulf and therefore abandonment of the military protection of its vast oil interests. When these withdrawals are completed, Britain will be completely at the mercy of external sources of vital fuel which it can no longer protect. And sooner or later, the United States armed forces are going to be compelled to step into this new vacuum—not so much in Southeast Asia where, compared with America's massive involvement, British military presence had already become purely symbolic, as in the Persian Gulf which had always been a British preserve without American interference.

At the tail end of the road to Suez, Great Britain has become merely Britain, an impoverished and powerless offshore island at the mercy of the United States. And the United States finds itself alone, without even the semblance of a European ally to help it police the world east of Suez.

The psychological consequences of the Suez Crisis were far-reaching in Britain. France took its political defeat with an amount of cynical philosophy; it was one more defeat on the long road of its shrinking world power, taking its due place between Dienbienphu and the final loss of Algeria. Britain was not accustomed to ringing defeat, nor to being publicly spanked by her elder daughter. Without any outside prompting, London had gracefully relinquished its hold over the various components of the British Empire and had withdrawn, and was still withdrawing, with great dignity. But the Suez Crisis was a traumatic experience—not only because it was a stinging defeat but because, as many Britons admitted at the time, it became a *moral* crisis of the first order. No such qualms tormented the French to whom international morality means little, and to whom the Suez adventure appealed in part precisely because it was morally indefensible; it tickled their cynicism pleasantly and they sighed with regret only because it had failed. To the British, it was an extreme emotional shock, and that shock produced in the British soul a quick and startling metamorphosis.

In the late 1950's and early 1960's, Britain underwent its first historic mutation since it entered the dour Victorian era. Centuries of world leadership and responsibility now lay behind her forever; her largest overseas offspring had taken over, with callousness and occasional brutality, but with commendable determination and efficiency. Almost with a sigh of relief, rid at last of a world empire on which the sun never sets, the British began to retrieve a lightness of heart and a careless joy of living that had disappeared under the heavy Victorian mask. Britain's younger generation quickly stripped off this Victorian mask of hypocrisy as its elders were stripping off the Empire. From now on, the Americans would have the pangs of conscience, not the British, who began to devote their newfound talents to the development of a new art of gay, careless, Bohemian living.

It all started during the dark and shameful days of Suez when thousands of puzzled and tormented Britons gathered at Trafalgar Square to protest the appalling fiasco, when the Speaker had to suspend the sitting in the hallowed House of Commons because of the undignified uproar caused by the protesting Labour members. Revolt was in the air and struck out in every direction at a traditional way of life. Following John Osborne's *Look Back in Anger*, one play after another began to hit the venerable ruling classes slowly collapsing along with the Empire they served. The Profumo scandal dealt a death blow to the Establishment's prestige and moral authority. Strange rhythms began to shake the stately mansions of London's West End. Carnaby Street became the mecca of the new foppish fads; all sex taboos collapsed in one great roar: "Merry Old England" had found a reincarnation.

It was no accident if, in the process, new centrifugal tendencies began to threaten to tear Britain apart, destroying the carefully built-up unity of the British Isles. The departure of Ireland in the 1920's was a first, ominous sign of the times, to be followed by spasmodic outbursts of anti-English nationalism in both Scotland and Wales. In the 1960's, however, anti-English nationalism acquired new momentum in both Celtic countries. The Scottish Nationalists claimed two thousand members in 1962; by 1967, the figure had swollen to sixty thousand, and a "Scots Nats" member was voted into Parliament, beating simultaneously both Labour and Conservative candidates, and claiming that the time had come to end the union with England that had lasted since 1707. And on the same venerable bench of the House of Commons sat a Welch Nationalist MP advocating a similar divorce from England.

Summing up the grave implications, a Scottish Nationalist wrote in the *Spectator:* "It was primarily the British Empire that made and kept us British. Now that it has gone, the word British is almost devoid of meaning." [29] With the Empire gone and grave economic difficulties ahead, the rise of regional nationalism is all but inevitable. Just as it would be unthinkable, today, that the states of Maine or California would want to secede from the Union—since the United States' imperial expansion is in full swing—it is quite possible that, some time in the future, a majority of the populations of both Scotland and Wales will opt out of Britain altogether and divorce the English as peacefully as the Norwegians divorced the Swedes at the turn of the century. This disintegration of British unity, and consequently power, would ultimately leave its fragments with little choice except some form of incorporation in a larger entity.

☆ VII ☆

Death and Transfiguration of the Commonwealth

The remarkable structure of the British Commonwealth, as distinct from the Empire, was born out of the trials and tribulations of the American Revolution. The loss of the greater part of their American possessions taught the British a bitter lesson which they were not likely to forget. And since they were in a position to send out waves of emigrants to populate largely empty overseas territories, they had many opportunities to start all over again and do a better job of it—eventually to grant them all the freedoms that had been denied their American cousins. So it was that the British Commonwealth of Nations grew organically into a worldwide federal republic whose federal links became increasingly tenuous until they consisted of hardly more than a symbolic allegiance to a common Crown and an emotional attachment to the mother country which behaved with such tolerant understanding.

Such was the situation in the first half of the twentieth century; two World Wars, far from strengthening these tenuous links, loosened them further, mainly because of the drastic shift in the center of gravity of the English-speaking world. And today, like a new star in the firmament whose gravitational weight increases steadily at the expense of the lesser star it is about to displace, the United States' increasing gravitational pull and power is gradually changing the orbits of Britain's former planets, prelude to a radical reorientation of Anglo-Saxondom's planetary motion. These orbits are increasingly revolving around Washington rather than London. Not only that; reduced from the rank of a star to that of a planet, albeit the weightiest of them all, post-Suez Britain herself is beginning to revolve around Washington in the same company as her former Commonwealth daughters.

All at once, the British Commonwealth is dying and being transfigured into an essential component of the emerging American empire.

In analyzing the evolving structure of this new English-speaking planetary system, one thing becomes evident: if there is any member of the British Commonwealth that, by rights, should have been long ago incorporated in the United States, it is Canada. Gigantic in geographical size, relatively small in population (one tenth that of its neighbor to the south), Canada shares a five-thousand-mile border, mostly artificial and arbitrary, with the United States. This border is an historical accident, not a geographic reality. Indeed, the United States almost seized Canada by force during the 1812 War but met the determined resistance of the Canadians and, in particular, the French Canadians who had become reconciled to London's tolerant rule and dreaded the all-absorbing domination of the Americans. Mindful of the sermons drummed into them by their clergy to the effect that "the best way to remain French is to stay British," they also recalled the fate of Louisiana and the swift disappearance of its French character.

Canada grew slowly in the shadow of its giant southern neighbor; but it grew in physical size only, not in spirit. It was never able to develop "Canadianism" into a definite personality with its own identity. There is no Canadian individuality, nothing that gives it its own specificity: "Canadians are generally indistinguishable from the Americans, and the surest way of telling the two apart is to make the observation to a Canadian," [1] said a wit. True enough, many Canadians still attempt to maintain, or rather to develop, a distinct national identity which can never emerge, for the simple reason that Canada is not one country but at least three—French Canada, centered around Quebec, the old British Canada founded by the United Empire Loyalists who turned their backs on the American Revolution and migrated to Ontario, and the new, modern Canada of the prairies where immigrants from all over Europe—Poles, Italians, Ukrainians, Germans—care not one whit for the ancestral quarrels between British and French Canadians. To these three major components can be added such disconnected fragments as British Columbia, cut off from the rest of the country by the Rocky Mountains and entirely focused on the Pacific, and the Maritime Provinces, equally cut off from the rest of English-speaking Canada by French-speaking Quebec. And all of them live, with different degrees of apprehension, in the shadow of the United States' overpowering influence in all walks of life.

Forgetting for a moment the massive presence of the southern neighbor, it is quite clear that Canada is virtually torn apart by inner forces, and that these forces have sharply increased since the war. Just as the racial problem has taken on an entirely different complexion in the United States because of the large-scale emigration of southern rural Negroes to the northern and western cities, the French Canadian problem has completely changed its nature as increasingly large numbers of French Canadians moved from the rustic countryside to the great cities. The French Canadian has always resented the English Canadian's superiority complex; but so long as he remained in his villages and hamlets as a docile "hewer of wood and drawer of water," there was no great political problem. The province of Quebec enjoyed a large degree of autonomy and the majority of its population still looked up to its French-speaking Roman Catholic clergy as its natural leader.

But things changed as the migration to the cities increased in momentum. Docility disappeared, and so did a great deal of clerical influence. French Canadians began to resent with increasing fierceness their inferior social position, their lower standard of living, and their inability to achieve equality in the social and economic life of the country. In the late 1950's and early 1960's, an ugly word began to appear with increasing frequency, in speech and in print, *séparatisme,* French Canadian nationalism pushed to the extreme of complete secession from the rest of Canada. French Canada is undergoing simultaneously an economic and a social revolution which is leading it away from the rest of the federation. The Quebec issue is now forcing the rest of the country to decide whether it wants to become a nation or whether it is going to break up. But how can it become a cohesive *nation* when one of its main components, French-speaking Quebec, feels that it is itself a nation—and is fast becoming one in sentiment? The French Canadians' situation is much like India's Moslems who *became* a nation in the early 1940's before the foundation of the state of Pakistan, which merely institutionalized what had already become a fact.

The majority of the English-speaking Canadians refuse to understand the depth of the French-Canadian feeling and still cling to the idea that, being a minority, the "pea-soupers" should comply with the wishes of the majority and cease thinking of themselves as a separate nationality. But the English-speaking Canadians are caught between the anvil and the hammer. They, in turn, live in dread of their southern neighbor. Gradually, United States financial groups and large corporations have come to own more than half of Canada's industrial plants and mineral wealth. The higher the standard of living of the Canadians, the more they want to raise it further, and the more they go on selling their resources to powerful American companies. Statistics are eloquent: in one typical decade, from 1952 to 1962, Canadians bought from the Americans fourteen billion dollars worth more in goods and services than they were able to sell them in return.[2] During the same length of time, American investors bought well over eight billion dollars' worth of Canadian industrial and mineral resources.

Political resistance to the trend occasionally crops up in Ottawa's neo-Gothic Parliament; but it is futile since, even in the realm of culture, whatever Canadianism ever existed is fast disappearing under the flood of Americanism that pours in irresistibly through five thousand miles of sievelike border—five thousand miles of common border along which (within less than two hundred miles' distance) the overwhelming majority of Canadians live, their cities strung along this thin ribbon of populated land like beads on a long necklace. While inhabitants of the Maritime Provinces look to Boston rather than Toronto as their main city, the Central Provinces look to Chicago and Minneapolis, and British Columbia to Seattle and San Francisco.

It is clear today that a substantial minority of Canadians believe that, in the long run, Canada will break up and that its fragments will be absorbed by the United States. Canada's inner centrifugal forces being what they are, "if the United States thought it in its self-interest today, as distinct from the past, to see Canada splintered so that the segments would clamor for statehood, there is little doubt that State Department practice would be to fan the flames." [3] Canadians who favor such a union with the giant southern neighbor usually belong to the low-income groups who believe that their standard of living would rise appreciably after incorporation.

More than anywhere else, it is in matters of military defense that Canada has become almost completely integrated in the American structure. In case of nuclear conflict with Soviet Russia, for instance, Canada would have to act as a shield covering the United States from the polar regions of Siberia—a shield which Washington rather than Ottawa would have to control. Canada's military orientation which used to be focused on Britain in an east-west direction is now entirely north-south—with control virtually vested south of its border, in Washington's Pentagon. Canadian defense can only be a hemispheric defense, especially in a nuclear age. The Canadian Air Force, long a step-child of Britain's Royal Air Force, is now completely Americanized in terms of weapons and procedure, and has fallen into the integrated structure of the hemispheric North American Defense Command (NORAD), which was established in 1958. That NORAD cannot be anything but an American show through and through is evident from the figures: Canada's R.C.A.F. has roughly fifteen thousand men in it, as against the

United States' two hundred thousand. It is on Canadian soil that the United States' first lines of radar warning are located—the Distant Early Warning Line (DEW) and the Mid-Canada Warning Line, built by American technicians and financed by the United States.

When differences of opinion arose between Washington and Ottawa, then under John Diefenbaker's premiership, over the nuclearization of Bomarc squadrons stationed on Canadian soil, Washington reacted with such verbal brutality that Prime Minister Diefenbaker had to resign. A general election was called and a new Prime Minister, Lester Pearson, took over and mended Canada's fences with the United States—by giving in to Washington's wishes. Most Canadians had to resign themselves to the fact that their country had become, for all practical purposes, part and parcel of the United States' hemispheric defense structure. Diefenbaker's outburst of anti-Americanism was, and could only be, a passing phase, a temporary revolt against the inevitable. As a member of the socialist New Democratic Party put it wistfully, "We can't contract out of North America." [4]

If Canadians have accepted the United States' military domination as inevitable, they are still fighting its cultural and especially economic domination—twenty billion dollars' worth (30 percent of America's total investments outside the United States) of Canadian mining and manufacturing wealth, of which about two-thirds is direct investment in subsidiary companies. It is not just passive ownership but actual *controlling* investment. If one recalls that at the turn of the century, Britain's investments of one billion dollars (75 percent of all foreign investments in Canada at the time) completely overshadowed the United States' 170 million dollars, one can clearly see the complete metamorphosis of the situation; in the 1960's, British investments have shrunk to a mere 15 percent of all foreign investments in Canada. As things stand in the late 1960's, the Americans control over half of Canada's mining and smelting, 95 percent of the automotive industry, 75 percent of the oil and 90 percent of the rubber industries, along with 65 percent of the electrical appliances.[5] All these percentages of American control increase steadily, year in and year out, in spite of Canadian efforts to legislate against them. Interest and dividend payments flowing out of Canada cripple its international balance of payments. But any practical steps to halt the trend or reverse it would lead to such a drastic fall in the Canadian standard of living that they could never be tolerated.

The violent reaction to Canadian Finance Minister Walter Gordon's mild attempt to do so in 1963 illustrates the stark impossibility of resisting this wholesale takeover: "So devastatingly hostile was the reaction that the effect on the government in the interval was almost traumatic," states an expert on Canadian affairs. What is clear is that an increasingly large proportion of Canadian businessmen are merely employees of American companies headquartered in New York, Detroit, or Chicago. And these American companies, parents of Canadian subsidiaries, owe their first allegiance to American, not Canadian, legislation and interests. As a result, no Canadian subsidiary dares contravene the United States' antitrust laws or the Trading with the Enemy Act. Inevitably, unobstrusively, American legislation applies in Canada in an extraterritorial way. It is also obvious that if the international market for goods produced on both sides of the border were to shrink substantially, American companies would probably not hesitate to close down their operations in Canada so as to maintain full production in the United States.

Those who believe that there is no threat to Canadian independence point to the fact that the United States was developed out of British capital in the nineteenth century. But that capital was in the form of redeemable bonds, whereas United States investments in Canada are in the form of outright ownership of subsidiaries. American investments, again, are *controlling* investments, providing not only the financial resources but the technical skills, the managerial know-how, the research and development, and the overall business policy. Furthermore, not only are a majority of the large Canadian corporations American-owned but they also happen to be in the most dynamic sectors of the economy. And, not content with mere economic activity, they have begun to lobby in Ottawa, contributing financially to

Canadian political parties and becoming involved in Canada's internal politics "for their own self-protection," [6] inevitably impinging on Canada's political freedom and sovereignty.

The ironic sidelight to this state of affairs is that French Canadians have long held the same complaint against English-speaking Canadians that the latter now raise against the Americans. For instance, they point out that almost 100 percent outside ownership now exists in Quebec whose industrial plants and mines all have their head offices outside the province. While French Canadians complain that their English-speaking compatriots relegate them to subordinate positions, the English-speaking Canadians now raise the same complaints on their own behalf against the Americans. To all this, many hardheaded Canadian economists reply that all talk of economic independence is pointless, that a full integration of Canadian and American economies is desirable, that the Canadian public should not be taxed for "the privilege of having a national identity," [7] and that they see no harm in an eventual political union as the ultimate consequence of an economic one. But, so far, recent surveys indicate that two Canadians out of three favor economic union with the United States—while the proportion is almost exactly reversed when it comes to *political* union. That one would inevitably follow the other is evident. Interestingly enough, the younger generation of Canadians seems to favor organic union with the United States to a far greater extent than the older one.

This changing attitude collides head-on with the rising challenge of Quebec's French Canadians for increasing autonomy, if not outright separation. And, simultaneously, the faint interest manifested only too occasionally by English-speaking Canadians in their French-speaking compatriots arises from their understanding that it is Quebec, and nothing else, that gives a certain distinct flavor to whatever Canadian identity there is, that it is in Quebec that lies the last-ditch defense of Canada *as a whole* against complete Americanization. But this interest remains faint, and relations between the two main components of Canada's population remained strained.

If this strain eventually led to a breakaway by the enormous province of Quebec, Canada's balkanization would inevitably follow. Completely cut off from the rest of the country, the Atlantic portion—the Maritime Provinces—would have little choice except seek admission into the United States. When Newfoundland, Canada's newest province, had to make up its mind about its political future after the Second World War, it was clear that "if Newfoundlanders had been given a free choice, 85 percent would have voted to join the United States." [8] But they were not given a free choice and eventually merged with Canada; it still remains, however, that a great many Newfoundlanders show more kinship with the United States than with the Canadian mainland "and the island's Prime Minister Joey Smallwood himself points to the traditional gravitation southward that has made Boston 'Newfoundland's biggest city.' " [9]

If the gravitational pull of New England on Newfoundland is enormous, it is just as great on the other Maritime Provinces—Prince Edward Island, New Brunswick, and Nova Scotia. As one Canadian remarked, "There's another kind of separatism in Canada. I found it during my ten years in the Maritimes: down there, they all want to join Boston. . . . The only difference, as I see it, between Quebec's separatists and the Maritimes' is that in Quebec they have a different language." [10] Ties with New England are immensely strong, including the presence of millions of Canadian immigrants in Vermont, Maine, Massachusetts, and New Hampshire. A survey revealed in 1964 that almost 40 percent of the Maritimers favored political union with the United States—the highest proportion in Canada at that time.[11] A breakaway by Quebec would inevitably throw them into the United States.

In what would be left of a truncated Canada, the three provinces in the central prairies would be next to feel the irresistible pull of southward gravity. Alberta, Saskatchewan, and Manitoba are, in many ways, the most Americanized of all Canadian provinces; their populations are more heterogeneous, springing originally from many parts of Europe; their common border with the United States is completely artificial and splits in two a huge region that geography had made one. Their citizens resent having to pay federal taxes to finance social welfare programs in the poorer Maritime Provinces and schools in hostile Quebec. Residents of Winnipeg go the theater in Minneapolis and Chicago, not Toronto or Montreal. For all that, secessionist sentiment is not as strong in the 1960's as it was in the 1930's, for plain economic reasons. But if the Canadian federation broke up, the probability is that "it would really come down to an economic evaluation of where we would get a better deal: in Ontario or in the States." [12]

As for British Columbia on the Pacific coast, it has never displayed much enthusiasm for Canada as an entity and, except for Quebec, has been demanding a greater degree of decentralization and provincial autonomy than any other province, one that would leave federal ties as tenuous as they could be, short of snapping them altogether. Separated from the rest of Canada by the towering Rockies, it inevitably tends to look south to California, rather than east to faraway Toronto and Ottawa. "What does Ottawa own?" asked Premier Bennett in a 1967 interview. "The federal government has nothing but the power to tax us. We have the wealth." [13] And indeed, British Columbia has increasing wealth in its lumber and paper industries as well as livestock and even minerals. It "is viewed as the province best able to go it alone should Canada ever fall apart. The ebullient Mr. Bennett never loses an opportunity to point this out." [14] Vancouver looks south to San Francisco and across the Pacific to Hawaii, while its wealthier citizens spend their winter vacations in Honolulu. And even the remote Yukon feels intensely the gravitational pull of nearby Alaska—whose purchase from the Russians in 1867 had been made in anticipation of a merger between Canada and the United States.

Canada's geographical immensity and relative emptiness make it difficult for its small population to have a sense of identification with it. As an eminent Canadian literary critic stated it, the basic problem of identity—"Who am I?"—is part of a bigger question: "Where is here?" [15] Life is not in the frozen north but in the warmer south; Canada's life currents do not flow along the parallels of latitude but along the meridians, linking every disconnected region of Canada with its American extension south of the border.

With this fact in mind, one has to recognize that the fuse that could spark the breakup of Canada is the growing mood of *séparatisme* of Quebec's French Canadians. Prime Minister Lester Pearson appointed a Royal Commission on Bilingualism and Biculturalism in 1963; in its first preliminary report, it had this to say: "All that we have seen and heard has led us to the conclusion that Canada is in the most critical period of its history since Confederation. . . . We must reiterate that we have found overwhelming evidence of serious danger to the continued existence of Canada." [16] Many English-speaking Canadians, who refuse to take the danger quite as seriously, nevertheless saw a real threat to federal authority in the agreement signed in 1965 between Quebec and France covering an exchange of professors—an agreement which Quebec's Education Minister Gérin-Lajoie described as "entente" and "accord," rather than a formal treaty. Quebec, so far, was just feeling its oats, testing Ottawa's reaction. And gradually, leading French Canadians began drifting away from Ottawa back to Quebec, no longer wanting to play a part in federal politics.

Into this complex and delicate situation, France's President de Gaulle decided to tread with heavy boots during his July 1967 visit to Canada. Traveling in a motorcade from Quebec to Montreal amidst enthusiastic crowds, de Gaulle whipped up successfully the atavistic separatism of the French Canadians, and his utterances became so undiplomatic that he had to cancel his visit to Ottawa: "French Canada is a country which is becoming master of itself," he proclaimed, adding more pointedly: "You are French, you are part of French Canada." And to cap it all, he cried, "Long live Free Quebec!" [17]

The hue and cry raised by de Gaulle's intrusion in Canada's internal affairs obscured a cardinal fact: that the great majority of the French Canadians approved his behavior. Quebec's Premier Daniel Johnson gave his wholehearted blessing to the French President's controversial words, while blaming the Federal Government in Ottawa for its own frosty response to de Gaulle. By and large, French Canadians welcomed the opportunity thus created to air Canada's most fundamental problem. And back across the Atlantic, de Gaulle soon proved that he had not uttered empty words but meant to follow up on his proposal to help French Canada achieve "freedom." In September 1967, the French Government announced that France would multiply its assistance to Quebec ten times over the following three years. A further announcement stated that the President of France would meet twice a year with the Quebec Government—the beginning of a *de facto* recognition of Quebec as an independent state. A new intergovernmental organism was created to handle the new contacts. And in the meantime, the Quebec Government lost no time in building up its embryo ministry of foreign affairs, the Ministry for Inter-Governmental Affairs.

While France can provide considerable leverage to the Quebec authorities in their dealings with Ottawa, it is not likely that the old mother country, after having ignored its stepchild for two centuries, can ever reestablish bonds of mutual affection. This was more in the nature of Charles de Gaulle's personal initiative than a spontaneous and belated remembrance of the French population as a whole. And, as usual with de Gaulle, he might end by defeating his own purposes. The end result of a breakaway by Quebec can only be the disintegration of the Canadian federation as a nation and the absorption of its remains by the United States—making it that much larger and more powerful, which is certainly not what de Gaulle had in mind.

For the time being, French Canadians are slowly feeling their way toward a new formula of "associated statehood," which might represent only a transitory phase, preparatory to an eventual bid for complete independence. But while the rest of Canada could find organic union with the United States, Quebec would have to settle for a form of independence under United States' protectorate which would safeguard its vital interests in such fields as military defense and freedom of navigation on the St. Lawrence. Indeed, the Pentagon lost no time in making plans for such a contingency. Its "Project Camelot," begun in 1962 as a study of all the "turmoil-ridden areas" of the world, focused on the problem of Quebec's *séparatisme* with such intensity that an uproar ensued in Canada, with John Diefenbaker, now a bitter leader of the opposition, asking the Canadian Government if it had protested such "an unusual course" on the part of the United States.[18] What is certain, at any rate, is that the best Quebec could ever hope for—in case it breaks away from the Canadian Federation—is a loose but stern American protectorate. Under no circumstances would it be allowed to enjoy untrammeled independence.

Thousands of miles to the southwest, all the way across the Pacific, lies Australia and its junior partner, New Zealand. Along with Canada, they make up the whole of the "white" British Commonwealth—and "white" Australia is and intends to remain since, unlike Canada, she lies on Southeast Asia's doorstep and will always remain a tempting field of expansion for would-be Asian immigrants from overcrowded lands. Australia is more than an island; it is a continent, almost as large as the whole of Europe or the United States, but whose interior is largely empty, a desert unfit for human habitation, populated mostly by quick-moving kangaroos and wallabies. From the first, immigrants from Britain clustered on the southeast coast of what is now New South Wales, in Botany Bay. The impetus to colonize Australia sprang from the loss of the American colonies, hitherto a convenient outlet for its convicts. That Australia was, at first, largely a collection of penal settlements has been overstressed to the detriment of the large number of freemen who emigrated "down under." What is clear, however, is the historical link between the American Revolution and the founding of Australia, which replaced Virginia and Maryland as the destination of shiploads of convicts.

Australia's first modest settlements grew slowly during the first half of the nineteenth century; political rights were quickly won by the rebellious "squatters" after the transportation of convicts had been discontinued and a new society began to grow on the Australian shores that resembled America's far more than Britain's. The hardworking squatters did not develop into a class of cultured and leisured gentry as in England; nor could the established Anglican Church make much headway against the opposition of Roman Catholics, Presbyterians, and all kinds of Dissenters. Nonconformists, Chartists, and radicals combined to build up an extremely equalitarian and democratic society; and in their opposition to Britain's Royal Governors, were joined even by the wealthy squatters who were violently antagonized by the Government's land policy.

Anxious to avoid the errors that had led to the loss of the American colonies, the British were not slow in granting a great deal of autonomy to their various Australian colonies—by now, settlements had begun to spread around Australia's east, south, and west coasts. Still, there was often tension between the Australians and their British overlords, and in a famous clash between British Commissioner Bigge and a leading Australian personality, the latter threatened "that people of New South Wales might look to the United States of America for help if, as seemed likely, the colony were to be 'goaded into rebellion.' " [19] The American example, and also potential assistance, was never far from Australian minds when in conflict with British authority.

The area of conflict shrank rapidly as the Australian colonies were granted an increasing amount of self-government. The tempo was largely dictated by the rising proportion of free immigrants and colonial freeborn as opposed to convicts. Immigration, almost entirely from the British Isles, came in discontinuous waves, depending on the prevailing economic conditions. On the whole, Australians displayed an urge to expand economically at a somewhat reckless pace, each period of expansion to be followed invariably by another period of depression and overall stagnation. Australia's motto was always "what America has done, Australia can and will do," [20] regardless of the differences in every respect except that of size. One of the major differences was that, whereas in the United States free enterprise had full play, the more socialistic Australians tended to look to the Government for assistance in large undertakings such as railroad building.

Lack of free play of individual initiative also introduced a certain Malthusian outlook which began to inhibit immigration. Around 1880, New South Wales and Victoria, and the other Australian colonies to a lesser extent, were no longer "immigrant communities." Not only was local labor hostile to assisted immigration; the whole Australian temper, like the American, was hostile to Europe's Old World "with its hereditary privileges, its landlordism, class distinctions and alleged oppression, not to mention its national rivalries and militarism." [21] These same reasons motivated America's isolationist sentiment; but the great difference is that they did not inhibit the United States' tremendous power of expansion whereas Australians exhibited no such expansionist mood, did not often welcome immigrants, and even found themselves unable to really occupy and populate more than a fraction of their immense continent. Unlike its American counterpart, Australian isolationism was really Malthusian. "Australia for the Australians . . . vested interests of wealth and caste are less potent than in other countries. . . . The intellect of the people is freer, stronger and more original than in the age-old states of Europe," claimed the *Bulletin* in 1887.[22]

Just like the United States, Australia took for granted the worldwide protection provided by Britain's Royal Navy, and never gave it a thought. It enabled the Australians to experiment with new social formulas and give free play to its Radical-Labour movement. Furthermore, Australia did not develop a ruling class comparable with the Boston Brahmins or the South's plantation aristocracy. Australian society remained fundamentally egalitarian as well as freedom-loving. The people were also intensely race-conscious and feared that an influx of Asian immigrants might drown them in their underpopulated land and destroy their way of life.

Almost at the same time as California, the various Australian states (before Federation came into being) began to curb Chinese immigration drastically. Despite China's official protests, and the embarrassment of the British Government, the Australians remained firm: "Neither for Her Majesty's ships of war, neither for Her Majesty's representative, nor for the Colonial Office, do we intend to turn aside from our purpose," stated the Liberal leader Sir Henry Parks.[23] The danger of Chinese immigration was only one of the bones of contention with the mother country. Australians, although not expansionist-minded, did take an interest in the islands located in their immediate vicinity; Queensland's desire to annex New Guinea in 1883 had been frustrated by Gladstone, and the big island's northeastern part had promptly been occupied by the Germans. It required a great deal of rough talk on the part of Australia's Alfred Deakin at the first Colonial Conference to nudge the British into doing something about France's intention to take over the New Hebrides.

Unlike Canada, however, where federal ties have weakened, and are still weakening, Australia, since the inception of Federation (1901), has developed federal power at the expense of the states. A true Australian nation came into being. One of the reasons is that the turn of the century witnessed the startling rise of the mighty Japanese Empire, and behind it, the beginning of Asia's awakening. Conscious of their precarious isolation, the Australians woke up to the fact that their security was dependent on Britain's Royal Navy and on the British Empire's overall strength. Japan's victory over Russia in 1905 spread a mild panic of the "yellow peril" variety. Furthermore, Britain was by far Australia's best commercial market, as well as the source of most of its immigrants. Quicker communications brought the home country closer. In this new mood, Australia began to revive assisted immigration, and two hundred thousand migrants came over between 1911 and 1914 alone.

The First World War saw Australia line up firmly with Britain and gave Australian troops the first real opportunity to display in front of the world their remarkable military qualities: "There are certain divisions," reported Sir Douglas Haig's chief of staff, "which if given a thing to do, would do it. All the Australian divisions are in that category." [24] The statistics were eloquent: the Australian Army Corps, while representing 10 percent of the British army on the Western Front, captured almost one quarter of the guns and prisoners taken. They fought just as effectively in the Middle East. All in all, the Australian people, although numbering only a few million, enlisted over four hundred thousand men for voluntary military service, lost sixty thousand men killed, and suffered total casualties of over two hundred thousand, the highest percentage of any British force. In fact, Australia lost more men than the United States—a fact of which Australian Prime Minister Hughes reminded President Wilson undiplomatically at the Versailles Peace Conference. More than any other event, it was the Gallipoli campaign that revealed to the world the great fighting qualities of both Australians and New Zealanders, and "Anzac Day has been observed ever since with a feeling of almost religious reverence in Australia. It was on this day, it is said, that Australia became a nation." [25]

Yet, World War I's hostilities never came near enough to threaten Australia's very existence, as the second one did. This helps explain why, in the midst of the boom-and-bust sequence of the 1920's and 1930's, Australia reverted somewhat to its old Malthusian outlook; immigration was slight and the birthrate alarmingly low. Malthusianism went hand in hand with a certain form of isolationism that was a duplicate of the United States'— indifference to whatever happened beyond the Great Barrier Reef where the Royal Navy took over the safeguarding of Australia's security. No wonder that, by and large, Australian public opinion was extremely favorable to the 1938 Munich agreement between the European democracies and the dictatorships—anything to avoid being dragged again into Europe's old quarrels.

But militarized Japan was flexing its muscles and moving ahead steadily toward the brutal construction of its "Greater East Asia Co-Prosperity Sphere." Here, at last, was a clear threat to Australia's own security, and exclusive reliance on Britain's Royal Navy and the great base at Singapore seemed insufficient to many; but little was done to really prepare Australia for the military threat that was going to materialize with such startling rapidity and effectiveness. Nothing brought home so clearly to Australians the fact that Britain could no longer defend them as Japan's all-out assault after Pearl Harbor. Their only trained forces were overseas—three divisions in the Middle East, two of which began their return home journey in 1942, and one which was captured in Malaya with the fall of Singapore.

It was World War II that tore Australia forever away from Britain and British protection: when Japan attacked in the South Pacific, only the United States could and did come to Australia's assistance. Britain, hard-pressed by Germany at the other end of the world, could do nothing. Australia's Prime Minister Curtin stated bluntly at the time: "Without inhibitions of any kind, I make it quite clear that Australia looks to America, free of any pangs as to our traditional links or kinship with the United Kingdom." [26] From then on, in the words of an Australian, "we pay perpetual appreciation to the U.S. for taking up the fight with us when times were very dark in this part of the world, and when little sympathy was extended from our traditional source of origin." [27]

Saved by United States assistance during World War II, linked with her in the ironclad ANZUS pact in the early 1950's, Australia has watched the disintegration of Britain's empire and power with misgivings. But the process has been as relentless as it has been inevitable: the Suez Crisis during which Australian Premier Menzies did his diplomatic best to help Britain regain control of the last geographical link between their two countries, Britain's withdrawal from Aden and South Arabia in 1967, the stepped-up pace of the British departure from Singapore and Southeast Asia, everything points to a slow collapse of Britain's power east of Suez—just as everything points to the inevitable rise of an American empire in Southeast Asia. This twin development leaves Australia no choice. Determined to make the best of it and cement their growing ties with the United States, the Australians have adopted an entirely pro-American foreign policy since the war, which often sets them against Britain's. The Australians refused to follow Britain's lead in recognizing Red China, and joined the United States in fighting the Vietnam War. Even in matters of trade, Britain's increasing inclusion in Europe's economic life is slowly cutting the last effective link between mother and daughter. On the other hand, Australia did not wait to increase its trade with the rest of the world: Red China absorbs two to three million tons of Australian wheat a year; Japan has become a major market for its wool. Along with Japan, Australia intends to become a major factor in the Far Eastern economy and already educates fourteen thousand Asian students in its universities. Geopolitical developments have increased the centrifugal tendencies inherent in the structure of the British Commonwealth, to the point where its British phase has almost passed out, and its American phase is beginning.

But other, internal and more subtle, processes are also beginning to Americanize Australia and alter her personality, hitherto
exclusively British. The massive postwar immigration of almost
two million Dutch, Poles, Italians, Hungarians, Greeks, Germans, and Yugoslavs has diluted the peculiarly British character
of the native population; and this immigration is continuing at
the rate of one hundred thousand a year. Along with the new
postwar native-born generation of Australians which has no personal memory of the old awe-inspiring British Empire, the immigrants have no atavistic feeling of loyalty to Britain and look
upon the United States as their natural leader. Signs of Americanization abound: the pound has given way to the dollar, the
armed forces use American equipment; Australians travel increasingly to the United States and attend American universities
in growing numbers. American investments "down under" pour
in at a much faster rate than Britain's, having already reached
the two-billion-dollar level in 1968, up from four hundred million in 1957, increasing at a current rate of two hundred million
dollars a year, and fast accelerating. Over five hundred American companies have a substantial stake in Australia. Large,
industrial-scale agriculture, financed almost exclusively by
American capital, is opening up virgin land. The nostalgia of the
older, pro-British generation of Australians is no longer a match
for the realistic pro–United States attitude of the younger one—
realistic because it faces hard facts without sentimentality. And
for the United States, Australia has truly become one of the
extensions across the Pacific of the old western frontier, ready
and willing to become a new, huge California with its vast and
largely untapped natural resources.

Hanging precariously on the outer rim of Asia—where a billion and a half underprivileged Asians are potentially hostile
because Canberra's immigration regulations cling tenaciously to
the "White Australia" policy, depriving them of resources and
wide-open spaces on their doorstep—Australia is bound by all
the laws of geopolitical gravity to fall into the American orbit,
dragging along with her New Zealand which, although more
staunchly pro-British, has hardly any more choice in the matter
than Tasmania. In times to come, Australia and New Zealand

are bound to join the United States organically. This integration can be made with even greater ease than Hawaii's, whose population is mostly of Asian extraction. Although Australia's population has increased by over 40 percent since 1947—the fear of God caused by the near-invasion of the Japanese having caused it to repudiate its former Malthusian attitude—it is still smaller than that of California.

Australia is a junior replica of the United States in the heyday of its massive immigration at the turn of the century. Its foreign policy, as stated by its Defense Minister in 1965, is that "containment of the Communist Chinese threat has become a primary Australian objective." [28] From now on, the United States can expect Australian participation in all its military undertakings in the Far East and Southeast Asia. An Australian volunteer in the Vietnam War stated his countrymen's outlook pungently when he asked: "Why fight someone in your bedroom when you can snoot [punch] him on the front lawn instead?" [29] In fact, Australia will eventually stand ready to act as warden of the United States' empire in Southeast Asia.

As one Australian put it succinctly, "Australia is sinking into the Pacific and a new state is rising which we might call Austerica." [30]

With all the compelling reasons for Canada, Australia, and New Zealand—the "white" dominions—to throw in their lot with the United States, to enter the Union as so many new states, there is one visible obstacle, and a major one. They would then be open to a vast influx of American Negroes. To take a simple example, Australia, which has spent most of its historical life defending its "whiteness," would have to accept the spontaneous immigration of one and a half million Negroes if it were to have roughly the same proportion of Negroes and whites that exists in the United States; Canada would have to take in over two million. This is one aspect of the situation that makes a formal amalgamation of these countries with the United States improbable in the short run. The ironic coincidence of Charles de Gaulle's 1967 visit to Quebec with the outbreak of the most violent Negro riots in some of America's largest cities must have tempered the sense of outrage felt in most of Canada at the French President's brutal intervention. The average reflective inhabitant of Toronto or Winnipeg must have thought, when Detroit burst out in flames lit by hordes of Negro rioters on Canada's very doorstep, "There but for the grace of God, and national separation from the United States, go we," and been induced to seek any form of accommodation with his French-speaking compatriots in order to preserve Canada's integrity. Few Canadians would be tempted to share in the United States' intractable racial problem.

What of the rest of the dying Commonwealth—the black, brown, and yellow Commonwealth, all these new African and Asian states that still look to London but are increasingly shifting their gaze in Washington's direction? Depending on their overall political orientation, whether pro-West, anti-West, or truly neutralist, many are bound to become client-states of the United States. Here again, whatever amount of British cultural implantation has taken place—in Malaysia or Nigeria, Jamaica or Ghana—this implantation, including the English language, legal framework, and parliamentary tradition, makes it easier for American influence to penetrate than in the former French, Dutch, or Belgian colonies, still under Continental cultural influence.

But the most crucial area is that of the Indian Ocean—India and Pakistan, along with Burma and Ceylon. More than anything else, it is the integrity of the Indian Union that is bound to be the United States' main concern—just as its disruption is one of Red China's main goals on the Asian mainland. Ironically enough, the drive to preserve India's unity, military safety, and economic progress is not only a primary Washington objective, but fast becoming one of Soviet Russia's major preoccupations as well. Indian unity is the one achievement that robs Red China of a dominant position on the Asian mainland; it constitutes the one, but slim, hope that another large Asian Power can be bolstered in such a way as to thwart Red China's ambition to be surrounded wholly by weak and dependent client-states. And in connection with the bolstering process, it is likely that the preservation of the English language's official position as one of the main elements of Indian unity will, in the long run, tighten the links between India and the United States.

The historical trend of our time decrees that the United States, whether it likes it or not, is becoming heir to the deceased British Empire and Commonwealth—that at the present stage of history, it is unthinkable that the balkanization of the world engendered by the liquidation of this global empire should last forever. Its official metamorphosis into a "Commonwealth" only barely disguises the fact that its center of gravity has been steadily shifting from London to Washington; the bifocal ellipse of the first half of this century is becoming a circle with its center in the United States. For all practical purposes, the "British" Commonwealth is dead—and transfigured into an American one.

☆ VIII ☆

Frontier Across the Pacific

In an increasingly balkanized world, America is inheriting, willingly or unwillingly, the remnants of all the collapsed empires of the past century and a half. Indirectly, the United States inherited most of the former Spanish Empire in the Western Hemisphere, object of the unilateral Monroe Doctrine. A large slice of it was appropriated outright at the conclusion of the Mexican War and nicely rounded off the metropolitan territory of the Union; small bits and pieces were secured in Central America for the purpose of building the Panama Canal—but without formally abolishing local sovereignty; others were retained in the Caribbean after the Spanish-American War; and over the rest of the "banana republics," *imperialismo yanqui* established a loose but effective economic dominion.

More recently, the collapse of the venerable Ottoman Empire opened the way for the balkanization, not only of the Balkans proper, but of the entire Middle East: with the elimination of the temporary European heirs who had carved it and parceled it out among themselves, the United States finds itself alone in defending it against the encroachments of Russian imperialism; and finds itself, more or less consciously, in the process of using the newborn state of Israel, a Western implantation in an Oriental environment, as an instrument by which to compel the most troublesome Arab states to accept its benevolent protectorate.

Lately, the disintegration or forcible liquidation of most of Europe's other colonial empires is also adding to America's imperial burden. The French, Dutch, and Belgian empires, so recently transformed into new and often artificial nations, have required the United States' intervention on more than one occasion—Indonesia in discreet fashion; the former Belgian Congo, more openly during its times of troubles in the 1960's; and the former French Indochina, in terms of a full-fledged war in the second half of the 1960's. One way or another, the perennial threat of Communist takeovers, real or imagined, has compelled Washington to take a hand in the running of these nations' affairs.

But it is probably the inheritance of Japan's Far Eastern empire that has become the most burdensome—not that the United States was actually reluctant to take it over, since it had no choice in the matter. Washington was never willing to accept what the Japanese euphemistically called the "Greater East Asia Co-Prosperity Sphere," regardless of the fact that, like so many former empires, it was a geographical and economic necessity in an area where nationalism can only develop on the local level. It was inevitable that, sooner or later, it would have to take over the task that Japanese imperialism was not allowed to accomplish.

But the fact that the United States was bound to collide with Japan in the Pacific has its roots far back in the nineteenth century past: long before the United States' western frontier had been overcome in the Western Hemisphere, it had already leaped across the Pacific. Even before they reached California, Americans had started trading with China from their East Coast ports; the acquisition of California and a long stretch of Pacific coast after the Mexican War added to their interest in the Pacific. Britain's victorious Opium War against China helped increase America's trade with that vast and mysterious empire. Robert Walker, Secretary of the Treasury, claimed in 1848 that "Asia has suddenly become our neighbor with a placid, intervening ocean inviting our steamships upon the track of a commerce greater than that of all Europe combined." [1] This new neighborhood, at one stroke, gave the United States a potential preponderance in the Far East where it could, whenever the development of its West Coast enabled it to do so, outstrip, in time, all its European competitors put together.

In the early 1850's, as noted in chapter I, expansionist Americans had all but decided that their continent had been "finished up" and, with their backs still turned on Europe, the Pacific and Asia beckoned the rising power of the young American nation. Matthew Perry was convinced that "American expansion was inevitable and equivalent to the progress of mankind." [2] The Japanese door had hardly been open for a few months when the Russian squadron of Admiral Putiatin tried to slip in, to the great annoyance of Perry, who wished to preserve an American monopoly in the land of the Rising Sun. But there could be no monopoly; once the door was opened, all the Great Powers came in; the resulting breeze of fresh air blew the old Shogunate away and ushered in the Meiji Era—the quickest, and most amazing metamorphosis of an oriental feudalism into a highly efficient, modern industrialized state.

The Christian missionary spirit, as well as trade and economic expansion, motivated the growing interest of the Americans in these distant shores; this missionary spirit was not confined to the export of the biblical message; it was just as much political and social, a genuine and naïve belief that America's republican institutions and democracy were the best political institutions, that they should be exported and assist in the overthrow of decrepit oriental despotisms. Blended with it, was a strong belief, in the words of William Allen White, that it was the Anglo-Saxon's "manifest destiny to go forth as a world conqueror. He will take possession of all the islands of the sea" [3]—a credo revived toward the end of the century. The growing might of the American navy, the writings of Alfred Thayer Mahan who wanted to establish Anglo-Saxon supremacy in the Far East, the search for new commercial markets in Asia, the imperialistic drive of statesmen such as Theodore Roosevelt, Henry Cabot Lodge, Albert J. Beveridge, and John Hay, everything drove the Americans to push their western frontier all the way across the Pacific.

Hawaii, the first stepping-stone, had become a commercial satellite of the United States during the last quarter of the nineteenth century when American missionaries became businessmen and developed huge sugar plantations. When Queen Liliuokalani ascended the throne in 1891, she adopted a policy designed to eliminate or at least curtail American influence. The American reaction was not long in coming: in connivance with the local Americans, the American navy landed marines and the unfortunate queen was deposed on January 17, 1893. A provisional government recruited among the American residents was formed and immediately opened negotiations for the annexation of the archipelago by the United States; but the scruples of President Cleveland prevented a successful conclusion of the business at that time, although the new Republic of Hawaii remained entirely in the hands of the small groups of local American residents.

Needless to add, the phlegmatic and easygoing Polynesians were not consulted in the matter. But the strangest part of the whole episode is that, at the time, the twenty thousand Japanese residents outnumbered the Americans ten to one—but were not consulted either. Formal annexation had to wait a few years, but there was hardly any doubt that it would come, just as it had in the case of Texas. In order to ease the way, the first of a series of war scares was conjured up in America—the scare that a swiftly modernized Japan was planning a trans-Pacific expansion aimed at invading California and the rest of the West Coast. The annexation was actually carried out during the Spanish-American War. The war itself and its aftermath implanted American power and sovereignty all the way across the Pacific; Guam was annexed, and the Philippines taken over in 1899—now viewed, in its turn, as a stepping-stone to the valuable China trade and a base for the protection of American missionaries on the Chinese mainland.

It is rather striking that, at the time when Cuba in the hands of the decrepit Spanish Empire was viewed as a potential threat to the United States, few Americans gave any thought to the fact that the takeover of the Philippines by the far more vigorous, expansionist-minded Americans was bound to be similarly interpreted in Japan. A cry of alarm was raised in Tokyo; from then on, an inevitable chain-reaction set in, compelling both Powers to develop their respective navies for the protection of their imperial outposts—America's Philippines and Japan's Formosa. Nonetheless, American opinion tended to be pro-Japanese in those days, largely out of pride that the United States' erstwhile pupil should have been capable of modernizing itself so fast that it was able, unassisted, to defeat in turn the huge Chinese Empire and the powerful "European" Russian Empire.

However, Japan's increasing power and population explosion prompted Tokyo to try and break down the obstacles to free Japanese emigration to Australia, Canada, and the United States; but in vain. Racial discrimination in the "white" areas around the Pacific increased rapidly; and for all their growing might as a nation, the Japanese, as well as the Chinese, had the strange feeling that they were looked down upon as second-class human beings who should remain on their side of the Pacific and not intrude in the white man's domains. In 1920, a distinguished member of the Japanese Diet spoke for most Japanese when he said: "America appears to think she is divinely appointed to rule the world with a big stick! What is the purpose of her colossal Navy if it is not to make her power supreme in every part of the Pacific? American statesmen . . . preach the doctrine of racial equality and equal opportunity and yet refuse to admit educated Japanese immigrants to American citizenship." [4]

The 1924 Immigration Act, with its amendment banning all future Japanese immigration to the United States, was bitterly resented in Tokyo as prime evidence of racial discrimination. To the West Coast Americans, Chinese immigration, which had been terminated in the 1880's anyway, was deemed less dangerous than the Japanese; Chinese immigrants busied themselves running small businesses (restaurants, laundries) that did not interfere with American businesses; Japanese immigrants competed directly and efficiently with American farmers and businessmen. Sooner or later, the American gates had to clang down on the Japanese inflow.

Simultaneously, it was in the first years of the century that a feeling of kinship between Australia and the United States became fully apparent. The visit of an American squadron prompted an Australian official to state that the presence of American battle-ships in the South Pacific was "a demonstration of white solidarity against the yellow races"; [5] to the Japanese, it became a vivid reminder of what they were beginning to term the "white peril," threatening to encircle the Pacific.

In spite of immigration laws, American public opinion did not look upon Asians with systematic hostility. During the first decades of the twentieth century, American missionaries began to flood into China; and as a result, America's views of China began to change for the better, as their views of Japan altered for the worse. A considerable number of American missionaries' sons, upon their return to the United States, were to play an important part in influencing their country's public opinion into adopting a set of sentimental views which vastly complicated the relationship between the two countries after the Second World War. Early in the century, the overthrow of the Manchu dynasty, the eminent part played by Chinese Christians, from Sun Yat-sen to Chiang Kai-shek and the Soongs, implanted in the minds of many Americans, including Woodrow Wilson and his Secretary of State, William Jennings Bryan, the idea that America had a noble mission to accomplish in the Far East—a mission to spread democracy and Christianity. Mission boards and their supporting American churches did a great deal to spread around the notion that the Chinese had become American wards—even though Chinese converts, "rice-Christians" for the most part, were few and far between.

Between the turn of the century and the 1920's, America's self-proclaimed Manifest Destiny had undergone a subtle change. It was no longer the rabid jingoism with its crass colonial-type imperialism based on the alleged superiority of the "Anglo-Saxon race," but a more mature and humane destiny to establish a world order based on a higher moral level—which, somehow, was never presumed to come into conflict with America's economic and strategic welfare. This new outlook shaped the United States' policy in the Far East in between the two World Wars— growing antagonism toward Japan and growing friendship for the Chinese who were then just beginning again to vent their hostility toward all Westerners, Americans as well as Europeans. The American Ambassador in Peking reported to Secretary of State Hughes in 1921 that "we are universally regarded by the Chinese people as their special friend" [6]—but six months later was forced to advise American tourists to avoid China! There was even talk during the next few years of war between China and the United States, all the way up to the actual reckoning of how many American divisions would be required to occupy the whole of China and put an end to its civil war. But all this ended when Japan invaded Manchuria; both the British and the Americans gradually came to the conclusion that Japanese imperialism was far more dangerous than Chinese nationalism, however hostile to the West the latter might be.

What is striking in the interwar period is that American interest in the Far East never flagged; as mentioned previously, isolationism applied to Europe, never to the Pacific area. Secretary of State Henry Stimson took a firm line against Japan in the Manchurian affair and went on to say, in October 1932, that the United States was "naturally destined for a leader in the promotion of peace throughout the world." [7] Japan's imperial expansion in the Far East, however, was, geopolitically, a natural and normal phenomenon; if it had to be countered on legal and moral grounds, war was inevitable. Indeed, looking back in 1947, Henry Stimson was able to say, "The lines of division laid down so clearly in February 1932, led straight to Pearl Harbor." [8] The narrow legalistic approach to the Sino-Japanese conflict involved steadily worsening relations between Tokyo and Washington; and President Roosevelt was the last one to object. In love with both the navy and China (where his father had made a fortune in the Canton trade), Roosevelt personally shaped America's Far Eastern policy in the 1930's. The development of a powerful American navy and sentimental friendship for China were the two explosive ingredients that were going to convince the Japanese that they would eventually have to fight the Americans—and that they had better strike first.

That Washington did not intend to let itself be deflected from its chosen collision course with Japan became plain as early as 1934 when rumors of a *rapprochement* between Britain and

Japan began to float around. Infuriated, Roosevelt instructed Norman Davis to communicate to the British Foreign Minister that if Great Britain "is even suspected of preferring to play with Japan to playing with us," the United States was determined to bypass Britain and negotiate directly with the British dominions around the Pacific.[9] In Roosevelt's mind, the Pacific was, or should indeed be, under a virtual American protectorate, and European interference with United States' policy in the Far East would not be tolerated.

In 1937 and 1938, many thoughtful Americans called for a reevaluation of their country's policy in the Far East. Japan had embarked on the conquest of China proper which, if successful, might have given it a complete mastery over the Far East and led straight to a showdown with Soviet Russia; in all likelihood, Japan would never have been able to absorb the whole of China, and some new balance of power would have been established between Japanese imperialism, Chinese nationalism and Chinese Communists backed by Soviet Russia's might. Whatever the outcome, it would have implied an American retreat to Hawaii; Washington either had to back down and retreat to the eastern Pacific, abandoning China to whatever fate was in store for her, or go forward, assist Chinese resistance, increase its naval might, and prepare for eventual war. The United States saw itself at "the Oriental cross roads of decision" and, with some hesitation, decided to harden its attitude against Japan.

Warnings as to the consequences were not lacking and prophetic voices were heard pointing out that if the equilibrium which was being sought in the Far East by the Asians themselves was to be disrupted by American interference, only Soviet Russia and the Chinese Communists would benefit. Pertinently, John V. A. MacMurray, former chief of the Far Eastern division at the State Department, pointed out that, whereas Japan's empire was bound to be geographically circumscribed and limited to the Far East and Southeast Asia, "the triumph of Communism in China would stimulate anew the revolutionary forces in every country." [10] And he added that it was a "delusive hope" to expect that the destruction of the Japanese Empire would cement good relations between the United States and China: "If we were to 'save'

China from Japan and become the 'Number One' nation in the eyes of her people, we would thereby become not the most favored, but the most distrusted of nations," prophesied MacMurray as early as 1935.[11]

With war looming in Europe, Britain felt helpless in the Far East and urged Washington to come to terms with Japan; France's collapse in 1940 made the British even more despondent. But the die was cast; decisions in Washington were increasingly in the hands of the "hard-liners." On June 26, Cordell Hull's political adviser attacked the British and Australian proposals for a softer policy toward Japan and criticized their "appeasement policies";[12] and Washington tightened further the economic screws.

In June 1940, Henry L. Stimson became Secretary of War and threw his considerable weight on the side of the "hard-liners." A year before, he had advised the State Department "to begin a frank attack in Asia instead of Europe," having "always found the American people much more willing to take an affirmative policy in Asia than in Europe."[13] No sooner had he become Secretary of War than he berated the British Ambassador, Lord Lothian, whose country was beginning to feel the full weight of the German Luftwaffe's bombing, for the British "timidity" in Asia. Starting in July 1940, Washington decided to halt all trading in aviation fuel, high quality iron, and steel scrap with Japan; in turn, Japan formally strengthened its links with Germany and Italy. Taking this effect for a cause, the American Government decided to simplify the global picture by assuming that ". . . there is at present going on in the world one war, in two theaters."[14] The convenient thesis of a single world conflict in which Japan, Germany, and Italy formed a cohesive team is not confirmed by a postwar examination of the record; on the contrary, it shows conclusively that their real ties were far weaker than assumed at the time. A quarter of a century later, the same psychological urge to oversimplify led the American authorities to continue talking in terms of an "international Communist bloc" long after the bloc had broken up, of a Sino-Soviet imperialism years after it became obvious that Chinese and Russians had become bitter enemies. At any rate, behind the 1940 thesis of "one world war" lurked the idea that American public opinion could be far more easily aroused and mobilized against Japan than against Germany—in effect, it was an indirect appeal to an atavistic instinct of racial dislike.

The economic screws were tightened further, and assistance to the Chinese Kuomintang was stepped up. On July 26, 1941, Roosevelt launched total economic warfare. All Japanese assets in the United States were frozen; the British Empire and the Dutch East Indies followed suit; and Japan's foreign trade came to an almost complete standstill. "As one Japanese expressed it, his country felt like a fish in a pond from which the water was being gradually drained away." [15] The encirclement, aimed at reducing Japan through its extreme economic vulnerability to the state of a small oriental power, was complete. Only war could break it.

In October 1941, Secretary of the Interior Harold Ickes had inscribed in his diary: "For a long time I have believed that our best entrance into the war would be by way of Japan. . . . Japan has no friends in this country but China has. And, of course, if we go to war against Japan, it will inevitably lead us into war against Germany." [16]

Indeed, it did. But the decision to compel Japan to go to war was to have far-reaching consequences in the entire Orient—the main one being that the United States was bound to fall heir to the Japanese Empire and, without wanting it, would be compelled to build an American empire in its place. Although many American leaders saw in the war against Japan a means to an end, the end being American involvement in the European war, American public opinion focused on the Far East rather than the Old World. When Winston Churchill visited Washington shortly after Pearl Harbor, he was amazed to find "the extraordinary significance of China in American minds," and that even among the higher ranking Americans it was "strangely out of proportion." [17] In 1942 and 1943, public opinion polls found that twice as many Americans pointed to Japan rather than Germany as their major enemy. Obviously, most American leaders gave very little thought to the ultimate disposal of the broken pieces of the

Japanese Empire, feeling that everything would fall into place by itself, giving no thought to the perennial fact that a power vacuum always has to be filled and that this filling process is bound to bring into conflict antagonistic expansionary forces— in this instance, Communist ideology and American power.

Having pursued an expansionary policy across the Pacific for generations, having decided to upset the local balance of power-in-the-making, they had no choice except become a major element in whatever new balance of power would be established after the crushing of Japan.

This crushing had another unforeseen consequence: in order to ensure that it would not be the West's gain, local Japanese representatives and military commanders in former Western colonies did their utmost to tear away what was left of European power and prestige, encouraged local anti-European movements, fanned all the flames of Asian nationalisms, to the point of handing over their weaponry to the local Communists whenever they happened to be the most powerful anti-Western group. For instance, the Japanese commander in the former Dutch East Indies, General Terauchi, was the first to proclaim the birth of the Indonesian Republic in 1945. Quite naturally, the Dutch were anxious to get back to their East Indies and strangle the nationalist movement at birth, before it had time to gather strength. But this could only be done with the full approval, and logistical assistance, of the United States; neither was forthcoming. According to Douglas MacArthur, "After the Borneo campaign, I had planned to proceed with the Australian troops to Java and to retake the Netherlands East Indies. Then, as in New Guinea, restoration of the Dutch government would have brought the return of orderly administration and law. But for reasons which I have never been able to discover, the proposed movement was summarily vetoed by Washington. . . . This reversal soon bore fruit in the chaos that ensued in that portion of Indonesia; it was a grave error and was the result of political meddling in what was essentially a military matter." [18]

But it was not political "meddling" and it was not "essentially a military matter." It was a conscious and deliberate American policy aimed at stripping European colonial Powers of their colonial empires in Southeast Asia, regardless of the chaos and power vacuums thus opened; and often, all they had to do was to let the already defeated Japanese complete their own work of anti-European destruction. Washington's attitude toward the French in Indochina was similarly motivated.

One thing was clear as soon as hostilities came to an end: whatever the fate of the Far East proper, for all practical purposes the Pacific had become an American lake, and the American navy was supreme, from coast to coast. The United States inherited all the Japanese-controlled islands in Micronesia and took over the Ryukyus and Okinawa for an indefinite period. After having been reshaped into an American protectorate with full internal autonomy but no real independence in foreign affairs, Japan adopted a suitably modest "low posture" attitude, becoming one of the most valuable and secure bases for the United States armed forces in the Far East. The Korean War ultimately enhanced Japan's dependence on American protection; Tokyo nationalists of the prewar school used to call Korea a "loaded pistol pointed straight at the heart of Japan"; [19] by extending its *de facto* protectorate over South Korea and building up its military power, Washington put its own finger on the pistol's trigger, adding another element to its already considerable leverage over Japan.

In the long run, it was in Southeast Asia that the United States was, and is, driven by historical compulsion to establish a *de facto* empire—driven to it largely because of the fall of mainland China to Mao's Red Army, and because the expansionary requirements of Red China, permanently on the edge of famine, pointed to the Southeast Asian breadbasket as being the major goal of its imperialistic drive. In an emotional sense, the metamorphosis of China into a xenophobic Power filled with hatred for the West, was resented in the United States as a personal insult; for sentimental reasons, which had, for a while, little to do with power politics, the Communization of the former Middle Kingdom was a stunning blow—whereas the October Revolution in Russia a generation before had triggered no such emotional outburst.

Many Americans felt that they had "lost" China; but what can one lose that one has never "had"? In fact, all that the Americans had was a "Pearl Buck" view of China and the Chinese which had little to do with the "real" China that came through brutally when the Red Army conquered the mainland. The sentimental link through the missionaries had made them feel that the Chinese were amiable wards who should be grateful for all the time and expenditure doled out to them by devoted Americans; they "knew" that the Chinese were the best cooks and launderers in the world, clever traders, individualists to the core, quaint ancestor-worshipers, and apparently anxious to be Americanized. When this picture postcard view of China and the Chinese was torn to shreds by the Red Chinese, and the displays of the Chinese's atavistic xenophobia assumed such unpleasant ferocity, American public opinion reacted as if stung in the soul. From then on, whether in uneasy alliance with Soviet Russia in the 1950's, or increasingly antagonistic toward Moscow in the 1960's, Red China became the main enemy of the United States —and, as such, the main catalyst of the expanding American empire in the Far East and Southeast Asia.

It was the change of Administration in Washington early in 1953 that really set the new course of American involvement on the far southern side of the Pacific. The situation in Europe had, by then, become geopolitically frozen and Soviet Russian communism could no longer be rolled back without all-out nuclear warfare. But in Asia, situations were still fluid, all at once full of danger and full of opportunity. The tone of the new policy was set forth by John Foster Dulles in 1952, a few months before he became Secretary of State, when he stated that "those who think only of Western Europe and of making it 'impregnable'— without regard to the Near, Middle and Far East and Africa— are just as blind as those who think only of the United States and of making it 'impregnable.' Policies that do not defend freedom in Asia are fatally defective." [20] He then listed twenty-odd nations lying next to the "Soviet World," living "close to despair because the United States, the historic leader of the forces of freedom seems dedicated to the negative policy of 'containment' and stalemate." He advocated moving rapidly out of the stalemate and added that he was in favor of committing "our offensive military power to the deterring of aggression and the preservation of peace." [21]

In Dulles' statements, one can find all the misconceptions and historical distortions that were going to lead from an attempt to defend a political "freedom" that Asians have never known (at least in the Western sense of the word) to the gradual and partly reluctant establishment of an American imperium in the Orient. Right from the start, Dulles served notice on the Europeans that the United States was angry at "the hesitancy of the British and the French to join with the Americans in making a bold and unified stand against the Red Chinese," and that "if things went wrong [with the European Defense Community] the United States might swing over to a policy of Western Hemispheric defense, with emphasis on the Far East." [22] The Atlantic Alliance was pushed into the background and the anti-Communist crusade in the Far East began to take precedence.

For the second time, it was happening. In the 1930's, Washington strove to destroy the balance of power that was being slowly established between Japanese imperialism, China's indestructible nationalism, and its equally vigorous Communist element backed by Soviet Russia's Far Eastern power. At the cost of a major war, it succeeded, only to discover a few years later that a new balance had to be established; and in view of the successes of the Communist movement in China and Vietnam, it could only be found on the Asian mainland *within* the Communist world itself—pitting the conflicting nationalisms and imperialisms of the Russians, the Chinese, and the Vietnamese against one another without external interference. If this new balance of power was not acceptable, and Dulles adamantly refused to accept it, the only alternative was a further extension of American involvement on the Asian mainland in order to create, more painfully still, another balance of power between a *de facto* American empire and its Asian enemies. The seeds of the Vietnam War of the 1960's were sown at the time, in 1954, when the French threw in the sponge after the debacle at Dienbienphu.

At this point, a historical flashback is required. Of all the nations dwelling along the borders of the immense Chinese Empire, the Vietnamese have been the most enthusiastic in their wholesale adoption of all the elements of Chinese culture and civilization, while remaining just as enthusiastically anti-Chinese in a nationalistic, political sense. A thousand-year domination by the Chinese Empire was overthrown in A.D. 938 and all subsequent efforts made by the Chinese to reestablish their imperium in Vietnam failed. From then on, and to this day, the great heroes in Vietnamese history, still alive in legends, songs, and poetry, were those remarkable personalities who fought the Chinese and kept alive Vietnamese nationalism—the Trung sisters, contemporaries of Tiberius, Ly-bôn who temporarily freed his country in the middle of the seventh century, and Ngô-Quyen who threw the Chinese out of Annam (North Vietnam) for good in 938.

Simultaneously, the dynamic Vietnamese were animated by an imperialistic instinct all their own. When they finally emerged as an independent nation in the tenth century, they occupied only the plains of the Tonkin Delta. Hardworking and prolific, they began to expand southward along the coastal plain, pushing before them or slaughtering the ancestors of the present-day Cambodians until they reached the area of Saigon in 1698 and the Gulf of Siam a half-century later. Nor would their expansionism have stopped there, had it not been for the arrival of the French colonizers who froze the political situation and the national boundaries as they found them—although even then, such was the power of the Vietnamese, that the whole of what became French Indochina (except the kingdom of Luangprabang) paid tribute to the Vietnamese Emperor and recognized his suzerainty. Politically, economically, and militarily, Vietnam's power was overwhelming; it was the intervention of the French and the imposition of their colonial domination that saved Cambodia and Laos from being swallowed up and digested by the far more vital Vietnamese.

In Vietnam proper (Tonkin, Annam, and Cochin China), the French found a remarkable civilization patterned after China's, a society dominated by Chinese-style mandarins recruited by intellectual examinations, a power structure based largely on the merit system; a people of great nervous energy and willpower who prized learning and moral dignity above all else, an imperial court at Hué organized as a small-scale replica of the Son of Heaven's court in Peking, a religion largely based on ancestor-worship, as in China. Quite naturally, the leading Vietnamese under French colonial rule had a tendency to seize upon the type of ideology that best suited them psychologically; and their mental framework being largely that of the Chinese, it is no wonder that as soon as the first Chinese Marxists appeared on the scene, a Vietnamese Marxist appeared almost simultaneously.[23] Mao Tse-tung, Chou En-lai, and Nguyen Ai Quoc (alias Ho Chi Minh) embraced the Communist movement at its inception; in fact, Ho Chi Minh took part at the historic congress at Tours, in France, where the final divorce between the French Socialist and Communist parties was proclaimed in the early 1920's. Soon after, he set out to build a Vietnamese Communist party, while realizing full well that, under the French colonial regime, Marxism would have to disguise itself as revolutionary nationalism for decades before he could hope to have at his disposal a pure, orthodox Communist party.

As in so many other parts of the world, it was the Second World War that gave his Vietminh movement its opportunity and enabled it to display the immense superiority enjoyed by all Communist-led revolutionary movements over those which are merely dedicated to a national struggle for independence. All the politico-cultural elements that were going to insure the eventual triumph of Mao Tse-tung's Red Army in China were present in Vietnam, especially in the north, but with an added complication: the superposition of a Japanese dominion on top of that of the colonial French. In 1945, however, a few months before the war ended, the Japanese did away with French rule and took over for a brief spell; the next decade following the war was filled with the unsuccessful attempts of the French to reestablish their domination.

In order to understand the bitterness of the struggle during these ten years, it is essential to realize that the Americans had already become involved in the problem—involved in the sense that President Roosevelt had made it clear as early as 1942 that he was opposed to a reestablishment of French domination in Indochina after the war, and in the sense that a tacit agreement between the United States and China's Kuomintang regime provided for a thinly disguised Chinese protectorate over North Vietnam.[24] When the Japanese abolished French rule at the tail end of the war, the Americans found themselves suddenly deprived of their main source of information and immediately sought to replace it. The best one available was the Communist Vietminh network, with which the OSS immediately linked up, committing the same error as the British in Greece and Malaya. Providing the Vietnamese Communists with a considerable amount of weapons and supplies, associating with them in their guerilla warfare against the Japanese, the Americans naïvely thought that they had recruited genuine allies in the war. In fact, the Vietminh played its own game with consummate skill, preparing its takeover of the country in the anticipation that Japanese rule would, in any case, some to a quick end. Again, it is worth recalling that, in their hour of defeat, the Japanese in Indochina, as elsewhere in the former European colonies in Asia, decided to hand over their weapons to Asian nationalists and not to their Western victors: in so doing, they gave meaning to their unsuccessful war against the West, and made sure that European domination could never be reestablished on the Asian mainland; their East Asia Co-Prosperity Sphere had collapsed; so be it. At least, their struggle to chase the white man out of Asia might still end in an Asian, if not Japanese, victory.

Having promptly come to the conclusion that the Vietminh was the most influential and effective party in northern Indochina, the Japanese decided to hand over power to the Communists in Hanoi and the north. However, the Vietminh was far weaker in the south and the Japanese found it more convenient to transfer power to a conglomerate of anti-Communist nationalists and religious sects. In all cases, and whenever feasible, the main purpose of the Japanese was to frustrate the inevitable return of the Westerners.

Meantime, the victorious allies had decided at the Potsdam Conference to slice Indochina in two, north and south of the sixteenth parallel, for the purpose of accepting the surrender of the Japanese: the north was handed over to the Kuomintang Chinese, the south to SEAC, Admiral Mountbatten's command. Strangely enough, the temporary wartime coalition between Americans and Vietminh was quickly reestablished in Hanoi, a coalition directed essentially at the prevention of a French return to northern Indochina. The Vietminh received assurances of American support in its forthcoming struggle against the reestablishment of French colonialism [25]—and simultaneously, the Americans supported the anti-Communist Kuomintang Chinese who occupied North Vietnam and were hostile to the Vietminh. In turn, the Kuomintang Chinese supported the anti-Communist nationalists in Hanoi. Out of this confusion, one thing soon became clear: Ho Chi Minh's Communists were in danger of losing control of the revolutionary movement; Ho Chi Minh, more patient and farsighted, was outflanked at every turn by the more violently anti-French nationalists. His cool Marxist analysis of the situation eventually classified his antagonists, in order of decreasing importance, as being the other nationalist parties, the Chinese army of occupation in Tonkin, and its American supporters; the French seemed almost harmless by comparison.

The Kuomintang Chinese appeared to have inherited the Japanese dream: the liberation of Asia from Western domination, but under Chinese Nationalist auspices, this time. Obviously, their chosen instrument in Hanoi could not be the Communist Vietminh but the right-wing nationalist parties such as the Dong Minh, Dai Viet, and other such groups, eventually linked organically in a "Nationalist Bloc." Meantime, the Americans had come to realize the mistake they had made in assisting the Vietminh Communists, shortly before they also realized that their Kuomintang allies in China were about to go down to defeat in front of Mao Tse-tung's armies (the Chinese army of occupation had, in the meantime, evacuated North Vietnam). In this complex situation, Ho Chi Minh moved with the cool assurance of an old professional revolutionist; he simultaneously made a serious effort to come to an understanding with France and gradually destroyed his nationalist rivals. But the French, having returned to North Vietnam on the heels of the departing Chinese, and haunted by old dreams of colonial glory, were in no mood to come to terms with him; inevitably, the first Vietnam War broke out in the fall of 1946.

This war drained the resources of a weakened France. But what soon made it more dramatic still, was the arrival of the triumphant Red Chinese on the Vietnamese border in 1949. The Vietminh was now backed by the formidable power of Red China. Even though France officially abandoned its sovereignty over Vietnam in December 1949, the war went on: France had not given it up in favor of the only effective force in the country but in favor of the former Emperor of Annam, Bao Dai. But if the backing of the Vietminh by neighboring Red China was an added headache for the French, the very existence of an expansionist Red China became a new headache for the Vietminh, which had not the slightest intention of letting itself fall into the wide embrace of its gigantic neighbor—whether Communist or not. Lacking the possibility of an understanding with the French, Ho Chi Minh had no other choice but to rely on Soviet Russia as the only available counterweight to Red China, while accepting an indispensable minimum of Chinese assistance for the duration of the hostilities. A new process of equilibrium was in the process of formation, a natural balance of power *within* the Communist world. The French should have then faced facts and let them be: the only effective barrier to China's domination of Southeast Asia that did not involve non-Asian Powers was Vietnamese nationalism.

Still, the French might have thrown in the sponge at that time, had it not been for the war in Korea which completely altered the policy of the United States. In the fall of 1950, the French Statesman Pierre Mendès-France made several speeches in the Assemblée Nationale in which he suggested granting complete independence to Vietnam and recognition of Ho Chi Minh's government as the legal authority in the country. But now, fear of American reactions, added to lingering sentiment for the preservation of France's colonial prestige, prevented the French Government from adopting this solution. And instead of frowning on

French colonialism, the Americans now began to see in the Vietnamese war another theater of operation against international communism.

American assistance began pouring into Vietnam, mostly to shore up the discredited regime of Bao Dai; Chinese assistance to the Vietminh was also stepped up—but only in limited amount since a total Vietnamese victory might curtail Chinese influence in Hanoi. That the French eventually suffered the catastrophic defeat of Dienbienphu in 1954 was not the doing of Red China but of the Vietminh themselves.

The French collapse at Dienbienphu marked a watershed in the long history of European domination in Asia. A dramatic symbol of the inability of European Powers to control any Far Eastern colony, it was promptly followed by negotiations with the victorious Vietminh and a settlement providing for a temporary partition of the country between a Communist-dominated north and a non-Communist south. The United States could have let well enough alone—that is, let the natural forces seek their own balance of power in that part of the world.

Had this been allowed to happen, it would no doubt have led, within a few years, to the complete takeover of South Vietnam by Ho Chi Minh, then to the probable "satellization" of Cambodia and Laos by the Vietnamese—in other words, under different political labels, the imperialistic drive of the Vietnamese, thwarted by the imposition of French colonial rule in the nineteenth century, would have been successfully resumed. But this concession made to Vietnamese imperialism would have been the best guarantee that, in its turn, Vietnam's local imperialism would have turned against China's far more powerful and dangerous imperialism, blocked its southward expansion and frustrated its attempt to grab the rest of Southeast Asia. Communist Vietnam's imperialism would have provided by far the cheapest and most effective barrier against Chinese expansion.

Again, this solution providing for a local, Asian balance of power, was not to Washington's taste. The fear of any American administration of being accused of "abandoning" South Vietnam as China had, presumably, been "lost" a few years before, clouded the vision of policy makers in Washington, making it impossible to devise and pursue an intelligent policy based on the realities of the situation. In addition, the indestructible conviction that the idealistic American can always succeed where the cynical European colonialist fails, was instrumental in dragging the United States into the Vietnamese imbroglio.

☆ IX ☆

The Hawaiianization of the Orient

National consciousness is rooted in some form of mythology or other, an outward expression of a society's collective unconscious. In reference to America's policy in the Orient, it is clear that prime responsibility lies with the historical mythology underlying American thinking about the United States' posture and role in the world. Eisenhower and Dulles expressed an atavistic belief, shared by most Americans, when they claimed that their country had a long anti-colonialist tradition and that this tradition gave it its unique moral stature among Western nations; and there is enough grain of truth in this view to make it plausible, while it is only part of the truth. They were not in the least bothered by the fact that this distorted vision of their true history was not shared by the rest of the world—certainly not by the Latin Americans to whom *imperialismo yanqui* had been the only threatening imperialism for more than a century, and certainly not by many Asian people who saw in American imperialism the historical heir to Europe's colonialism—just as, two thousand years ago, the Orient saw in Roman imperialism only an extension and fulfillment of the Greek imperialism it was supposed to do away with. American presence in the Far East had been acquired by military and commercial force, and had no greater moral justification than that of any European colonial power—however sincere the belief of the Americans in their national mythology and however genuine their idealism. But this mythology had, and still has, great hold over the American imagination and is largely responsible for the repeated collisions between American undertakings based on it and the intractable reality concealed behind it. Out of these repeated collisions between myth and reality, arises slowly the great American empire to come, born unconsciously, and then reluctantly, of this disregard for unadorned facts.

The belief that American-style democracy must spread around the world, by missionary persuasion if possible, by force if necessary, is far more ancient than the relatively recent appearance of international Communism. One is reminded of a famous conversation between Walter Hines Page, the farsighted American Ambassador at the Court of St. James's at the time of the difficulties with Mexico in 1913, and Sir Edward Grey, British Foreign Secretary:

> GREY: Suppose you have to intervene, what then?
> PAGE: Make 'em vote and live by their decision.
> GREY: But suppose they will not so live?
> PAGE: We'll go in again and make 'em vote again.
> GREY: And keep this up two hundred years?
> PAGE: Yes. The United States will be here two hundred years
> and it can continue to shoot men for that little space of time
> till they learn to vote and rule themselves.[1]

This missionary urge to compel aliens to abide by a democratic process which may be quite unsuitable to their national temper can only result in the involuntary buildup of an empire; in this context, the Communist urge to convert aliens to Marxism-Leninism is only the mirror-image of America's far more ancient democratic spirit; and the clash between their contending imperialism, preordained generations ago, has become the main political leit-motiv of our times.

By now, under the sway of John Foster Dulles in his capacity as Secretary of State, the American nation was ostensibly engaged in an anti-Communist crusade which made (with the exception of Yugoslavia) hardly any distinction between different brands of communism. International communism and the Sino-Soviet Bloc were seen as two sides of a monolithic movement calling for containment all around the rim of Eurasia. The Americans, profoundly hurt by the fall of mainland China to Mao Tse-tung, saw in the eventual triumph of Ho Chi Minh's Communists in Vietnam an extension of the China debacle—whereas it would, in all probability, have been quite the reverse. Furthermore, being unable or unwilling to understand the religious-like appeal of Marxist ideology for many leading Vietnamese, being blind to the fact that, unless proper native leadership can be generated, it is impossible to build up a successful anti-Communist movement, and that proper leadership is primarily based on the human quality of this leadership, the Americans were led into an active intervention in a local situation which they misunderstood completely.

The Eisenhower Administration was quite unwilling to "settle" and made this clear to General Paul Ely, chief of the French General Staff: "Dulles and Radford both spoke about victory, no concessions, positions of strength, and did not even let themselves be drawn into a discussion about how, at Geneva, a rapid termination of the war would be reached." [2] Instead of letting a situation in which they were not directly involved develop all by itself, the Americans, once again, decided to take a hand and frustrate the natural course of events that would have established a new. and purely Asian, balance of power in Southeast Asia. In Washington's view at the time, "A complete Communist conquest of Indochina would have had far graver consequences for the West than a Red victory in Korea." [3] But the reality of the situation was that a Communist Vietnamese conquest of Indochina would have set up a strong and viable state, whose only likely aim, from then on, would have been to block the extension of Red China's influence in Southeast Asia by resisting the imposition of a Chinese protectorate.

Nevertheless, and in spite of Dulles' efforts to "internationalize" the conflict and launch his anti-Communist crusade in Southeast Asia, the Geneva Agreements were signed in July 1954, extricating the French forces from their disastrous predicament in Indochina. The British played a vital part in these negotiations and their success in bringing them to a successful conclusion infuriated Dulles; a serious breach began to split the traditional Anglo-American association, to reach its widest extension two years later, at the time of the Suez Crisis. Nor would the Americans accept or endorse the Geneva Agreements. The new artificial state of South Vietnam stretching from the seventeenth parallel to the Gulf of Siam, was devoid both of true leadership and national consciousness, and whatever power there was fell into the hands of Ngo Dinh Diem, a narrow-minded, incompetent Vietnamese Catholic and anti-Communist nationalist. While refusing to endorse the results of the Geneva Conference, the United States turned out to be the only Power eager to assume an obligation to defend these results. What, for the participants of the Conference, was merely a face-saving device which in no way obligated them to safeguard the temporary settlement arrived at, was taken at face value by the Eisenhower Administration. As for the proviso that elections were to take place, it could only be a farce and the South Vietnamese representatives never accepted it. Thus, the United States came to occupy, of its own free choice, the position of sole guardian of South Vietnam's independence and territorial integrity.

Led into this trap by its uncompromising anti-Communist crusade, Washington then proceeded to shore up Diem's regime; worse still, Dulles, haunted like so many of his compatriots by the idea that any association with "colonialist Powers" such as France and Britain would harm America's moral stature in Asia, decided to "go it alone" in Saigon. The creation of the SEATO pact, the stillborn brainchild of Dulles, did nothing to ensure the territorial integrity and independence of South Vietnam which could only be achieved by some settlement *inside* this artificial state. How artificial it was, the United States soon discovered. Contrary to widespread belief at that time and later, Diem never drove the remnants of the French army out of South Vietnam, quite the contrary. It was the French who kept him in power at a time when he had no police, no army, no government nor administration, and no popular support; it was the French Government's own decision, and no one else's, to withdraw the French authorities from the administrative management of South Vietnam's public utilities and from the newly formed Vietnamese army.[4] But when the French attempted to curb Diem's incipient dictatorial rule and counteract the civil war he began against the semiautonomous religious sects (Cao Dai and Hoa Hao), many Americans saw in this French opposition a desire "to protect their commercial interests." [5] The more the French warned the Americans that Diem was dictatorial and dangerously incompetent, the more the Americans warmed up to him. Senator Mike Mansfield, who later was to become a determined opponent of the use of military force in Vietnam, sowed the seeds of this American military involvement when he stated, in his October 1954 report, that "in the event that the Diem government falls . . . the United States should consider an immediate suspension of all aid to Vietnam and the French Union forces there." [6]

Washington became determined to push the French out of Vietnam and eliminate their influence in Saigon. Less than a month after the signing of the Geneva Agreements, President Eisenhower decided that aid to Indochina would be given directly to the Associated States rather than through the French. From then on, the gradual establishment of the United States' *de facto* protectorate over the non-Communist part of Indochina was launched. Elimination of French influence, knowledge, and military support, was the natural counterpart of Washington's increasingly uncompromising support of Diem. Senator Mike Mansfield, head of a special subcommittee on Indochina, shaped congressional policy along this disastrous course of unconditional support of Diem and elimination of the "colonialist" French; thirteen years later, the same Senator, now majority leader, urged in the midst of the raging Vietnam War that the whole mess be dumped in the lap of the United Nations' Security Council (August 28, 1967).[7] Congressman James F. Richard, shortly before becoming Chairman of the House Foreign Affairs

Committee, made a public statement in which he urged that in Vietnam "the task of building up an anti-Communist force be assumed by the United States." [8] Britain's Anthony Eden and France's Pierre Mendès-France made a last attempt to reestablish a Western policy partnership in Vietnam in December 1954, to no avail. Dulles made it plain that Washington would view the final exit of the French from Indochina without any displeasure.

Disgusted, the French gave up and gradually withdrew, leaving the Americans to cope alone with the problem; Britain's diplomatic influence was eliminated just about the same time. Several years later, under another administration, the American Government attempted to undo the harm and invite the Europeans back into Vietnam; and again, but in reverse, this time, to no avail.

When, animated by his virulent dislike for French colonialism and its alleged misrule of its Indochinese colony, President Franklin Roosevelt made his incredible offer of Indochina as an outright gift to China, Chiang Kai-shek refused point-blank and pointed out quite rightly that the Vietnamese had a long tradition of hostility to the Chinese.[9] Nevertheless, Washington had insisted that the French should not return to Indochina and had handed over North Vietnam to the Chinese as a zone of occupation after World War II. In the ensuing conflict between the returned French and Ho Chi Minh, the United States had, at first, favored Ho Chi Minh. Was he less of a Communist in 1946 than he was in 1966? As a British commentator wrote at the time, "in the international field, the Americans show a tendency to kick into their own goal." [10] Quite suddenly, in American eyes, the whole picture turned from white to black (or red) after Mao Tse-tung had conquered mainland China—as if the enduring fact of Vietnamese hostility to the Chinese, whatever their political persuasion, had evaporated overnight; it simply needed to be fitted into a new context.

At any rate, America's growing influence in Saigon had delivered South Vietnam to Ngo Dinh Diem, whose repressive rule was theoretically justified by the threat of Communist subversion. Diem had turned against practically everyone else in South

Vietnam, except his Roman Catholic coreligionists—the Hoa
Hao, the Caodaists, the Buddhists, liberals, socialists and democrats, and all those South Vietnamese who had friends or family
north of the seventeenth parallel. Diem was not only a fanatic;
he was also a hopeless administrator. The late 1950's, far from
being used for the gradual buildup of a South Vietnamese nation
and army, were years of slow disintegration. The Americans increased their assistance and sent one mission after another to
Saigon—to no avail. In October 1961, another mission under
General Maxwell D. Taylor, urged Diem to undertake badly
needed reforms and liberate all the genuine nationalists who
were held in jail. Diem's response was to initiate a violent press
campaign against American attempts to "infringe on Vietnamese
sovereignty." [11] Intimidated by the very man they had put in place
against French advice years before, the Americans backed down;
they had not yet learned to play the true game of imperialism in
that part of the world. Diem felt that, by now, the United States'
prestige had become so involved with his own rule, that he had
them by the throat; and the Americans behaved as if he had.

The 1961–1962 winter was a turning point. Diem was getting
completely out of hand, ignoring American advice, attacking the
United States' alleged trespassing on Vietnam's independence,
tightening the screws on all his political opponents. The only
progress made in South Vietnam was made by the Communist
Vietcong. Eventually, a handful of Buddhist leaders started an
open, gruesome but spectacular mass movement; Diem's violent
repression outraged American public opinion. Washington could
no longer close its eyes to the progressive disintegration of the
South Vietnamese state and army, and belatedly, cut off part of
its economic assistance. At that, Diem decided to reply by making his boldest move yet: his brother Ngo Dinh Nhu started
flirting with Ho Chi Minh, and contacts were established between Saigon and Hanoi.

Once more, the United States was offered a way out of the
imbroglio and could have retired gracefully, bowing to the inevitable and calling Diem's bluff—if it was a bluff. But after all
these years of costly assistance and eroded prestige, America's
cup of bitterness overflowed; Washington's assistance over the

years now amounted to a substantial investment which had to be recouped. The Americans decided to throw good money after bad: it became clear that Diem's fate was sealed. The days of a loose American protectorate were over; the time for a military takeover had come, and other, more pliable Vietnamese "leaders" would have to be found.

A number of Vietnamese nationalists and army officers, encouraged by the altered atmosphere in America, hatched a plot, keeping Washington informed of its progress after having been assured that the Americans would not stand in the way. Washington gave it its full blessing, although the assassination of Diem and Nhu added an unwelcome touch of tragedy. But the situation kept deteriorating after November 1963; while the Vietcong made steady progress and came to control most of the South Vietnamese countryside, at least by night, military coups succeeded one another in Saigon where no real political leadership emerged. Time and again, rumors went around that some prominent elements of the army were about to stage a coup in order to come to terms with Hanoi and neutralize Vietnam—which might, again, have offered the Americans a way out; but the Americans steadily increased their assistance and supervision, making it plain that they were not seeking a way out but, on the contrary, were prepared for further involvement.

Every coup was followed by American disappointment in the new leaders; but they never appeared to be able to find adequate substitutes of stature. Unlike the South Koreans, who were more amenable to American advice and who also generated better leadership, the South Vietnamese vented their frustrations against their American partners without being able to lead their own people. One involvement leading to another, Washington finally decided, in the spring of 1965, to send American ground troops to prevent the otherwise inevitable collapse of South Vietnam into the arms of the Vietcong. At last, the Americans were irretrievably sucked into Southeast Asia.

Once the American military buildup started, the whole picture began to change. South Vietnam is not and has never been a "nation"; ethnologically, its population is part of the Vietnamese people; politically, it consists of the old French colony of Cochin

China and most of the former French protectorate of Annam. Politically and socially, it is a conglomerate of disparate elements —Roman Catholic refugees from the north, remnants of those religious sects (Cao Dai, Hoa Hao) temporarily crushed by Diem, large and conflicting Buddhist associations—and the vast bulk of the peasants working in their rice paddies who would gladly be rid of both Hanoi and Saigon.

The plain fact is that, unwittingly, the United States had set itself the task of actually *creating* a nation in South Vietnam where none existed before; its massive intervention in the internal civil war of the Vietnamese, if successful, was inevitably bound to result in the painful birth of an artificially created South Vietnamese nationalism, irretrievably tied to American apron strings. This slow process was marked by numerous crises— political upheavals in Saigon where instability is endemic and where Buddhists, students and squabbling military leaders and politicians often seemed unable to get on with the nation-building job. When such a crisis broke out in the spring of 1966, many a voice was heard in the Pentagon expressing impatience and advocating a complete American takeover in South Vietnam: "Let's take this thing over or get out; we cannot go on like this: either we have to command the political or military situation, use our power to change it radically, or give it up as a hopeless job." [12]

Such remarks are likely to be heard frequently in the future— to be followed, usually, by effective action. Ability for self-rule, democratic-style, is a rare quality among nations, especially nations-in-the-making with which the United States happens to be involved; the temptation to "take this thing over" and "make 'em vote," whether they like it or not, will recur with increasing frequency—the inevitable wages of involvement.

South Vietnam is the focal point of the struggle for Southeast Asia, the military spearhead of the anti-Communist crusade— but not the only piece of real estate that the Americans wanted to save in that part of the world. While Cambodia turned neutralist, ostensibly with an anti-American bias, Laos was partitioned between a nominally neutral segment and a Communist

Pathet Lao protectorate of the North Vietnamese. Thailand was also drawn into the crusade, when it became plain that Chinese-sponsored and North Vietnamese–led guerillas had started operating in the northern jungles. Most important of all, in 1965 a revolution took place in Indonesia which decapitated, at the cost of over half a million lives, the powerful Communist influence in the immense archipelago and shifted governmental power into the hands of a pro-Western, businesslike triumvirate, backed by the Indonesian army. However, it was felt, in Washington, that the whole American position in Southeast Asia depended on safeguarding South Vietnam itself from a Communist takeover. The geographical configuration of the country supposedly made it suitable for American military intervention—an extremely narrow width and an elongated coastline along which the United States navy's immense firepower could be brought to bear with great effectiveness.

Thus, the decision taken by President Johnson in 1965 was wholly logical; his massive military intervention in Vietnam's civil war was in line with the consistent, if partly unconscious, policy of previous Administrations—since, time and again, the alternate solution of letting South Vietnam slip into the clutches of Ho Chi Minh, in the hope that a united and powerful Communist Vietnam would stand as a sturdy barrier against Chinese expansion, had been rejected. From then on, it became increasingly clear that there was no pulling back from escalating commitments, each new commitment sucking the United States deeper into further commitments until the United States shall have built up its protectorate in the Orient—extending to the border of Burma its indirect dominion which stretches already from South Korea to Taiwan and the Philippines. The United States now holds firmly a number of footholds on the Asian shores on the far side of the Pacific, increasingly involving in its destiny the fifteen million Australians and New Zealanders of European descent, who represent the southern anchor of the United States' Asian empire.

What is left of European presence in the Pacific is disappearing fast. Britain's accelerated departure from Singapore and Malaysia is cutting off its last military link with its sister states "down under." France's scattered islands in Polynesia are restless. Early in 1968, the French Polynesian territorial assembly renewed its demand for greater autonomy and expressed its reluctance to allow French nuclear tests in its territory.[13] Eventual independence for Polynesia is only a matter of time. In truth, no other power is left in the world's greatest ocean that can possibly challenge America's right to rule all the waves of the Pacific, except the coastal waters of Red China and Soviet Russia. In contrast to the attitude of French Polynesia, where half of the voters in the March 1967 election wanted outright independence while the other half wanted internal autonomy, the vast archipelagoes of Micronesia (Mariana, Caroline, and Marshall islands), wrenched from the Japanese after the war, are sure to remain under American control, under one form or another. The hundred thousand Micronesians are scheduled to vote on their future status in the early 1970's, and soundings of their political opinions in 1967 indicated a marked preference for incorporation by the United States.[14] Micronesia, as well as French Polynesia, are destined to become, in time, wholly owned subsidiaries of Hawaii.

In fact, the most important phenomenon in the Pacific and the Far East is a steady process of "Hawaiianization." The cultural impact of hundreds of thousands of American combat troops, at work or on leave throughout the Orient, is a dynamic phenomenon of incalculable importance which is gradually changing the cultural face of that part of the world. When World War II came to an end, American tastes and customs began a peaceful invasion of the Pacific's Asian shores, profoundly altering social customs, traditions, and tastes. Symbolic of this Hawaiianization is the increasingly popular custom among Far Eastern and Southeast Asian women to westernize their oriental eyes with the assistance of Japanese-invented surgery.

The war in Vietnam has increased the tempo of this Hawaiianization. Thousands of young American servicemen (thirty thousand a month in 1967), granted leave for "R & R" (rest and recreation) began roaming the streets of Bangkok, Manilla, Singapore, Penang, Kuala Lumpur, Hong Kong, and Taipeh—wearing Hawaiian-style sports shirts, well equipped with cameras and binoculars, making an impact on the far side of the Pacific that far exceeds the effects of Asian influence on the Americans. Slowly, American pop music, dancing, and bowling are taking over the cosmopolitan cities of the Far East, while a strange pidgin American is on its way to becoming the lingua franca of the Orient. Commodore Perry would undoubtedly be proud of the achievements of his compatriots in the century following his eloquent plea for American expansion across the Pacific, which he equated with the "progress of mankind." [15] In the long run, this cultural impact may well rank, historically, as the major by-product of the United States' protectorate over the Far East and Southeast Asia.

This involvement is no temporary affair. It is a lasting one, the natural culmination of an involvement that started over a century ago. Not least among the various elements of this involvement was the United States' long occupation of the Philippines. And when, in 1967, in the midst of the fearful race riots that erupted in the black ghettos of America's largest cities, many liberal Americans complained that the efforts and expenditures caused by the Vietnam War could be put to better use in the cities of the United States, they could have recalled the contents of a letter written by James Bryce, the celebrated author of *The American Commonwealth,* to Theodore Roosevelt in 1898. In the aftermath of the Spanish-American War, he mused:

> How stupendous a change in the world these six months have brought. Six months ago you no more thought of annexing the Philippine Isles and Porto Rico than you think of annexing Spitzbergen today. In the interest of the United States, I am uneasy at the change, because the new enterprises you will enter are enterprises for which your Constitution and government have not been framed. . . . I am more anxious to see the American people purify city government and do certain other jobs at home than to see them civilize the Malays and aborigines of Luzon.[16]

James Bryce was right; he was uneasy because he felt that the United States had assumed an imperial role and might acquire a taste for it.

It now seems that the taste is acquired, and to some, is not so bitter after all. In 1967, General Earle G. Wheeler made no bones about the fact that American involvement in Asia was a long-term one and would last "at least until the turn of the century." [17] Secretary of State Dean Rusk added that "it will be useful for some time to come for American power to be able to control every wave of the Pacific, if necessary." [18] Many statesmen in Southeast Asia seem to agree. One of the most outspoken, Singapore's Prime Minister Lee Kuan Yew, stated emphatically in 1967 that even former colonial countries "may very well prefer a permanent American military presence" in order to ward off the threat of communism.[18]

The real threat overhanging the Far East, Southeast Asia, and even Burma and India, is not so much communism *per se,* that is the contagious expansion of a Marxist *ideology,* as the ethnic, flesh-and-blood expansion of Red China and the Red Chinese. Thanks to an irrepressible birthrate, continental China is bursting at the seams; even in normal times, the Chinese have trouble feeding themselves. The socialization of agriculture, the experimentation with the "communes," the "Great Leap Forward" and, more recently, the Cultural Revolution with its attendant civil war and anarchy, have done nothing to increase China's ability to feed its fast-growing population. Hence, the inevitable imperialism of the Chinese, Red or otherwise, especially toward Southeast Asia. Except for Vietnam and Java, Southeast Asian lands are not overpopulated and can be net exporters of foodstuff.

The natural immigration of the Chinese since the second half of the nineteenth century has been so massive that, in the 1960's, Southeast Asia harbors well over sixteen million of them, scattered throughout Vietnam, Thailand, Burma, Malaysia, Singapore, Indonesia and the Philippines. Whatever the political persuasion of those nations' leaders, they have to take into account the enduring hostility of their populations toward the Chinese settled in their midst—even in places such as Singapore where the Chinese are actually in a majority.

As an example, in 1967 alone, widespread outbreaks of anti-Chinese violence occurred all over Southeast Asia. In Malaya, racial warfare between Malays and Chinese reached such a pitch of violence in the northwestern part of the country that the Malaysian Government had to mobilize the army and civil defense groups along with the police; significantly, the outbreaks of anti-Chinese violence were apparently triggered by the ever-present Chinese secret societies.[19] Across the sea, the wild Dayaks of Borneo went on an anti-Chinese rampage in the area of Pontianak in the fall of 1967, and over thirty thousand Chinese refugees streamed into the cities; in this case, the ostensible provocation for this outburst was the presence of a handful of Chinese Communist guerillas operating along the border between Sarawak and Indonesian Borneo.[20] Again, in the summer of 1967, anti-Chinese riots swept Rangoon for several days, straining the relations between neutralist Premier Ne Win of Burma and Peking, almost to the breaking point.[21] Even anti-American Prince Norodom Sihanouk cracked down on Cambodia's four hundred thousand Chinese about the same time, just as they were about to fall under the spell of Peking's cultural revolution. Threatening Peking with a virtual severance of diplomatic relations, he arrested key men in the pro-Chinese plot, fired two cabinet ministers, banned all privately owned newspapers as well as the Khmer-Chinese Friendship Association, re-established Cambodian control over all Chinese schools, and forbade any kind of Maoist teaching to Chinese students.[22]

All this took place in the space of one year. This underlying sentiment of hostility toward the Chinese makes it highly unlikely that ideological exports from Red China can gain much acceptance among the native Southeast Asians. In fact, more than once, the basic incompatibility between the physical presence of millions of hardworking and aloof Chinese and the spread of Mao Tse-tung's gospel has tripped local Communist parties into disaster—such a one as befell the Communist party of Indonesia in 1965.

America's armed presence in Southeast Asia benefits from this underlying reality and finds discreet support among many local leaders who are vocal in denouncing American imperialism in public. This is all the more important in that Chinese communism is animated by an imperialistic drive all its own and on different levels—a specifically *Chinese,* ethnic imperialism which aims at the extension of China proper into Southeast Asia, the Himalayan mountain ranges and the Soviet Far East. But beyond it, Chinese communism is endowed with a global vision; in this vision, the new version of communism, as reshaped by Mao Tse-tung and as expressed by his Defense Minister Lin Piao in September 1965 (shortly after the buildup of a huge American army in Vietnam started in earnest), claims that "revolutionary power" resides in the worldwide countryside and not in the worldwide cities; peasants rather than urban and industrial proletariats are destined to be the vanguard of the worldwide revolution.[23] In this new political scheme of things, North America and Western Europe (with the potential addition of Japan and Soviet Russia) are the world's cities, whereas Asia, Africa, and Latin America are the world's "countryside." Revolutionary wars throughout the underdeveloped lands of Asia, Africa, and Latin America would become part of a global strategy aimed at encircling the hated "cities," primarily the geographical areas of the despised civilization of the West. Active revolutionary struggle is no longer the prerogative of the industrial proletariats working through crippling strikes and urban revolts such as Petrograd's October Revolution, but of armed guerillas in the wild countryside—in jungles, rain forests, swamps, inaccessible mountains and deserts. Drawing on the historical instance of their conquest of the Chinese mainland, Mao Tse-tung's followers are completely dedicated to this new form of revolutionary warfare which is, indeed, highly applicable to large areas of the world's "countryside."

This global vision and worldwide revolutionary action is bolstered by a new technological sophistication that will, in time, make Red China into a highly dangerous antagonist—to the extent that the devastation of the Cultural Revolution is repaired and that the centrifugal tendencies released during its virtual civil war are brought under control. Ever since Red China exploded its first nuclear device in October 1964, it has presented the rest of Asia with a new and unforeseen menace—and no one more so than Soviet Russia whose five-thousand-mile border with the renovated Celestial Empire bristles with mutual hostility. Peking has laid claims to a large slice of eastern Siberia on the grounds that it was formerly part of the Chinese Empire; their claims to suzerainty over a large part of the Southeast Asian breadbasket rest on more shaky historical, but far stronger economic, grounds. Having assumed the task of containment all by itself, and by establishing its *de facto* empire in Southeast Asia, Washington is gradually setting up a giant nutcracker with Soviet Siberia in the north as the other limb. Between them, and in tacit alliance, they may hope to contain Red China's vigorous imperialism.

The American "protectorate" over Japan is, by far, the most important element in the United States' imperial position in the Far East and a vital element of the nutcracker's northern limb. Having, through force of arms, stripped Japan of all its imperial possessions and reduced it to a small demilitarized archipelago off the coast of Asia, having inherited military control of South Korea (the "loaded pistol" pointed straight at the heart of Japan), maintaining large military bases in Japan proper and controlling the seas around it and the air above it, Washington is strategically in full control of this nation of a hundred million industrious souls. Retention of Okinawa as its main military bastion in the Far East (regardless of the wishes of the Japanese-speaking Okinawans themselves) is an additional element in Washington's immense leverage which compels Tokyo to follow constantly a "low posture," pro-American line in its foreign policy. In February 1967, it was announced that Japan would consult regularly with Washington on all matters likely to come before the United Nations General Assembly—implying an American mortgage on the course of Japan's foreign policy.[24]

The United States' imperial control over Japan is multidimensional, but a great deal of it is due to the economic leverage provided by Japan's inherent poverty in natural resources—depending, as it does, on imports for 96 percent of its iron ore, 99 percent of its petroleum, 75 percent of its zinc, 85 percent of its copper, and so on. Japan's sources of raw materials around the Pacific, whether in its former "Greater East Asia Co-Prosperity Sphere" or in the Western Hemisphere, are now all included in the United States' Pacific empire; Japanese access to these sources of raw materials is entirely dependent on American goodwill and its naval control of the world's largest ocean. Another important element of this leverage is the enormous market America provides for Japan's vital exports and the equally enormous source it provides for its vital imports. Roughly one third of Japan's total foreign trade is conducted with the United States, while another third is conducted with countries included in the United States' *de facto* empire: Japan has become an economic, as well as strategic, captive of America. Its last position of defense against this economic "satellization" is slowly crumbling—its stringent capital-investment law that limits foreign ownership to 15 percent of existing Japanese firms and 50 percent of new ventures, is being eroded, under American pressure; a new program of "capital liberalization" will eventually open the land of the Rising Sun to a tidal wave of American investments such as is now engulfing Canada and Western Europe.

Except for Western Europe, other commercial markets outside America's imperial orbit are largely negligible. Red China has proved disappointing in the extreme—partly because of the American-dictated embargo on the export of strategic goods to mainland China; in the late 1950's, Japanese trade experts had figured that Sino-Japanese trade could have jumped immediately from the meager yearly total of 100–150 million dollars to four or five times that amount; [25] but the embargo has been maintained throughout the 1960's and, a decade later, trade between the two countries had not yet reached 500 million dollars a year.[26] Of course, the compensation for this loss of Chinese trade is the huge Pacific area market provided by America's military expenditures, starting with the Korean War in 1950, all the way to the Vietnam War in the late 1960's; no item has been more responsible for the staggering increase in Japan's industrial production than the enormous demands made by America's military empire in the Orient.

The only other important trade partner could be Soviet Russia, which, through lack of manpower in Siberia's vast emptiness, is hard put to develop its Far Eastern possessions. As their relations with Red China deteriorated in the 1960's, the Russians switched from hostility to friendliness in their relations with Japan. In the late 1960's, they have become eager for Japanese assistance in the development and exploitation of Siberia's virtually limitless reserves of oil, iron ore, lumber, coal and nonferrous metals; the Japanese were not slow in responding to these overtures, and agreements were signed with the Russians providing for Japanese assistance in laying down trans-Siberian pipelines, oil drilling, improving Soviet harbors (Nakhodka, Vanino, Vladivostok, Mago), providing lumbering machinery, developing the copper resources buried north of Lake Baikal, in the Udokan Mountains.[27] This economic assistance could well prove crucial to the Russians in their efforts to defend and retain eastern Siberia in the face of Red China's aggressive claims to the immense territory. In the long run, Washington might find it wise to encourage Japanese participation in the economic buildup of the Soviet Far East as a counterweight to the growing menace of Red China's imperialism. Whatever the Americans decide in the matter, is and will be decided in the light of Washington's own imperial interests in the Far East, and it is obvious that Tokyo dare not take any initiative in the matter without American approval.

The process of Japan's "Hawaiianization" is so relentless that the Land of the Rising Sun cannot really resist it; in compensation, Japan's own cultural contributions to Hawaiianization (Zen Buddhism, architecture, interior decorating, gardening style, eye-westernizing surgery) is by no means negligible and is likely to rise in the future. The continuous intermingling of cultural elements around America's *mare nostrum*—reminiscent of the Hellenization and Romanization of the eastern Mediterranean, two thousand years ago—depends a great deal on the economic and military strength of the United States' oriental empire, in which Japan is included as the most important and powerful element. In turn, this empire is not conceivable without lasting American control over Japan, which Washington dare not relax without facing the danger of a collapse of its entire position in the Far East.

This implies a lasting involvement of the United States in the Orient, one from which there will be no pulling back for generations. Americans are involved, and irretrievably so, in South

Korea as well as Taiwan, in the Philippines where their huge naval base at Subic Bay and the equally large air base at Clark Field are vital components of their military power in that part of the world, in Thailand were they have been busy developing an enormous logistical structure since the mid-1960's, in Indonesia which they are discreetly committed to salvage from economic and political disintegration. If the Hukbong Magpapalaya sa Bayan (Tagalog for People's Liberation Army) rises from its ashes to start guerilla warfare in the Philippines and threatens the stability of the Manilla regime, Washington is bound to intervene. If the North Koreans attempt to infiltrate South Korea and start guerilla warfare south of the thirty-eighth parallel, the United States' fifty-thousand-man garrison will inevitably be drawn into the conflict. A direct Red Chinese threat to Formosa would inevitably suck the Americans into a military confrontation with Peking. There is no escape from pyramiding commitments, commitments which go far beyond external aggressions and include, not merely "indirect" aggressions but the slightest threat to the precarious political stability of all Asian regimes under America's virtual protectorate.

This is not to say that American garrisons cannot be reduced, bases closed, and American-occupied territories handed back to local authorities. Swift technological progress will soon allow entire American armies to be flown to any spot in the world in a matter of hours; careful planning beforehand will have made sure that they can arrive in bathing trunks and find on the given spot all the stores and equipment required to outfit them immediately. Just the same, indirect political control will become far more efficient; American proconsuls discharging their imperial missions will still be known as ambassadors, but they will effectively pull all the important political strings with the assistance of computerized information and efficient CIA task forces. To a limited extent, it is already happening. In other words, under familiar labels and within the framework of traditional forms, a new imperial infrastructure is being built, responsive to Washington's will and no one else's. Local political leaders will seem to emerge out of a natural, "democratic" process of local political selection; in fact, they will be created out of whole cloth by imaginative officials in Washington; and soon, in the increasingly Hawaiianized atmosphere of the Asian shores of the Pacific, permeated with all the refinements of Madison Avenue publicity (Pacific style), it will be possible to metamorphose docile underlings into Southeast Asian generals, prime ministers, and presidents, ready and willing to do the bidding of their transpacific masters.

☆ X ☆

Latins, Guerillas, and Anarchists

Except for Western Europe, no area in the world is quite as important to the security and welfare of the United States as Latin America—that immense southward extension of its own land which stretches all the way down to the antarctic. It is its only true continental border, since Canada can be considered a sister state, and a captive one at that. Mexico, Central America, and the Caribbean, on the other hand, are profoundly alien lands on the very doorstep of the United States; this double feature of profound alienness, yet immediate proximity, creates a very specific context for their political relations. Less proximate, but just as important, South America represents the normal and natural outlet for the vast surplus of energy of the North Americans, a natural area of expansion for United States' interests, the first area in the world where *imperialismo yanqui* became a byword before, translated into numerous languages, it became fashionable elsewhere.

Balkanized remnants of the great Spanish and Portuguese empires, none of the states of Latin America appear to have yet found a social and political equilibrium; they have not yet been able to condense into coherent political units, that is, well-defined, homogeneous nations. It is not, as in Asia, the problem of adapting old and alien civilizations to the Western-oriented modern age, of tearing out immeasurably old roots and destroying venerable symbols. Latin America part and parcel of Western Civilization, even if it is of the Iberian-Catholic variety whose peculiar form of Roman Catholicism has shielded it from both Reformation and Enlightenment; of its old Indian civilizations, nothing is left but a few atavistic customs still prevailing among some of the more remote and scattered of the Indian populations.

This explains why Latin America does not quite know what it is or what it should be; Latin Americans have not yet found themselves. When they shook off Spanish and Portuguese rule, they also shook off centuries of intellectual and cultural stagnation. Unable and unwilling to tie themselves culturally to Britain, although eager for Britain's political protectorate, they turned to France, a sister Latin nation. But there was no real cross-fertilization between them; this cultural marriage remained sterile and no offspring was born. With the advent of industrialization and speedy communications, of social revolutions which overthrew many Francophile oligarchies, of the slow rise of mass-consumption societies that are irresistibly drawn to the North American model, divorce between the Latin sisters was well on its way. Once again, Latin America is in a quandary. Just as it could not tie itself culturally to Britain in the last century although eager for its political and economic support, it has no conscious desire to be drawn culturally to the United States, even though condemned to a one-sided imitation of its alien way of life. As the Brazilian Afranio Peixoto put it in the 1920's: "We have abandoned the Old World, and we have not yet found the New." [1] Latin Americans can no longer balance, as they could in the nineteenth century, Britain's politico-economic alliance against French culture's irresistible seduction. In the second half of the twentieth century, Latin America has become, against its own will, a cultural as well as a political and economic captive of the United States.

In fact, the only recognizable element of Latin America's personality lies in its desperate determination to be *different* from the United States—hence the agonizing nature of its utter dependence on its support and assistance, the occasional violence of its anti-American reactions, and the deep-seated feeling of impotent frustration which springs from its wounded pride and feeling of lost dignity. Latin Americans suffer mostly from an acute crisis of identity which twists their souls—drawn by the sheer force of political gravity into the orbit of North America, yet infuriated by this historical and geographical compulsion. This is nowhere more apparent than in the establishments of higher learning south of the Rio Grande; it is essentially in the universities that the major centers of anti-United States feelings are located. Rather than the labor unions and the urban proletariats, it is the intellectual elites that give vocal expression to the widespread antagonism toward the northern giant. In Latin America, where the prestige of the academic *licenciado,* professor or doctor, is much higher than in the United States, whatever public opinion there is is largely shaped by the intellectual elite. Yet, this leadership itself is faltering to the extent that the quality of higher learning in Latin America is rather poor and that the brain drain debilitates it further. An already insufficient investment in education is compounded by a poor national return on whatever investment there is, since the best students often choose to emigrate to the United States or to Europe. It is estimated that at least half of the best students in medicine and engineering leave Latin America each year; this professional emasculation deprives most Latin American nations of essential leadership and stabilizing elements.

In turn, the poor quality of college graduates is detrimental to business and compels many business firms to import at great cost foreign technicians since they cannot find them on the spot. Furthermore, lack of engineers and economists results in the frequent inability of Latin American countries to present worthwhile projects to the international authorities that are able and willing to finance them—for instance, the Alliance for Progress according to which the United States is pledged to provide annually a billion dollars' worth of public funds. Frequent rebellions against the demands and requirements of the International Monetary Fund make it quite clear that Latin American nations do not take kindly to foreign dictation, even of a strictly technical, non-political nature.

In most cases where international authorities insist on steps being taken to curb bank credit, cut down government expenses, fight inflation, and liberalize foreign trade, they have to face the danger of nationalistic backlashes. The mass resignation in April 1966 of the eight members of the Alliance for Progress' panel of economic experts in protest against United States "domination" suggests that any form of assistance to Latin America can be expected to run into this kind of trouble.[2]

The crux of the matter, of course, is that it is impossible to provide meaningful international assistance to developing countries without some curtailment of their sovereignty. It is even more impossible to conceive the possibility of relationships on a basis of pseudo equality between such a giant as the United States and miniature states such as Panama, where the Canal Zone alone contributes a hundred million dollars annually to the national economy, more than the total budget of the state; where one single commodity such as oil provides 90 percent of the foreign earnings and almost a third of the national output while employing less than 3 percent of the labor force, as in Venezuela; or where another commodity, coffee, produces 70 percent of foreign earnings, as in Colombia; or again, where Ecuador's economy reels when Japan shifts most of its purchases of bananas (Ecuador's major export) to Taiwan.[3] In its present state of balkanization, Latin America can have neither political nor economic weight. Nor can the endemic political and social instability of its member nations create the climate of confidence and feeling of security required for rapid economic development.

Latin America's quenchless thirst for foreign capital boosted its medium and long-term external public debt from a little over four billion dollars in 1956 to over eleven billion in 1966.[4] In these ten years, the total of all foreign development loans and grants came to be completely absorbed by debt repayments, implying that Latin America's future is mortgaged to the hilt. Export earnings depend to a great extent on the prices of raw materials, many of which are kept low because the United States subsidizes its own producers of sugar, cotton, and wheat who compete directly with Latin American producers. These subsidies are conditioned by the United States' internal political situation, regardless of their heavy impact on scores of Latin American nations who then have to beg for direct grants of loans from Washington—increasing the humiliating nature of their one-sided dependence on the United States.

Not only size and economic weakness limit the effectiveness with which Latin American nations can hope to stand up to the giant of the north; the psychology and social structure of their people puts them at an enormous disadvantage. By and large, Latin Americans are far more individualistic than North Americans (which does not imply that they are more individualized). They lack a strong social consciousness but have a far greater feeling for family solidarity and loyalty. Families in Latin America hold together inwardly as nowhere else in Western countries; inevitably, this strong sense of clannishness inhibits social consciousness, for which it is a substitute. Lack of social cooperation thwarts the development of homogeneous nations and therefore decreases their ability to deal with such a colossus as the United States from a position of *national* strength.

However, there is a silver lining to the cloud: strong individualism and lack of social consciousness avoids the pitfall of tense race relations such as exist in the United States. This is vital in Latin America whose diverse populations result from the blending together of immigrants of European and African origins, often implanted in the midst of, or side by side with, massive Indian populations, resulting in an infinite variety of color blends ranging from pure white, pitch black, and copper-colored to a wide assortment of mulattos and mestizos. If consciousness is focused on the individual and the clannish family rather than society as a whole, relations between races are the exclusive prerogative of the individual and never become a *social,* and therefore racial, problem as such. Racial consciousness (in the United States and wherever it exists) derives from a cohesive society's collective psychology and strong sense of social solidarity which establishes group-distances between well-defined racial clusters.

With all that, many Latin American nations whose populations are largely colored, are still dominated by small groups of white elites. The potential for revolutionary trouble is considerable among the large unassimilated Indian populations of the Andes who are ruled by these white oligarchies and have not yet been brought into the twentieth century, either socially or economically. These as yet unawakened Indian masses who, with their separate languages and customs, live like foreigners in their own countries, are likely to wake up eventually and exert a revolutionary form of pressure against their white rulers. This additional weakness, which makes it easier for the United States to exercise a form of mild protectorate over them, makes it also probable that these countries will one day present the United States with a revolutionary threat of the first magnitude.

As in many other parts of the world, the United States' overwhelming economic power makes itself felt throughout Latin America, especially in the tropical belt. While the United States' total private investments in the area, at roughly eleven billion dollars, is relatively small compared with its much larger stake in Canada, for instance, it is even more significant *politically* in that Latin America is much poorer than Canada, and is split up into over two dozen separate sovereign states; and in many instances, North American economic power can be brought to bear more effectively on the political scene in banana republics than in large and relatively powerful countries such as Canada—or Argentina and Brazil. Latin America's only defense against such extraterritorial power has been, and remains, the expropriation and nationalization of foreign business concerns. This has been tried, with greater or lesser degrees of ultimate success, in a half a dozen lands south of the Rio Grande. The United States' reaction has often been violent, when decent financial compensation was not forthcoming, and more than one Latin American country has felt the full power of its armed intervention. But overall, the United States' economic power is such, and Latin

America's need for its assistance is so great, that the entire Western Hemisphere can be looked upon as an economic appendage of the United States.

This was not always so. Before the First World War, Britain and Continental Europe had a very large stake in the area; but two World Wars shattered this economic predominance and delivered the main economic sinews of Latin America to its North American neighbor. Having become the world's greatest creditors, the North Americans were in a position to buy out many European concerns and start many more on their own; and in some areas, such as Central America, this process had already been under way before World War I; under the Taft Administration, American banks began replacing their European counterparts, mostly in order to avoid European armed intervention in the Western Hemisphere and substitute, when need be, American marines.[5]

This economic domination was exercised to greatest effect in the Caribbean, Central America, and the northern part of South America, a region where the exploits of the Standard Fruit and Steamship Company, the United Fruit Company (*La Frutera*), and scores of North American-owned utility (*Empressa Eléctrica*) and transportation companies became legendary. Many of these banana empires dominated their Caribbean republics politically, raising the same specter of *el peligro yanqui* (Yankee peril) that the W. R. Grace Company (*Casa Grace*) raised down South America's west coast. But whereas, in former times, economic interests could pressure Washington into "sending the marines" whenever the local situation was slipping out of *yanqui* control, the situation was gradually reversed after World War II. In the present post-capitalist era in which private corporations, however large, have fallen to a great extent under the American Government's control and regulations, and in which *el peligro yanqui* has assumed the new look of a protective military and strategic imperialism, American corporations and private banana empires are more likely to be Washington's imperial tools than vice versa.

If, on March 23, 1953, the United States Government officially assumed the defense of American private interests in Guatemala, it was no longer out of genuine concern for the financial stakes of the United Fruit Company; on the contrary, the misfortunes of *La Frutera* were only the convenient excuse for the overthrow of the left-wing Guatemalan regime of Colonel Jacobo Arbenz Guzmán by the CIA-backed legionaries of Castillo Armas. Many, in Latin America and elsewhere, saw in this action a continuation of the traditional dollar diplomacy, but it was no longer anything of the kind: it was an entirely new form of protective, strategic *yanqui imperialismo,* triggered by the threat of Communist penetration in the Western Hemisphere. Whenever "Marxist" revolution and expropriation of private concerns seems acceptable to Washington for specific geopolitical and strategic reasons, it not only tolerates them, but actively encourages and supports them—as in Bolivia in the 1950's, for instance, where the revolutionary regime favored the United States' political and financial support rather than Soviet Russia's.

The United States' economic hegemony in Latin America is gradually becoming a function of its geopolitical interests in the Western Hemisphere instead of being based on a cluster of private, feudal banana empires, as in former days. To a far greater degree than elsewhere, it meshes with Washington's economic assistance schemes and government agencies—such schemes as the Alliance for Progress and such agencies as the Inter-American Development Bank. Even the 1957 Punta del Este declaration of purpose on the creation of an economic integration of the Americas and a Latin American common market, bears all the earmarks of a *political* move designed to assist multinational projects and ease the hitherto rugged path of North American economic penetration south of the Rio Grande—rugged because of the economic backwardness of the region, the limited local markets, the political instability, and perennial threat of expropriation. American economic penetration in Western Europe and Canada is due to the initiative of private corporations in search of greater financial profitability; but in Latin America, it is not so much the lure of business profit as strategic requirements that prompt Washington to attempt to raise the standard of living south of the Rio Grande, in order to ward off an extension of Communist influence in the Western Hemisphere's underbelly.

In imitation of the United States, the presidential rather than the parliamentary form of government was adopted throughout Latin America. As in the United States, what matters politically is the man who rules rather than the assembly which is supposed to control and check—but, unlike its northern counterpart, rarely does either in Latin America. Being primarily individualists with only a rudimentary social consciousness, Latin Americans have no gift for local government: they are not truly *citizens* but individual nationalists who have great verbal but no factual respect for law and legality. Inevitably, there are few legal or social checks on the potential tyranny of the executive power which, ultimately, tends to be dictatorial. By and large, Latin American masses, like masses everywhere, favor personal rule, even tyranny or demagogic dictatorship "à la Perón." It is usually the wealthy oligarchies that resist personal rule, unless it is their tool, in which case (increasingly rare nowadays) the ruler is likely to be a mere reactionary puppet. Arbitrary power is the result, backed by constitutional provisos enabling the chief executive to decree states of emergency and suspend constitutional rights whenever he feels so inclined. But perhaps the major difference between the North American and the Latin American political temper in practice is that, whereas the road to political power in the United States usually lies through financial success, the easiest road to financial success in Latin America lies even more frequently through political power. Unless he is already endowed with considerable private means, the Latin American official who does not take advantage of his position to feather his nest is a rare bird indeed.

Furthermore, Latin American countries are largely ruled through *personal* contacts, opening wide all doors to graft, nepotism, and inefficiency. There is no real permanent bureaucracy, no processing of state matters through an impersonal, nonpolitical machinery. The chief executive, rarely encumbered with a troublesome congress or legislature, has all the spoils of political victory at his disposal, dispenses all the choicest plums of his large patronage to his political clients. Being unfettered by a permanent body of officials and civil servants endowed with statutory protection, all his appointments are perforce "political"; everything is *politized*. The conquest of power, by legitimate or illegitimate means, changes over completely the administrative apparatus of the land according to the most venerable spoils system.

Mexico's one-party system is a unique and remarkable exception to the rule. An outgrowth of one of the few authentic social revolutions in the Western Hemisphere, Mexico's Partido Nacional Revolucionario has ruled the country continuously since the revolution, which overthrew Porfirio Díaz, came to an end. Adapting itself to the changing requirements of the times, undergoing countless metamorphoses, it is a self-perpetuating Establishment for the training and disciplining of the country's technicians, economists, and officials, and in full if indirect control of the lives and destinies of most businessmen, physicians, lawyers, artists, bankers, and engineers—of Mexico's professional elite, in fact. The PRI can swing right (as under Miguel Alemán) or left (as under Lázaro Cárdenas) with easy flexibility. Nothing of any importance in any walk of life can happen without the approval and cooperation of the PRI. Yet, it tolerates small opposition parties, fully respects freedom of opinion, skillfully weaves its way between the opposite dangers of anarchy and dictatorship. The PRI nominee for President (who is invariably the President-elect) is chosen by a mysterious process behind the scenes, very much like the head of Britain's Conservative Party in the old days.

The remarkable feature of the system is that, although authoritarian, it never degenerates into a personal dictatorship; its direction is collective, recruited largely by co-optation. Even more remarkable is the total lack of interference of the military in the political life of the country. And although left-wing sentiment is highly vocal, communism as such has little appeal since the country is economically prosperous and socially progressive. This progressivism, again, is rare in Latin America; from the end of the Second World War to the late 1960's, the rate of illiteracy has been cut from 52 percent to 28 percent, the result of a long-term campaign launched in 1944 by President Manuel Avila Camacho, considerably accelerated in the 1960's by Presidents Adolfo Lopez Mateos and Gustavo Díaz Ordaz. More remarkable still, the Mexican Government spends four times as much on education as it does on national defense—an order of priorities unheard of in the rest of Latin America.

The likely reason for this striking state of affairs, which is unique in Latin America, is that the PRI is a political front for a far more powerful, but secret, organization—Freemasonry. In Protestant countries, Freemasonry usually establishes itself as a welfare society on the pattern of the Rotary Club. Not so in Roman Catholic countries, where it tends, because of the Church's intense hostility, to become a counter-Church of its own, preserving a great deal of secrecy and wielding a political power out of all proportion to its limited membership. In the case of Mexico, Freemasonry has been firmly entrenched and influential for over a century, and largely ruled the country under the dictatorship of Porfirio Díaz, when the Roman Catholic Church was in disfavor.

An American diplomat who was appointed to the American Embassy in Mexico City at the time, stated that "Mexican Freemasonry . . . was an astonishing institution, having little resemblance to Masonry as it is practiced in the United States. To many military and governmental jobs Masonic membership was a prerequisite. Soon after my arrival I was approached by a Jewish Mason who invited me to become a member of the thirty-third degree. . . . He assured me that without a Masonic degree it would be difficult for an American to conduct even official business in Mexico." [6] Since then, the Mexican Revolution has come and gone, with its savage persecution of the Catholic Church, ultimately strengthening the influence of Masonry in the country. Today, most high party officials are known to be Masons and their Masonic Lodges constitute a highly secret network that stands off the Catholic Church's precarious influence.[7] It seems clear, therefore, that Freemasonry is the *connective tissue* holding the PRI together, very much as, but to a far more effective degree, it controlled and held together the apparently unstable politics of France during the seventy years of its Third Republic. This connective tissue has been fought over for a long time by the main antagonists within world Masonry—the atheistic, French-inspired Grand Orient, and the milder theistic Scottish Rites of Anglo-American persuasion—with definite signs that the Anglo-American variety is slowly winning out, perhaps even providing, now or in the future, an ideal channel of communication through which the United States might presumably make its influence discreetly felt.

Mexico's remarkable stability, while it lasts, is a boon to the United States since it is its closest neighbor, the only Latin American country with which it shares a continental border—a geographical fate which inspired dictator Porfirio Díaz to exclaim despondently: "Poor country, so far from God and so close to the United States!" Somehow or other, its stability has not been an example to the rest of Latin America which is cursed with endemic instability, in addition to its fragmentation into multitudes of small, medium, and large states, lack of national cohesion, poverty, and the highest rate of population increase in the world. Latin American psychology, largely inherited from Spain (except in Brazil), but profoundly influenced at times by various strains of Indian temper, has no built-in balance between violent passion and complete indifference or outright apathy. Latin Americans swing rapidly from one to another, making political stability difficult to achieve for any length of time; they are too impulsive for normal democratic processes and have no gift for parliamentary debate, making it appear that political stability is incompatible with political freedom in the North American sense of the word.

This incompatibility between stability and liberty has generated Latin America's contribution to the roster of political systems in the nineteenth century: military dictatorship. Napoleon once said that a revolution is an idea in command of bayonets. Abstract ideas or political ideologies have usually been absent in Latin America—until quite recently. But there, as elsewhere, bayonets are usually essential to the conquest of power, since it is primarily this conquest that is aimed at, rather than the concrete application of specific ideologies. Whenever there is a complete lack of respect for the law and a complete absence of powerful and autonomous social organisms in their own right, military power becomes the main arbiter of politics. This has usually been the case in Latin America since its independence: the government may rule without, but never *against,* the army.

For long a specific political institution of Latin America, military dictatorship has lately become a worldwide phenomenon which sheds additional light on its specifically Latin American aspect. And as in the Western Hemisphere, it generally results from the collapse or orderly liquidation of great multinational empires, along with their time-hallowed institutions and venerable symbolism, usually followed by the balkanization of their former territories—which is the case in most of the developing world, in Asia and Africa. Being rarely engaged in waging external warfare against neighboring states, the national military establishments have plenty of scope for making their political influence felt inside the country. This is especially true of Latin America where no formal war between two nations has taken place since the disastrous conflict between Bolivia and Paraguay, in the 1930's, over the possession of northern Chaco.

Nevertheless, a new situation developed with alarming speed after World War II, and especially after the outbreak of the war in Korea. Frightened by the progress of international communism all over the world, the United States decided to assist friendly governments everywhere with vast quantities of weaponry. Quite naturally, within the framework of this policy, Latin American states were not the last to benefit from this new largesse: from an annual rate of two hundred thousand dollars in 1952, the United States' military assistance jumped to eleven million the following year, thirty-four million in 1954, to well over a hundred million dollars ten years later.[8] At the same time, the United States looks upon other (European) suppliers of weaponry to Latin America with a jaundiced eye. In 1967, for instance, Washington vetoed the sale of six Canberra bombers by the British to Peru, a veto technically justified by the 1950 agreement according to which no military hardware manufactured with American financial assistance could be sold without Washington's permission. Washington's all-out struggle to keep the Latin Americans from buying French Mirages by threatening to cut off economic and technical aid to the guilty states, is another case in point.[9]

The political implication of Washington's military assistance is, of course, that American supplies and weapons, along with military training, are invariably used whenever the military overthrow a civilian government. For instance, a hue and cry was raised when a U. S. Sherman tank crashed through the gates of Pizarro Palace in Lima to overthrow the constitutional regime of President Manuel Prado y Ugarteche; no less significant was the fact that Colonel Gonzalo Briceno, who led the attack, was trained at the U. S. Ranger School at Fort Benning, Georgia.[10] This isolated incident symbolizes the increasing meshing of the Latin American military with their North American counterpart. New bonds of friendship between Latin American military leaders themselves have been established thanks to the numerous training programs sponsored by the United States, to conferences for inter-American defense in Panama and elsewhere, along with extensive exchange of officers between one Latin American country and another, as well as joint investigations or tight collaboration in military intelligence on Communist activities. The American-run Escuela de las Américas in Panama is at once the headquarters and training center of the American Special Forces and their Latin counterparts who specialize in jungle warfare and counterinsurgency. Both North and South Americans are linked by close ties of friendship and solidarity, strengthened in anti-guerilla combat, increasing further the mutual interpenetration of all their armed establishments. The most promising Latin American students are drawn to the United States where, provided by Uncle Sam with scholarships, they move on to higher military studies in unconventional warfare at Fort Benning or Fort Bragg, North Carolina. From there, they are sent back to their respective countries as missionaries of the "American way of life," military-style.

No great imagination is required to understand that, the military buildup in Latin America taking place as it does under the exclusive auspices of the Pentagon, there is or may be a tacit understanding between the military forces of these countries and the United States' own defense establishment which bypasses, in effect, the *political* control of their respective governments. As early as 1946, under Pentagon pressure and in spite of the State Department's objections, President Truman decided "to standardize military organization, training methods, and equipment throughout the hemisphere with the evident hope of ultimately producing an inter-American army under United States' generalship." [11] From then on, the Pentagon began to develop its own foreign policy in dealing with Latin American military establishments, hardly taking the State Department into consideration. The Pentagon-sponsored "Project Camelot," already referred to in connection with Canada, raised a furor throughout the hemisphere in 1965 with its sociological study on "the potential for internal war" in Latin America, and even upset the United States embassies concerned when it was revealed that it had not been cleared by the State Department.[12] The increasingly important role played by the Pentagon in Washington's policy-making (for instance, the decision to send marines into Santo Domingo in 1965) raises the spectre of more or less permanent military control in most of Latin America under the Pentagon's auspices—the main justification being, as usual, the struggle against Communist subversion.

It is not necessarily that the Latin American military enjoy the exercise of direct political authority. On the contrary, there is plenty of evidence that present-day military leaders, unlike their forebears, would much rather work through civilian politicians, whenever they can be found with the required qualifications, and remain discreetly in the background, exerting their influence indirectly. There is just as much evidence that this new breed of military, perhaps under North American influence, displays a far greater concern for social reform and public responsibility than the politicians. At any rate, the rapidly growing revolutionary threat to many Latin American nations may no longer leave them much choice.

A closer look at the subcontinent's revolutionary past may help us see the shape of things to come. Latin America's first fundamental social revolution started in Mexico, when international communism was not even on the map. And although it lasted well into the 1930's, it remained aloof from other revolutions, especially from Communist influence. Uncontaminated by foreign intrusion, it merely stepped on the toes of foreign investors and represented no real threat to the security of the United States, even though it took place right over its border, and provoked the intervention of American armed forces. Mexico made no attempt to export its revolution to other Latin American countries and confined its revolutionary activities strictly to its own society. The second social revolution took place in Argentina during the Second World War when dictator Juan Domingo Perón, partly out of anti-American spite, displayed feelings of kinship with Fascists and Nazis, although carrying out a left-wing prolabor revolution in his own country. It was largely an urban, proletarian movement; in its efforts to mobilize Latin American political resources and feelings against the United States, it attempted mainly to organize labor unions throughout the hemisphere; and it was mostly ineffective. Perón's threat could have been made good if the Germans had won the war or at least reached a stalemate; their utter defeat deprived him of his international leverage and weakened his economic base. Furthermore, geographical distance alone (Buenos Aires is closer to Madrid than to New York) would have made it difficult for Argentina to become a threat to the security of the United States. Perón's revolutionary influence soon came to an abrupt end. But for the first time since Bolívar, an attempt had been made to build a hemisphere-wide movement against the hegemony of the United States; it was not to be the last.

The third revolution, the Cuban one, is far more significant and pregnant with far greater potential for trouble. This one represents a direct threat and a challenge, not only to the security of the United States whose southern coastline lies barely ninety miles from Cuban shores, but to the social structure of the whole of Latin America. Its peasant-based type of revolutionary action focuses on outright guerilla warfare throughout the hemisphere. As in China, and unlike Soviet Russia, the social landscape of Latin America makes for a far more fertile soil for Castroites than it ever did for *Perónismo*—just as China's social and cultural landscape favored Maoism at the expense of the more orthodox form of communism imported from Moscow. Perón operated out of a highly sophisticated nation with the highest overall standard of living in Latin America and a hardly disguised contempt for other, poorer and more backward Latins. His urban revolutionary appeal was slight in those areas with greatest revolutionary potential: the Indian-populated Andes, northeast Brazil, Central America, Guyana and the Caribbean— those very areas that were immediately canvassed by Castroites with their bearded bohemianism and guerilla warfare apparatus, so different from Perón's well-tailored, almost elegant, brand of social reform.

A great deal of ink has been spilt over the nature and degree of Fidel Castro's involvement with communism. The involvement is real but does not and never did imply any kind of subordination to Moscow or Peking. It is a brand-new form of Communist action, adapted to the Latin temper, a tropical, wordy, exhuberant, romantic communism, completely *sui generis*. North Americans misunderstood the real nature of the problem and a pointless controversy raged on for years as to the true character of that baffling revolution. It should be recalled from the start that, almost alone among all Latin American nations, Cuba was an economic colony of the United States, in the full sense of the word. In fact, it was touch and go whether, after the Spanish-American War, the island would be incorporated into the United States along with Puerto Rico or set on the course of political independence. After a number of American military interventions, Cuba merely sank to the position of a powerless economic appendage; United States investments, to the tune of roughly two billion dollars, came to dominate all its strategic industries and services—telephone, electricity, railroads, raw sugar, cattle ranches, oil, and major tourist facilities. Several attempts at revolution came to nothing thanks to the ominous presence or threat of United States marines.

Fidel Castro's successful revolt, overthrowing the gory dictatorship of Fulgencio Batista, was followed by a period of transition. After this short breathing spell, he promptly expropriated all the vast American holdings and launched the most profound social revolution ever attempted in Latin America. The United States had reluctantly accepted Mexico's expropriation of American property decades before, without raising the spectre of communism; not so this time. It was Castro's Agrarian Reform Law that made North Americans prick up their ears and wonder whether Castro was not, after all, a dyed-in-the-wool Communist [13]—regardless of the fact that, at that time, Cuba's bona fide Communist party (Partido Socialista Popular) had next to no influence on the Revolutionary Government.[14]

From then on, one misreading of the true situation after another brought matters to a head—from the disastrous Bay of Pigs expedition in 1961 to the fateful nuclear confrontation with Soviet Russia in 1962. The truth of the matter is that Fidel Castro's advisers had always inclined toward Marxist socialism as a vague intellectual framework, but not toward a formal allegiance to a Communist party, mostly because their revolutionary temper went far beyond the rather timid and compromising policies of the Cuban Communists, or of most Latin Communists for that matter. Thus, the real situation was far worse than the most rabid anti-Communists in North America could have imagined who, in their rather naïve outlook, always thought of communism as the worst political and social menace one could conceive.

The real situation was that Cuba had fallen into the hands of genuine, uncompromising revolutionaries, dedicated men who were determined to overthrow the entire social order and worked at it with fanatical zeal. Growing American hostility and the threat of actual American military intervention on the old pattern, added to the economic chaos introduced by the complete socialization of Cuba's economy, brought about Castro's uneasy military and economic alliance with Soviet Russia. Without Russia's economic assistance, the whole Cuban revolution would have come to a dismal end; as for the military alliance, it provided Cuba with a useful leverage to offset the United States' crushing superiority—which leverage was brutally snatched from Castro's hands when Moscow, intimidated by Washington's determination, withdrew its missiles in the fall of 1962.

From then on, although desperately in need of Russia's economic assistance, Castro decided to go his own revolutionary way, regardless of the Communist toes on which he was treading. One would have thought that after Russia's bitter retreat in the fall of 1962, Castro would have turned to Peking for support; but he did nothing of the kind. He proceeded to do what Mao Tse-tung had done a generation earlier; to create his own brand of revolutionary communism, adapted to the time and place where he intended to exert his influence—that is, the whole of Latin America in the 1960's and, possibly, beyond. Although Nikita Khrushchev told President Kennedy at the Vienna meeting in 1961 that he did not consider Castro a Communist, Castro now insisted more than ever on keeping the label, and soon made plain that he was in the process of developing his own trademark without any advice from the foreign old-timers.

At the Afro-Asian-Latin American Solidarity Conference held in Havana in January 1966, Fidel Castro lashed out at Red China for halving both their exports of rice to, and purchases of sugar from, Cuba; the Chinese replied with equal sharpness, threatening an open break between the two countries.[15] A year later, when Russian Premier Aleksei Kosygin went to Cuba, after the Glassboro meeting with President Lyndon Johnson, to complain about Castro's peculiar brand of revolutionary warfare, Cuba's dictator told him in plain words to mind his own business —a bitter pill for the head of the biggest Communist Power, which was then pumping over a million dollars' worth of economic aid daily into Cuba.[16] While Soviet Russia was trying to increase its influence in Latin America through an expansion of trade and active diplomatic work—with the cooperative assistance of the local regular Communist parties—Castro bluntly stated that this policy could only assist the very oligarchies he, Fidel Castro, was pledged to overthrow. Nor was this an empty threat.

Cuba's Dirección General de Inteligencia was set up in the 1960's to become the fountainhead of armed subversion throughout the Western Hemisphere, organizing and supporting thousands of armed guerillas in a half-dozen countries in the late 1960's. In Venezuela, Peru, and Guatemala, thousands of regular soldiers began chasing a few hundred guerillas and terrorists; in Colombia, the indigenous guerilla warfare which had, hitherto, been plain banditry, was being gradually "politized" by Castroite agents. A small handful of guerillas settled themselves in Bolivia, hundreds of miles southeast of La Paz, to make life miserable for the Bolivian army; and hundreds of Castroite terrorists began to roam the jungles of Guatemala. Many of these guerilla expeditions fared badly, at first—especially in Bolivia where the American-trained and -advised army eventually captured and killed Castro's erstwhile companion, Ernesto "Che" Guevara; and in Peru where the army successfully put down the first uprising in the Andes. These first failures did not discourage the Cuban leaders who remembered Castro's 1953 failure at the Moncada Fortress. They went right on working on the start-up of new operations in another half-dozen countries—Paraguay, Guyana, Honduras, and Panama, among others.

Yet, in most instances, not only did the guerillas receive no assistance from the local Communist parties; most of the time, they found them intensely hostile. When a squad of Cuban and Venezuelan terrorists landed on the Venezuelan coast in the spring of 1967, with the ostensible aim of linking up with hundreds of guerillas already ensconced high up in the Andes, Venezuela's clandestine Communist party's central committee bitterly denounced the "insurrectional line" of the Cuban-trained guerillas and even paid for newspaper advertisements to make sure everyone would know exactly where it stood. Meantime, Douglas Bravo, head of the Venezuelan guerillas, while endorsed by Fidel Castro as the "authentic leader" of the Marxist-Leninist revolution, was expelled from the Venezuelan Communist party.[17] In its daily *El Siglo,* the Chilean Communist party attacked the Castroites with rare violence—while the Chilean socialists found themselves, out of anti-Communist spite, defending Castro-style guerilla warfare against the Communists who are supposedly to their left! [18] The Chilean Communist party's denunciation was then reprinted in Moscow's *Pravda* with an accompanying article blasting Castro's meddling in the revolutionary affairs of other Latin American countries and complaining that Castroite "adventurism" would damage the entire Communist movement in the hemisphere and might end by providing a free "gift to imperialism." [19] A few months later, Rodolfo

Ghioldi, member of the Argentine Communist party's executive committee, took the defense of Russia's efforts to improve relations with the existing Latin American governments and lambasted the Cubans for committing every sin under the Marxist sun—Maoism, Trotskyism, anarchism, petty bourgeois nationalism—and pointed to Che Guevara's death and the collapse of guerilla movement in Bolivia in 1967 as a perfect example of the futility of guerilla warfare in general.[20] Reprinted in *Pravda,* it betrayed the repressed anger of Moscow at Cuba's open defiance.

To settle matters once and for all, a gathering of all the Latin American revolutionary organizations took place in Havana during the summer of 1967—boycotted by the Communist parties of Venezuela, Argentina, and Brazil. What was significant about this meeting was not the endless squabbles and petty quarrels between delegates, but the general atmosphere and the conclusions hammered out at Cuba's dictation—the complete rejection of "satellization" by Peking as well as Moscow; the clear statement that a "third road to revolution" was valid, not only for Latin America, but for the whole world; the major slogan, uttered again and again, "the duty of every revolutionary is to make revolution"; the complete absence of any portrait of Marx and Lenin while a huge portrait of Simón Bolívar dominated the proceedings; the forceful rejection of theoretical dogmatism and philosophical hairsplitting which is one thing the Russians and the Chinese share a taste for; the emphasis on concrete situations and violent action; an even more specific condemnation of Peking's communism as being "dogmatic, sectarian, and unsuited to Latin America." [21] Quite clearly, a revolutionary movement was developing in Latin America, masterminded in Cuba, which owed no allegiance to either Moscow or Peking. And perhaps the most significant, as well as ironical, symbol of the true position of Castroism is the fact that Che Guevara's death went unlamented in Moscow, while stirring up such a feeling in Franco Spain that the main Falangist newspaper in Madrid deplored his death openly and compared him with Simón Bolívar and José Martí who, a century and a half ago, wrenched Latin America forever from the tyranny of Spanish rule,[22] Thus, by this odd fusion of political extremes, there was "fascist"

Spain deploring the death of the United States' most bitter Communist enemy in Latin America—while Moscow contemplated it almost with relief!

The truth of the matter is that Castroism is not communism at all but a reincarnation of what was, at one time, its worst enemy —anarchism. The hidden similarities between Castroism and anarchism are no accident; the plain fact is that, of all possible revolutionary types of action, anarchism is the one most suited to the individualistic and undisciplined Latin temper; nor should it be forgotten that Cuba remained under Spanish rule and influence until the very end of the nineteenth century, far longer than any continental Latin American nation, and as such provided a natural springboard for the penetration of Spanish-type anarchism in the Western Hemisphere.

A glance at the history of anarchism in Spain is bound to throw some light on the future of Castroism in Latin America— from its inception in 1868 when the Italian Fanelli, a disciple of Bakunin and a companion-in-arms of Garibaldi, arrived in Madrid and lit the fire, all the way to the eve of the Spanish Civil War when the movement had mushroomed to include roughly two million members, as against only a few thousand Spanish Communists. The difference between the two movements cannot be more pungently expressed than by stating that, whereas the anarchist wants to *be,* the Communist wants to *do.* Both Latins and anarchists want, above all, to strike an attitude, to safeguard the individual's dignity against real or alleged offenders; they are not determined "doers" or silent "builders"; they are actors. Life is a grand stage and the acting is more important than the play. In anarchism, the revolutionary Latin finds a highly congenial movement, one which is not burdened with Marxist philosophy or Leninist dogmatics, one which does not want to capture state power and instill discipline, but wants to destroy both state and concentration of power. Bakunin was a Russian, but he could just as well have been a Latin when he wrote: "All exercise of authority perverts and all submission to authority humiliates." [23]

While anarchism had its "terroristic" vogue throughout Europe around the turn of the century, it was only in Spain, and to a lesser extent in Italy, that it became a mass movement with re-doubtable potential. An international anarchist conference held in Berlin in 1922 specifically repudiated the Leninist theory of the dictatorship of the proletariat and advocated the outright abolition of every state function in social life. By then, the only mass movements left in Europe were Spain's dreaded Federación Anarquista Ibérica and the huge Confederación Nacional de Trabajo, the powerful gathering of Spanish trade unions; their equivalent in Italy, prior to the advent of Fascism, were the Unione Anarchica Italiana and the Unione Sindacale Italiana; they all went down the drain of history under the forthcoming dictatorships of Mussolini and Franco. Nor was there much possibility of European anarchism leading anywhere since it sought, not the conquest of political power, but its suppression; its main claim to fame in Europe rested on the important part played by the militarized anarchists during the Spanish Civil War.

The main point, however, is that it flourished temporarily in Latin countries and that it struck a chord in the Latin soul, the chord of instinctive passion, of striking attitudes of protest, of individual, unorganized violence and desire to shock. Just as important: whereas Marxism-Leninism basically apes the mate-rialism of the so-called capitalist societies and wants a fairer dis-tribution of material goods, the anarchist is essentially ascetic; while he thirsts for total freedom, he also thirsts for the leisure of the simple rural life and for the retrieval of an individual dignity lost in the soulless machinery of an increasingly complex indus-trial society. The strict discipline of the Communists and their Jesuitical habit of subordinating moral principles to political ex-pediency repels the anarchist.

In a sense, Hispanic anarchism owed little to Bakunin's theo-ries and far more to the first guerillas of modern times, to the Spanish *partidas* who fought Napoleon's invasion of Spain. As Gerald Brenan noted in *"The Spanish Labyrinth";*

> If anyone doubts that much of what is called "anarchist" today is merely unadulterated Iberian, let him compare the famous call for "organized indiscipline" pasted up by the F.A.I. on the walls of Barcelona in August 1936, at the time

when Durruti's column was getting ready for its march on Saragossa, with the description by an intelligent eyewitness of the organization of the guerilla war against Napoleon: "After the regular armies had all been beaten . . . one saw growing up a system of war in detail, a *kind of organized disorder* which perfectly suited the unconquerable character of the Spanish nation and the unhappy circumstances in which it found itself." [24]

Thus, in the Latin-Iberian framework, guerrilla warfare and anarchism are intimately connected; and it is this connection which might well be vitally important in the Latin America of the near future. While some form of guerilla warfare is endemic in many parts of Latin America and eventually conquered Cuba in the late 1950's, nothing has given greater impetus to the movement than the fierce and spectacular resistance of the Vietnamese Communist guerillas to a powerful American army in the 1960's. This resistance against America's military might armed with the latest gadgetry will, in years to come, prove to be one of the decisive catalysts of Latin America's guerilla warfares. Not that they can ever be replicas of the Vietnam War; temperamentally, Vietnamese and Latin Americans are poles apart. The Latin American dream is to fulfill Bolívar's dream; their latent anti-North Americanism is nourished by memories of the heroic deeds of the *Libertador* rather than by the writings of Marx, Lenin, and Mao Tse-tung. They have hated the enterprising and successful *gringos* for generations—out of wounded pride, but also out of an instinctive desire to find a scapegoat on which to blame their own shortcomings. Often arrogant, willing to destroy rather than to build, they are likely to find in guerilla warfare just the kind of natural outlet for what is, essentially, a retrograde impulse. And indeed, anarchism, as compared with Marxism-Leninism, is fundamentally retrograde, looking back to the legendary *Siglo de Oro* of the remote past, rather than forward to the highly technological and organized future.

But it is also far more honest, ascetic, and dedicated to the promotion of human dignity than Marxism-Leninism. Fidel Castro proves to be, deep down, a true anarchist when he emphasizes the "inalienable rights of the *human person*—political, social, economic and cultural," emphasis which has always been lacking in true communism.[25] He was not lying when he stated, in a televised speech on May 21, 1959: "Our revolution is neither capitalist nor communist! Our revolution has a position of its own. . . . We want to liberate man from dogmas. . . . We have been placed in a position where we must choose between capitalism which starves people, and Communism which resolves the economic problem but suppresses the liberties so greatly cherished by man. I know that Cubans and all Latin Americans desire a revolution that may meet their material needs without sacrificing their liberties. . . . Capitalism sacrifices man; the communist state sacrifices man. It is for this reason that we are trying to make our own revolution. . . . Our revolution is not red, but olive green, the color of the rebel army that emerged from the heart of the Sierra Maestra." [26] In fact, it is black as the anarchist flag of the pre-World War II generation.

Subsequent flirting with communism and increased dependence on Soviet Russia's economic and military assistance obscured the real nature of Castroism in the early 1960's—but in the latter 1960's, the atavistic anarchism of Castroism showed its true colors again at the Havana meeting of the Organization of Latin American Solidarity in 1967. In truth, OLAS is a barely disguised reincarnation of Europe's defunct anarchist movement, adapted to the Latin America of a later generation. Hector Mujica, spokesman for the Venezuelan Communist party, was perceptive when he stated angrily that "Fidel Castro is no Communist. . . . He is an anarchist and an adventurist who dreams of spreading disorder and chaos everywhere for his personal self-gratification. He is a *caudillo* who rules his island with his family and a gang of personal followers." [27] Indeed, true Communists hate nothing more than anarchy, the bottomless pit into which most revolutions are tempted to fall and against which Marxism-Leninism fights with ruthless, inhuman discipline.

In short, the quarrel between Castroism and Soviet-style communism is mainly a replay of the quarrel between the Communists and anarchists of an earlier generation—a precious indication that, in spite of temporary reconciliations and alliances of convenience, the chasm between them is so great as to be unbridgeable. For years to come, the vital tension within the Latin American revolutionary movement will be this tension between the black (or olive green, in its new incarnation) anarchist, bent on the destruction of the hated superstructure of civilization (state power, bureaucracy, military and political discipline, capitalist social distinctions, as well as the Communist establishments and "new classes") and preserver of the individual's dignity—and the red Communist, positive, constructive, disciplined, fighting the capitalist world on its own grounds with its own materialism, determined to subordinate and even sacrifice individual dignity, with its Jesuit-like discipline, to the all-encompassing state.

The anarchist spirit is strong today, not only in Latin America but throughout the world. The same search for dignity which motivates the Latin American revolutionary animates the Arabs, the American Negroes, and in general most of the socially or nationally depressed peoples' leaders who despise the bourgeois, middle-class mores of the suburban West and hate with a passion the crushing Communist conformity and suppression of individualism. That, nowadays, most of the anarchist element is forced by circumstances into the Communist mold, in which it fits so ill, is an example of historical *pseudomorphism*—an historical equivalent of what is known in mineralogy as the shaping of a specific mineral into the form proper to another, usually because of external geological pressure. In a political context, this implies employing the framework of one political faith to achieve the opposite aims, forced into this pseudomorphism by the pressure of a common enemy—in this instance, the expanding American empire.

It may well be that the Chilean Communist party's denunciation of Fidel Castro's revolutionary action as eventually providing a free "gift to imperialism" will turn out to be prophetic. It is obvious that the United States will not remain idle in front of a clear threat—the greatest challenge to its influence ever built up in the Western Hemisphere. Che Guevara, the "anarchist tramp" who had mysteriously faded away from Cuba in 1965 in order to organize guerilla warfare all over Latin America, wrote that "given suitable operating terrain, land hunger, enemy injustices,

etc., a hard core of thirty to fifty men is, in my opinion, enough
to initiate armed revolution in any Latin American country." [28]
He then added: "One does not necessarily have to wait for a
revolutionary situation to arise; it can be created. . . . In the
under-developed countries of the Americas, rural areas are the
best battlefields for revolution." [29] He was to pay with his life for
his boldness—but his death is more likely to make him a martyr
and an example than the last of his breed.

As a form of armed struggle, guerilla warfare, while eminently
suited to the Latin temper, is likely in the future to be broader
than is commonly assumed—may even, in fact, become more
international in character. It is by no means fanciful to anticipate
the birth of true international brigades made up of younger men
from countries other than those of the Western Hemisphere—
young idealists of anarchistic bent who will believe that they are
fighting for a just cause, young men thirsting for adventure and
fleeing from the dullness of urban middle-class life, young men
who are desperate for an ideal and believe that they can find
their innermost selves through a freely determined exposure to
individual danger. There is abroad, in contemporary Western
society (on both sides of the Atlantic) a profound sickness of the
soul, a spirit of revolt against the neat and pat life of suburbia,
against middle-class ideals and mores. This disease is spreading
fast among the younger, postwar generation who have never
been exposed to the actual dangers of regular warfare, nor to the
idealism that sustained their elders in armed combat between
1940 and 1945. The unbridled use of drugs and narcotics is only
one aspect of this permutation which, in fact, aims at the overthrow of Western society's foundations. These internal émigrés
of violent disposition who seek for complete release from the
fetters of an increasingly organized society, and for some lost self-
identity, are likely to turn to guerilla warfare for a purpose—
which will be ready and waiting for them in remote jungles and
mountains where they will find a welcome release from the rou-
tinism of civilized life.

It is not only young idealists of anarchistic bent who may be
tempted to join guerilla action. There are signs that elements of
the Roman Catholic clergy are all set to become involved too,
carrying a crucifix in front of them. The saga of the Colombian

priest Camilo Torres-Restrepo, chaplain of the University of Bogotá, is already becoming a legend all over South America.[30] Having joined a Castroite guerilla group in 1965, he was killed the following year by a detachment of the Colombian army; and, more influential in death than alive, he has awakened in the younger, more idealistic segment of the clergy throughout Latin America a new revolutionary spirit, which might even threaten a schism in the Latin American Church.[31] And this spirit is not even confined to the Latin American clergy. In January 1968, the rather startling news was released by the headquarters of Maryknoll, the American Roman Catholic missionary order, that a group of their missionaries had sought out and linked up with Castroite guerillas in the jungles of Guatemala, and had planned to smuggle light arms into the country for their benefit. Ordered back home to Ossining, New York, and suspended from priestly duties by their horrified superiors, the American mission- aries themselves explained that "American military and eco- nomic pressure were bringing on a revolution in Guatemala," and that in the guerilla army roaming the jungles of Guatemala, "there's a Communist here and there in the movement, but they're rare birds. The left has very much a Christian mystique." [32]

The fight against this challenge is likely to increase the United States' political and military involvement in Latin American affairs, to the extent, at least, that the local national forces will no longer be able to suppress the guerillas without substantial North American assistance—especially if, as seems probable, the guerillas coordinate across national boundaries and straddle the frontiers of neighboring countries in order to take advantage of divergent national policies—as Mao Tse-tung's troops straddled the borders of several Chinese provinces in order to take advan- tage of the conflicting policies of local warlords. And if the Or- ganization of American States, which largely follows the wishes of Washington, decides on the creation of a multinational OAS force in order to cope with this problem, it is likely that Washing- ton's Pentagon will be in *de facto* control of it. Whatever the type of response to the revolutionary challenge, it is likely to drag the United States into an increasing interference in the internal affairs of the Latin American nations concerned.

In the latest instance, President Lyndon Johnson did not hesitate to "send the marines" into the Dominican Republic in 1965, thus taking it upon himself to intervene unilaterally and in full violation of Articles 15 and 17 of the Organization of American States to which the United States had solemnly committed itself at Bogotá in 1948. The probability that the rebel (Constitutionalist) forces were about to defeat the forces of the existing government, possibly facing the United States with the threat of a new Cuba, left Washington little choice but to break its pledge and reestablish, by force of arms, a government subservient to its authority. The OAS meekly followed suit and, belatedly, legitimized this high-handed intervention.

Undoubtedly, the willingness and ability thus displayed by the United States to make its imperium respected in the Caribbean is bound to have some salutary effect on all would-be revolutionaries, while raising the expected outcry in Latin America and in the United States itself, and, again, tarnishing its image as a moral, idealistic Power. Quite unbothered by this fact, the United States House of Representatives promptly passed a resolution "calling for the unilateral use of force against any threat of communism in the hemisphere, which is to say, in clear and open violation of the OAS charter. The United States was promptly rewarded for the House of Representatives' action by unanimous expressions of outrage in Latin America, including resolutions of condemnation adopted by the Congresses of Colombia and Peru and by the Latin American Parliament representing fourteen countries." [33]

In the long run, the inevitable sequence of events is obviously that such strong interference on the part of the United States cannot help but promote further the revolutionary action it is fighting—this Western Hemisphere brand of Communism-anarchism gradually monopolizing and exploiting the latent feeling of hostility toward the United States which is atavistic throughout Latin America. Simultaneously, the ruling oligarchies and the middle classes of Latin America will be increasingly inclined to rely on United States' strength and determination to ward off the revolutionary threat to their welfare. The coming politico-military emergencies are certain to stimulate further this unending process. In other words, and as is the case with many other areas of the world, the United States and Latin America are now irrevocably trapped in a mechanical process of involvement with one another leading, eventually, to an involuntary but increasingly effective domination of the entire hemisphere by the United States.

The shape that this North American domination will assume in this part of the world depends, to a considerable extent, on the power of expansion of Castroism and the degree of success with which its guerillas meet throughout the hemisphere. Cuba's "continental strategy" visualizes an increasingly coordinated network of widely scattered guerilla operations, acting on the assumption that most Latin American societies are rotten to the core and are likely to collapse under the attacks of armed groups; that North Americans are bound to intervene militarily, thus increasing the anti-*gringo* feelings of the local populations; and that, eventually, the pressure of public opinion in the United States will compel Washington to abandon Latin American oligarchies to their sad fate.

More likely, the increasing successes of the guerillas might eventually compel the North Americans to invade Cuba and snuff out Havana's poisonous influence. This would not necessarily mean the end of hemisphere-wide guerilla warfare, but would undoubtedly prompt the Americans to revive their turn-of-the-century plan to incorporate Cuba, lock, stock, and barrel, into the United States—at great expense since it would imply lifting the Cuban standard of living up to Puerto Rico's, for instance. Indeed, the undoubted success of the Puerto Rican experiment is a portent of things to come in the Caribbean and Central America. If one could apply the unwieldy expression "Puerto Ricanization" to the process whereby the United States would extend its direct sovereignty to the Western Hemisphere tropics, the nature of its domination would become plain: not a "colonial" rule but a steady process of *organic* absorption such as is digesting Puerto Rico itself.

It is no accident or coincidence that Venezuela's former President Rómulo Betancourt who took over from a dictatorship and set up an excellent businesslike government in his country, had spent a great deal of his exile in Puerto Rico and had "brought back to Venezuela plans and institutions derived from the Puerto Rican experiment." [34] Intensely disliked by both right and left, under constant threat of assassination by such opposite dictators as the Dominican Republic's Trujillo and Cuba's Castro, Betancourt's rule in Venezuela was typical of those that, if long-lasting, might avoid the need for a "Puerto Ricanization" of the area.

In the long run, however, the Betancourt type of democratic stability is not likely to last and Puerto Ricanization appears to be the only political and economic solution in the Caribbean. In setting up the Alliance for Progress under the leadership of the Puerto Rican Teodoro Moscoso, President Kennedy made full use of Spanish-speaking Puerto Ricans to put his message across to Latin Americans; in the Dominican Republic, after the downfall of dictator Trujillo, President Kennedy and Puerto Rico's Governor Muñoz-Marín acted as a team, as a similar President-Governor team may one day operate in post-Castro Cuba. As one expert on Latin America pointed out, the implications of the Kennedy-Muñoz "Doctrine" and policy ". . . are far-reaching. The eventual creation of a Dominican Commonwealth analogous to Puerto Rico, is a possible outcome. The extension of similar methods to a liberated Cuba is another possibility. Washington and San Juan were forging a potent new instrument for use throughout the Caribbean and Central America." [35]

No such process, in any case, can be visualized for South America proper, where North American hegemony will retain the features of a loose protectorate, especially in the more distant south where massive countries such as Argentina and Brazil will retain a measure of autonomy and where Castroism may be less of a danger than regular communism. But all over the hemisphere, the fate of Castroism will depend to a large extent on its relations with the regular, old-line Communists; and so will the effectiveness of the counter-guerilla warfare directed from Washington depend on its ability to split the hostile twins.

☆ XI ☆

Race and Africa

In the long run, nothing will have quite as much influence on the development of the American empire, its extension, character, and duration, as the nature of race relations *within* the United States—race relations implying primarily the relationship between Negroes and whites, and only secondarily community problems affecting other minorities such as Puerto Ricans, Mexican Americans, Indians, Chinese, and Japanese. The problem affecting the relations between Negroes and whites is of much vaster dimensions—vaster because of the figures involved, since Negroes make up almost 12 percent of the total population of the United States, and also vaster because of the greater depth of feeling involved in black-and-white relationship.

If we look back at the turn of the century, when the United States was first beginning to flex its imperial muscles, it is quite clear that the main obstacle to imperial expansion was the fear of having to absorb too many nonwhite people as eventual citizens —since the whole ethos of the American nation was opposed to *colonial* extension in the sense of keeping alien populations in indefinite subjugation for the benefit of the mother country. There had been enough trouble with the American Negroes after the Civil War to give the anti-imperialists plenty of ammunition. Rather than respect for democratic tradition, it was racial prejudice that stood in the way of the acquisition of a much larger empire than actually came into Washington's possession. The racial argument was used time and again by the anti-imperialists, unsuccessfully in the case of Hawaii, but more successfully when it came to contemplated annexations in Central America and the Caribbean. Besides, the new, and more sophisticated form of colonialism—economic colonialism—could very well be divorced from a strictly political domination; pseudopolitical independence was quite compatible with economic colonialism on a grand scale (as in Cuba), and had the additional advantage of avoiding the massive intrusion of alien populations into the United States—such as the postwar immigration of Puerto Ricans flooding New York City. Therefore, the future development of the American empire depends, not only on the United States' ability and willingness to absorb large colored populations from other lands and grow organically, rather than colonially, but also on the ability of its society to resolve its only major social problem—the integration of its own Negro population.

As a general rule, racial conflict acquires dangerous political overtones only when the dominant racial group manifests a high degree of social cohesion and consciousness (as in the United States, Great Britain, Australia, and South Africa) and strives successfully for democratic equality *within* the group—whereas, as we have seen in the case of Latin America, where social conscience is weak and strong family ties prevail over social solidarity, no racial problem exists as such, since there can be no conflict between extremely weak or even nonexistent social organisms; there is hardly any group-consciousness, and it is all a matter for the individual and his family to settle for themselves. In the first type of society, which concerns us now, collision between the drive for democratic equality and the existence of different compact racial groups, becomes inevitable.

White leaders in the United States have failed, quite naturally, to advocate boldly the only long-term solution to the problem:

total miscegenation. This solution has been rejected in both theory and practice for generations; it is now further removed from actualization than ever, in spite of a marginal amount of blending: the races are being increasingly polarized and are moving full speed away from each other. Prior to the First World War, the great majority of Negroes were impoverished farmers and sharecroppers living in the South's rural areas. But two World Wars made great demands on the available surplus of labor, including black labor, which began to migrate toward the large cities of the North and West; further, the increasing mechanization of agriculture and the steady disappearance of the small, uneconomical farm, drove millions of other Negroes who might have remained in the southern countryside to the North and West, changing the whole racial landscape of the United States. Migrating from the legally segregated society of the South to the *de facto* segregated society of the North, these millions of Negroes began to carve out huge ghettos for themselves in every large city in the country; but, in the process of migrating, they also underwent a psychological and social mutation, from illiterate, isolated, and easily intimidated sharecroppers of the rural South to members of huge angry and volatile masses of Negroes compressed in the great urban slums. Thrown together by the thousands in the black ghettos, the American Negroes became more conscious of their racial unity and the frightening power which this new feeling of kinship, uniting millions of underprivileged colored people, gave them.

The great melting pot which was so successful in amalgamating immigrants of European descent failed to boil when it came to the Afro-Americans. They remained separate; and soon, sensing that this separation would never end, they began searching for a new, separate identity. The first mass movement among the American Negroes appeared, significantly, at the end of the First World War—the amazing and short-lived Universal Negro Improvement Association of Marcus Garvey who urged Negroes to give up all hope of assistance or understanding from American whites, heaped contempt on the heads of the Negro middle class, exalted everything black, and advocated a return emigration to

Africa, of which he became the first self-appointed "Provisional President."

But Africa was not for the giving; it was mostly under European domination, without any prospect of become independent. Garvey's eventual fiasco put a temporary end to this dream of a return to the "homeland" beyond the seas. Besides, what was Africa's public image in those days?—Darkest Africa replete with savages and cannibals, painfully but gloriously discovered by European explorers and civilized by European missionaries; the Dark Continent which was alleged to have made no contribution to human culture or civilization, populated mostly by primeval tribes. There was in this picture nothing to be proud of, no glorious past, no great inheritance to claim. Humbled at home, American Negroes could not even look back to Africa with pride of ancestry; nor could they look at the African present with any hope since even the local kings and tribal chieftains on the African coast, whose ancestors had sold their ancestors into slavery, had become the obedient subjects of white European rulers. In fact, American Negroes made a conscious and deliberate effort to dissociate themselves from all past or present association with Africa, from their own "blackness," from all Negroid features, color, and kinky hair. But all the cosmetics and hair-straighteners, in the end, could not wash away their skin color. Rejecting Africa, the American Negroes had come to reject themselves.

But while the Second World War was generating vast changes in the American Negro's geographical location and psychological disposition, it was also profoundly altering Africa's own historical picture and political landscape. Not only had archeologists and anthropologists discovered an ancient Africa worthy of respect, replete with ancient African empires and rudimentary civilizations; not only had African art been exerting a powerful influence on Western art; now, at last, enfeebled Europe was gradually withdrawing its soldiers and administrators: the era of decolonization was at hand. Suddenly, in the late 1950's and early 1960's, dozens of African nations emerged to political freedom, taking their rightful place in the United Nations on a footing of complete equality with the world's other nations—black

African kings and presidents, prime ministers and ambassadors in full regalia, received at the White House with full honors— black Africans who appeared to be proud of their African features and identity.

The rise of free and independent African states had a profound impact on the American Negro by restoring his pride in his *négritude* and confirming the possibility open to him of separate development; henceforth, he would be different from the white man, but not inferior. Before World War II, Africa made a powerful contribution to Negro self-contempt; now, suddenly, it contributed as much to his self-pride. African independence gave him an international leverage, or at least the illusion of one, which he had never suspected. It gave him the courage to challenge the white man and demand his fair share, or what he thinks is his fair share, of the national pie. As a Harlem resident, referring to the American Negro, put it: "More and more, the black man here is moving toward an African frame of mind." [1]

Whatever the future course of race relations in the United States, this course is going to have a profound impact on its relations with black Africa—a continent which its imperial worldwide drive cannot ignore; and whose liberation from the fetters of European colonialism has had an almost traumatic effect on its internal race relations.

This impact has to be seen in relation to the growing importance of the Negro in the American social and political structure—especially in its military segment. The rapidly increasing proportion of professional Negro soldiers and officers in the American armed forces makes it plain even today. Roughly one quarter of the American soldiers fighting in Vietnam, the first major conflict in which American troops fight on a fully integrated basis, are Negroes whose rate of reenlistment is considerably higher than that of the whites. In 1966, for instance, the rate of first-time Negro reenlistment was more than three times that of white servicemen, or well over 60 percent as compared to 20 percent for the whites. [2] The social and economic causes of this high rate are obvious—better and more secure income than in civilian life, the dignity of uniform and rank granted according to individual merit, the absence of racial discrimination in what is essentially a man's world.

In view of the Pentagon's increasing weight and influence in America's power structure, it is interesting to note that it has come to the foreground of the struggle to eliminate discrimination against Negro servicemen, even in areas *outside* those under purely military jurisdiction: fighting for open housing to put an end to discrimination against Negro military personnel,[3] fighting to salvage a hundred thousand poverty-crushed youths each year during their military service, and training yearly three quarters of a million men leaving the military in order to enable them to fulfill useful roles in the more competitive civilian life.[4] In other words, that temple of social and political conservatism which is the Pentagon is becoming, with its immense resources and power, a prime agency for social reform—not out of pure altruism or charity, but with an eye to training and preserving a useful pool of ex-military men in the most deprived segment of American society—that is, mostly in the Negro community. The sudden emergence of the Pentagon as the prime guardian of Negro rights, a task that should have been fulfilled under normal circumstances by civilian agencies—is likely to have far-reaching consequences.

Simultaneously, it is also evident that American Negroes are going to take an increasing interest in African affairs, and are likely to exert a growing influence in the former Dark Continent. What this interest and influence are likely to be will depend largely on the kind of social and economic settlement reached by the races within the United States itself. In the past, American Negroes took an interest in Africa as a land of opportunity to which they might return from their enforced *diaspora* and thus escape the overpowering structure of the United States' white society. So far, it has remained a dream without actualization. However, like the Jews' return to Israel after nineteen hundred years of exile, and other vast transfers of population that have taken place in our century, an important movement of American Negroes to some parts of Africa cannot be ruled out in the future. As Gunnar Myrdal pointed out in his classic *An American*

Dilemma: "Many Negroes in America feel an emotional attachment to Africa and its population. And because of their color they would, with greater ease, gain the confidence of the African Negroes." [5] He then goes on to quote one of the leading American Negroes, W. E. B. Du Bois, who stated:

> . . . my plan would not decline frankly to face the possibility of eventual emigration from America of some considerable part of the Negro population, in case they could not find a chance for free and favorable development unmolested and unthreatened, and in case the race prejudice in America persisted to such an extent that it would not permit the full development of the capacities and aspirations of the Negro race. [6]

This, of course, had already been tried in the nineteenth century, but not on a massive scale: the foundation and settlement of the Republic of Liberia by a few thousand American Negroes. Since white Americans had no interest in colonizing any part of the Dark Continent, Liberia was left to shift for itself, and, in no time, the immigrant American Negroes had practically enslaved the much larger native population, instead of offering a haven to other Negro refugees from America. Then, in the twentieth century, the United States began displaying more interest in the backward state on the West African coast; the Firestone Company pioneered its economic development, World War II prompted the Americans to establish military bases at Fisherman's Creek and Roberts Field—garrisoned by American Negro troops; in fact, it became America's only "banana republic" in Africa—by no means an answer to the problem.

A large-scale migration of millions of American Negroes to Africa is improbable, if only because of the logistics involved. What is not impossible, however, is a limited migration to various parts of Africa where they could settle and occupy key professional functions for which no Africans are qualified. True enough, the rare American Negroes who have attempted to establish their racial kinship and have gone to Africa for the purpose, have quickly come to realize the size of the cultural and psychological gap which separates them from most Africans. The American Negro in Africa usually feels more American than any white American. The African returns the compliment and usually has a poor opinion of the American Negro with his psychological complexes derived from a background of ancestral slavery and social inferiority—which he is not equipped to understand since his African environment, even under the loose supervision of European colonial rulers, was always culturally and socially Negroid.

Furthermore, most black Africans still live socially in a tribal environment, and their nationalism is essentially tribal, and remains largely indifferent to "racial" problems in a social context to which they were never exposed. It is only with the new urban, detribalized Africans of the large modern cities mushrooming all over Africa that the American Negro will be able to communicate and establish some kind of link based on the racial issue. But as things stand now, the American Negro is still shocked by the visible remnants of African culture and traditions, by the psychological disposition of the African with its reliance on some forms of magic and fetishism; he is shocked, as many white Americans in Europe, by lower standards of living, faulty plumbing, the lackadaisical attitude of Africans in business, their corruption and political taste for tyranny, and the contempt felt by many African rulers for their fellow "citizens" whom they usually treat as lowly subjects.

But, however large the gap which separates them, the American Negro will never remain indifferent to Africa and is likely to take an increasingly active interest in its political and economic development. Early in 1967, when political wrangling in Nigeria between tribal and military leaders threatened to lead to a collapse of the federation, four American leaders offered to mediate the dispute so that "the largest, richest and in many respects most promising nation in black Africa, may fulfill the destiny it so rightly deserves to the benefit of Africa, the world and *ourselves* [author's italics]." [7] Disappointment with a probable lack of progress and stability in Africa may very well instill in a number of qualified American Negroes the desire to actually *colonize* their African cousins and bring them up to date by imparting to them all the blessings of the "American way of life"—Negro style. All they will need in order to do so is the blessing and assistance of the United States' white establishment, which they are likely to get if it serves its purpose—unlike Black Power advocate Stokely Carmichael whose 1967 visit to Tanzania and other "neutralist" African countries was aimed at encouraging left-wing guerilla warfare and developing anti-American sentiment in Africa.

The United States has, or soon will have, a real strategic, economic, and political stake in Africa. Without being at all inclined to dominate and rule Africa in the old European colonial style, the Washington authorities will soon discover the extreme convenience of tightening the links between a qualified portion of their own American Negroes and Africans. Even after decolonization, the French have made good use of French Negro citizens from the West Indies, some of whom are occasionally found in key administrative positions in independent African nations. And as late as 1967, for example, over half the members of Senegal's Cabinet held French passports and citizenship. It is quite likely that, sooner or later, Washington will follow in the footsteps of the French and begin placing trusted American Negroes in key positions throughout the continent, many of whom could even become citizens of the African countries in which they reside while serving the interests of the United States. And from the standpoint of the English-speaking Africans themselves, nothing could be more fruitful than a close relationship with choice American Negroes; out of this cross-fertilization, could emerge a modernized Africa to which the Afro-Americans could contribute technical skills and a rudimentary knowledge of American-style democracy; in return, the Africans could teach the American Negroes how to conjure their purely *racial* complexes and restore, as their political independence has already begun to, their pride in their *négritude*.

The United States' involvement in black Africa is already considerable, especially in the economic field; American interests, often through the intermediary of European affiliates, and to the tune of well over two billion dollars, are by no means negligible. On the other hand, some parts of Africa, such as Dakar in Senegal and South Africa, are of considerable strategic importance,

which importance will grow to the extent that Communist penetration and subversion manages to establish strong footholds in
some African "Cuba" or other. So far, neither the Russians nor
the Chinese have been really successful in their attempts at penetration—the Russians, because of their white skin, even less so
than the Chinese who have made strenuous, and not always un-
rewarded, efforts in east and central Africa (Tanzania, the
Congo-Brazzaville, Burundi). To the extent that Communist
efforts at subversion have already been made, the United States
has already felt compelled to interfere—as usual, in the stickiest
situations since they are the very situations that Communists are
likely to exploit. Such a situation developed in the Congo, shortly
after the formal ending of Belgium's colonial rule.

American involvement in the Congo began in 1960, when the
Soviet Union attempted, through the agency of the Congo's first
Premier, leftist Patrice Lumumba, to turn the whole country into
a Soviet outpost in the heart of Africa. Opportunism rather than
an ideology he could not even understand induced Lumumba to
play the Russian game; but to the great alarm of the West, he
played it to the hilt; and so did the Russians, whose sudden
interest in the Congo was quite easy to understand; Oleg Pen-
Kovsky's diary gives us the reason:

> There is a shortage of atomic raw materials needed for the
> atom bombs and missiles with nuclear warheads. . . . Almost
> all the ore containing uranium comes to the Soviet Union
> from Czechoslovakia. . . . In view of this shortage of atomic
> raw materials, it is small wonder that our government is so
> interested in establishing Soviet control in the Congo. The
> largest uranium ore deposits are in the Congo. When Lu-
> mumba was temporarily in power, the Soviets sent twenty-
> three planeloads of officers (including generals) there via
> Egypt and the Sudan. . . . The primary task of this mission
> was to establish Soviet control over the uranium ore in the
> Congo.[8]

Russian supplies began to pour into the country, while hundreds of Russian and Czech technical and diplomatic advisers
fanned out across the Congo, masterminding the crushing of anti-
Lumumbist rebellions. Washington lost no time in exerting its

influence on President Kasavubu, Lumumba's bitter rival, who dismissed his Premier—who, in turn, dismissed his President. The Congo collapsed into anarchy and Lumumba was eventually assassinated. This gave Kasavubu a free hand and, at Washington's instigation, he promptly evicted the Russian and Czech embassies, along with their numerous personnel.

This did not dispose of the Communist stronghold in Stanleyville where Antoine Gizenga inherited Lumumba's mantle; a form of protracted civil war ensued which, along with the secession and eventual reincorporation of the Katanga, lasted a number of years. Throughout this whole period, the involvement of the United States grew along with the protracted civil war. Both the American Embassy and the CIA found themselves virtually ruling some parts of the vast country and, to a great extent, even displacing the Belgians, whose influence had been declining steadily. By 1967, President Mobutu and his key ministers were largely under the direct influence of American Embassy officials, and even the Belgians found themselves compelled to deal with the Congolese Government through the agency of the Americans.

Belgium still assisted the Congo financially to the tune of seventy million dollars a year, and technically through the presence of some forty to fifty thousand teachers, technicians, missionaries, planters, and businessmen; but paramount influence was wielded by the United States which provided, not only just as much financial assistance, but also the strategic support and planning required to guide the Congolese Government's day-to-day operations. Angry as they were at this American paramountcy, the Belgians had to accept it and learn to cope with it. The revolt of the last remaining mercenaries in the summer of 1967 incited Washington to send three U.S. Air Force C-130 transports with a hundred and fifty American servicemen to give the Congolese army logistical support against the mercenaries— and incidentally touching off an angry debate in Congress over this overextension and additional involvement in Africa, in the midst of the Vietnam War.[9]

Large as the United States east of the Mississippi, the Congo is the heart of Africa and cannot be allowed to collapse. Like it or not, the United States is going to be involved for a long time, as it has been since 1960, and as it is likely to be in most African countries that are all at once strategically located, well endowed in natural resources, and threatened with Communist infiltration, as the Congo was in the early 1960's.

In the long run, however, no area in black Africa is likely to be of greater interest to the United States than southern Africa, and especially its hard core, the Republick van Suid-Afrika— Afrikaans for Republic of South Africa. In the second half of the twentieth century, the Republic (till 1961, "Union") is a re-markable anomaly—a state based frankly and openly on com-plete white supremacy, that is on the absolute, legal domination of fifteen million people by that one-fifth of the population whose skin happens to be white. And that one-fifth, in turn, is politi-cally, if not economically, dominated by its Afrikaans-speaking members who constitute a slight majority of the white popula-tion. Being the only independent African state that is run by whites (Rhodesia can be considered a *de facto* extension of the Republic), it is also, by far, the most powerful economically and militarily, as well as the most stable politically. In spite of their violent feelings of hostility, the other Negro-run states of Africa find themselves powerless to destroy it.

Afrikaners are a remarkably dour, bigoted, unimaginative, and stubborn lot, who are quite prepared to flout world public opinion and follow their own way, regardless of criticism. Most leading Afrikaners belong to the secret Broederbond association and are determined to apply kragdadigheid ("unyielding strength") to the solution of their racial problem. Politically organized in the Nationalist party, they came to power a few years after the end of World War II. But it was the Sharpeville riot and massacre that led Prime Minister Verwoerd to set up a far more authoritarian regime than the rather liberal democratic system that he had inherited from his predecessors. The already strong police force was considerably strengthened, the Anti-Sabotage Act enabled it to arrest or confine to his house anyone suspected of "liberalism," and various other provisions for "emergency" measures began to turn the Republic into a police state. Finally, in the summer of 1967, the Government disclosed its decision to raise South Africa's armed forces from thirty thousand to a hundred thousand men over a period of ten years, establishing the draft for all white South African males. Obviously, leading Afrikaners expect real trouble in years to come, and they may be right.

Applying systematically their policy of *apartheid,* the leading South Africans are determined to force the Negro majority into a number of autonomous *Bantustans* scattered throughout South Africa's territory, states reserved exclusively for Negroes and where whites will not be allowed to reside or own property—just as the Bantus will have no right to reside permanently in white areas. A steadily tightening legislation attempts to decrease white reliance on black labor while technological improvements and automation are partly substituting for Negro employment in white-owned industries. In other words, the leaders of South Africa, moving against a worldwide trend, are systematically retribalizing their Africans, rooting them back in the soil, stripping them of all possibility of receiving a modern education by encouraging them to remain faithful to their native dialects and encouraging, in Bantu areas, the authority of the traditional chiefs.

What they are doing, in fact, is attempting to solve a *social* problem by transforming it into a *political* one, recreating out of their black proletariat their own partly forgotten tribal nations (Zulus, Xhosas, Tswanas, Vendas, etc.); eventually reaching the point where the Republic of South Africa will become a crazy-quilt of small Bantu nations speaking different tongues, scattered throughout the huge white territory (the "White Homeland") and whose available labor will be hired as needed on a temporary base by white industry and agriculture. Transkei, the first Bantustan to come into existence, is the model for others to follow, with which, as M. C. Botha, the Minister of Bantu Administration, stated in 1967, the Government of the Republic will conclude "international agreements" in no way different from those it is already concluding with an increasing number of African client states—independent and sovereign states in law, but *de facto* protectorates of South Africa. Thus Lesotho, Botswana, and Swaziland, former British protectorates wedged into South

Africa and never ruled by Pretoria, are bound to fall into the South African orbit because of their extreme weakness and poverty.

Not only that; South Africa is actively trying to recruit other African client states beyond its borders, and its trade agreement with Malawi was truly described by Prime Minister Vorster as a "breakthrough" in South Africa's new policy—while its opponents contend that Malawi is merely the first of the Bantustans north of the Limpopo. Malawi's social and economic posture left it no choice, as President Hastings Banda understood only too well; providing thousands of young Malawians to work the South African mines (where they receive far higher salaries than would ever be available at home), in exchange for vastly increased imports of South African goods, the Malawinian Government even began to use South African mercenaries to train its armed forces. And, of course, white-dominated Rhodesia, ever since Salisbury trumpeted its unilateral declaration of independence in 1965, has become South Africa's major bastion in the north.

Any policy which is systematically applied over a long period of time and with utter determination is bound to be successful. African Negroes, inside and outside the Republic, are unable to prevent it. Run with discipline and efficiency, the Republic of South Africa has granted the highest standard of living in Africa, not only to its whites but to its Bantus as well. Year in and year out, thousands of black Africans stream *into* the Republic from other African countries in search of better jobs and higher salaries. The oppression is real, and so is the resentment, not only of the few educated Negroes but of a handful of liberal whites; but law and order are maintained and peace of a sort between multitudes of separate communities—not only Bantus and whites but Cape Coloreds and Natal's Indians, all of whom are rigidly segregated according to the Group Areas Act. A glimpse of what would happen if this rigid segregation was not applied can be obtained by looking at the record of the frightful outbreak of Zulu violence against the Durban Indians in 1949.

With all that, it still remains that South Africa is not living in a vacuum but in a troubled world, a world in which there is hardly any sympathy for its social and political system. If we listen to the voice of Alan Paton, one of its rare and eloquent white liberals, this is the dark outlook for South Africa's future without taking into account the possibility of external interference:

> One thing is certain. Nonwhite opinion will grow in unity and strength. Nonwhite labor will grow more powerful, even though it is not permitted to organize itself lawfully, as is the case today. . . . More and more will white people have to choose between white domination and the common society. *Total apartheid* will be seen as a fantastic impossibility, and the policy of *white leadership* will be seen as halting between two opinions. Who will win out, the group for white domination, or the group for a common society? If white domination wins, some violence, whether of internal revolution or external interference, must be expected. Domination by a minority is an unstable condition. Suppose those who support the *common society* achieve a majority. Will the common society continue as a true democracy, or will it be followed by *black domination*, the great revenge? This, of course, is a possibility, and one that is much feared.[10]

Alan Paton has been quoted at length because he gives us the framework within which to think about the future. South Africa, however ruthless its Afrikaner leadership, is an unstable society in which the white minority lives dangerously. As Chief Albert Luthuli claimed, "For Africans, the promotion of Bantu Self-Government Act [establishing the Bantustans] is the end of a long road of subjection and tyranny. For the whites, it is the abandonment of any pretence of the rule of law, the beginning of the long-drawn-out, agonising end." [11] Yet, the Republic of South Africa is a wealthy, powerful country, led by determined men. More than that, it is of immense strategic importance, which importance is highlighted whenever the Suez Canal is blocked by warfare in the unstable Middle East. And its wealth and relative isolation from any powerful and hostile neighbor makes it a truly independent country—more independent than any European country, completely out of the control of the leading Western Power, the United States.

It is not likely that this state of affairs can last very long—that the United States can tolerate this true independence forever.

And lately, leading South Africans have taken to veiled threats against the West, implying, for instance, that if the arms embargo imposed upon their country by the United States and Great Britain were to be maintained, South Africa might well turn neutralist. In 1967, Foreign Minister Hilgard Muller stated plainly that in view of the increasing importance of the sea route around the Cape of Good Hope, the arms embargo policy was "shortsighted, incomprehensible and unforgivable," and went on to add: "Many South Africans are beginning to ask themselves whether the country's traditional loyalty toward the West does not hold for her more disadvantages than advantages and whether we would not be appreciated more if we were less loyal to the West." [12]

Such blunt form of blackmail might well backfire since South Africa, having no friend in the world, has no place to go; and if acted upon, could well antagonize the leading Western countries to the extent of triggering a more violent reaction.

Sooner or later, the United States is going to move to extend its imperium to the southern part of Africa, and bring the Republic under some form of control or other; that much is certain; but what kind of control? To take an extreme and unlikely possibility, the United States could move to consolidate white supremacy in South Africa. Its own intractable racial problem and the rising white backlash it is bound to generate within the United States could well bring some American sympathy over to the side of the proponents of white supremacy in South Africa. The majority of white American southerners, of course, sympathize in full with South Africa's present leaders and would be the first to rise against any attempt to join an international action against the Republic; so far, Rhodesia serves as a lightning rod and, to an extent, shields South Africa from direct attacks; from present attitudes toward Rhodesia, one can gauge future attitudes toward South Africa, and the amount of support the Republic's present leadership could expect in the United States. We can transpose, for instance, the amendment offered on October 10, 1967, by Senator Byrd of Virginia, warning the Administration against joining an armed crusade against Rhodesia [13]— and, instead of Rhodesia, read its South African extension. Not only does the present white South African leadership enjoy some substantial support in the United States; it might very well be, in the future, that frightened by rising Bantu opposition and rising threats from the rest of Africa, the South African leaders decide that a loose form of American protectorate might be the lesser of two evils; and that a tacit alliance between South Africans and American southerners and anti-Negro white backlashers would block any attempt to dismantle South Africa's apartheid policy.

But all this is unlikely. The reverse is more probable. Precisely because of its own racial problem, the United States is more likely to indulge in the oldest ritual in the world, the search for an external scapegoat: by sacrificing on the altar of world public opinion South Africa's white leadership, the United States' white leaders may hope to placate their own angry Negro minority at home. Black magic and the celebration of "scapegoatism" are not dead yet.

On a more mundane, down-to-earth level, it is clear that, in years to come, nothing is as likely to win the sympathy of African and American Negroes, as well as that of assorted Asian and Arab public opinions, not to mention liberal and leftwing radical opinion in all Western countries, than the destruction of South Africa's white establishment's policy and power—destruction which, alone in the world, the United States would have the power to carry out, in the guise of a humanitarian crusade. But the approval of world public opinion, for whatever it may be worth, would only be the small change of all the potential benefits such a forthright policy would bring to the United States. The destruction of South Africa's white power structure might even have to be followed by a massive emigration of a substantial part of its white population, on the pattern of the massive emigration of a million European settlers out of Algeria in the early 1960's.

In turn, this white emigration could, conceivably, make room for a substantial immigration of American Negroes, however unpalatable this solution would be to the local Bantus who could provide no trained leadership on which to build a viable state. Chief Albert Luthuli, on a visit to the United States, was struck by the interest displayed by American Negroes in South Africa; he was asked many times: "Can we come over there and assist you?" to which he invariably replied: "It would be heartening if you could, but for one thing the South African Government wouldn't let you—certainly not with that motive. For another, you'd find yourselves foreigners in the continent of your origin. But we're glad of your interest in any case, and to the extent that you fight segregation here, you help indirectly." [14] Clearly, the welcome mat would not necessarily be spread out for American Negroes in a Bantu-dominated South Africa, but the leaderless Bantus could hardly expect to resist their forcible intrusion if it were encouraged and assisted by Washington. The net result, in this case, would be the creation of a gigantic "Liberia" in southern Africa, but one that would not be allowed by Washington to drift aimlessly as its West African predecessor did in the nineteenth century.

Dominating South Africa through the agency of its own American Negroes implanted there, the United States would control a strategic area of prime importance overlooking all the southern hemisphere sea lanes connecting Europe with the Far East. It would also control the world's richest diamond and gold mines—not an inconsiderable advantage for the United States' leaders, coping with a precarious balance of payments situation, to be able, at last, to state that the dollar is as good as gold— because it would then control *politically* most of the free world's gold production. Nor should it be forgotten that South Africa is a prime source of uranium, the vital ingredient for the mushrooming uses of peaceful as well as military nuclear power. In addition, South Africa is generously supplied with platinum, coal, iron ore, manganese, chrome, asbestos, lead, zinc, copper—a true cornucopia.

While a great deal of this speculation may sound rather farfetched, a close look at South Africa's international relations since the end of World War II might make it sound more plausible. While world public opinion has, for long, condemned the policy of apartheid and expressed its disapproval in strong moral terms, it still remains within the prerogatives of a sovereign country to determine its own social policy as it sees fit. And even then, in an unprecedented interference of the United Nations

Security Council in a member country's internal affairs, a motion was voted in 1964 requesting the other member nations to ban all sales of arms to South Africa in protest against its policy of apartheid; among others, Britain and the United States decided to comply with this request. Irritated at the lack of concrete results a few years later, the United Nations General Assembly urged, in the fall of 1967, a worldwide trade boycott of South Africa as "the only means" of ending her policy of apartheid, drawing the Security Council's attention to the "grave situation" created by South Africa's racial policy.[15]

All by itself, South Africa's internal situation would hardly justify sterner measures than some form of trade boycott; and the strictures of the United Nations may be put down to growing irritation in the 1960's at the part played by South African mercenaries in the Congo and elsewhere, just as United States' impatience may well be justified by repeated incidents provoked by the visit of American warships to Capetown, Durban, and other South African ports and the petty harassments inflicted by the South African authorities on the Negro members of the ships' integrated crews.

On legal grounds, however, the Pretoria Government finds itself in a weaker position in other quarters, which might conceivably warrant escalating the United Nations' action all the way up to outright military intervention—Washington willing, of course. The Union of South Africa inherited after World War I a League of Nations' mandate over the huge former German territory of South-West Africa and, without formally incorporating it into the Union, ran it as if it would inevitably, some time in the future, become part of it. When the United Nations took over from the deceased League of Nations after World War II, it made numerous attempts to assert its authority over the territory, but in vain. From 1945 to 1966, South Africa ignored seventy-five resolutions of the General Assembly, including the one passed in October 1966, terminating South Africa's mandate over South-West Africa—a resolution which the South African Government promptly termed "illegal." The following spring, in 1967, a special session of the General Assembly was called to consider the problem and find ways and means of implementing the United Nations' decision to oust South African authority from the territory. But how? Only one country in the world would have the mobile military strength to back up the United Nations' resolution—the United States; and Washington was in no mood, in the midst of the war in Vietnam, to saddle itself with another conflict on another distant continent. Although the Afro-Asian bloc, strongly assisted by most Communist states, advocated the use of force, none of them could provide the military muscle to do so. In the end, all the United Nations could achieve was to appoint a Council for South-West Africa, and direct it to take over the administrative functions of the territory and help prepare it for independence—all of which remained a futile gesture. Such instructions will remain dead letter for as long as Washington does not put military teeth into them.

In the meanwhile, quite undaunted, the South African Government went ahead with its plan to extend the policy of Bantustans to South-West Africa and announced that it was offering "self-determination" and perhaps eventual independence to Ovamboland—a parched plain lying in the north of the territory and containing almost half of its population. There was a general outcry on the part of the Afro-Asians and even the United States felt compelled to disapprove. Until then, America had tried to smooth things over and attempted, through discussions and talks, to persuade the Republic of South Africa to take the United Nations' resolution into account. But the Ovamboland offer, shrewdly calculated to impress part of world public opinion, made the United States' efforts in favor of a peaceful solution seem pointless.

As an editorial in the *New York Times* pointed out at the time: "Mr. Vorster's tactics may achieve their immediate objective of sowing confusion and dissension at the United Nations; but over the long haul they only make more probable a showdown between South Africa and most of the rest of the world" [16] —which showdown can only end, in years to come, in a military confrontation between America's armed might and the obstinate rulers of South Africa. Meantime, in one of his most violent speeches, the American Ambassador at the United Nations attacked the South African Government in December 1967, accused it of brutality in South-West Africa and of breeding violence by "closing the avenues of peaceful dissent," [17] putting the South Africans on notice that, sooner or later, Washington might have to contemplate some drastic steps to apply the United Nations' will in that part of the world.

Since World War II, Washington has displayed a remarkable eagerness to intervene militarily in all quarters of the globe. One can conceive, therefore, that at some time or other, when there is no other war on hand, the United States' leaders will come to see all the advantages implied in the destruction of South Africa's white establishment's power and independence, and in the extension of its *de facto* protectorate over its territory—because any, even peaceful, defeat in the matter of South-West Africa would begin to sow the seeds of defeatism in some parts of South Africa's white population. Rising tension between the Republic and world public opinion would probably encourage many among South Africa's English-speaking whites to emigrate permanently to other, less threatened lands—leaving in South Africa the hard core Afrikaners who have nowhere else to go. In other words, a determined policy on the part of Washington could so soften up and weaken the South Africans that they would hardly be in a position to put up a serious armed resistance to the military application of Washington's policy.

Taking all this into account, the most probable development, in years to come, seems to be a forcible tearing of South-West Africa out of the clutches of the Republic, carried out, militarily, if need be, by the United States and assorted satellites in the name of the United Nations and world morality, followed by a rising chorus of anti–South African incantations throughout the world—inevitably followed by a steady white emigration *out* of South Africa, thus weakening the very basis of white supremacy. In addition, it should be expected that some form of Bantu guerilla organization, encouraged by these developments, would begin effective operations in the wilder parts of the Republic, linked with terrorist organizations in the cities. And, finally, as a precondition, Rhodesia would have had to be disposed of, since it has become, for the time being, South Africa's advance bastion facing the heart of black Africa.

It is symptomatic that, in August 1967, the outlawed Rhodesian and South African nationalist parties (the Zimbabwe African Peoples Union of Rhodesia, and the African National Congress, of South Africa) announced the formation of a military alliance pledged to overthrow their respective white governments, and made no bones about admitting that they were using arms supplied by Communist countries—while stating that they would, of course, welcome weapons from non-Communist quarters. Almost simultaneously, the Rhodesians announced that their security forces had clashed with African guerillas south of Victoria Falls and that, for the first time, a detachment of South African military had been flown to Buluwayo and sent to join the Rhodesian forces in the Zambezi Valley.

Guerilla warfare alone could never hope to topple the white regimes in southern Africa; but in conjunction with international military action against South-West Africa, stimulated by the clear evidence that world public opinion was putting teeth into the United Nations resolutions, there is a definite possibility that guerilla action could have a seriously demoralizing effect upon the white populations of southern Africa, who have very few friends in the world. This, in effect, would deliver the whole area into the hands of the United States who would, then, become the arbiter of the situation and, in effect, the "protector" of whatever settlement takes place in that part of the world.

☆ XII ☆

Empire and Nation-State:
The Future of Europe

Fanning out across the world, America's influence and interference have been compelled, out of a legitimate preoccupation
with its own self-protection, to fill the numerous power vacuums
opened up by the collapse of Europe's worldwide empires.
Rather fitfully, depending on the mood of its public opinion and
the personality of its various Chief Executives, the United States
had attempted to cope with one emergency after another, patch
up local quarrels, set new states up on their wobbly feet, extend
economic aid, and lend military assistance right and left. Everywhere, in Asia, Latin America, and Africa, its major concern has
been to dam the Communist flood which threatens to submerge
the "developing" world where living standards are drastically
lower than in Europe and North America—Lin Piao's "world
cities." In the process it has decisively assisted the destruction of
Europe's "colonial" rule and influence, gradually cutting off the
Old World's extensive power relationships with Africa and Asia;
at Suez, in 1956, it crushed just as decisively France and Britain's last attempt to "go it alone" and restore Europe's power

position in the Middle East; it is reorienting the Commonwealth's scattered "white" dominions into becoming American outposts and detached elements of the United States' strategic power; it is being led to interfere with increasing vigor in the internal affairs of Latin American nations as they are likely to be increasingly threatened by revolution and gnawed at by guerilla warfare; it is building up a *de facto* empire in the Far East; and already, it has become the warden of the Congolese heart of Africa, prelude to the eventual development of an Afro-American empire which is barely visible over the future's horizon.

All this, without being consciously *willed* by one man or group of men, is happening unobstrusively and inevitably. Each new emergency has to be coped with on the spur of the moment and each emergency is responsible for the development of new tools and instruments—economic, military, and intelligence tools which, once created for a limited and temporary purpose, tend to perpetuate themselves and acquire an autonomous life of their own. In turn, these instruments beg to be utilized, and often tend to create the very emergencies that justify their existence. This is the familiar landscape through which the reluctant imperialists proceed on the road to empire.

In the process of development, two major and related events of considerable magnitude have taken place, two events produced by two World Wars that propelled two non-European Superpowers to the fore while destroying all European Powers: the anti-Western revolt of all submerged civilizations from Morocco to China; and the increasing concentration of the inward-looking West Europeans on their own small, bustling, and relatively prosperous half-continent, leaving the United States to deal as it can with the anti-Western revolt which is sweeping through the world. While by no means stripped of all its illusions and mythology concerning world affairs, the United States has embarked on a definite course of action regarding the world at large; and given the physical means to do so, any policy which is pursued with a certain persistence eventually succeeds.

Regarding Europe, however, America has no definite policy and seems puzzled in the second half of the 1960's. Yet, of all areas of the world, Western Europe is the one most vital area from the standpoint of America's own safety, one that can never be allowed to fall into hostile hands. Combined with Soviet Russia's might, it could easily challenge the global power of the United States. Included in the United States' orbit, on the other hand, it would give Washington true mastery of the world—an unchallengeable mastery against which any other combination on earth would be powerless. For two decades after the Second World War, the North Atlantic Treaty Organization embodied, in loose form, this combination of power which deterred Soviet aggression and Communist subversion in Western Europe. But during these two decades, the spirit of the organization and the strength of its alliance were undermined by the relentless transfer of global power and responsibilities from Europe to the United States and by the accumulated resentment of some Europeans at the shrinking of their world status.

For these resentful Europeans who wanted neither American nor Russian protectorate, there was a third geopolitical possibility: European unification, and its emergence as a third Superpower in its own right; but the inner logic of their passionate resentments against each other and their mutual distrusts prevented them from boldly, and quickly, taking this course of action; the very being of Europe's component nations is intimately connected with their narrow, parochial, deeply rooted chauvinisms, not with the fragile concept of a European community—which only came into temporary and short-lived existence in its free Western half when under the threat of Soviet aggression. Reluctant to face facts and sacrifice their petty nationalisms for the sake of a greater and more significant nationalism on a Continental scale, they sought refuge in the wholly negative policy of retrieving their outdated parochialisms and undermining the entire concept of Europe's *political* unification. It is easy to blame one or several statesmen for this state of affairs; but it is more fruitful to realize that if they have their negative way, as they do, it is mostly because Europeans have a profound aversion to sacrificing their national identities on the altar of Continental unification. Hostility, fear, and contempt are the main ingredients of Europe's nationalisms and, though muted at present, they have by no means disappeared. Even within single and relatively small states, separate would-be nations coexist with greater or lesser difficulty in a state of permanent tension—Flemings and Walloons in Belgium are constantly at loggerheads; Basques and Catalans are thorns in the flesh of Spain; Welsh and Scottish nationalists threaten Britain's unity; northern and southern Irishmen cannot stand each other.

Europe's greatest contribution to modern politics is not the exaltation of nationalism as such, but the concept of the *nation-state*: to each well-defined nation must correspond an independent and sovereign state in a precisely delimited territory. It is in the name of the nation-state ideal that Germany and Italy forged their belated unity in the nineteenth century; and it is in the name of the same ideal that such multinational entities as the Ottoman and Austro-Hungarian empires were smashed into small, unstable, and mutually hostile nation-states in central and eastern Europe. As other empires crumbled throughout the world, the same balkanization took place, with increasingly disastrous and eventually ridiculous results, until the world's map began to look like an incomprehensible crazy-quilt in which such microscopic states as Honduras and Lesotho are presumed to have the same sovereign rights as the United States or Soviet Russia. The small, weak, and artificial newborn nation-state is ideal fodder for expansive imperialism; and there is every prospect that the absurd extension of this principle will inevitably give way to other modes of political organization. In many cases, it is not even applicable: most articulate Arabs feel part of one Arab *nation* split up among many states, but all their efforts to gather into one *state* are doomed by geography and their individualistic temper. India is, basically, a conglomerate of many different nations gathered, through the temporary intrusion of British imperialism, into one federal state.

While thriving in many ex-colonial areas, the nation-state is probably on its way out of Europe, its birthplace—but not because of any looming European unity. True enough, the European Common Market has slightly dented the hitherto unrestricted sovereignty of its member states—but only on economic grounds; the eventual entry of Britain, however painful and long delayed is certain to restrict further the Common Market's unifying role to a strictly economic one—if it is still in existence by then. The European nation-state is on the way out, mostly because it has become too small, both militarily and economically. Not only that; Europe itself—that is, Western Europe, since any hope of unification with Eastern Europe is largely chimerical—is already, in many respects, too small by comparison with the Superpowers. Even politically united, Western Europe would be at the strategic mercy of the United States; even united, the Continent would control neither the seas around it nor the air above it; it has lost control of its African underbelly, of the Suez Canal which connects it with East Africa and Asia, of the Mediterranean which is in the hands of the American Sixth Fleet; unlike the United States and Soviet Russia, it does not possess in the ground all its required sources of fuel and raw materials. Just as important, European nations have proved, since World War II came to an end, that they have not even had the will to fight for their own survival; with the exception of West Germany, Europe's member states have never contributed their pledged quotas of military forces and hardware to NATO, with the absurd result that, again with the exception of West Germany, the United States army in Europe is greater than that of any European nation-state—and in the specific instance of actual firepower, with no exception at all.

All this suggests that since the European nation-state is historically doomed, and since Europe's political unity appears to be unrealizable, some other, more practical solution will have to be found—indeed, has already been found in the nebulous shape of a North Atlantic community in search of institutionalization. A retrospective glance at the postwar decades brings out clearly its inevitability.

Throughout the 1960's, it might seem that France was the main obstacle to the creation of a politically unified Europe; however, if we take a closer look at the historical record and put Charles de Gaulle back into proper perspective, it will be clear that, after World War II as after World War I, Britain was the main obstacle—a shrewd, cunning obstacle made formidable because it had centuries of traditional British diplomacy and quasi-religious fervor to back it up. No European country reacted with such harsh hostility to Aristide Briand's 1929 proposal for a "federal bond" between European nations; and Aristide Briand was a leading *French* statesman, as was Édouard Herriot, who endorsed his proposal. Indeed, between the wars as after World War II, French personalities and statesmen were the leading advocates of some form of European unification; and in the aftermath of the Second World War, it was such leading French statesmen of diverse political persuasion as Paul Reynaud, Léon Blum, Paul Ramadier, and Édouard Herriot, a survivor of the first "European" effort of the 1920's, who played a leading part in sponsoring various schemes of European unification.

In the middle and late 1940's, an influential, discreet, and far-sighted segment of France's elite, led by Jean Monnet and Robert Schuman, rescued the European idea from the dustbin into which the statesmen of the 1930's had thrown it, and presented it anew to a Europe that had undergone the ordeals and devastations so clearly prophesied by Eduard Benes. It is difficult for us to appreciate, decades later, the remarkable courage required by such Frenchmen who suggested shortly after the end of the war —while the memory of so many victims of German aggression and atrocities was still vivid, while anti-German sentiment was at fever pitch and the thirst for vengeance seemingly unquenchable —that all should be forgiven and forgotten, and that a start should be made immediately toward the unification of the Old World. Had it not been for the first dream of the 1920's, it would not have been possible to suggest to the French people that all their suffering would be wasted unless former enemies joined in building a better future together.

Monnet and Schuman spoke for France, but not for France alone; they spoke for the rest of Continental Europe that was still mute, painfully picking itself out of the rubble. The French voice was the only one heard on behalf of the Continent at international gatherings of the Great Powers. Strangely enough, even de Gaulle joined the Europeanists in opposition to the Morgenthau plan to destroy Germany's heavy industry; before the war was even over, he had spoken of Germany as a "great, and certainly a guilty, people, but nevertheless a people whose destruction the higher insight of Europe cannot permit." [1] Yet, the war was over, dismemberment of Germany was the first task to which Charles de Gaulle and his successors applied themselves. And when he went to Moscow to sign a new treaty of alliance, it seemed that France was getting ready to revert to the old fruitless policy of holding Germany in check by allying itself with a Soviet power that was a far greater menace to all concerned than a mutilated Germany could ever become.

De Gaulle's postwar dream was to preserve the illusion of France as a great Power by playing off Communist East against English-speaking West, with himself in the middle as the spokesman of Continental Europe. This policy experienced an early collapse. The alliance with Moscow did not prevent de Gaulle's exclusion from the ill-fated Yalta Conference, and did not prevent Stalin from adopting a contemptuous and even hostile attitude toward his only Continental ally, or from countering French policy in Germany all along the line: and at the July 1946 Council of Foreign Ministers, Soviet Foreign Minister Molotov stated plainly Soviet Russia's support for a politically unified Germany and opposition to the political separation of the Rhineland. De Gaulle's resignation in 1946 did not immediately alter the postwar expression of France's foreign policy. Georges Bidault persisted in playing the game of an illusory balance of power between East and West; attempting to sit between two stools, he was unable to realize that he was, in fact, sitting on the floor, wrapped in the prevailing mist of French illusions.

The mist lifted with terrible swiftness in 1948, and the French suddenly saw the situation as it really was. France, and the whole of Western Europe, were in ruins, on the brink of starvation and economic collapse. The prompt institution of the Marshall Plan, its concomitant gathering of European statesmen around the same bargaining table, and the initiation of economic planning on a European scale caused the first breach in the nationalist illusions of the French leaders: France's bankruptcy was part of a Continental bankruptcy. Panic spread quickly throughout Western Europe when Soviet Russia displayed its ruthless imperialism, crushed what was left of freedom in Central and Eastern Europe, and blockaded Berlin. France's bourgeois nationalists suddenly woke up to the startling realization that a large number of Soviet armored divisions were only hours away from their borders, ready to join with a powerful French Communist movement already inside the gates. The presumed great power of their country disappeared like a puff of smoke; far from being an arbiter between East and West, France discovered that she was rushing to join the ranks of those who took shelter under the United States' nuclear umbrella.

It was not Washington that imposed the Atlantic Pact on more or less reluctant partners but the French Premier of the day, Henri Queuille, who, on February 25, 1949, made a desperate appeal for American protection. This was promptly acknowledged and answered when the United States signed the Atlantic Pact on April 4 of the same year, less than two months later. The United States sincerely thought of the alliance as one in which European nations would participate fully in the common military defense of Western Europe. This, however, the latter had no intention of doing, feeling economically unable to shoulder the burden. The mood in France had turned to outright defeatism, and while the French nationalists attempted to preserve the remnants of the colonial empire against African and Asian subjects who had become infected with the same nationalist disease, they relied on America's nuclear hardware for protection in Europe. In effect, however much they might deny it or minimize it later, they had asked for and accepted an American protectorate for years to come. This protectorate had a price tag: unification of Western Europe, as willed by the United States in an effort to strengthen the defense of that split Continent.

Georges Bidault had at last picked himself up from the floor and, his balancing act between East and West having utterly failed, he began to promote the economic unification of Europe as a prelude to some form of political federal union. But he encountered the same immovable obstacle: Britain. Try as he might, he never succeeded in convincing the British that an Anglo-French union (actually suggested by Winston Churchill in 1940) was the first step, and an essential step, toward the unification of the Old World—or rather, the British understood it only too well and wanted no part of it. The swift resurgence of

Germany's economic power after 1948 made such a step even more urgent. The French did not want to be left alone with the Germans on the Continent; only an Anglo-French-Benelux union could possibly digest such an enormous lump as Germany. But nothing came of the French move.

Not only old atavistic instincts, not only special ties with the United States and the Commonwealth, but five years of war had effectively reoriented Britain away from Europe, toward the high seas and the world beyond. Terribly weakened economically, almost bankrupt, Britain believed that its only hope to retain World Power status was to keep out of Europe and strengthen the ties binding her to the worldwide English-speaking community. British insularity proved, in the end, far tougher than French nationalism. France had temporarily thrown nationalism overboard for a multitude of reasons which had little to do with the wishes of the United States. French leaders and politicians had reached the conclusion that nothing short of Europe's unification could shake France loose from its economic inertia and vitalize its ossified bureaucracy and outdated social structures, along with creeping parliamentary paralysis at the top. Britain obstinately barred the way and adamantly refused to join in building a united Europe.

Winston Churchill had suggested, in the late 1940's and out of power, the gradual setting up of some form of "United States of Europe"; but, when he returned to power, he did strictly nothing to implement it. Nor can it be forgotten that in his Fulton, Missouri, speech of March 5, 1946, he called for an alliance of the English-speaking people—and never squared this proposal with that of a "United States of Europe." On the other hand, overcoming their fear of Continental solitude with Germany, the French began moving in that direction when, in May 1950, Foreign Minister Robert Schuman proposed the setting up of a "High Authority" to control the entire West European production of coal and steel—first step toward a European federation, and first step of the forthcoming Franco-German *rapprochement*. But when the French invited the British to take part in talks about the "Schuman Plan," they were turned down cold. The same thing happened a few years later when the Common

Market was founded. Every step of the way, the British were requested to join, and every time they refused. Even in political and military matters, the British very conscientiously sabotaged all and every "European" effort—from the Council of Europe in 1949 which the British joined but emasculated, to the European Defense Community which they virtually destroyed by refusing to join it—wittingly or unwittingly reviving the French fears of Germany's ascendancy in an integrated, purely Continental army.

The British not only refused to cooperate. When the foundation stone of the Common Market was being laid by the Treaty of Rome, Britain decided to erect a hostile counterorganization, the European Free Trade Area (EFTA), whose failure was as remarkable as the Common Market's success.

All this was an instinctive reaction conditioned by the historical past. The move toward European unification was led by staunch Roman Catholics—France's Schuman, Germany's Adenauer, and Italy's de Gasperi, a trio of remarkable men known in Britain as the dreaded "Black Front." Hundreds of years of atavistic hostility to the potential disruption of the Continent's balance of power, the conservative Anglican dislike of the Vatican and anything connected with popery, the Labour Party's dislike for the social and economic conservatism traditionally attributed to Continental Roman Catholics—everything conspired to induce the British to launch their postwar offensive against a successful integration of the Continent. After all, as Winston Churchill, newly reelected Prime Minister in the early 1950's, told Konrad Adenauer, Britain was a "neighbor of Europe" but not *in* Europe.[2] Mindful of the shadow of Pope Pius XII in the background, his Labour opposition was just as adamantly determined to keep out of Europe and preserve the outdated balance of power; Britain's left-wing press damned the "Black Front" for "attempting to establish a Catholic-dominated alliance after the pattern of Metternich's Holy Alliance, aimed at delivering Europe to a reactionary-clerical despotism." [3]

Britain's attitude, in effect, gave French *nationalisme intégral* a new lease on life. While the sheer momentum acquired by the European movement brought into being a number of supranational entities (the Coal and Steel Community, Euratom, the Common Market), French nationalism revived, fanned by de Gaulle's parliamentary mounthpiece, Le Rassemblement du Peuple Francais. Strong enough to destroy France's own scheme for the creation of an integrated European army (the European Defense Community), French nationalism was nevertheless unable to carry out the reconquest of the nation's Far Eastern dominions or even to hold on to its African empire. Wasting its few military resources on these ill-fated undertakings overseas, France was even too weak to claim its share of power and responsibilities in NATO's integrated structure.

Throughout de Gaulle's twelve years of exile from the responsibilities of power, his policy had remained consistent in its shrill nationalism and anti-Anglo-Saxonism, although it was slightly ambiguous regarding the concrete problems presented by the revolt of the French colonies—which he would, undoubtedly have liked to retain as an essential element of French *grandeur*. In the light of his violent opposition to the United States' military policy in the Vietnam of the 1960's, it is worth recalling that, prior to Dienbienphu, de Gaulle advocated a total mobilization of French power to crush the Vietminh "rebellion." [4]

Nevertheless, as a modern disciple of Machiavelli, skilled in the art of exploiting the inevitable, de Gaulle soon made up his mind that decolonization was inevitable; and he was able to rise to power out of the wreckage of the Fourth Republic in 1958, determined to remain in the Elysée Palace for as long as he chose to. There was no real break in continuity between the Fourth and his Fifth Republic. Indeed, since he had for so long overshadowed the Fourth Republic, and had enjoyed a certain veto power through the workings of his parliamentary devotees (often in conjunction with the Communists), his accession to the presidency merely symbolized the return of France's outdated parochial nationalism to the seat of supreme power in Paris.

Charles de Gaulle's Fifth Republic, internally stable, endowed with a rudimentary form of nuclear power (*Force de Frappe*) and a large hoard of gold, and still exerting substantial influence throughout French-speaking Africa, was at last free, as soon as Algeria became independent, to turn on its Anglo-American partners and protectors. In his progressive shift toward a neutral-ist position, de Gaulle dealt what might prove to be a deathblow to NATO, and decisively curbed the Common Market's drive toward some form of political unification, compelling it to re-main merely an instrument of economic welfare. For whatever it might be worth, he temporarily raised French prestige through-out the neutralist world, pulled Uncle Sam's beard in Latin America and Southeast Asia (but with no concrete results). Yet, at times of acute international crisis in the early 1960's, he proved to be a loyal ally of the United States, perhaps even stauncher than the British: the Berlin Wall crisis in 1961, and more especially the Cuba crisis in 1962, saw him line up firmly with America.

Charles de Gaulle was fully aware of the historical drift of the Western world toward some form of political unification under American hegemony, and was determined to fight it with all his might. In his press conference of October 28, 1966, he made his position clear: after stating that France's policy was above all "aimed essentially at France's present and continued independ-ence," he spoke of his loyalty to France's allies but served notice that he wanted no part of what he called the "supranational myth." He warned that he would refuse to let France become absorbed in supranational organizations where, in his own words, "political protection, military force, economic power and the many-sided aid of the United States predominate"; such "or-ganizations would have been for us nothing but a cover for our submission to the American hegemony. Thus France would have disappeared, carried away by flights of fancy." [5]

It is rather de Gaulle's policy that is "carried away by flights of fancy," since he can raise nothing but the flimsiest barriers against the growing ascendancy of American influence through-out the world. At times, indeed, Charles de Gaulle behaves like an unconscious harbinger of American imperialism by delib-erately weakening all the Western elements that could conceiva-bly stand up to this American hegemony—attempting to disrupt Canada so that its broken pieces would inevitably fall into the United States, weakening Britain so as to drive it further into America's arms, fighting European unity and therefore weakening the resistance of a small balkanized Continent. Simultaneously, the United States' policy, coping with one emergency after another without any long-term vision of its relationship with Europe, poured a great deal of fuel into de Gaulle's anti-American engine. There is no doubt that the resurgence of the spirit of nationalism in France—a belated reaction to its collapse in 1940, a psychological compensation for the humiliation felt ever since—did a great deal of harm to both the solidarity of the Atlantic Alliance and the drive toward European unification. It did not play, on the stage of world politics, the beneficent part de Gaulle claimed for it—except, perhaps, insofar as the nationalist disease began spreading to Central and Eastern Europe where it weakened Soviet Russia's grip on its satellites. But much of the blame for these harmful developments must be laid to the clumsy handling of de Gaulle by the Anglo-Americans themselves since the Kennedy-Macmillan meeting in Nassau, December 1962.

At this meeting, without consulting any of their other partners, the British and American leaders decided to establish a NATO multilateral nuclear force, adding the usual polite but meaningless formula—"in the closest consultation with other NATO allies." In mid-January, however, de Gaulle refused to go along and announced that France would build its own nuclear weaponry in order to preserve its military independence. The plain, hard, inescapable fact is that Britain and the United States have always had, and always will have, a "special" relationship which will always raise hackles on the Continent. Of course, this "special relationship" itself has considerably altered over the years, especially since the Suez fiasco. While Anthony Eden's successor, Harold Macmillan, assiduously repaired the damage done to British-American relations (and all the while insisting that Britain was still "Great" Britain), he charted a new course of utter subservience to American wishes; and when he went to Moscow in 1959, he made sure beforehand that he had Secretary of State Dulles' permission to do so. A well-known American journalist makes no bones about the fact that "Many Americans . . . have been gratified by the deference, at times verging on servility, showed to United States interests and policies by Prime Minister Macmillan and the majority of his associates in the cabinet." [6] But then, it was already well known that twenty years before, when he was British Minister Resident in Algiers during World War II, Harold Macmillan had stated his belief that "These Americans represent the new Roman Empire and we Britons, like the Greeks of old, must teach them how to make it go." [7] Macmillan, the wily, self-styled "Greek," was determined to beat the other European "Greeks" in the race to become the prime adviser to the Roman-Americans. Under Macmillan's leadership, Britain took a big step toward further "satellization" —and pushed France on its road toward increasing neutralism.

Coincidentally, Harold Macmillan himself decided that the time had come to face facts on the Continent. The unexpected success of the six-nation Common Market, combined with Britain's own economic stagnation, was compelling the British to change their views. On August 2, 1961, Prime Minister Macmillan announced in the House of Commons that Britain would seek admittance to the Common Market—an historic announcement which implied, in fact, that Britain was no longer able to preserve its insularity in a world of Superpowers. Breaking with a thousand year old tradition, the British had come to admit that, now, they were only one of Europe's offshore islands. With mixed humility and cunning, the British paid their respects to an unexpected Continental success but fully intended to get in on the venture and wrest control of it from the arrogant hands of Charles de Gaulle; this they could hope to achieve by preserving their vital financial position in world trade, their extensive connections with the Commonwealth and, more important, their "special relationship" with the United States.

In other words, by becoming the vital *hinge* between the Continental Six and the outside world, they could influence both in turn to their own advantage by playing diplomatically one against the other. By dragging in some of their EFTA partners, the British could further hope to dilute the overwhelming Franco-German leadership. Once admitted within the organization, stated a noted journalist at the time, "Britain may influence the direction of this mighty force and lead it toward a greater amalgamation of power with the United States, Canada, and perhaps Australia and New Zealand in a great community of the free" [8]—the very concept that would hitch the Common Market to the English-speaking chariot and which Charles de Gaulle abhors. Needless to say, the Kennedy Administration was fully in favor of the scheme. And no great foresight was required to foretell that de Gaulle would slam the Common Market's door in Britain's face—which he did in January 1963.

Years went by and power shifted from the Conservatives to Labour in London; but the problem and the attitudes hardly changed at all, except that Britain's economic predicament was becoming steadily worse, and that the British had not given up hope of joining the Common Market—on their own terms and determined to shift its course toward the "high seas." The same Harold Wilson who, in 1967, started banging on the doors of the Common Market seeking admittance—doors against which the full and considerable weight of Charles de Gaulle was brought to bear again in order to keep it closed—stated, in October 1963, the perennial British view of the matter in the following terms: "We regard an Atlantic partnership—indeed, a wider-than-Atlantic grouping, covering the Commonwealth and Latin America—as the objective. We felt that membership in EEC would have been worthwhile as a stepping-stone to this wider free world unity." [9] Harold Wilson's, and indeed Britain's, atavistic policy has not changed and will not change: Britain's entrance into the Common Market can only be a "stepping-stone" to a wider Atlantic Community, never to a united Europe standing on par with the world's two Superpowers.

To a great extent, large and distant as it is, there is no doubt that America is bound to adopt some elements of the British attitude toward any attempt at European unification of a strictly "Continental" variety, that is, a European union from which Britain would be excluded. Charles de Gaulle's attitude can only reinforce the United States' suspicion that a Europe *politically* organized without Britain and the United States would be a Europe organized *against* them. This is the whole reason for America's enthusiasm about Britain joining the Common Market— once inside the gates, Britain would be America's broker and would keep the door open for her. De Gaulle was perfectly right in stating that Britain would become a Trojan Horse within the

Common Market; and, in the long run, he can do nothing about it; it is bound to happen.

Had the political unification of Europe really been one of Washington's objectives, it would have been wiser to encourage rather than hinder the *rapprochement* between France and Germany that had been worked out between de Gaulle and Adenauer. At the above-mentioned press conference, de Gaulle stated with repressed anger: "It is not our doing if the preferential contacts ceaselessly developed by Bonn with Washington have deprived the French-German agreement of inspiration and substance." [10] The fact is, and will remain, that London will never completely trust a real, durable alliance between France and Germany, inevitable cornerstone of Europe's *political* unification, around which other Continental countries could then agglomerate; for this "Frankenreich" monster, the British will always have a mixed feeling of fear and hostility. This would be true in the best of circumstances, that is, even if France was headed by a friendly government; how truer it is when Charles de Gaulle is lord of the Elysée Palace! And when it comes to European matters, British views and influence are still paramount in Washington.

One must never lose sight of a fundamental fact of political history: with the exception of Britain and a few minor countries in northern Europe, the United States, alone in the world, has preserved the same political system and the same Constitution since it became a nation in the eighteenth century. At great cost in bloodshed, it has not only preserved the Union but strengthened it and increased its size while preserving a remarkable political stability and the rule of law. It has been free of the social upheavals and revolutions that have ravaged and still are ravaging the rest of the world; its compact society has been able to evolve creatively, achieve an unparalleled standard of living, and develop peacefully the new political and social institutions that changing conditions required. Alone among all the Western democracies, it has been able, without any breach in the Constitution, to develop an equally unparalleled concentration of Executive power with which to deal with unexpected emergencies.

In other words, in spite of wide and often furious differences of opinion as to the proper course of action in given circumstances, the United States presents itself to the world as a compact block, in space as well as through time, united with its past and its traditions, looking far into the technological future, united in whatever present course of action has been decided upon by the people's chosen leader whom they will follow, on the whole, with discipline and loyalty, even if they disagree with his policy. This is true of no other free country in the world; in particular, it is true of no country on the European Continent. Quite apart from the fact that it is today the greatest Superpower, the United States enjoys a comparatively superb *political metabolism* which only a few others, and much smaller countries, can enjoy. It is in terms of the molecular structure of their respective social organisms that the United States and Europe's nation-states should be compared; and, apart from the racial problem which is the only seriously disruptive element in American society, the comparison, in terms of social efficiency and power-breeding, is all to the advantage of the United States.

Without referring to European nation-states such as Italy and Germany that were not even united until the second half of the nineteenth century, we can select France as a perfect instance of poor political metabolism, of endemic instability. When the United States achieved its independence and adopted the Constitution under which Americans still live today, France was still in the age of its *ancien régime*—absolute monarchy; overthrown in 1789, it gave way to a chronic instability which has been France's trademark ever since: the great Revolution itself, ending in the Directoire and Consulate, followed by Napoleon's First Empire, the restoration of the monarchy in 1815, overthrown by the 1830 revolution in favor of Louis-Philippe's "bourgeois" monarchy, in turn overthrown in 1848 by the advent of the Second Republic, which gave way three years later to Louis Bonaparte's Second Empire which crumbled in the aftermath of the Franco-Prussian War. We then have to record the advent of the Third Republic—a seventy-years'-duration miracle, which came to an end in the military debacle of 1940. After a remarkable display of disunity and inner squabbling among themselves during the war, the French then set up the Fourth Republic after World War II, and saw it disintegrate in 1958, to be replaced by Charles de Gaulle's Fifth Republic—the last one, to date. Quite clearly, this turbulent history shows that France has not yet found its true political balance and cannot present itself to the world as an organized, disciplined, purposeful nation determined to control its independent destiny. How then can it pretend to challenge, for any length of time, other nations that are not only much larger, wealthier, and more powerful, but also politically and socially far more stable?

To make matters worse, both France and Italy harbor within their body-social large Communist parties, whose membership is made up of internal *émigrés* recruited in their vast proletariats and who care not one whit for the present bourgeois regimes and national aspirations. Able to muster anywhere from one-fifth to one-quarter of the total voting strength, these large, undigested Communist movements represent a potential threat of real magnitude for the bourgeois leaderships of both France and Italy; in times of real crisis, their potential power might be such as to throw their countries' frightened middle classes at the mercy of some external protective force—the United States' for instance. More particularly in the case of France, the existence of such a large, disciplined, and enduring Communist party actually mortgages its middle class, inasmuch as it represents an ineradicable check on its power of leadership and freedom of decision—as was dramatically demonstrated in 1940 when many French Communists collaborated with the invading Germans in the aftermath of the Hitler-Stalin Pact.

The West European Communist parties may no longer be subservient to Moscow as they were in Stalin's days; they still remain ideologically linked with Soviet Russia and are prepared to work and risk for the sake of Russia's national and imperial strategic interests—all the while believing that they are working for world revolution. It is essentially a religious-like feeling of brotherhood within the embrace of a faith blindly adopted which links all West European Communist parties to their Mecca in Moscow. Their power of disruption is immense, their discipline fearsome; Communists in France and Italy never miss voting with almost religious obedience whereas their opponents, who believe in freedom and democracy, often have a poor voting record.

In France, in particular, with its deeply rooted revolutionary tradition going all the way back to the Great Revolution of 1789 and the Commune of 1871, the Communist party, with over four hundred thousand dedicated members organized in nineteen thousand closely knit cells, is a world of its own, a country within a country, with its own doctors, lawyers, bankers, publishing houses, bookstores, publications, film directors, theaters, sports teams, women's associations, boy scouts, poets, and even night-club singers. The only French political organization headed by full-time professionals entirely devoted to the party, it resembles a crusading Church rather than a political party; its fanatical members have more in common with religious leaders than politicians. Largely in control of Paris' famous Red Belt with over three million inhabitants in fast spreading industrial suburbs, they run their model local governments with ruthless and incorruptible efficiency. They are clever enough to capitalize on every social problem that presents itself, regardless of the issues involved; and with jesuitical skill, they will just as well stand up for the small farmer and pass themselves off as the champions of the small privately owned farm, as they will for the poorest member of the industrial proletariat. And for all the changes that have taken place, both in Soviet Russia's structure and that of international Communism at large, they remain as emotionally dedicated to Moscow as Moslems to Mecca. They are a power to be reckoned with under any circumstances, a political tapeworm in the bowels of France.

Even in Britain, whose political metabolism is far superior to France's, and where communism is not a social problem and does not command the allegiance of entire social classes, Communists expertly steal away the leadership of labor unions from their legitimately elected leaders to promote devastating strikes and weaken further Britain's alarmingly weak economy. Indeed, Prime Minister Wilson made no bones about it when, on October 24, 1967, he bluntly stated that he had evidence of a Communist plot to wreck Britain's economy.[11]

All this is poor ground for the development of any significant power base, even on a semi-Continental scale—Eastern Europe being out of the picture of any unification scheme, for the time being. On the other hand, this is fertile soil for the gradual implantation of foreign influences and the concealed application of a determined political will from abroad. Even Gaullism cannot put up much of a resistance; the self-assured expression of postwar French nationalism will not outlive Charles de Gaulle. It may still find instinctive expression in small, unimportant ways, but it will never recapture the unified, purposeful, and dramatic expression he gave it in the 1960's. The spectacular French crisis in May 1968, with its student rebellion and paralyzing general strike, underscored the fundamental weakness of an old country led by rigid, backward-looking mandarins who have proved incapable of adapting France's antiquated social and academic structures to the requirements of an increasingly technological age. In a revolutionary atmosphere of impending civil war, the entire Gaullist edifice began to show signs of disintegration, slowly dragging along with it to its eventual doom its brilliant paraphernalia of independent foreign policy, nuclear *force de frappe,* and vast gold hoard. And so will Europe's last flame of independent spirit be snuffed out—leaving the Old World divided against itself in so many ways, at the mercy of the non-European Superpowers.

Without even noticing the steady erosion of their outdated "sovereignty," the weak and disparate European nations, unable to truly unite into a new organic whole, are doomed to fall into a Superpower's orbit. Already at the time of the Marshall Plan, then through the agency of the Atlantic Alliance and NATO, it became clear that multiplying relations between a Superpower and smaller nation-states could no longer use the normal diplomatic channels which are the traditional means of contact between "sovereign" nations. Soon flooded by the swelling mass of contacts required by one emergency after another, these diplomatic channels were quickly replaced by direct links between the powerful American departments and their weak European counterparts, power flowing directly from the strong to the weak pole.

This international phenomenon is made possible by the decline of legislative influence and the steady enhancement of executive authority in every country. Even in Britain where the Mother of Parliaments is still enthroned in its Gothic palace, the decline of the power and influence of the venerable House of Commons is startling. Britain is no longer ruled by its MP's but by a strong, discreet caste of sophisticated bureaucrats whose citadel is Whitehall and against whose entrenched and enduring power elected representatives can hardly do anything. Power is steadily passing into the hands of the permanent officials, out of those of Parliament—and into the hands of the Prime Minister, out of those of the Cabinet. Nothing has done more to enhance this bureaucratic power than the vast nationalization of private business and industry carried out by the Labour governments— to the point where over 40 percent of Britain's total investments is owned by public authorities. And what is true of Britain, as a relatively new feature in its history, has long been true of France whose talkative *députés* have never had much share of real power since Napoleon established a permanent bureaucracy of mandarins.

One can therefore understand that this erosion of legislative power everywhere is leading to direct confrontations between bureaucracies, bypassing Congresses and Parliaments, leading in turn to either conflict or subordination and virtual integration of bureaucracies serving, ostensibly, different countries. For instance, the direct *gearing* of a particular American department, agency, or even private company, onto their European counterparts can only lead to *de facto* integrations. In the 1950's this was particularly noticeable in military matters; in the 1960's, it is becoming increasingly evident in economic matters. This progressive symbiosis, by increasingly meshing their respective bureaucracies and administrative apparatuses and industrial corporations at the highest level, along with their military establishments and their technological centers, can only lead to growing unification on an "Atlantic," and no longer European, level. An equally gradual atrophy of West European nations' sovereignty and political independence will automatically lead to

Washington's assumption of "European" responsibilities, leading eventually but inevitably to an "Atlantic Empire" of which the United States will have become the nucleus.

This new form of transatlantic imperialism is slowly becoming multidimensional as American influence comes to be exercised in a wide variety of realms—*vertically*, linking American groups in Europe (military, diplomatic, business, intelligence, cultural) to their headquarters in the United States; and *horizontally,* in more discreet fashion, linking these American groups transplanted in a European country with one another, joining them in a common, and partly instinctive, effort to dominate the European nation-state in which they live, upholding and assisting each other in such a way as to increase tenfold the effectiveness of their influence. A perfect example of this imperial network in action on a *horizontal* plane was given in January 1968 by Germany's Social Democrat member of the Bundestag, Martin Hirsch, when he accused American officials in Germany (where they were entitled to monitor West German communications for defense purposes) of handing over confidential German business information to competing American firms; and he added that "there is a much closer contact between American government and military officials and business" than is usual in Germany.[12]

The second half of the 1960's has witnessed a bold attempt to dismantle part of the intricate machinery linking both continents on the North Atlantic when Charles de Gaulle expelled the NATO headquarters and entire military paraphernalia from France. This, many took to be a sign of the times, a normal return to old-style national independence, a sort of "business as usual" reversal due to the gradual thawing of the Cold War freeze. They are likely to be just as shortsighted as those who saw in the American isolationism of the interwar era a decisive return to "normal" conditions—instead of seeing in it the swan song of "business as usual." There will never be a return to "normal" conditions in those terms. The old-fashioned nation-state is dying on its feet, not without making a great fuss about it. It is happening, inevitably.

What gives it its disturbing feature, to many, is that every sacrifice of national sovereignty falls on the shoulders of Europe's weak nation-states, not on those of the United States. When, shortly before the Nassau meeting between President Kennedy and Prime Minister Macmillan, the Americans offered, in exchange for the ill-fated Skybolt, to sell Polaris missiles to London, they insisted in exchange that Britain's Polaris force would have to be "irrevocably" committed to NATO—in other words, irrevocably under ultimate American command. This the British indignantly refused, claiming that the terms should be the same as those originally set for the Skybolt. The Americans can afford to commit "irrevocably" anything they please to a supra-national organism such as NATO because they are in ultimate control of it; it all amounts to shifting it from their right to their left hand. This is not the case with the European nation-states, whose sovereignty and independence are being steadily eroded, whose freedom of choice shrinks relentlessly.

The inescapable wave of the future is not a revival of the European nation-state but its gradual atrophy. If the fact is not faced, if the Europeans attempt to fight the inevitable, they can only further fasten the alien grip on their destiny—enhancing the *imperial* nature of the alien hegemony, since imperialism is essentially the predominance of the part over the whole. European institutions are slowly crumbling under the onslaught and European power is fast slipping away. What Europeans will now have to struggle for is no longer the retention of an illusory sovereignty, the chimera of the eternal nation-state; they must and will struggle for fair representation within the North Atlantic community—a concrete "reality" on every level, which is growing by leaps and bounds and is begging for some form of institutionalization. They must transform what is fast becoming a partly invisible, unavowed empire into a visible, institutionalized community in which political representation and distribution of power will be evenly shared by all on both sides of the Atlantic.

America's imperial burden is becoming increasingly heavy and the only way its innumerable commitments can be met is for the imperial body to grow up organically, cell by cell, to the size required to shoulder this increasingly weighty load—in other words, by organic union with Western Europe, Canada and Australia. It was striking, for instance, that early in 1968, at a time when the United States was having considerable difficulty enlisting the manpower required to prosecute the war in Southeast Asia, it was disclosed that about five hundred Britons were volunteering every week to serve with the American forces in Vietnam. In March 1968, an American Embassy spokesman in London stated that "we would have no trouble in raising a British division or two to serve in Vietnam." [13] Indeed, with the disintegration of the British Empire and other European colonial empires, a great deal of Europe's newly available manpower could very well beef up America's own strained resources in the buildup of its empire. But Washington's bureaucratic leaders, stuck in old grooves and lacking in imagination, could not even bring themselves to amend the old legal proviso that foreign volunteers would have to pay their own fare to the United States!

The institutionalization of the Atlantic community would be beneficial to all concerned on many grounds—the military burden in defense of Western Europe would be more equally shared, and so would the defense of the West's (no longer just the United States') imperial positions throughout the world; the deficit in the United States' balance of payments, which is largely the counterpart of Continental Europe's surplus, would disappear overnight, and so would all trade barriers; a grave international problem would become a minor domestic one. The weight and might of this confederation of five hundred million free citizens would be such as to make it invulnerable to the aggressions of any other combination of Powers in the world.

Nothing remains static in life and in history; what does not move forward constructively, moves backward destructively. The American failure to take the lead, in the late 1950's, in transforming NATO into a tight Atlantic union or confederation —as urged by many of its farsighted Canadian and European allies—led straight to a breakdown of Western solidarity and a virtual collapse of NATO itself, not to mention the possibility of rising protectionism, trade wars, and monetary chaos. Had the same imagination that had led to the Marshall Plan and the North Atlantic Treaty Organization been displayed ten or fifteen years later, on a *political* level this time, Charles de Gaulle would never have had a chance to disrupt Western solidarity.

This disruption is only a temporary setback, however; there is some evidence that the wisest of France's Gaullist leaders themselves are uncertain as to whether they can reestablish the French nation-state's full independence. When, in a 1967 television appearance, French Premier Georges Pompidou compared de Gaulle to Philopoemen, the last of the great Greek leaders to resist the Romans, he was quite obviously trying to pay him a compliment in thus describing him as the last European who is willing to stand up to the spreading hegemony of the modern Romans. Did he also slyly intend to convey the notion that de Gaulle's entire crusade was a *"baroud d'honneur"*—a glorious fight for a lost cause—and that it would go down in history as being just as doomed from the start as that of the great Philopoemen—because neither could or would unite Greeks and Europeans in a common stand against Roman and American hegemonies?

Europe's historical greatness sprang in ages past from the stimulating rivalries between its component states and nations; America's own greatness, on the contrary, sprang from its relentless striving toward union, even at the cost of a major Civil War. Of what European statesman could it be said, as Alexander Stephens said of Abraham Lincoln, that "The Union with him, in sentiment, rose to the sublimity of religious mysticism"? [14] The principle of *unity* is incarnate in the American body politic, and it is only under American leadership that such overall unification of the West can take place—West European unity being included in it as one of its components. And only then can Marshal Lin Piao's "world cities" roll back the revolutionary threat flung at Western Civilization from the depths of the "world countryside." This unification can come by stealth, as it has for two decades of crisis and international emergencies; or it can come openly through free debate and the conscious will to evolve toward a North Atlantic Confederation. In any case, the two continents bordering the North Atlantic are already being integrated in more ways than one. Probably the most dramatic in the 1960's is the *economic* way of integration.

☆ XIII ☆

Economic Hegemony

America's growing hegemony in the realms of economics and technology amounts to a entirely new form of imperialism, largely invisible and unobstrusive to all but the technicians involved. This peaceful invasion is worldwide; but it is in Western Europe that its political repercussions are likely to be the most far-reaching, the Old World whose antiquated social and economic structures are slowly crumbling and are, simultaneously, being rebuilt by the influx of American managerial know-how and technological proficiency. Europe is having its old face lifted, but when the new face appears after surgery, it is an American, and no longer a European, face.

Throughout the nineteenth century, European capital had poured into North America, as it did into every other continent —fresh capital that, along with America's own native capital, built railroads and industrial plants and developed the United States. Two World Wars have decisively reversed the flow, and the two decades following the end of World War II have witnessed the most extraordinary outflow of American capital and business know-how which is threatening to submerge most of the non-Communist world. In fact, the economic expansion of America's giant corporations is in the process of leading to their virtual control of the free world's key industries.

This process is so startling and so relentless that it is raising a hue and cry all over the world: in October 1966, the Canadian Liberal Party's policy conference in Ottawa was requested "to do something to halt the spread of United States control of Canadian industry"—by which time, roughly half of Canada's industry and more than half of Canada's mineral resources were already in American hands. In June 1966, George C. McGhee, United States Ambassador in Bonn, speaking to the Rhein-Ruhr Club of Düsseldorf, felt compelled to deny that "United States investment represents a threat to German economic independence." [1] Belgian economic circles criticize their Government for inducing Americans to take over a large slice of their industrial potential by providing incentives for investments in underdeveloped areas such as West Flanders, or soft areas such as the declining coal mining regions; but, in reply, the Belgian Government points out that the same incentives are offered to Belgian companies who refuse to take advantage of them; and adds, hopefully, that American companies are oriented only toward profits, not politics.[2] Labor troubles plague many American-owned automobile plants in Britain; typical was the trouble, in the autumn of 1965, at the General Motors-owned Vauxhall automobile factory in Luton where, to the cry of "bloody Americans," British workers threatened to break into the office of the American director of manufacturing.[3] The impact of American management concepts sparked as much trouble at the Chrysler-owned Rootes Motors plant at Linwood, near Glasgow. Wholesale dismissal of French workers at General Motors' Frigidaire plant in Gennevilliers and in 1962 at Remington Rand's Caluire factory near Lyons, triggered a short-lived attempt on the part of the French Government to halt, in the early 1960's, the inflow of American capital and control.[4] Even in microscopic, neutral Switzerland, the takeover of the Raffineries du Rhône, the first Swiss venture into oil refining, by Standard Oil of New Jersey, prompted an outburst of anti-American feeling, pungently expressed by one disappointed stockholder who stated: "I am no Gaullist, but with the way American business is taking over in

Europe, I say that the United States is losing more friends all the time." [5]

The fact is that the expansion of America's economic power and influence throughout the world is irresistible. The bare statistics, alone, are staggering. Whereas in 1950, United States' assets and investments abroad totaled an already impressive amount of 31.5 billion dollars, this figure had leaped to 106 billion, fifteen years later. During the same fifteen years, American private investments climbed from 19 to 80 billion, while the United States Government credits and claims went from 12.5 to 25 billion. The most significant segment of this remarkable ascent is the rise of direct private long-term investments from less than 12 billion in 1950 to over 57 billion in 1966. [6] These figures represent, not only the actual stakes owned by American interests in foreign lands but also the direct application of their management and economic overlordship abroad. Broken down geographically, in 1966 American ownership reached over 17 billion dollars in Canada, almost 11 billion in the rest of the Western Hemisphere, over 16 billion in Western Europe, 2 billion in Africa, 3.5 in Asia, and again 2 billion in Australia and the South Pacific. In actual fact, however, these figures represent only the book value, which underestimates to a considerable extent the actual market value of these investments. [7] The rapid pace of this economic invasion can be gauged from the fact that in the late 1960's, America's private business concerns invested abroad somewhere between 8 and 9 billion dollars a year. For purposes of comparison, it should be noted that American corporations were spending well over 60 billion dollars a year on new plants and equipment at home, over six times as much as in the rest of the world.

From these astronomical figures, it is clear that the United States corporations focus heavily on Canada and Western Europe, that is, on the most industrialized countries outside the United States itself—with the exception of Japan which protects its native ownership against foreign takeovers. This economic invasion is highly profitable: total sales of foreign affiliates of American corporations reached roughly 43 billion dollars in

1966, having more than doubled since their 18 billion sales in 1957, yielding a net total profit of about 6 billion dollars in 1966.[8] But again, in terms of ultimate political implications, it is American industry's invasion of Western Europe that is most significant. One third of all the automobiles manufactured in Europe are built in American-owned or -controlled plants; American firms control between a quarter and a third of the oil industry's market in Britain and the Common Market. In tires, earth-moving equipment, razor blades, sewing machines, and countless other industries, their share is even larger. By 1967, American firms had a stake of almost 6 billion dollars in Britain alone, produced 10 percent of its manufacturing output, 17 percent of its exports, employed already one out of sixteen British workers, controlled about 7 percent of the country's total industrial assets— and at the present rate of growth, would control one quarter of Britain's entire economy by 1980. In many ways, and to an increasing degree, the centers of economic decisions in Europe are shifting to the United States; European industry is now faced with the threat of becoming a mere subcontractor of American industry.

In spite of occasional outbursts of anger at America's "economic imperialism," it is usually the Europeans themselves who invite American participation, and eventually American control, in all industrial sectors where American technological advance has become unchallengeable—in the techniques of management, cost accounting, marketing, publicity, and in all advanced technological fields where their immense superiority in research and development tells, along with their ability to tap an enormous capital market which is rarely available to European concerns. Furthermore, most American subsidiaries in Europe now have a considerable capacity for self-generated growth and are becoming increasingly independent of United States' financing. As early as 1965, over half of the funds required for the expansion of American firms in Europe were borrowed on the European market, one-third was derived from subsidies extracted from European governments and from local financing, and only one-tenth came directly from the United States. The non-American share of this financing increases constantly: for the first three quarters of 1967, the flow of dollars from the United States for the financing of direct corporate investments was down 14 percent from the same period in 1966,[9] while American subsidiaries raised increasing amounts of money on the spot—in the Old World, mainly tapping the Eurodollar debenture market. In other words, American corporations are no longer taking over European industry with their enormous financial resources, since they finance these takeovers mostly with *European money:* they are taking over primarily with organizational ability and constructive imagination. Nor is this invasion merely an altruistic missionary effort to teach the Europeans how to do business: their profit margins, along with their growth rate, average twice that of their European rivals.

In all this, they receive considerable assistance from the Europeans themselves. Rather than merge with European competitors and pool two weak firms, many European concerns are only too happy to find security in the ample bosom of some giant American corporation that can and will provide the safety of its size, its technological and managerial know-how, and its vast financial means. Size is often of the essence—the sales of General Motors alone exceed the gross national product of nine out of ten of the worlds nations, and its capitalization, in the 1960's, is larger than the total capitalization represented on the Paris stock exchange. It is easy to understand the feeling of security engendered in those who are absorbed. American business in Europe has an additional, and highly important, advantage: unlike most of its European competitors, it thinks "European," not local or national; it is mentally geared to tap the whole European market, not merely that of France, Britain, Germany, or Italy. Thinking in terms of a single continental market, with a sales network covering the whole continent and straddling dozens of nation-states, with a uniform accounting system, the American subsidiary is in truth more typically "European" than any European firm rooted in one single country. Up to 1967, only one European merger had taken place in the Common Market (the German Agfa and the Belgian Gevaert companies), ten years after its birth! Separated by a multitude of different national fiscal systems, patent laws, trade unions, rules of competition, languages, traditions, and tastes, with miniature stock exchanges and capital markets that are totally inadequate, the Continental Europeans are beginning to discover that it is the Americans who are thinking European and making a united Europe— albeit, increasingly as an economic subsidiary of the United States.[10]

Nothing can really stand in the way of the American economic juggernaut, not even the blatant use of local political pressure—the last-ditch defense of the antiquated nation-state; too many counterpressures can be brought to bear. The takeover of Machine Bull by General Electric is a case in point. When General Electric offered to buy 20 percent of France's largest, and ailing, manufacturer of computers and data-processing machines in 1964, the French Government refused to grant permission— the main reason being the previous refusal of the United States Government to allow France's Atomic Energy Commission's purchase of a large IBM computer required for its nuclear research center at Saclay.[11] And who had to give in first? The French Government, for compelling financial and technological reasons. Eventually, Machine Bull was allowed to go into partnership with General Electric (prelude to its absorption, with the exception of a subdivision engaged in French defense work); it had been soon discovered that France could supply neither the technological know-how nor the capital required to save Machine Bull from bankruptcy . . . and Charles de Gaulle finally received his IBM computer in 1966.[12]

It is not only the United States Government that prevents France, for instance, from blocking new American investments —to single out the most hostile country in Europe in the 1960's. Aside from the fact that, as a member of the developing Common Market, the French nation-state has already lost part of its sovereignty, and therefore partial control of its economic destiny, investments that should have gone to France in 1964 and 1965 went instead to its Common Market neighbors [13]—General Motors switched a new plant from Strasbourg to Antwerp, a major petrochemical plant, planned for Bordeaux, was eventually built in Belgium.[14] From there, these concerns can just as effectively compete in France, once tariff barriers have dropped within the Common Market. Realizing, at last, that resistance was worse than useless, the French authorities gave in late in 1965 and the American flood was resumed. It was made plain that no single European country can operate a restrictive policy all by itself. Even the present Common Market has already become too small for effective resistance to the invasion from overseas: an enormous amount of work still remains to be done on the unification of European tax systems and corporate statutes as a preliminary to all-European mergers which, alone, could stand up to American competition. In fact, the emergence of the Common Market has benefited primarily the European subsidiaries of American corporations, because only the Americans were *mentally* geared to take advantage of it.

The fact that, so far, America's direct investments in the Common Market represent already 7 or 8 percent of total manufacturing capacity is not as important as the fact that these investments are concentrated in specifically vital sectors, servicing growth industries; and the fact that these investments have grown from 600 million in 1950 to 6 billion dollars in 1965 and roughly 7 billion dollars in 1967, can well be interpreted as an actual takeover-in-the-making of the vital sinews of Europe's industrial power. The process is irresistible, inasmuch as the United States' leadership in research and development is steadily widening the technological gap which separates Europe from America.

It is not that European governments lack the will to stem the tide; they often do, and not only in France; but most of the time, unsuccessfully. A perfect symbol of the insidious inevitability of American power's extension is the history of Rootes Motors Limited's acquisition by Chrysler Corporation. Anthony Wedgwood Benn, Britain's Minister of Technology, told the House of Commons on January 17, 1967, that Rootes was insolvent—its insolvency being largely attributable to the British Government's austerity program. The Minister of Technology then stated that

the previous Conservative Government had tied the hands of its
Labour successor by letting Chrysler buy a minority interest in
Rootes as early as 1964, which had then led to full integration of
marketing and managerial activities—such integration implying,
evidently, the American takeover of marketing and management
owing to their unquestioned superiority in these fields. The result
was that Rootes could no longer be merged with another British
automobile company. Some members of the House of Commons
then suggested that it be bought out by the British Government
itself. Again, Anthony Wedgwood Benn proved that it was too
late: the current expansion plans of Rootes depended entirely on
the 1964 agreements on technological exchanges with Chrysler.[15]
In other words, owning only a minority interest in the British
firm, Chrysler had come to dominate the situation so completely
through its managerial, marketing, and technological superiority,
bolstered by its enormous financial resources, that the British
Government itself could no longer prevent the complete final
takeover by Chrysler—an 85 percent ceiling being agreed to as a
face-saving device. And right away, the Americans took charge;
the American chief executive went through the company "like a
whirlwind" according to the phlegmatic but startled British and
"reshaped it down to grassroots with Chrysler men in key positions." The board of directors remained, but power was instantly
shifted to a new administrative committee in which key positions
were handed over to Chrysler men. Toward the end of 1967, the
Sunday Telegraph could only conclude that "Rootes is responding
to American surgery." [16]

The political impact of this rapid expansion can be far-reaching.
Quite obviously, although America's giant corporations are
often euphemistically dubbed "multinational," they remain, in
fact, subservient to the Government of the United States. And an
American company's foreign affiliate can presumably get its
parent company into trouble if, even with the consent of the host
government, it sells prohibited goods to a Communist country
that is not in good standing with Washington; quite likely, the parent company can then be prosecuted for violation of the United
States Trading with the Enemy Act. Needless to say, the parent

company will use its unlimited authority over its foreign affiliates to make them comply with the wishes of the Government—of the United States Government, that is.

For instance, for all the virulent nationalism proclaimed by President de Gaulle, France could not sell Caravelle jetliners to Red China because American electronic equipment is an important component of the aircraft, which component falls under the sway of the United States Trading with the Enemy Act. Toward the end of 1967, under the Cuban Assets Control regulations, Washington's Treasury Department forbade the 65 percent American-owned Clayson Company of Zedelgem, in Belgium, to accept a 1.2 million dollar order from Cuba—triggering a predictable outburst of Belgian resentment at "American interference in Belgium's internal affairs," and compelling the Government in Brussels to attempt, through diplomatic channels, to induce the American Government to rescind the order.[17] In other words, American power makes itself felt in an extraterritorial way—and the governments of the nation-states, who feel their sovereignty slipping away unobtrusively, attempt to fight back.

President Lyndon Johnson's sweeping orders, issued in January 1968, that West European subsidiaries of American corporations send home the major portion of their earnings, prompted France's Finance Minister Michel Debré to issue veiled threats of reprisals;[18] it soon became clear that such subsidiaries could well be faced with the choice of violating either Washington's executive order, or the standard corporate law of the host countries: a contest of *political* power was on. Just about the same time, in January 1968, William Gordon, President of Canada's Privy Council, presented to the Cabinet a copy of the Task Force report on the growth of foreign ownership and control; the Task Force had dealt at length with the fact that Canada's sovereignty was being eroded by the extraterritorial claims of the United States and, among other items, strongly recommended legislation "to block Canadian-based companies from abiding by foreign court decisions affecting their parent companies."[19] All this is very well; but, in the long run, who needs whom? And who is politically, militarily, economically, and technologically in the stronger position?

However international it may appear, an American-controlled "multinational" corporation is driven to organize itself on two distinct levels: 1) Increasing *strategic centralization* in matters of overall planning and global policy, which is carried out in the United States; 2) Increasing *tactical decentralization* of all other functions, giving foreign subsidiaries and the host governments the illusion of greater independence than they actually possess.

The most striking aspect of this economic onslaught came out of a report from the United States Council of the International Chamber of Commerce, forcefully rejecting the thesis that the voluntary restraints on the outflow of dollars, set up in 1963, would cure the perennial deficit in the United States' international balance of payments.[20] On the contrary, it urged that all government assistance be given to a carefully planned, long-term expansion of American investments and business on the grounds that "this is the only way, consistent with maintaining our worldwide economic position, that the continuing, ever-growing commitments of the United States can be met." [21] Thus, a self-perpetuating mechanism is being set up, requiring ever more American economic involvements in other countries in order to pay for the United States' increasing *political* commitments abroad, with the result that they, in turn, require added *political* involvement for the protection of these economic stakes, and which in turn can only be paid for by additional economic penetration.

However, on January 1, 1968, this self-perpetuating mechanism was brought under Washington's administrative control by President Lyndon Johnson's executive order prohibiting private American investments abroad without the approval of the Secretary of Commerce. The ostensible reason for taking this drastic step was the worsening American balance of international payments' deficit, in turn triggered by the vast expenditures of the Vietnam War and the speculative attacks on the dollar stimulated by Britain's devaluation of the pound sterling in 1967. But since, as has been pointed out previously, American subsidiaries in Europe were already financing nine-tenths of their expansion by raising money *outside* the United States, the progress of America's growing economic hegemony will be merely slowed down, not halted. Quite obviously, it is not in the United States' interest to halt a process which generates abroad net receipts for America—inflows from interests, dividends, royalties, fees, incremental exports, etc.—at an annual rate of 4 billion dollars, which more than counterbalances the 2.5 to 3 billion dollars outflow.

The basic problem is that, in the late 1960's, the United States Government was spending abroad, on foreign aid, tourism, and military deployment, at twice the rate at which the private sector was generating additional surpluses. However, the point has already been reached where European prosperity itself is at stake, inasmuch as American investments in the Old World's industries have now become a vital component of Europe's economic expansion. If American investments were totally cut off for any length of time, European industry would stagnate and fall back further in terms of technological and managerial competitiveness; on the other hand, it would eventually be counterproductive for the United States in the sense of aggravating rather than solving its balance of payments problem.

Looking at the *political* implications of President Johnson's executive order, it is clear that by bringing private American investments overseas under Washington's direct control, the American Government will be able to shift these investments from hostile countries (France, for instance) to other, more friendly lands. It is therefore a political weapon of awesome power that could conceivably bring the hostile country to its knees, since by cutting off the flow of American investments it would also be knocking a great deal of its industry out of world competition. Directing the flow of American investments, for instance, to the other Common Market countries at the exclusion of France would, in time, ruin the French economy and allow the wholesale takeover of what would be left by its more prosperous Common Market partners.

The truth of the matter is that the intermingling of the American and European economies has reached such a stage that any large-scale tampering with the present transoceanic currents can only harm both interdependent economies; and that the growth of America's economic hegemony is intimately connected with the unparalleled postwar prosperity, which is already well into its third decade. Any successful effort to fight this growing hegemony along the lines laid down by the French economist Jacques Rueff (de Gaulle's mentor in the science of economics) could only result in triggering a worldwide depression.

Key to the rapid development of American economic power in all its aspects is its single-minded emphasis on research and development—"R & D." Being usually the pioneers in both peace and war technologies, Americans are always exploring new technological territory, always solving problems that no one has ever had to face before. Unlike their more tradition-bound and static European cousins, they conceive life in dynamic terms; they live in the stream of time as fish in a swirling river—where Europeans would like to believe that this swirling river is only a placid lake. Being pioneers in research in most fields of human endeavor, they are bound to be leaders in most key technologies.

Here again, statistics are eloquent. In 1939, Europe and America both spent roughly 500 million dollars a year on R & D. A quarter of a century later, America was spending at the yearly rate of 24 billion dollars, as against 7 or 8 in Europe. Du Pont, the chemical giant, was then spending as much money on research as the whole of France's private industry; as national entities, France was spending roughly one billion and Britain two billion dollars on R & D. Such differences are out of all proportion to the respective differences in size and wealth—but whereas American consumer industries, for instance, spend about 4 percent of their turnover on research, comparable European firms spend 1 percent or less. All told, the United States spends ten times the per capita figure and four times the total of what the whole of Europe spends on R & D.[22]

In order to get a bird's-eye view of the rising importance of research and development in this new technological age, the following figures should be kept in mind: whereas total American R & D expenditures in 1921 were roughly 150 million dollars, representing 0.2 percent of the gross national product with a percentage of government financing of 17, comparable figures in

1967 were 24 billion, representing 3.1 percent of GNP, with a percentage of government financing of 63. The full meaning of this disparity does not lie only in the remarkable increase in the percentage of GNP devoted to R & D, but also to the fast-rising percentage of government financing. And while European governments spend only small amounts on research, the United States Government alone' spent 15 billion dollars in 1967. In 1966, for instance, the American defense budget allocated about 10 percent of the total, or over 6 billion dollars, to R & D. Thousands of new weapons are simultaneously on the drawing boards of the Pentagon's eighty-three laboratories and arsenals, as well as on those of universities and private industry.[23]

Government expenditure on *development* (roughly 10 billion dollars in 1967) focuses on space, supersonic transport aircraft, nuclear reactors and weapons, health care, telecommunications, weather forecasting, advanced mail-handling systems. Government expenditures on *research* (roughly 6 billion dollars in 1967) focuses on space, medical research, basic scientific research, and housing and urban renewal problems. Of all this 15 billion dollars in government money in 1967, the Government actually performed only 14 percent, industry 70 percent, and the universities the rest.[24]

The important element here is the indirect commercial fallout from space and defense R & D. "Spin-off" products, applicable to the civilian market, are now flooding the world. The Boeing 707 was largely an offshoot of the KC-135 military jet tanker. A giant antenna built at Stanford to study the detection of hostile missiles was eventually used to bounce radar signals off the sun. Space research, under the guidance of NASA, has generated thousands of new inventions and has been a leading factor in the development of microcircuitry, diagnostic equipment, cyogenic surgical innovations (brain and eye surgery), weather forecasting (and, eventually control).[25] Even warfare yields a precious technological fallout, such as a new foam tested in 1967 in the tanks of the HH-3E helicopters and assorted aircraft fighting in Vietnam, which foam, when mixed with fuel in the aircraft's tanks, apparently prevents explosions or fire; no sooner had it been successfully tested when commercial applications for the safety of all aircraft were under study.

This transfer process from space and defense innovations to the broad industrial market has already yielded new products such as pliable films and laminates to be used in a wide range of temperatures and radiation, metal coating with Teflon, electron-beam guns for improving vacuums, endless-loop tape recorders, electrometer tubes to monitor radiation. A continuous stream of technological breakthroughs in lasers, ion propulsion, super-conductivity for electric transmission, silicon solar-cells, even in food packaging for space travel, have moved Germany's finance minister Franz-Josef Strauss to exclaim that "every dollar spent for space research in the United States, ten years ago, is worth four times as much in economic value today." He should know, since Germany, in spite of its own advanced technology, spends four times as much on American patents in chemicals, engineer-ing, and metals as it earns on its sales of technological know-how to the same industries in America. All told, the patent gap costs Europe half a billion dollars a year, and European industries are increasingly functioning under foreign licensing agreements— already halfway to becoming American subsidiaries; "Some evi-dence of the effectiveness of the greater American research and development effort is provided by statistics of patents and pay-ments for technical know-how, licensing fees and so forth. Amer-ican receipts from Western Europe exceeded payments by a ratio of 5 to 1." [26]

The world is now fast moving out of the era of audio-visual communications into a new era dominated by computer com-munications. The United States' predominance in this field is overwhelming, both in terms of production and utilization. In 1966, for example, out of 36,000 computers in use throughout the world, 30,000 were in the United States, and most of the others abroad were of American manufacture. And here again, the military uses of computers give America not only a precious advantage in terms of defense, but a means of financing research and experimentation which supplements the purely civilian ex-penditure. The military uses of computers are increasing at a geometrical rate of progression: IBM 7010 and 1460 computers, mounted on railroad cars, control the American army's supply system in Europe, keeping track of a quarter of a million stocked items, and handle 10,000 requisitions a day from 1500 units scattered throughout the Old World, continuously matching supply and demand in Europe.[27] IBM 1041's are moved right behind combat troops in Vietnam and are linked with a vast computer network extending back through Saigon and Okinawa all the way to Hawaii. "Project Mallard" is developing an all-embracing tactical communications system which will be common to the field armies of the United States, Canada, Australia, and New Zealand—virtually integrating the armed forces of these nations into the United States' defense apparatus, at the highest technological level. Millions of dollars spent on Mallard R & D are expected to mushroom up eventually to a billion dollars' expenditure on the system's development. Further research expenditures on computers for a Tactical Operations System (TOS), Tactical Fire Direction System (Tacfire) and a Combat Service Support System (CS3), to be tested by the Seventh Army in Europe, will further the growth of the whole computer industry, inducing most of the major American computer manufacturers to compete for government contracts. Save Soviet Russia, no other country in the world has the resources or the will to devote so much time and money to this kind of research—with the result that the United States, alone, will benefit from its industrial "spin-off."

The gap between the effort put into research in the United States and that of the rest of the world widens constantly, without any prospect that it can be narrowed in the near future. Not only wealth and size militate in favor of America; psychological attitudes toward the whole problem are radically different on both sides of the Atlantic. Pure research is still excellent in Europe; all the evidence suggests that the real bottleneck lies between the laboratory and the consumer's market. Timidity, conservatism, lack of entrepreneurial spirit, and lack of risk capital too often paralyze the European; market research, which is highly developed in the United States, is still in its infancy in Europe. It is the superior management of most American companies that is responsible for this far more efficient and rapid transfer of knowledge from drawing boards and laboratories to consumer shelves —superior management largely due to the fact that American business leaders are often young, willing to experiment and take risks which the older European managements would not dare to take. Furthermore, American experts and specialists of all kinds move back and forth freely between the universities, government, and business—whereas, in caste-conscious Europe, these are closed circles. One of the results is that, while 40 percent of the United States' large and extremely numerous universities offer graduate courses in business management, European companies and universities refuse to treat business as a legitimate academic science.[28] The situation here is increasingly grave, inasmuch as the time span between technological breakthroughs and their commercial applications narrows constantly: 79 years were required to bring forth the commercial applications of the flourescent lamp; 33 years for the vacuum tube; 5 years for radar; 3 years for transistors; and 2 years for solar batteries. Very recently, in the case of integrated circuitry, commercial application has taken place almost simultaneously with development. This bottleneck between development and commercial application, which is fast disappearing altogether in America, still looms as large as ever in Europe.

Not only are national markets far too small in Europe; nationalism still intrudes into technological research at the highest level, and duplication of efforts is standard in many European research undertakings. The recurrent woes of the European Atomic Energy Community (Euratom) are typical; it has become almost impossible to coordinate multitudes of strictly national projects. Early in 1967, the French and the Germans were working on fast-reactor projects along parallel lines, without in the least coordinating their efforts, even though they both belong to the Common Market. Worse still, and as if to underscore Europe's overall weakness, they could lease the required plutonium only from the United States, since it is the sole supplier— when, lo and behold, Washington decided to change its policy after the Euratom budget had been approved, from leasing to outright sale, putting it beyond Euratom's financial resources.[29]

In spite of official denials, the aim was quite clear: to pressure the Euratom countries into agreeing to the nuclear nonprolifera- tion treaty as proposed by the United States at the Disarmament Conference in Geneva. But far from seeing the light and strengthening their common nuclear organism, the Europeans proceeded to weaken it further. In December 1967, the Common Market Council of Ministers, meeting in Brussels, cut down Euratom to a small, marginal research center by giving it a re- search budget characterized as the "minimum of the minimum," and described by another as a plain "catastrophe." [30] And why? First of all, because the Italians complained that they had not received a "fair return" on their contributions to previous bud- gets; then the French insisted that future cooperation in long- term research programs should be "à la carte," leaving individual countries free to choose the projects in which they were willing to participate, rejecting the rest. As a result, joint research on thermonuclear fusion and nuclear-propelled ships had to be abandoned; no work was done on fast-breeder reactors, and key installations were condemned either to fall into disuse for lack of funds, or to pass under various national controls. Thus, not only was Euratom dependent on American-supplied (with Washing- ton's permission) enriched uranium and plutonium, making it in any case a technological protectorate of the United States; internecine rivalries, snowballing into multitudes of frustrations and resentments, prevented the Europeans from ever agreeing on *European* research, leaving the United States (and presumably the Russians) to reap the immense and exclusive benefits of an increasing technological monopoly (or, again, duopoly with the Russians).

It is obvious that one of the main pillars of R & D in the United States is government expenditures; figures make it quite clear; and nothing like the immense amounts devoted by the Pentagon and NASA exists in Europe where the endemic lack of funds, and governmental economy drives, undermine most Eu- ropean efforts to remain in the technological race with the two Superpowers. In such an industry as aerospace, government as- sistance plays a vital part, and it is easy to understand why the American aerospace industry, with 25 billion dollars' worth of annual sales, is flourishing, while its European counterpart, with only 2.5 billion dollars' worth of sales, is weak—especially in Britain. Even more startling is the fact that output-per-head in the American aerospace industry is seven times that of its European equivalent. No wonder the 85 percent of the non-Communist world's requirements for aerospace equipment and components is supplied either directly by American manufacturers or by foreign companies under United States license.

One of the worst blows that struck Europe's aerospace progress was France's cancellation, on July 5, 1967, of the Anglo-French V-G swing-wing aircraft. This highly sophisticated strike-and-reconnaissance aircraft with its variable geometry design was described in a 1966 defense White Paper by Britain's Minister of Defense Denis Healy as "both operationally and industrially, the core of our long-term aircraft program." [31] But a budgetary squeeze in Paris, caused by the mushrooming of France's expenditures on its miniature nuclear weapons system, prompted it to withdraw from the 800-million-dollar V-G project, leaving Britain's aircraft industry high and dry, to face the loss of its first-rate designers and engineers to American firms, and increasing dependence on America's aerospace production. In another instance, having had the lead in the study and designing of air-buses, the British, German, and French Governments put together an aircraft manufacturing company—but just as fast as they put it together, they began quarreling, slowing down the work to a crawl while the Americans were drawing up their own plans to catch up and overtake the Europeans.

If we now take a step back in time, and analyze this complex phenomenon which is America's growing economic hegemony in the light of history, it is clear that what really widened the technological gap beyond closing between Europe and America, was the Second World War which, indirectly, sowed the seeds of the United States' remarkable progress. First of all, it really launched the American Government into the R & D business; federal contracts were distributed right and left, leading to an intense cross-fertilization between three major partners—government, industry, and the universities—who have been working hand-in-glove ever since. Furthermore, it revolutionized management techniques to a degree unparalleled anywhere else by developing the joint technological-entrepreneur spirit in management; and especially by developing a new managerial technique known as "systems management" based on the teamwork of highly different industries and technological disciplines aiming at the solution of complex problems that none of them could solve all by itself. This interdisciplinary, multi-industry approach yielded rich dividends, the richest being, of course, the harnessing of nuclear power.

The technological gap can no longer be closed.[32] In the whole range of the new science-based industries, in aerospace and computers as well as in the electronic and communications industry, the United States' lead can no longer be overcome—to a great extent because the Europeans can never agree among themselves; they have become economic and technological captives of the New World.

To make matters worse, a brand-new problem arose after the Second World War: the so-called brain drain. As a general rule, the brain drain afflicts the whole world to the extent that most of the talented engineers, scientists, physicians, and teachers abandon poor countries in favor of rich ones. All the trained personnel and intellectual elite, whose skills are desperately required in their homelands, migrate to Western Europe and the United States—some because they find no ready employment for their talents in their misruled countries, some because they cannot resist the lure of better salaries, greater research facilities, and a more stimulating life in highly industrialized countries. This movement takes place on two distinct geographical levels: at the lower level, Western Europe pumps its former colonial empires of local talent; a 1966 report of the United Nations' Special Fund gives the following typical instances: Togo sends more physicians and professors to France than France sends to Togo; there are more specialists of all kinds from the Commonwealth working in Britain than there are British specialists working in the rest of the Commonwealth.[33]

At the highest level, however, the brain drain ultimately operates for the benefit of the United States, which is the end of the migration line—and at that end, only the most talented are to be found, the rest remaining in Western Europe. The same Special Fund report specifies that 5,000 engineers migrate to the United States every year and that between 1949 and 1961, for instance, 43,000 scientists and engineers moved permanently to America; and that, for another example, 14,000 highly trained Argentinians came to the United States between 1950 and 1964.[34] In 1966, 1,143 Indians held faculty positions in American colleges and universities, as against 192 American scholars similarly employed in India.[35] Almost 10 percent of all Indians holding medical degrees were working in the United States and Britain; in March 1967, for instance, two thousand Indian doctors took the examination of the Educational Council for Foreign Medical Graduates, which establishes qualifications for work in American hospitals. The trend is still upward, for the simple reason that it is found cheaper to import talent than to develop it at home. A 1967 report to the British National Conference on Social Welfare estimated that the United States had imported a total of one hundred thousand physicians, engineers, and scientists since 1949, at a total saving of about four billion dollars—which is what it would have cost to train them in the United States.[36] The same report added that, in medicine alone, 20 percent of the annual additions to the American medical profession was made up of foreign doctors; in 1965, for instance, 28 percent of the internships and 26 percent of the residencies in American hospitals were filled by foreign graduates.[37]

It is not only the medical profession that is drained. In the 1960's, for instance, an average year saw 3 percent of Western Europe's new graduates in science and 9 percent in engineering leave for the United States. In 1966, Britain's aerospace industry lost 1300 top technicians—520 directly to the United States and 344 to American firms in Britain. In October 1967, the British government-sponsored Committee Manpower Resources for Science and Technology reported that Britain loses over two-fifths of its annual output of engineers and technicians, and a quarter of its new science graduates.[38] There are so many instances of this relentless hemorrhage of talent that one is hard put to choose the most striking example. For instance, on November 16, 1967, the *New York Times* reported the following:

> The House of Commons broke into an uproar today over
> Government charges that the Westinghouse Electric Corpora-
> tion had tried to buy secrets of Britain's advanced nuclear
> technology "on the cheap" by offering inflated salaries to
> British scientists. . . . Prime Minister Wilson supported his
> Minister of Technology, Anthony Wedgwood Benn, to shouts
> of approval *from all sides* [author's emphasis]. . . . Mr.
> Wilson added that the Westinghouse policy seemed to be to
> "buy British scientists, whose training had been very expen-
> sive and borne by this country, and who would of course
> carry a great deal of the secrets in which the British publicly
> owned Atomic Energy Authority were far ahead of some of
> these American firms."

The additional fact that, for once, British technology had a
definite edge on its American counterpart in the peaceful uses of
nuclear energy only made matters worse, and the brain drain
more damaging. What irritated the British further was that, while
American salaries average three times those of the British, in this
particular case Westinghouse was alleged to have offered five
times the British rate for scientists experienced in fast-breeder
reactor systems. Quite obviously, Westinghouse found it more
convenient and cheaper to hire the scientists away than buy the
licenses "on a proper commercial basis," as the British Government would have it.

Inevitably, the first to be alarmed by this trend and to coin the
expression "brain drain" were the British, who lose a considerable part of their technological lifeblood to the United States, year
in and year out. Even the alarm sounded in September 1966 by
Kenneth Robinson, Britain's Health Minister, seems powerless to
check it: "Britain simply cannot afford to train doctors for the
purpose of swelling the membership of the American Medical
Association," [39] he pleaded, while six hundred local physicians
were undergoing testing and examinations for practice in the
United States. One quarter of the new doctors graduated annually by British medical schools emigrate. In turn, they are
replaced by Indian and Pakistani doctors, who are already in
terribly short supply at home. Occasionally, an outburst of increasingly rare patriotism thwarts this trend, as in the remarkable

instance of the frustrated takeover of Edwards High Vacuum International, a British engineering company, by Varian Associates, a California corporation. While the board of directors was strongly tempted to sell out for a price of fourteen and a half million dollars in 1966, they were warned "in the strongest terms" that the senior executives and many of the staff might not be willing to work for the company if control passed into American hands, stating that the results of years of research in the specialized field of vacuums and compressors should be kept in Britain and not be transferred abroad. With a sigh of regret, the directors gave up the deal.[40]

But as a rule, any effort to stanch the drain is doomed to failure, unless it further fastens the American grip on foreign brains. A perfect instance is the suggestion put forth by William A. Douglass, president of the American talent-scouting firm of Careers, Incorporated. While engaged in December 1966 in interviewing six hundred British engineers eager to go to the United States for the benefit of seven American aerospace, computer, and electronic companies, he suggested that British and American companies pool their technical skills in a joint research organization powerful enough to win contracts from the United States; but, as pointed out by Sir Solly Zuckerman, scientific adviser to the British Cabinet, this Anglo-American research organization would merely substitute an "internal" brain drain for an external one, in the sense that talent would be drawn by American-scale salaries from British to American projects, and that the fruits of this brain pool would go almost entirely to the United States.[41] A perfect example of "internal" brain drain was the capture of the Earl of Cromer, prestigious former Governor of the Bank of England, by IBM in 1967. The shock experienced and expressed without the usual British understatement came not only from the fact that an internationally respected British financier should go to work for an American firm, but that he would lend his prestige and authority to the greatest American manufacturer of computers, just at the time when everything was being done in Britain to build a viable computer industry—IBM having captured only a third of the British market at the time.[42]

In April 1967, a two-year study of the problem was released by Washington's Interagency Council on International Education and Cultural Affairs. This report, prepared for the American Government, concluded that the "brain drain has been exaggerated by other countries and that no steps should be taken to curb the migration of scientists and engineers to the United States." [43] Indeed, no. Why should the United States deprive itself voluntarily of the indirect benefits brought on by its higher standard of living and greater research facilities? And, short of government controls and restrictions on the movements of technicians from one country to another, what steps could be taken? This process works through natural osmosis and cannot be reversed in free societies. But the dramatic results are there: the suction effect exercised by the United States on foreign talent amounts to a form of intellectual emasculation of the rest of the world and, in effect, to an intellectual imperialism that is far more effective than all the old-fashioned, more conventional forms of imperialism. Not only is America's mental productivity increased; that of its allies and satellites is weakened by the same amount.

Thus, as far as the eye can see, Europe is increasingly condemned to be a major exporter of brains and a major importer (under license) of technological progress.

This vast expansion of American economic power throughout the world requires plenty of financial fuel; and thanks to the almost unlimited financial market in the United States—where not only the enormous amounts but also the velocity with which money circulates is far greater than in the more static, and far smaller, marketplaces of Europe—this financial fuel has always been forthcoming. Even when the United States' precarious balance of payments situation compels American corporations' affiliates to seek abroad the capital required for their expansion, they are able to do so with conspicuous success. More than two decades after the end of World War II, American subsidiaries in Europe are so well entrenched and so far better managed than European firms that they can better afford the higher interest rates and the risks involved; they no longer require the protective shield of the mother corporation and the inexhaustible capital market in the United States.

But in the late 1940's the situation was quite different. Great as was the national wealth of the United States at the end of World War II, this tremendous extension of American economic power abroad could never have taken place if the dollar had not become the chief reserve currency, with the British pound sterling (in which 40 percent of the world's trade was still conducted) playing distinctly second fiddle. Since the collapse of the gold standard in the early 1930's, it was a foregone conclusion that some other form of reserve medium for the world's currencies would have to be created—either one or two main reserve currencies, or a new artificial unit. The collapse of the gold standard simultaneously removed the severe, and at times brutal, discipline imposed on the world's commercial transactions— brutal discipline from which no nation, however powerful, could escape. This collapse meant that, if and when the United States found itself compelled to play the part of provider to, and policeman of, the world, the American Government could impose the dollar as the chief reserve currency—with obvious political implications, inasmuch as the United States itself could create at will, within limitations set by domestic inflationary considerations and external balance of payments' problems, the currency with which to pay for its vast acquisitions.[44]

The Bretton Woods Agreement had specified that international debit balances should ultimately be settled by transfers of gold. It also added that although gold remained the ultimate kingpin of the system, the use of automatic credits at the exclusion of all political privileges was necessary. However, a spontaneous development, strongly assisted by the active policy of the United States and the existence of a dangerous shortage of dollars abroad, relegated gold to a subordinate position and set up the dollar as the main component of international reserves. The main reason for this, of course, was that Washington adamantly refused to revalue the price of gold; alone, of all the world commodities, gold has been maintained artificially at the price fixed in the early 1930's. Thus relegated to a subordinate position, it became increasingly inadequate to finance an enormously expanding international trade—hence, the crucial role of reserve currencies; and, in turn, the crucial importance of the United States' power to control and regulate world trade through its control of the main reserve currency; had the price of gold been adequately raised, the importance of reserve currencies would have been far less, and the control of the United States over the world's monetary flow would have been considerably weaker. In the long run, it always boils down to a matter of *control,* that is of sheer, unadorned power—quite justified nowadays on strictly technical grounds since it is evident that gold does not provide the flexibility required by modern economic structures.

In the early postwar years, the main incentive for preferring dollars to gold was that dollar claims are interest-bearing, whereas gold is sterile. Then, as the dollar shortage disappeared with the economic resurgence of Europe in the 1950's, the full political power of the United States began to put pressure on all non-Communist states to keep their reserve dollars and refrain from converting them into gold—with remarkable success. Furthermore, while the International Monetary Fund had been set up at Bretton Woods for the specific purpose of stabilizing international monetary exchange rates and financing current deficits of member states, it soon became a choice instrument of American policy for the specific purpose of protecting the dollars' increasingly vulnerable position in the 1960's. While all IMF loans extended throughout the world were made conditional on IMF approval of the internal economic and financial policies of the recipient countries (thus effectively limiting the extent of their national sovereignty), no such condition was imposed on the United States, nor on Great Britain. In 1965, for instance, both English-speaking nations had jointly appropriated half of the IMF's resources for their own use. This implied that the IMF was, in effect, financing the export of American capital (and additionally bolstering Britain's weak pound sterling); it also implied a serious distortion of the original purpose of the IMF, but an inevitable distortion in view of the plain fact that the United States' economic power is immense (ten times that of the IMF's second most powerful member country) and that the soundness of its economic health is vital to all other non-Communist nations.

Lacking the severe disciplinary effect of the former gold standard, the present gold exchange standard has enabled the United States to create for itself the large funds that have been flooding the world and given them virtual control of important segments of the world's industries. The simple fact that most foreign countries were compelled, by Washington's political leverage, to keep a substantial part of their credit balances in dollars, enabled the United States to finance its vast economic expansion with the savings of their creditors rather than with their own: and so, while Europe's central banks accumulated the dollars that poured in and earned a modest return on the money, American subsidiaries earned a 10 percent return on their investments in Europe. The additional fact that it enabled American banks to create dollars in foreign countries, not only allowed American corporations to buy up huge slices of these countries' industries but compelled their governments to fight the inflationary pressures that flowed inevitably from this additional creation of unwanted dollars.

One of the by-products of this state of affairs is that America is becoming banker to the world, slowly but inexorably displacing Britain whose remarkable mismanagement of its impoverished estate is gradually destroying sterling's role as reserve currency and chief medium of world trade. The staggering expansion of American banks in Europe in the 1960's illustrates this change, partly as a result of the equally staggering expansion of American business concerns in the Old World. And not only did the Interest Equalization Tax imposed by the Kennedy Administration effectively prevent foreign institutions from raising money in the United States; it also induced many American banks to "go international," buy into European banks or set up their own branches in Europe and exploit the enormous Eurodollar market, prelude to their eventual financial hegemony in Europe: no wonder that, even if most of their assets are still in London, the Chase Manhattan, for instance, is already the second largest commercial bank in France.[45] Having become banker to the world, in addition to being its policeman, the United States has been able, until now, to use the position of the dollar as a reserve currency to throw a truly imperial mantle over the non-Communist world's industrial and economic resources, with far-reaching political consequences.

Toward the end of the 1960's, however, ominous signs appeared, indicating that this expansionary mechanism was beginning to run down—mounting dollar claims abroad, torrents of gold flowing out of Fort Knox, a slight but alarming contraction in the world's total gold reserves in 1966 and 1967, everything indicated that it was time to shift gears. After four years of discussion, the ten leading nations in the International Monetary Fund agreed, in 1967, on a far-reaching reform of the international monetary mechanism—"the most ambitious and significant effort" since the 1944 Bretton Woods conference, in the words of Henry Fowler, United States Secretary of the Treasury.[46] This reform amounts to the creation of a new reserve medium to supplement gold, dollars, and pounds: a special drawing right (SDR), of which 70 percent represents a permanent new currency with which to lubricate the world's increasingly rusty mechanism.

Although, in a sense, an American victory, and for some time to come a purely nominal gesture, it had to be paid for by the granting of a veto power to the Common Market countries (who have 17 percent of the vote), thus theoretically ending the absolute domination of the English-speaking countries. But it remains to be seen whether, in case of disagreement, some clever maneuvering on the part of the United States cannot split the Common Market's voting block to its own advantage—if the Common Market itself survives Charles de Gaulle's reckless policies.

At every turn, in the late 1960's, the irresistible force which is American worldwide expansion encounters the same immovable obstacle—which is de Gaulle. Here again, it is in order to destroy America's ultimate control of the world's international monetary machinery that France set out on its gold-accumulating course—gold being a completely neutral, nonpolitical entity to which even the most powerful country in the world has to bow, unless it can destroy its role as the ultimate reserve unit. It is on *political* grounds alone that France decided to challenge America's economic and financial hegemony by striking at its Achilles' heel—the half-empty Fort Knox. This challenge flung at Washington entails great risks of dismantling the world's international monetary system before the SDR has had time to begin functioning, triggering the first worldwide depression since World War II; it also entails the risk of American retaliation against France's own economy. At any rate, in the name of the preservation of the outdated sovereignty of the nation-state, it represents a last retrograde effort to dismantle America's economic imperium, just as it is about to shift its monetary basis from dollar-reserve to SDR-reserve—SDR-reserve being just as much under Washington's overall control, through its overwhelming power in the IMF, as was the outright dollar-reserve. Ultimately, there can be no question that the SDR, or a similar type of credit-creating mechanism, will become the main component of the world's monetary reserves, and is eventually destined to dethrone gold. But, in the meantime, the struggle is on between the forthcoming SDR and a revaluation of the price of gold.

While America's economic hegemony is worldwide (at the exclusion of Communist countries), its impact on European developments is particularly significant and its political implications far-reaching. In effect, the increasing meshing of the economic structures of the two continents bordering the Atlantic can only lead to a profound, if gradual, change in their political relationship. Unifying Western Europe under its economic imperium because, to a large extent, only American businessmen seem to have the ability to think "European," the United States is going to be compelled to interfere increasingly in the *internal* political affairs of Europe—as it already is in Canada—in order to protect its vast investments in the Old World. American firms in Europe stand in little danger of nationalization for the simple reason that, as the example of Rootes' takeover by Chrysler demonstrates eloquently, no nation-state can nationalize foreign brains, technology, marketing ability, or managerial know-how. But nation-states may take some steps damaging to American interests, even though they be self-defeating in the end; and it is not likely that the United States would refrain from forcible (even if underhanded) interference in the internal affairs of these nation-states if some of its vast interests were threatened by local political action.

As has already been pointed out, old-fashioned nation-states are, ultimately, on the way out; their sovereignty is increasingly jeopardized, not only on political but on economic and techno-logical grounds. Looking to the future, some American busi-nessmen have put forth some bold proposals that would further undermine what is left of their sovereignty. Rudolph A. Peter-son, President of the Bank of America, in a 1967 speech in London, stated that the economic cohesion of the Atlantic com-munity was vital to world prosperity; and he advocated the proliferation of multinational corporations established on both sides of the ocean, since it seemed that business was perhaps better equipped to handle international relations than govern-ments. Going one step further, former Under Secretary of State, George W. Ball, put forth the more audacious suggestion that multinational companies be withdrawn from the jurisdiction of individual nation-states through international treaties providing for the creation of "international company laws," thus avoiding "the stifling restrictions imposed on commerce by the archaic limits of nation-states." [47] In this perfectly honest and forthright suggestion, one can nevertheless perceive the ghostly contours of a more comprehensive economic hegemony, exercised extraterri-torially by American business interests in Europe, depriving the nation-states of their last possible defense against wholesale takeovers—their territorial sovereignty. If and when this comes to pass, European nation-states will have ceased to exist in all but the name.

This perfectly logical development would, in effect, create *de facto* an economico-technological Atlantic community whose next logical step would be a *political* institutionalization of this community—politics being usually the camp followers of eco-nomics and technology, rather than the other way around. But, quite obviously, if George Ball's additional suggestions—multi-national investment guarantees, merging national patent systems, common approach to antitrust problems, free flow of technology

—were adopted with the addition of tariff barriers, America's economic takeover of Europe would become complete and irrevocable. The only hope, then, for the European business managers would be to work their way up *within* the multinational structures of the American-dominated corporations, as *individuals*. Only a completely united Europe could prevent this takeover; and, as we have already seen in many instances, there is not a shred of evidence that Europe can ever unite politically of its own free will; in fact, all the evidence points to the fact that most of the individual molecules that make up Europe's disjointed economic body would much prefer, consciously or unconsciously, to become an organic part of America's economic power structure—rather than come to terms with one another in order to make Europe a living organism. It is the gradual, irresistible intermingling of their complementary molecular structures that is slowly giving birth to a *de facto* Atlantic community under America's economic hegemony, merging in one superorganic entity the United States, Canada, and Western Europe.

From all the evidence, one can only conclude that European unification as such will probably remain a figment of some imaginations and a typical instance of wishful thinking; and that the only possibility that has any chance of becoming a reality—because already based on another underlying reality—is the unification of the entire North Atlantic world, of which an eventually united Western Europe would be only one of the components. And just as the world of Classical Greece could only find its eventual unity *within* the confines of the much vaster Roman Empire, contemporary Europe—Western Europe, that is, since the eastern part of the Continent will remain in the orbit of Soviet Russia for the foreseeable future—will find its true, and only, unity in the much larger framework of an institutionalized Atlantic community.

☆ XIV ☆

The Great Condominium

Charles de Gaulle has one nightmare—an understanding, amounting to a tacit alliance, between the United States and Soviet Russia. At one of his press conferences, in the fall of 1966, he expressed himself quite forcefully on the subject, insisting that the world cannot be allowed to fall under the spell of "two Superpowers who alone have the weapons to destroy every other country." But he acknowledged the shadowy existence of this double hegemony by adding that this "spell had to be broken. We have broken it. We are breaking it, as far as we are concerned with the only means at our disposal." [1] By mixing his tenses in one single paragraph, de Gaulle shows that he is not sure whether this understanding between the Superpowers belongs to the past, the present, or the future. It is, in fact, a nebulous, imprecise convergence of worldwide interests in an increasingly chaotic world, made more chaotic still by the rivalry between the Superpowers themselves. But many straws in the wind appear to indicate the inevitability of this coming-together and the steady approach of the Russo-American Condominium—the concrete, inescapable manifestation of de Gaulle's nightmare.

Labeled by President Lyndon Johnson "Peaceful Engagement," this trend, temporarily overshadowed by the long-drawn-out war in Vietnam, appears irresistible. One of the most significant straws in the wind blowing through the 1960's was the Consular Treaty, signed in June 1964 and ratified by the United States Senate in March 1967 by a resounding vote of 66 to 28.[2] There had already been some limited agreements in the past; but all of them, dealing mostly with cultural exchanges and aviation matters, had been governmental decisions rather than formal treaties. The Consular Treaty, on the other hand, became the first bilateral treaty concluded between the two Superpowers since the distant days of the Czars. The more important cluster of outer space and nuclear test ban treaties are multinational, involving many other nations. This one is not only bilateral but includes features such as the granting of diplomatic immunity from criminal charges to their respective consular officials which exist in no consular agreements signed by the United States with other nations. Although of scant practical significance, it has considerable symbolic meaning—symbolism highlighted by the fact that the United States Senate ratified it by a large majority at a time when fighting in Vietnam was extremely bitter and when emotionalism over it was such that American public opinion was largely unfavorable to its ratification.

Other signs of a gradual thawing have appeared in this decade. Cultural exchanges between the Superpowers have proliferated in the 1960's, although slowed down by the Vietnam War—exchanges of scientists and scientific equipment, joint space studies and countless other forms of technological collaboration in such wide-ranging fields as the preservation of endangered animal species or scientific studies of American geologists in Russia, or again swapping American computer equipment against the right of American scientists to work with the most recent Soviet particle accelerators—most of which are merely projects on which technicians from both countries would like to get started. Nor should it be imagined that such exchanges are one-sided: by devoting an enormous proportion of their resources to such undertakings, the Russians are technologically ahead of the Americans in some fields—in the late 1960's, for instance, on planetary exploration, on which the Russians probably spend ten times as much as the Americans.

These straws in the wind came to join other such straws—such as the Soviet–United States draft treaty to stop the spread of nuclear weapons. During the Geneva talks, the world saw the astonishing spectacle of the two Superpowers aligned against the overwhelming majority of the world's nations, in defense of their joint predominance. They were both jointly pelted with objections and blamed for wanting to deprive other nations of nuclear weaponry while preserving their freedom to keep and add to their own stockpiles; for refusing to offer non-nuclear states *joint* guarantees of protection against nuclear aggression or even blackmail; and for denying non-nuclear countries the right to develop nuclear devices for such peaceful uses as mining and engineering work[3]—such as was undertaken by the Americans on December 10, 1967, in New Mexico when a thermonuclear device, equivalent to twenty-six thousand tons of TNT, was detonated deep under the surface of Carson National Forest in order to free natural gas trapped in the rock formations.[4] This first test of a new technology was the fruit of a joint effort of private industry and the American Government—giving the United States, and presumably Soviet Russia, an inestimable advantage over all other nations that would subscribe to the nuclear nonproliferation treaty.

The substance of the reproaches flung at the Superpowers is of merely technical interest; what is of great import, however, is the fact that, in spite of their disagreement over details, the United States and Soviet Russia stood shoulder to shoulder in defense of their joint nuclear predominance. When the United States and Soviet Russia submitted identical drafts of a nuclear nonproliferation treaty to the Geneva Disarmament Conference on August 24, 1967, the whole world was put on notice that, in a limited way and at the highest technological level, and in spite of sulking on the part of the French and the Chinese, the world as a whole was slowly but irresistibly sliding under the overall protectorate of the Great Condominium.

How did it come about that the two rivals, seemingly situated at the opposite poles of political persuasion, one the arch-apostle of free enterprise and democracy, and the other the holy land of Marxism-Leninism, have gradually and in spite of countless brush-fire wars all over the globe, begun to join hands in a common effort to establish some law and order in the world's political jungle? This convergence has been long in the making and its origins can be traced to the beginning of the Kennedy Administration and its repudiation of the simplistic Dulles policy of "massive retaliation." Even before the fateful nuclear confrontation over Cuba in the fall of 1962, farsighted Germans had become alarmed at the signs of Russo-American *rapprochement,* possibly at German expense. But repeated crises interrupted, and still interrupt, the budding honeymoon—the assassination of President Kennedy, the downfall of Nikita Sergeevich Khrushchev, the intensification of the war in Vietnam, and the Middle East crisis in 1967. Nevertheless, the slender thread between them never snapped completely; both had their difficulties with their allies and satellites—Soviet Russia with Yugoslavia and Rumania's virtual exit from its block, the United States with Charles de Gaulle's envious hostility. Both were becoming concerned with Red China's fast-developing nuclear potential and Peking's arrogant xenophobia. More than anything else, both were deeply worried by the danger of miscalculation arising out of a small local conflict developing into an all-annihilating mushroom cloud and the extinction of life on this planet. But it would be a grave historical error to view this *rapprochement* as being the work of one or several specific American Aministrations, temporary leaderships in Moscow, or chance events in the political evolution of the world. The Russo-American Condominium of the future has its roots even deeper in the remote past and in order to gauge its inevitability, we must look back at the historical record and let it speak for itself.

In spite of the fact that Czarist Russia, throughout the nineteenth century, looked upon the young and "revolutionary" United States with suspicion, their interests coincided more often than they diverged. Both opposed Napoleon; and when the United States went to war against Britain in 1812, the worried Czar offered himself as mediator. Again, the Crimea War of 1856 saw American public opinion swing toward the Russians; in return, the Russians stood firmly by the side of the Union during the Civil War and turned down British suggestions to grant diplomatic recognition to the Confederacy. Fundamentally, Russian policy throughout the century was to prevent any tight alliance between the two English-speaking Powers, fearing a domination of the world by "the ambitious projects and political egotism of the Anglo-Saxon race," explained the Russian envoy to Washington during the Civil War.[5] And basically, the Americans saw in Russia a new nation like their own, standing apart from the "decrepit" Europeans. Alexander II's emancipation of the Russian serfs in 1861 generated a wave of enthusiasm in the United States, and *Harper's Weekly* went so far as to advocate a Russo-American alliance against France and Britain, concluding that "Russia, like the United States, is a nation of the future." [6]

But both were taking a collision course in their respective westward and eastward expanions—the United States across the Pacific and Russia across Siberia into Manchuria. Direct collision was avoided because Japan, "playing our game" as President Theodore Roosevelt stated it,[7] chose to take it upon itself to throw the Russians back into Siberia. But from then on, without ever getting very emotional about it, the Americans took a more jaundiced view of Russia; their unfavorable view was not improved by the pogroms which prompted millions of Russian Jews to emigrate to the United States; nor was it improved, either, when the October Revolution and its frightful carnage transferred Russia, almost overnight, from the far right to the far left of the political spectrum.

It was only after the conclusion of World War II that tension, for the first time, rose to a high pitch between the two nations, now promoted to the exclusive rank of Superpowers. In that new position, the United States was merely inheriting Britain's traditional geopolitical role—temporarily foresaken during the two World Wars because of the more deadly German challenge. The old British-Russian rivalry was metamorphosed into an American-Soviet struggle, considerably enlarged to include the entire world and the whole gamut of ideological conflicts.

Almost a century and a half ago, Alexis de Tocqueville wrote: "There are at present two great nations in the world, which started from different points but seem to tend towards the same end. I allude to the Russians and the Americans. Their starting point is different and their courses are not the same; yet each of them seems marked out by the will of Heaven to sway the destinies of half the globe." [8] Since the distant days when this prophecy was uttered, many events have taken place in the world; many empires have come and gone; Russia underwent the ordeal of wars, invasions, and revolution; the United States was almost torn apart by the Civil War, went into isolationism, and suffered a catastrophic economic collapse in the 1930's. Yet this prophecy rings truer today than ever.

Only one thing was missing in this oracular pronouncement: they can indeed each "sway the destinies of half the globe"; but in this nuclear age, they can only do so *jointly,* or rather in full agreement with one another, not against one another. In order to do so jointly, they have a ready-made tool at hand, a tool that has never really been tried yet, because it can only function as an organ of the forthcoming Condominium: the United Nations. Only once did the United Nations function as the exclusive tool of the United States: during the Korean War, when the Russians were careless enough to vacate their seat on the Security Council. Determined never to let that kind of mistake be repeated, the Russians, from then on, were always on hand to interpose their veto and paralyze the functioning of the United Nations whenever it suited them. But if, for other reasons, the United States and the Soviet Union happened to agree on a common course of action, such as the 1956 condemnation of the French, British, and Israelis during the Suez Crisis, the United Nations becomes a truly effective organization—all at once the moral tribunal of the world and a forceful peacemaking agency, whenever backed jointly by the two Superpowers.

Many elements are going into the making of this approaching Condominium, most of which spring from Soviet weakness rather than strength—basically, the weakness of a relatively young country, ruled within the framework of a rigid ideology and ossified political system. Historical youthfulness, in the barbarian rather than decadent sense of being ill-adapted to the times, is a temporary weakness, not a strength. Lenin himself was conscious of it when he wrote, in 1923, "Russia stands on the border-line of civilized countries." [9] Simultaneously, from both the Russian and the American viewpoint, there has been for over a hundred years, a certain aura of decadence about Europe.

From the start, the Soviet leaders looked not to Europe but to the United States as a model of economic development and efficiency, to be imitated and then surpassed. This competitive spirit, in spite of being bolstered by a deep faith in the virtues of the Marxist-Leninist ideology, was also imbued with admiration for the economically advanced land in the Western Hemisphere. Reporting from Soviet Russia, in 1929, Dorothy Thompson was struck by the fact that "Russia has respect for only one other country and believes she can learn from only one other nation: the United States. For Europe Russia has only contempt. Europe she regards as a continent in decadence, which must in the course of time fall completely under the domination of the United States, if the European proletariat does not seize power— and so come under the influence of Russia. Europe she regards as already beaten in the struggle for world power. . . . When they look ahead to the ultimate Armageddon—and Russian communists are accustomed to looking ahead many decades, being, in this respect, superior to the leaders of most countries—they foresee that the final struggle is to be not between England and Russia, but between the United States and Russia." [10]

Written already far back in the past, these words reflected a prophetic insight. In the meantime, Hitler's Third Reich came and went, bringing Soviet Russia closer to collapse and total ruin than ever before or since. Russian sentiments toward the United States are still very much as Dorothy Thompson described them in the late 1920's: "There are many ways in which the Soviet civilization copies America and rejects Europe. . . . The new Russian civilization has, as a result, many aims in common with the American." [11] And many a time, she heard the boast of some simple Russian: "Some day soon it will be like America here in Russia." [12]

This general attitude was confirmed by no less an authority than Joseph Stalin himself. In his work *Leninism,* Stalin exemplified both this admiration and simultaneously his abiding faith in the superiority of his ideology: "American efficiency is that indomitable force which neither knows nor recognizes obstacles; which, with its business-like perseverance, brushes aside all obstacles; which continues at a task once started until it is finished, even if it is a minor task; and without which serious constructive work is inconceivable." [13] However, he then added: "But American efficiency has every chance of degenerating into narrow and unprincipled commercialism if it is not combined with the Russian revolutionary sweep" [14]—Stalin, who swept millions of Russians out of their lives, never understood that "commercialism" is one of the keystones of civilized life.

To these encomiums mixed with Marxist reservations written over a generation ago, one could add the same blend which is to be found in the work *Businesslike America,* published in 1967 and written by Nikolai N. Smelyakov, a deputy minister of foreign trade and formerly the head of Amtorg, the Soviet Trade Agency headquartered in New York. While condemning capitalism as such, he praises just about every feature of the United States' business organization, with the obvious implication that his fellow Soviet citizens would do well to adopt many elements of this remarkable structure. Coming at a time when the Soviet press was filled with denunciations of American "racism" and "imperialism," this was high praise indeed—praise which was not intended to flatter American cars but to prod his own countrymen into greater efficiency and productivity.

Many foreigners have been struck by this Russo-American convergence, by the profound desire of the Russians to become the Americans of the twenty-first century. For instance, Cubans in the 1960's, describing the Russian advisers who were pouring into their home island, were reminded of Americans of earlier times, "a little coarse, clods of earth." And they were struck by the fact that "They're desperate to catch up with the United States and become the Americans of the future: they admire Hemingway more than they admire Fidel." [15]

The weaknesses of the world's second Superpower spring from both its internal and its external circumstances; both of them are equally instrumental in influencing Moscow to seek a *rapprochement* with Washington. On the home front, it is clear that the Soviet leaders had not waited for the latest economic appraisals of America's economic superiority to begin overhauling their own creaky system. Reconstruction of wartime devastation and the maintenance of a huge defense apparatus had compelled the Russian authorities to starve the consumer into drab austerity all through the 1950's. Nevertheless, this wholly socialized economy grew by leaps and bounds; but as it grew, so did the inefficient bureaucratic controls, slowly paralyzing economic progress in the late 1950's and early 1960's. The annual rate of increase in investments dropped 50 percent from 1959 to 1964, while the economic rate of growth dwindled from 6 percent in the 1950's to 2.5 percent in 1962 and 1963. Alarmed, the Soviet leaders promptly decided to scrap many of the controls, decentralize their industrial operations, and restore the profit motive at the center of every industrial and agricultural undertaking: profit rather than total output would become the new yardstick of Soviet economic success.

It was in 1965 that the new system was launched under the inspiration of Yevsei Liberman, professor of economics at Kharkov University. It was suddenly rediscovered that the idea of profitable undertakings, incentives for workers, and relative independence for enterprises had been Lenin's all along—or so *Pravda* would have us believe, defending the Soviet system's profound reforms against accusations that it was indirectly returning to capitalism.[16] Regardless of doctrinaire interpretations, the fact is that up to 1968, the new planning methods had been extended to over six thousand enterprises, mostly large industrial plants, accounting for 40 percent of the Soviet Union's total industrial output.[17] Following the "principles of Lenin," each "reformed" factory is now presumed to work profitably, fully paying for all its expenditures and showing a profit, most of which can be plowed back into the enterprise itself rather than providing for an enormous centralizing bureaucracy in Moscow. Most of the bottlenecks of the Khrushchev era disappeared, along with the unrealistically high quotas set in Moscow. Profits in the "reformed" industrial plants rose 24 percent in 1966, as against only 8 percent for the entire Soviet industry. In 1967, total industrial output was up 10 percent, as against a planned increase of hardly more than 7 percent.[18] Labor productivity went up as production costs went down. The same profit-making incentive was introduced in agriculture and a thousand state farms were switched over to the new system in 1967. Instead of relying on the state for capital investments, state farms would retain part of their profit for their own use, including wage bonuses for their workers, and each state farm would succeed or fail according to its own efficiency.[19]

The result of this transformation in depth of the Soviet economy is a remarkable growth, in spite of the fact that 20 percent of its gross output goes into defense spending, as against less than 10 percent in the United States. Another result is awakened consumer appetite; consumers are getting more demanding, just as production under the new system is made more responsive to demand. But the fundamental result of this drift away from orthodox Marxism is that Soviet society, becoming more and more consumer-minded, is also drifting away from its revolutionary past which, in the form of austerity and drabness, had stayed with it until the early 1960's: Soviet society is gradually becoming conservative, because it is beginning to have something to "conserve."

The impact of these structural changes on the Soviet political system are also far-reaching. Gone are the days when the Kremlin was an awesome blend of a Mongol horde holding the entire Soviet people in bondage, and a Byzantine court catering to the whims of Stalin, the oriental despot. The abolition of terror, which had prevented any kind of social crystallization and stratification from taking place, was bound to be followed by this typically post-revolutionary crystallization and stratification. The result is that power is no longer concentrated at the top but emerges more or less anonymously as the result of the interaction of powerful and semiautonomous pressure groups, institutions, and vested interests—the armed forces, the scientists, the literary intelligentsia, the technocrats and industrial managers, the security and intelligence agencies. The whole atmosphere has changed, the psychological temper altered. To a degree, there is now the rudimentary rule of abstract, impersonal law; the power apparatus is becoming slowly institutionalized.

All this can be seen in countless forms—the growing indifference toward ideology as such, especially among the Soviet students, the "silent generation" whose focus is almost exclusively on its personal affairs and is profoundly bored by Communist ideology, in spite of all the efforts of the Central Committee's propaganda apparatus; [20] the growing strength of Russian nationalism *per se* and the resolution of its "identity crisis" by increasing references to the Czarist past, now seen in a more favorable light when compared with the gory aftermath of the October Revolution; the emotional attitude of even confirmed atheists toward their own Orthodox Church. Western observers have been struck by the enthusiasm with which more than a million Russians have become members of the new All Russian Society for the Preservation of Memorials of History and Culture.[21] There is no desire to return to prerevolutionary conditions; but there is a strong sentimental feeling for Russia's past history.

More than anything, the extraordinary rebirth of Russian poetry in the 1960's can be seen as a religious awakening in literary form; and it is no accident that Russian poets are in the vanguard of the increasing demands for spiritual and intellectual freedom—and land in jail for their pains. Typical is the poetic vision of Andrei Sinyavsky (Abram Tertz) which gives us, in capsule form, the contemporary Russian's understanding of his country's revolutionary experience:

> We did not want salvation for ourselves, but for all of humanity. . . . We set about to correct the universe according to the best of all models, the shining model of the Purpose which we approached ever more closely.
>
> So that prisons should vanish forever, we built new prisons. So that all frontiers should fall, we surrounded ourselves with

a Chinese Wall. So that work should become a rest and a pleasure, we introduced forced labor. So that not one drop of blood be shed any more, we killed and killed and killed . . . O Lord, O Lord—pardon us our sins! [22]

As time goes on, and as the Russians are coming out of their generation-long nightmare, as Stalinism recedes into an increasingly distant past, they will revert to their traditional *weltanschauung*—but refreshed and made new by the ordeal through which they went. Their nominal, and in many ways sincere, attachment to Marxism-Leninism will not necessarily waver; the internationalist outlook will remain intact and they will still "want salvation . . . for all of humanity." But what the Soviet intelligentsia want now, and will want increasingly vociferously, is freedom of thought and expression at the highest literary level; they reject the demands made by the Communist party on their thoughts and emotions. When Alexander Solzhenitsyn blasts censorship, when Andrei Voznesensky strips away the mask of hypocrisy worn by Moscow's rulership, they are actually burying the revolutionary past and overthrowing the deadly conformity imposed on the Russian people in the name of Leninist orthodoxy. Andrei Voznesensky, greatest among the new poets of the younger generation, stated in 1967: "Before, with us, art looked outward—at things, the economy, and so forth. Now it looks inward. What has taken place in Russia in recent years is an upsurge of popular—to a foreigner it might even seem religious —interest in poetry. People are unbuttoning themselves. There is a kind of spiritual communion." [23]

Clearly, Russians are rediscovering their Russianness, their Slavic soul. In the process, they are becoming conscious of their inheritance, that of the Czars. Since World War II, communism has spread far and wide throughout the world, both as ideology and as power-structure; and as it spread, it assumed many strange shapes and colors; it soon began to emancipate itself from Russian tutelage, digested anew by the non-Russian people who absorbed it, and made into new ideologies such as Titoism, Maoism, and Castroism, with probably more to come. Eventually, it even turned viciously against its Russian coreligionists; it is probable that nothing helped more to force the Russians to become conscious that they were one with their Czarist past than the virulence with which Red China attacked them—and attacked them not only on "revisionist" grounds, but on national grounds as well. And here, we have our finger on Soviet Russia's second group of weaknesses, those depending on external circumstances.

In the late 1960's, the unity of the international Communist movement lies in ruins, shattered by its own success and its enormous power of expansion. True enough, Marshall Tito's breakaway in the late 1940's was a nasty blow; but it remained isolated, without imitators elsewhere. The triumph of Mao Tse-tung's Red Army in China was ample compensation in the eyes of true Communist believers in Moscow. But there followed a steady deterioration of relations through the 1950's which led to a parting of the ways in the 1960's, to the point where Peking decided to set itself up as a rival Communist Mecca to Moscow's. Here again, before the official break between Russians and Chinese, a new revolutionary explosion in Cuba gave the Kremlin some gratification as Fidel Castro appeared to move gradually into the Soviet orbit. But then a new parting of the ways took place after the fateful nuclear confrontation of October 1962— not so violent and dangerous as the Chinese one, since, at the yearly cost of half a billion dollars in aid, the Russians can still claim an ostensible alliance with Cuba; but Cuba no longer follows Moscow's advice, and calmly proceeds either to capture the leadership of Latin America's Communist parties, or to ignore them if they refuse to follow its revolutionary path of guerilla warfare.

In the meantime, Moscow's grip on its East European satellites weakened perceptibly. In spite of the ruthless crushing of the Hungarian rebellion in 1956, the process of emancipation behind the Iron Curtain proceeded steadily in the 1960's; some satellites such as Rumania went all the way to open defiance; and Albania had long ago switched over to the Red Chinese side. Others, for strictly geopolitical reasons, remain loyal, regardless of their populations' feelings of distaste for both communism and Russian imperialism: such is the case with Poland and, to a lesser extent, Czechoslovakia; and again others, such as East Germany, are outright satellites whose very existence depends on Soviet military presence. The fissiparous tendencies within the Communist world are not confined to those countries where Marxist-Leninists are in power; they extend to all the Communist parties strewn across the non-Communist world where they freely criticize Moscow—or Peking, or Havana, or each other; and where they occasionally split along factional lines, as in India, between pro-Russian and pro-Chinese.

The 1967 spring meeting of European Communist parties at Karlovy Vary, in Czechoslovakia, was symbolic of this growing confusion. Called for the purpose of displaying Communist unity to the outside world, scheduled to discuss only innocuous topics on which all good Communists should agree (condemnation of NATO, of German "revanchism" and American "aggression" in Vietnam), it turned out to be a startling display of disunity. One quarter of Europe's thirty-one Communist parties made it clear that they refused to follow the Soviet line even on topics of relatively minor importance; six parties (Albania, Yugoslavia, Rumania, Holland, Norway, and Iceland) flatly refused to attend the meeting; Sweden sent only an "observer" who refused to sign the final declaration; even some of those who attended the meeting, such as the British, published violent denunciations of some aspect or other of Soviet policy. The next gathering of world Communist party leaders in Budapest (February–March 1968) produced a similar display of disunity—with no representation from China, Albania, Yugoslavia, Cuba, North Korea, and North Vietnam; with a spectacular withdrawal of the Rumanians, the absence of the Japanese, and representatives of only half of the Indian Communist Party; with the anger of the Italians at Moscow's persecution of its unorthodox intellectuals and the Hungarians grumbling at Soviet Russia's support of Middle Eastern and other regimes throughout the developing world that clamp down on their domestic Communist parties. The Russians, at all such meetings, usually get blamed for concentrating on daily tactics rather than long-term strategy and ideology—as if to point out the obvious fact that the Russians are now more interested in the political leverage they can extract from the worldwide Communist movement, of which they are the

nominal leaders, than in the welfare and progress of the movement itself.[24]

For true Russian believers in Marxism-Leninism, the shatter-
ing of communism's international unity in the 1960's is a dismal
tale which destroys all the ecumenical pretensions of their faith
and cannot help but throw them back upon themselves, thus
reinforcing their own Russianness at the expense of their internationalist outlook. True enough, they have no intention of
throwing away the important leverage given them by their belonging to, and fitfully leading, a powerful worldwide movement.
First of all, Marxism-Leninism still remains, up to a point, the
only mental framework they know and understand; they are not
about to discard it in favor of what we call "freedom of thought"
—which, to them, is merely a frightening mental chaos. But also,
and except for immense China where geopolitical considerations
alone would make for a revival of hostility regardless of the
regime in Peking, worldwide communism still retains a certain
awe of Moscow. This immense fund of goodwill and respect is
not about to be sacrificed by a narrow-minded interpretation of
Russia's national interests.

However, it is also clear that these Russian national interests
predominate to an increasing degree—nor have they ever been
entirely forgotten, especially at the height of Stalinism. After all,
the erection of Stalinism as the official doctrine, in opposition to
Trotsky's internationalism, was the first indication of an obscure
revival of the specifically "Russian" consciousness. The Second
World War was not won by Communist ideology but by Russian
patriotism; the extension of communism to Eastern Europe was a
by-product of Russia's military victories, not a voluntary acceptance of this new ideology by East Europeans; its extension beyond the borders of Soviet military power was largely a result of
Western blunders during the war, since, from Yugoslavia and
Greece to Malaya and Vietnam, its devotees were the benefici-
aries of ample Anglo-American supplies and support—but, also,
it was a result produced by genuine, home-grown Communists
who adapted Marxism to their own atavism, without any regard
for specifically Russian interpretations. In this case, most notable

in China, it lost no time in turning against its Russian mentor and setting itself up as a rival.

In fact, it is beginning to dawn on the Soviet leadership that, far from putting an end to "capitalist" or "bourgeois" contradictions, to religious inspirations and national aspirations, the extension of communism merely revives them in a new guise, and presents them in a new dress. The articulations of the profound splits within the Communist world (as distinct from superficial and temporary ones) follow very precisely the geopolitical lines of cleavage separating the world's great cultures from one another; doctrinal quarrels are merely intellectual rationalizations of profound impulses—so it was when both Christianity and Islam started breaking up into their different components on geographical, linguistic, ethnic, cultural, and economic grounds, masquerading as theological differences.

This being the case, it is obvious that Soviet Russia's Communist proselytism has suffered an irreparable blow. Only too often, the extension of the Communist power-structure to new areas has only resulted in creating more efficient and fanatical enemies for the Russian people; in creating dangerous rivals for the allegiance of other Communists throughout the world; and in creating a dangerous group of doctrinal critics who tear apart, verbally, the "deviations" of the Russian leadership from *within* the Communist movement itself. Is there a Russian today who does not long for the good old days when China was a power vacuum, mute, in chaos, in the hands of inefficient, conflicting warlords?

The result, throughout the past two decades, has been, in the midst of an extraordinarily successful expansion of communism throughout the world, a succession of disastrous defeats for Soviet foreign policy—only partly compensated by the defeats suffered by the West itself (the "loss" of China, European decolonization, revolution in Cuba, chaos in the Congo and in Vietnam). The six-day Arab-Israeli war in June 1967 brought to a temporary climax this long string of Soviet defeats. It is not only that two billion dollars' worth of Soviet military equipment was lost by the Arabs in a single week—at no expense to the

United States, whose position in the Middle East was considerably strengthened by Israel's own strength. It is also that its efforts to prop up, at great expense, the Egyptian economy were nullified at one stroke. But this indirect defeat merely capped its long string of previous defeats: the vast investment lost in China, a billion dollars' investment in Indonesia lost in the anti-Communist bloodbath of 1965, one and a half billion dollars' worth of aid to India which has not resulted in any appreciable increase in Indian Communist power nor prevented the Indian Communist party from being split right down the middle between pro-Peking and pro-Moscow wings. With the demise of Patrice Lumumba in the Congo and Kwame Nkrumah in Ghana, its influence in Africa has collapsed—not permanently, to be sure, but to the extent of providing an unforgettable lesson: Russians are white men, too, and that ethnological fact will always limit their influence on the vast nonwhite populations of the world.

The Soviet economy is not so strong that it can afford to keep Castro's Cuba afloat at a cost of half a billion dollars a year, only to watch Castro attempt to eliminate Soviet influence in Latin America. In this particular context, it is mostly a matter of deciding whether Castro's nuisance value to the United States is greater or lesser than it is to the Russians who are footing the bill. All this, following upon earlier defeats of the 1940's and 1950's in Iran, Greece, Turkey, Berlin, and Korea, makes it plain that Soviet Russia's freedom of maneuver in foreign affairs is becoming increasingly limited. And in their disillusionment about the doubtful benefits accruing to them from the worldwide expansion of communism, the Russians can well ponder Lenin's prophetic words, uttered against those West European "petty-bourgeois democrats," who "call themselves Marxists" and who disputed the possibility of building up a Marxist socialist state in such a backward country as Russia: "Our European philistines are not even aware that the coming revolutions in Eastern countries which have a vastly greater population and are distinguished by a vastly greater diversity of social conditions, will undoubtedly present them with still greater peculiarities than the Russian Revolution." [25] Could Lenin have foreseen the actual threat that the communization of China would present to Russia?

Perhaps the most striking aspect of this situation is that the Soviet leadership is no longer interested in the expansion of communism *per se* but only in its own worldwide power contest with the United States. One proof is the immense amount of military and economic aid extended to Arab states, all of which, with the possible exception of Syria, do not even tolerate a Communist party in their midst. The progress of Marxism-Leninism in the Arab world is almost nil; but the Arabs tend, atavistically, to be anti-Western: hence, it is more profitable for the Soviet leaders to forget about the staunch anticommunism of the Arabs and develop their nuisance value to the West. After their remarkable victory in June 1967, the Israelis revealed that among the captured Soviet weapons in the Sinai, was an enormous quantity of highly sophisticated weaponry of the latest manufacture, such as had not been distributed by the Russians to their East European Communist "allies" who are members of the Warsaw Pact.[26]

In other words, the Russians will go far in supplying those non-Western people, regardless of their attitude to communism as such, who are in the direct firing line of the United States or its allies and satellites; they will do so for their own "Russian" geopolitical reasons, not in any hope that their assisted allies will become part of the fractured Communist fraternity. In 1967, the cost was high and the result disastrous because of the Arabs' shortcomings and the Russians' lack of control over them; the price was even higher in terms of the temporary alienation of all the non-Communist but left-wing movements in Western countries, all of which were, to a man, in favor of Israel and profoundly shocked by Moscow's one-sided policy. In turn, this loss of left-wing goodwill was harmful, both to the local Communist parties in the West, and to Soviet Russia's campaign to arouse world public opinion against the United States policy in Vietnam. It even had a nefarious impact on the Communist structure of some of its East European satellites, notably in Poland and Czechoslovakia—not to mention the disaffection of some of its own Russian Jews. But the traditional century-old Russian policy of acquiring a zone of influence in the contiguous Middle East overrode all objections and cast aside all obstacles. At any time, under any circumstances, Moscow would be happy to trade the Middle East against Southeast Asia—an impossible trade, in any case.

Internal and external problems and weaknesses have profoundly altered the Soviet Union's outlook. Regardless of internecine intrigues within Moscow's leadership, regardless of the temporary shifts of influence between Russian hard-liners and soft-liners, this profound alteration will have consequences with which all future Soviet governments will have to reckon. One is the change in depth of the Soviet people's social metabolism: its growing emphasis on its "Russianness," its development toward an increasingly consumer-oriented society, and hence its growing conservatism. The other, looking outward, is its growing disillusionment with the expansion of communism *per se,* its increasing emphasis on the protection of its own geopolitical position as "Soviet Union" rather than holy land of international communism—without in any way intending to throw away the precious leverage it possesses as important member and nominal head of the worldwide Marxist faith. Furthermore, twice during the 1960's—in the fall of 1962 and in June 1967—Moscow refused to push its nuclear confrontation with America to the danger point and hastily backed away from the brink; nor did the United States recklessly push its advantage in these circumstances.

The cool-headed *apparatchiks* who now lead the Soviet Establishment are no longer revolutionaries, even though they may be fervent Marxists. They are realists, whose apparently reckless moves in foreign policy spring more from misinformation and misunderstanding of the opponent's reactions than desire to upset the world's applecart; and the area of misinformation and misunderstanding is shrinking perceptibly as both the United States and the Soviet Union begin to learn the rules of this new game of international chess. The Russians want to preserve and increase the material gains obtained since the Second World War, not throw them away for the sake of their ideology. As a result, the Soviet Union has become almost respectable as a Superpower—in a Western sense, that is: a pragmatic preoccupation with economic prosperity and power, and increasing, if still limited, liberalization, at home; a desire for peace whenever its vital interests are not threatened, abroad.

When, in September 1965, the Soviet Union arbitrated the reestablishment of peace between India and Pakistan and sponsored the Tashkent Agreement, it not only acted as an honest broker; it also acted with the full approval and backing of the United States. Both Superpowers share the same concern for the safety and welfare of India—not so much out of an altruistic feeling for the welfare of the Indians, as out of a common distrust of the Chinese menace in the Himalayas. Sensing this unity of purpose, India lost no time, when the nuclear nonproliferation treaty came to be discussed, in announcing in April 1967 that it would not agree to sign it unless both the United States and the Soviet Union would give New Delhi a *joint* guarantee against a nuclear attack by Red China.[27]

Very slowly, but surely, the shadowy outline of the Great Condominium is becoming visible; the vague contours of this worldwide understanding are beginning to emerge out of the fog which is surrounding us. The Condominium will be essentially a tacit alliance between two imperial *states,* not between irreconcilable and competing ideologies. It will be the partial conjunction of their national and imperial interests that will serve as foundation for their virtual alliance which will, in no way, put an end to their rivalry. Indeed, the prospects are that they will continue to compete through multitudes of local conflicts; and the increasing power of the Soviet navy, the determination of the Russians to have a military capability of striking at a great distance from their borders, proves that they will persist in exporting their influence to distant shores and assist their—Communist or non-Communist—allies everywhere, thus nursing a precious element of their worldwide political leverage, compelling the United States to fight and attempt to destroy their influence locally, or come to terms with them and accept the establishment of various local Soviet spheres of influence.

The Russo-American Condominium will never be an official affair; it will never be embodied in a formal, all-inclusive treaty of alliance or a stated partition of the world into precisely delimited spheres of influence. It will eliminate neither countless rivalries nor peaceful quarrels. But it has been, and continues to be, in the making. Every world crisis brings it closer, and it is already an accomplished fact at the highest technological level—where only the most extraordinary breakthrough in technological research could upset the present balance of power and terror.

However vague its contours, the Great Condominium is bound to fill many of the world's nations with consternation.[28] It already has, to an extent, in connection with the debates on the nuclear nonproliferation treaty. The West Germans protested that it should not become the instrument of a "greater inequality among nations"; [29] Italy's Socialist deputy premier Pietro Nenni, stating that he favored the treaty, nevertheless added: "It is true that it sanctions the supremacy of Washington and Moscow in nuclear armaments. And this cannot make us happy. But this is a fact whose negative aspects certainly cannot be corrected with the spread of nuclear arms." [30] Harlan Cleveland, American Ambassador to NATO, complained that while the Europeans had been urging for years the two Superpowers to settle their differences, they were now complaining about a "Soviet-American condominium." [31] West German Chancellor Kurt Georg Kiesinger lamented that the United States and the Soviet Union were attempting to create an "atomic confederacy." [32] In December 1967, "resentment at the Soviet Union and the United States for 'backstage' efforts to agree between themselves on nuclear and space treaties has erupted into open revolt by some non-nuclear countries here," reported an American correspondent from Geneva.[33] And in a January 1968 issue of the *Bayern-Kurier,* West German Finance Minister Franz-Josef Strauss blasted out that "NATO would be turned into a comedy, because it would have to renounce the whole concept of who the enemy was, after the sly [Russian-American] goings-on in Geneva. . . . The Common Market would stagnate in the case of a signing. We would accordingly have to look forward to becoming a nation of shopkeepers. . . . The reservations of France would degrade the Elysée [German-French Friendship] Treaty to a historical paper." [34] The mere fact that both Superpowers work in a common interest, even if they hardly admit it in public, raises the spectre of "parallelism." All these are European complaints. What of those to be heard in the future among the Afro-Asian "neutralists" who played East against West so profitably for years?

The fact is that the United States and the Soviet Union both spend altogether well over a hundred billion dollars a year in armaments, and they could both use a sizable portion of these gigantic sums for their own internal welfare. But this cannot be done unless they establish this Condominium; and this, in turn, however great their mutual desire to do so, cannot come about quickly for fear of losing allies and satellites. But only thus can a reasonable world order come about; only thus can the United Nations function as it was intended that it should. And the place where this world order can be displayed to greatest effectiveness, where the Condominium may become a political reality of the first magnitude, is Europe, on both sides of the Iron Curtain. Here is where Charles de Gaulle's recurring nightmare might well become concrete reality.

The Condominium would imply an actual freezing of the *de facto* situation in Eastern Europe, an overall acceptance of the *status quo* on the Continent. More than anything else, it would imply final acceptance of Germany's postwar borders with Poland and its indefinite partition into two separate states. West German Chancellor Kurt Georg Kiesinger understood this so well that, in March 1968, in the first "state of the nation" speech ever delivered in the Bundestag, he claimed that West Germany and Western Europe should seek their future *outside* the framework of a "North Atlantic imperium," arguing, quite correctly, that "such a solution would transform the demarcation line which divides Germany and Europe into a permanent border wall." [35] This is precisely what the future is most likely to have in store for Germany and Europe; and the North Atlantic imperium is the natural corollary of such a permanent demarcation line. The time is long past when, to the leaders of the Kremlin, the communization of Germany was the first order of the day—

as it was after Lenin had seized power in Petrograd, and again after Stalin had pushed his armies beyond Berlin. The time is long past when the Soviet leaders would gladly accept the unification of Germany provided it took place under the aegis of the German Communist party. Stalin himself is alleged to have stated repeatedly that communism fitted Germany as a saddle fits a cow—an un-Marxian remark, but a revealing one.

The Russians no longer want a united Germany, whether Communist or not; they are quite content with a Western Germany separated from their sphere of influence by another buffer German state under their military control. They are not happy to watch West Germany develop the most powerful army and the most prosperous economy on the Continent; but that is a minor inconvenience compared with the nightmare of a united Germany of eighty-five million disciplined, warlike, and technologically competent people ready to strike out again. The trauma of World War II, the devastating invasion and the twenty million Russian lives sacrificed, is still with Moscow's leaders, and will be for a long time. More than one responsible Soviet Russian must recall Heinrich Heine's verse:

> Denk' ich an Deutschland in der Nacht
> Dann bin ich um den Schlaf gebracht

and like the poet himself, be robbed of their sleep if, in the night, they think of Germany.

The Russians are without a shred of illusion concerning the sentiments of *all* Germans toward them. Even East Germany they consider a captive state, no more, no less. It is well worth quoting at length Oleg Penkovsky's remarks, dating back to 1961:

> There is talk in senior military circles, especially among Kupin's group and others stationed in East Germany, that in case of a Berlin crisis or a war we would have to kill both West and East Germans. Everything is ready to fight, not only against West Germany but East Germany as well, because both sorts of Germans are basically anti-Soviet. . . . Fedorov specifically told me that the military, in spite of their great strength, are afraid that the Germans will set up barricades, trap them, and make it impossible for them to get

back to their bases. The Soviets stationed in East Germany are afraid that during the very first night of hostilities the Germans will begin to massacre all the Soviet military personnel in East Germany.[36]

This, of course, suggests that a reunited Germany would tend, if only on account of the pent-up frustrations of the East Germans themselves, to be violently anti-Russian—a prospect which would in no way induce Soviet Russia to allow it, having already to contend with an increasingly hostile Red China in the back.

In the Russians' preference for a permanently split Germany they are fully backed by many of their satellites. Whatever misgivings the Poles and the Czechs may have on other grounds, they are at one with their Russian overlords on that question. Furthermore, since the Wall sliced Berlin in half in 1961, East Germany has almost become a going concern and an industrial power in its own right; it has accelerated its separate development, moving away from its skin-deep Western traditions and from the rest of Germany. It is all too often forgotten that German unity was a very recent affair, brought about by war in 1870; that what one war had put together, another might tear apart; and that there is no particular reason why one nation should not be split up into several states. Bismarck's entire policy since 1866 has been repudiated; the Second and Third Reich have collapsed in ruins and will not be rebuilt. The forceful and artificial unification of the whole of Germany into one nation-state has been undone, never to be put together in our lifetime. Were it not for the Communist fact in East Germany, most Westerners could and would agree that a partitioned Germany is desirable—just as desirable as the separation between the West German state and Austria.

While the partition of Germany is the core of the European problem, it is not the sole element. For those who remember Eastern Europe between the World Wars, the petty national rivalries, the oppression of minorities, and all the evils of an absurd balkanization, an enforced peace is clearly the only solution. The world cannot afford to see the Poles, Czechs, Slovaks, Rumanians, Hungarians, Croatians, Slovenians, Serbs, and Bulgars at each other's throats again. The *Pax Sovietica* that was imposed upon them after World War II had plenty of evil features; but through fire and bloodshed, it has imposed peace upon them. The course of world history has determined that peace in Eastern Europe could only be imperial and imposed from the outside; the same course of world history has also determined that this imperial peace would be imposed by the Slavs and not the Germans. At great cost in suffering, a balance of power has been achieved between East and West across the body of Europe, cutting the Continent in half—a well-deserved punishment for its suicidal conflicts. In spite of all the pious wishes expressed in the West, this balance of power is not about to be disrupted. The last, and most propitious, time for such disruption would have been in the fall of 1956 when Hungary revolted; the divided West did nothing and forfeited its right to tear down the Iron Curtain. Since then, a tacit acceptance of the situation has become evident, accompanied by the hope, in the West, that the Curtain would just melt away in time. And melt to a certain extent, it has, in the 1960's: increased economic, cultural, and touristic exchanges between the two halves of the Continent have multiplied.

Just as many signs indicate that many developments in Eastern Europe appear to parallel those that symbolize the profound changes in Soviet Russia itself—a new historical consciousness, a new fascination with the national pasts which many mistake for a rebirth of anti-Communist nationalism, but is nothing of the sort. An effective rebirth of anti-Communist and anti-Russian nationalism died in Hungary in 1956. What is taking place, however, is a rebirth of sorts, a rebirth of national consciousness and specificity which is mildly anti-Russian but hardly anti-Communist— not that the Russians trust their European satellites wholeheartedly, since Marshal Varentsov is alleged to have remarked in 1961: "They say we must give our brother Slavs missile weapons. We give them missiles now, and later they will stick a knife in our back." [37]

Polish Premier Gomulka reminded General de Gaulle, during his 1967 visit to Poland, that all the former victims of Germany still look, and will go on looking, to Soviet Russia as their natural protector. True enough, the further removed from Germany, the greater the freedom from Russian supervision they can afford; Yugoslavia, Albania, and Rumania can all behave like autonomous entities and, occasionally, flout Russian wishes; even the Czechs and Slovaks felt free, early in 1968, to over-throw the "Stalinist" regime of Antonin Novotny, and initiate a new economic policy under the guidance of Ota Sik, the Czech equivalent of Russia's Yevsei Liberman. But the terrible example of Hungary will always be there to remind them that they can never cross the threshold of Soviet Russia's own imperial security —in other words, that they remain potential hostages of the Superpower to the east.

There has never been, and never will be, as far as the prophetic eye can see, a "Europe from the Atlantic to the Urals." Not only is Russia, with its immense Asian extensions, another continent *sui generis;* it has firmly established its paramount influence on its side of the Curtain and nothing will remove it short of a nuclear conflict. Nationalist rebellions may occur, but never to the extent of prying Soviet paramountcy loose from Eastern Europe. Charles de Gaulle's vision of the Europe of the future, rid of the domination of the Superpowers, is sheer utopia. But this gradual freezing of the situation in Europe cannot come about without entailing great dangers for the Western alliance, already considerably shaken by de Gaulle's own gradual with-drawal into an increasingly "neutralist" position. As time goes on, however, it becomes more and more apparent that Charles de Gaulle could only be, and quite unconsciously, a stalking horse for the Russians who are aiming at far bigger game— nothing less than the worldwide Condominium with the Ameri-cans. By playing up to the Lord of the Elysée, Moscow could only hope to induce the Americans to accelerate the establish-ment of this Condominium.

The wave of anti-Americanism that swept through West Ger-many when Bonn first perceived the ghostly contours of the Russo-American Condominium that was beginning to take shape, had nothing to do with Gaullist propaganda. Germany began to fear that it would become the major casualty of this dual hegemony, that it not only would be asked to accept its new borders with Poland and its *de facto* partition into two antagonistic states, but would be forever barred from any kind of peaceful nuclear development as well. Chancellor Kurt Georg Kiesinger rose to power on this wave of anti-Americanism, fair warning that the making of the Condominium would have to be compensated for, somehow. Like many other Europeans, he staked his hopes on European unity; but he also staked his hopes on the preservation of NATO and the Atlantic Alliance. Given all the elements that go into making the *reality* of the situation, it is clear that a united Europe, operating independently of both the Soviet Union and the United States, is and will remain a myth, an unattainable goal. As to NATO, shorn of its geographical keystone which is France, it is fast becoming a ghost from the increasingly distant past, cut into separate portions covering the North Sea and the Mediterranean, geographically unconnected with one another. Its only remaining reality rests on the large West German army and the quarter of a million American troops stationed in Western Europe.

The true compensation for the Great Condominium to come would be, and eventually has to be, the deliberate creation of a North Atlantic Confederation. The web of political, military, economic, financial, and cultural connections between the two shores of the ocean is becoming so tight, so thick, and so strong that it can never be torn apart—not even by Charles de Gaulle at his worst—and that it is in increasing need of institutionalization within a new and adequate political framework. In days to come, when Britain will have joined whatever Common Market there is and Charles de Gaulle will only be a nameplate on a grave, when the web across the North Atlantic has become tighter and stronger yet, the urge to unite across the ocean will become much stronger than the urge to unite merely that half of Europe that lies in the west. New Soviet threats toward Western Europe are not necessarily required to impel both Americans and Europeans toward this new political formula. The main agent, the honest (but interested) broker, is likely to be Britain; only thus could Britain be persuaded to accept the unification of Western Europe—which would then become only part of a much larger unit; and only thus could West Germany be persuaded to forgo its dream of reunification and fully accept the inescapable establishment of the Condominium.

The tacit understanding that is developing between the two Superpowers is all but inevitable; it would probably have come about without the existence of nuclear power which now makes it imperative for the survival of the entire human race. Historically, and except for the Cold War, the Americans and the Russians had maintained distant but friendly relations, without any basic cause for quarrel. Geographically remote, yet both rooted in a Christian outlook, they were never emotionally involved with one another—as Americans had become involved in China, both as missionaries and as resentful hosts to Chinese immigrants on the West Coast. As Alexis de Tocqueville had already pointed out long ago, there were great similarities in their historical and geographical circumstances—westward the course of empire for the United States, and eastward for Russia; both conquered vast empty spaces, and both were marked by the "Frontier" experience—rough-riding cowboys in the Far West, cossacks in Siberia. Yet, for all that, material development has been far swifter in America than in Russia; it still is today. In the Condominium to come, at least in its early stages, the Russians will definitely be the junior partners—very much as the Parthian realm, ostensibly an enemy, was in fact the junior partner of the far more extensive and powerful Roman Empire. American achievement has always been, and remains, the yardstick whereby the Russians measure their own achievements; their major and often stated goal is to overtake the United States, economically and technologically.

Respect is not all one-sided, and more than one American respects the recent achievements of the Soviet Russians in science and technological developments, as others admire Russia's great prerevolutionary literature and music. There is no need to embrace the "convergence" theory according to which Soviet society is bound to evolve toward some form of capitalist organization while the Westerners are marching full speed ahead toward socialism. The two realms will develop differently, according to their own atavistic inclinations—but keeping all the channels of communication open, and opening new ones. They will continue to compete with one another on many levels; but they have been, for years, building the chessboard and defining the rules of this new worldwide game, rules and regulations forged during the numerous international crises; the chessboard is now about completed and the rules set.

Like civilized chess players who would not dream of throwing the chessboard at each other, Americans and Russians will abide by the rules of the game as they have been developed—not forgetting that they are not always in full control of their chessmen who may, at times, be motivated by other considerations than those of their patrons. They will come to accept each other's empires and zones of influence—and, hopefully, in the more or less distant future, will focus their competitive instincts on a peaceful exploration of outer space, while jointly ruling the earth.

BIBLIOGRAPHY

AGAR, HERBERT, *The Price of Union,* Boston, Houghton Mifflin, 1950.

BARCK, JR., OSCAR, *A History of the United States Since 1945,* New York, Dell Publishing Company, 1965.

BATOR, VICTOR, *Vietnam—A Diplomatic Tragedy,* London, Faber and Faber, 1967.

BELOFF, MAX, *The United States and the Unity of Europe,* London, Faber and Faber, 1963. Washington, D.C., The Brookings Institution, 1963.

BENOIST-MECHIN, JACQUES, *Sixty Days That Shook the World,* New York, Putnam's, 1963.

BISHOP, JOSEPH BUCKLIN, *Theodore Roosevelt and His Time,* 2 vols., New York, Scribner's, 1920.

BOWEN, CATHERINE DRINKER, *John Adams and the American Revolution,* Boston, Little Brown, 1950.

BRENAN, GERALD, *The Spanish Labyrinth,* Cambridge, Cambridge University Press, 1943. New York, Cambridge University Press, 1950 (2nd edition).

BYRNES, JAMES F., *Speaking Frankly,* New York, Harper & Brothers, 1947.

CARR, EDWARD HALLETT, *Conditions of Peace,* London, Macmillan and Company, 1944.

CHALANDON, ALBIN, *Le Système Monétaire International,* Paris, Conseil Economique et Social, 1966.

CLARK, GERALD, *Canada: The Uneasy Neighbor,* New York, David McKay, 1965.

COFFIN, TRISTRAM, *The Passion of the Hawks,* New York, Macmillan, 1964.

DEAN, VERA MICHELES, *The United States and Russia,* Cambridge, Harvard University Press, 1948.

DESNOES, EDMUNDO, *Inconsolable Memories,* New York, The New American Library, 1967.

DEVILLERS, PHILIPPE, *Histoire du Viet-Nam,* Paris, Editions du Seuil, 1952.

EDEN, ANTHONY, *Facing the Dictators,* Boston, Houghton Mifflin, 1962.

——— *The Reckoning,* Boston, Houghton Mifflin, 1965.

——— *Full Circle,* Boston, Houghton Mifflin, 1960.

EISENHOWER, DWIGHT D., *Whitehouse Years,* Vol. II, *Waging Peace 1956–1961,* London, Heinemann, 1965. New York, Doubleday, 1965.

FOCH, F., *Mémoires,* 2 vols., Paris, Librairie Plon, 1931. New York, Doubleday, 1931.

FREEMAN, C., AND YOUNG, A., *The Research and Development Effort,* Paris, Organization for Economic Co-Operation and Development, 1965.

FULBRIGHT, J. WILLIAM, *The Arrogance of Power,* New York, Random House, 1966.

FURNISS, JR., EDGAR S., *France, Troubled Ally,* New York, Harper & Brothers, 1960.

GARRETT, GARET, *A Bubble That Broke the World,* Boston, Little Brown, 1932.

DE GAULLE, CHARLES, *Mémoires de Guerre,* 3 vols., Paris, Librairie Plon, 1954. Published in the United States as *War Memoirs of Charles de Gaulle,* 3 vols., New York, Simon & Schuster, 1960.

GERARD, JAMES W., *My Four Years in Germany,* New York, Hodder & Stoughton, 1917.

HENDRICK, BURTON J., *The Life and Letters of Walter H. Page,* 2 vols., London, Heinemann, 1922.

HERRIOT, EDOUARD, *The United States of Europe,* New York, Viking, 1930.

HULL, CORDELL, *The Memoirs of Cordell Hull,* 2 vols., New York, Macmillan, 1948.

JAPAN EXTERNAL TRADE ORGANIZATION, *Foreign Trade of Japan, 1966,* Tokyo, 1966.

JUNGK, ROBERT, *Brighter Than a Thousand Suns,* New York, Harcourt, Brace & World, 1956.

KEYSERLING, HERMANN, *Europe,* New York, Harcourt, Brace & Company, 1928.

KINTNER, WILLIAM R., *Peace and the Strategy Conflict,* New York, Praeger, 1967.

KOHN, HANS, *World Order in Historical Perspective,* Cambridge, Mass., Harvard University Press, 1942.

LANGER, WILLIAM R., AND GLEASON, S. EVERETT, *The Undeclared War,* New York, Harper & Brothers, 1953.

LAYTON, CHRISTOPHER, *Trans-Atlantic Investments,* Paris, The Atlantic Institute, 1966.

LENIN, V. I., *Marx, Engels, Marxism,* London, Lawrence and Wishart, 1936.

LICHTHEIM, GEORGE, *Europe and America,* London, Thames and Hudson, 1963. Published in the United States as *New Europe: Today and Tomorrow,* New York, Praeger, 1963.

LIDDELL HART, B. H., *The Other Side of the Hill,* London, Cassell, 1948. Published in the United States as *German Generals Talk,* New York, Morrow, 1948.

LUDENDORFF, ERICH, *Souvenirs de Guerre,* 2 vols., Paris, Payot, 1921.

LUETHY, HERBERT, *France Against Herself,* New York, Praeger, 1957.

LUTHULI, ALBERT, *Let My People Go,* New York, McGraw-Hill, 1962.

MAO TSE-TUNG AND CHE GUEVARA, *Guerilla Warfare,* London, Cassell, 1962.

MACARTHUR, DOUGLAS, *Reminiscences,* New York, McGraw-Hill, 1964.

MARX, KARL, AND ENGELS, FREDERICK, *The Civil War in the United States,* New York, International Publishers, 1937.

MCNEILL, WILLIAM HARDY, *The Greek Dilemma,* Philadelphia, Lippincott, 1947.

MIDDLETON, DREW, *The Supreme Choice: Britain and Europe,* New York, Knopf, 1963.

MORGENTHAU, HANS J., AND THOMPSON, KENNETH W., *Principles and Problems of International Politics,* New York, Knopf, 1952.

MORISON, SAMUEL E., AND COMMAGER, HENRY STEELE, *The Growth of the American Republic,* 2 vols., New York, Oxford University Press, 1953.

MURPHY, ROBERT, *Diplomat Among Warriors,* New York, Doubleday, 1964.

MYRDAL, GUNNAR, *An American Dilemma,* New York, Harper & Brothers, 1944.

NEUMANN, WILLIAM L., *America Encounters Japan,* New York, Harper & Row, 1965.

Newsweek's History of Our Times, 1951, New York, Funk and Wagnalls, 1952.

NICHOLSON, IRENE, *The X in Mexico,* London, Faber and Faber, 1965. New York, Doubleday, 1966.

OLSON, PAUL R., AND HICKMAN, C. ADDISON, *Pan American Economics,* New York, John Wiley, 1943.

PATON, ALAN, *South Africa and Her People,* London, Lutterworth Press, 1957. Published in the United States as *The Land and People of South Africa,* Philadelphia, Lippincott, 1955.

PEEL, THE HON. GEORGE, *The Enemies of England,* London, Edward Arnold, 1902.

PENKOVSKY, OLEG, *The Penkovsky Papers,* London, William Collins Sons, 1965. New York, Doubleday, 1965.

PFLAUM, IRVING P., *Arena of Decision: Latin America in Crisis,* New York, Prentice-Hall, 1964.

QUINTANILLA, LUIS, *A Latin American Speaks,* New York, Macmillan, 1943.

RAYMOND, JACK, *Power at the Pentagon,* New York, Harper & Row, 1964.

DE RIENCOURT, AMAURY, *The Coming Caesars,* New York, Coward-McCann, 1957.

———— *The Soul of China,* New York, Harper & Row, 1965.

———— *The Soul of India,* New York, Harper & Brothers, 1960.

ROBERTSON, TERENCE, *Crisis: The Inside Story of the Suez Conspiracy,* New York, Atheneum, 1965.

RODRIGUEZ, MARIO, *Central America,* New York, Prentice-Hall, 1965.

ROMIER, LUCIEN, *Qui Sera le Maître: Europe ou Amérique?,* Paris, Librairie Hachette, 1927.

SANDS, WILLIAM FRANKLIN, *Our Jungle Diplomacy,* Chapel Hill, The University of North Carolina Press, 1944.

SCHEER, ROBERT, AND ZEITLING, MAURICE, *Cuba: An American Tragedy,* Harmondsworth, Middlesex, Penguin Books, 1964. Originally published as *Cuba: Tragedy in Our Hemisphere,* Chicago, Black Cat Press, 1963.

SCHLESINGER, JR., ARTHUR M., *A Thousand Days,* London, Andre Deutsch, 1965. Boston, Houghton Mifflin, 1965.

SHAW, A. G. L., *The Story of Australia,* London, Faber and Faber, 1962.

STALIN, JOSEPH, *Leninism,* London, Lawrence & Wishart, 1940. New York, International Publishers, 1942.

STEEL, RONALD, *Pax Americana,* New York, Viking, 1967.

THOMAS, HUGH, *Suez,* New York, Harper & Row, 1967.

THOMPSON, DOROTHY, *The New Russia,* London, Jonathan Cape, 1929. New York, Holt, 1928.

DE TOCQUEVILLE, ALEXIS, *Democracy in America,* 2 vols., New York, Knopf, 1945.

TRUMAN, HARRY S., *Memoirs,* Vol. I, *Year of Decisions, 1945,* London, Hodder & Stoughton, 1955. New York, Doubleday, 1955.

———, *Memoirs,* Vol. II, *Years of Trial and Hope, 1946–1953,* London, Hodder & Stoughton, 1956. New York, Doubleday, 1956.

TULLY, ANDREW, *CIA: The Inside Story,* New York, Morrow, 1963.

TYRNER-TYRNAUER, A. R., *Lincoln and the Emperors,* London, Rupert Hart-Davis, 1962. New York, Harcourt, 1962.

WELLES, SUMNER, *The Time for Decision,* New York, Harper & Brothers, 1944.

WIGHTON, CHARLES, *Adenauer,* New York, Coward-McCann, 1963.

WILSON, HAROLD, *Purpose in Politics,* Boston, Houghton Mifflin, 1964.

WISE, DAVID, AND ROSS, THOMAS B., *The Invisible Government,* London, Jonathan Cape, 1965. New York, Random House, 1964.

NOTES AND REFERENCES *

Introduction

1. Riencourt, *The Coming Caesars*, p. 331.
2. *Washington Post*, November 22, 1967.
3. *Ibid.*
4. *International Herald Tribune*, December 11, 1967.
5. *Ibid.*
6. Riencourt, *op. cit.*, pp. 332–333.
7. For further elaboration on the cyclical aspect of historical evolution, see Riencourt, *op. cit.*, Introduction and Epilogue.
8. Kohn, *World Order in Historical Perspective*, p. 113.
9. Riencourt, *The Soul of China*, pp. 51–61, and *The Soul of India*, pp. 81–89.
10. Kohn, *op. cit.*, pp. 141–142.
11. *New York Times*, November 4, 1967.
12. Fulbright, *The Arrogance of Power*, p. 53.
13. *Ibid.*, p. 53.

I—The Roots

1. Morison and Commager, *The Growth of the American Republic*, i, p. 141.
2. *Ibid.*, p. 143.
3. *Ibid.*, pp. 143–144.
4. Bowen, *John Adams and the American Revolution*, p. 205.
5. Morison and Commager, *op. cit.*, i, p. 226.
6. *Ibid.*, p. 390.
7. Agar, *The Price of Union*, p. 308.
8. *Ibid.*, p. 319.
9. Tyrner-Tyrnauer, *Lincoln and the Emperors*, p. 16.
10. Morison and Commager, *op. cit.*, i, pp. 610–611.
11. Tyrner-Tyrnauer, *op. cit.*, p. 22.
12. *Ibid.*, p. 69.
13. *Ibid.*, p. 72.
14. Marx and Engels, *The Civil War in the United States*, p. 46.

* Dispatch, rather than publication, dates are used in newspaper references, except when quoting editorials and columnists.

15. Tyrner-Tyrnauer, *op. cit.*, pp. 76–77.
16. Morison and Commager, *op. cit.*, i, p. 714.
17. *Ibid.*, ii, p. 315.
18. *Ibid.*, p. 323.
19. *Ibid.*, p. 320.
20. *Ibid.*, p. 325.
21. *Ibid.*
22. *Ibid.*, p. 335.
23. *Ibid.*, p. 339.
24. *Ibid.*, p. 351.
25. Agar, *op. cit.*, p. 650.
26. Gerard, *My Four Years in Germany*, p. 32.
27. Morison and Commager, *op. cit.*, ii, p. 406.
28. *Ibid.*
29. Peel, *The Enemies of England*, p. 11.
30. Hendrick, *The Life and Letters of Walter H. Page*, i, pp. 144-151.

II—The Suicide of Europe

1. Morison and Commager, *op. cit.*, ii, p. 451.
2. Garrett, *A Bubble That Broke the World*, p. 8.
3. Gerard, *op. cit.*, pp. 144–145.
4. *Ibid.*, p. 167.
5. Keyserling, *Europe*, p. 115.
6. Hendrick, *op. cit.*, ii, pp. 269–271.
7. Morison and Commager, *op. cit.*, ii, p. 483.
8. Ludendorff, *Souvenirs de Guerre*, ii, p. 256.
9. Foch, *Mémoires*, ii, pp. 79, 115.
10. Eden, *Facing the Dictators*, p. 408.
11. Wighton, *Adenauer*, p. 35.
12. Romier, *Qui Sera le Maître—Europe ou Amérique?*, pp. 26–29.
13. *Ibid.*, p. 81.
14. Herriot, *The United States of Europe*, p. 3.
15. *Ibid.*, p. 51.
16. *Ibid.*, p. 55.
17. *Ibid.*, p. 259.
18. Beloff, *The United States and the Unity of Europe*, p. 1.
19. Welles, *The Time for Decision*, p. 108.
20. Carr, *Conditions of Peace*, p. 170.
21. Garrett, *op. cit.*, p. 60.
22. Keyserling, *op. cit.*, p. 119.
23. *Ibid.*, p. 133.
24. *Ibid.*, p. 120.
25. Garrett, *op. cit.*, p. 95.
26. *Ibid.*, p. 26.
27. *Ibid.*, p. 71.

28. Eden, *Facing the Dictators*, p. 371.
29. *Ibid.,* p. 606.
30. *Ibid.,* p. 609.
31. *Ibid.,* p. 616.
32. Benoist-Méchin, *Sixty Days That Shook the West*, pp. 35–36.
33. *Ibid.,* p. 109.
34. *Ibid.,* p. 113.
35. *Ibid.,* p. 126.
36. Liddell Hart, *The Other Side of the Hill*, p. 141.
37. Benoist-Méchin, *op. cit.,* p. 165.
38. *Ibid.,* p. 333.
39. *Ibid.,* p. 349.
40. *Ibid.,* pp. 487–488.

III—Pearl Harbor: The Genesis of Empire

1. Langer and Gleason, *The Undeclared War*, p. 170.
2. *Ibid.,* p. 172.
3. Eden, *The Reckoning*, p. 155.
4. Langer and Gleason, *op. cit.,* p. 231.
5. *Ibid.,* p. 233.
6. *Ibid.,* p. 708.
7. *Ibid.,* p. 852.
8. *Ibid.,* p. 757.
9. *Ibid.,* p. 867.
10. Neumann, *America Encounters Japan*, p. 276.
11. Morison and Commager, *op. cit.,* ii, pp. 696–697.
12. Jungk, *Brighter Than a Thousand Suns*, p. 46.
13. *Ibid.,* p. 87.
14. *Ibid.,* p. 105.
15. *Ibid.,* p. 80.
16. *Ibid.,* p. 114.
17. *Ibid.,* pp. 168–169.
18. *Ibid.,* p. 171.
19. *Ibid.,* p. 178.
20. MacArthur, *Reminiscences*, p. 163.
21. *Ibid.,* p. 169.
22. Morison and Commager, *op. cit.,* ii, p. 669.
23. Eden, *The Reckoning*, p. 447.
24. *Ibid.,* p. 454.
25. *Ibid.,* p. 461.
26. *Ibid.*
27. *Ibid.,* p. 470.
28. *Ibid.,* p. 529.
29. *Ibid.,* p. 526.
30. de Gaulle, *Mémoires de Guerre*, ii, p. 224.
31. Lichtheim, *Europe and America*, p. 28.
32. de Gaulle, *op. cit.,* ii, p. 238.

33. Eden, *The Reckoning,* p. 542.
34. Byrnes, *Speaking Frankly,* p. 63.
35. Eden, *The Reckoning,* p. 593.
36. *Ibid.*

IV—Cold War: The Establishment of Empire

1. Hull, *Memoirs,* ii, pp. 1314–1315.
2. Barck, *A History of the United States Since 1945,* p. 37.
3. *Ibid.,* p. 38.
4. Lichtheim, *op. cit.,* p. 13.
5. Byrnes, *op. cit.,* p. 53.
6. McNeill, *The Greek Dilemma,* p. 89.
7. Truman, *Years of Trial and Hope,* p. 111.
8. *Ibid.,* p. 112.
9. Barck, *op. cit.,* p. 114.
10. Morgenthau and Thompson, *Principles and Problems of International Politics,* p. 237.
11. MacArthur, *op. cit.,* p. 375.
12. *Ibid.,* p. 387.
13. Garrett, *Wall Street Journal,* January 3, 1952.
14. Steel, *Pax Americana,* pp. 15–16.

V—The Tools of Empire

1. Reston, *International Herald Tribune,* July 22–23, 1967.
2. *New York Times,* October 29, 1957.
3. Raymond, *Power at the Pentagon,* p. 111.
4. *Ibid.,* p. 15.
5. *Ibid.*
6. *Ibid.,* p. 81.
7. Eisenhower, *Waging Peace,* p. 616.
8. *Ibid.*
9. Coffin, *The Passion of the Hawks,* p. 11.
10. *The Times* (London), December 14, 1967.
11. Raymond, *op. cit.,* p. 68.
12. Hull, *op. cit.,* ii, pp. 1109–1110.
13. Tully, *CIA: The Inside Story,* p. 21.
14. *Ibid.,* p. 17.
15. Wise and Ross, *The Invisible Government,* p. 349.
16. Speech at Yale University, February 3, 1958.
17. Penkovsky, *The Penkovsky Papers,* p. 182.
18. *New York Times,* February 22, 1967.
19. *New York Times,* April 14, 1967.
20. *New York Times,* February 21, 1967.
21. *New York Times,* March 8, 1967.
22. Associated Press, February 16, 1967.

23. Wise and Ross, *op. cit.*, p. 349.
24. Schlesinger, *A Thousand Days*, p. 463.
25. United Press International, July 21, 1967. Also, *Le Monde*, July 15, 1967.
26. *Le Monde*, June 5, 1967.
27. *New York Times*, October 31, 1967.
28. Coffin, *op. cit.*, pp. 1–2.

VI—The Road to Suez

1. *Newsweek's History of Our Times*, 1951, p. 219.
2. Eden, *Full Circle*, p. 236.
3. *Ibid.*, p. 237.
4. *Ibid.*, p. 470.
5. *Ibid.*
6. Barck, *op. cit.*, p. 308.
7. Eden, *Full Circle*, p. 478.
8. Robertson, *Crisis*, p. 177.
9. Eden, *Full Circle*, p. 521.
10. *Ibid.*, p. 524.
11. *Ibid.*, p. 540.
12. *Ibid.*
13. Thomas, *Suez*, p. 56.
14. *Ibid.*
15. Eden, *Full Circle*, p. 604.
16. *Ibid.*, pp. 605–606.
17. *Ibid.*, p. 609.
18. *Ibid.*
19. *Ibid.*, pp. 622–623.
20. *Ibid.*, p. 628.
21. Murphy, *Diplomat Among Warriors*, p. 391.
22. Thomas, *op. cit.*, p. 149.
23. Eden, *Full Circle*, p. 632.
24. *Ibid.*, p. 634.
25. *Ibid.*, p. 635.
26. *Ibid.*, p. 641.
27. Barck, *op. cit.*, p. 310.
28. Eden, *Full Circle*, p. 646.
29. *New York Times*, November 16, 1967.

VII—Death and Transfiguration of The Commonwealth

1. Clark, *Canada*, p. 4.
2. *Ibid.*, p. 72.
3. *Ibid.*, p. 46.
4. *Ibid.*, p. 82.
5. *Ibid.*, p. 90.

6. *Ibid.*, p. 97.
7. *Ibid.*, p. 100.
8. *Ibid.*, p. 212.
9. *Ibid.*, p. 222.
10. *Ibid.*, pp. 236–237.
11. *Ibid.*, p. 239.
12. *Ibid.*, p. 315.
13. *New York Times,* January 3, 1967.
14. *Ibid.*
15. Clark, *op. cit.*, p. 367.
16. *Ibid.*, p. 414.
17. United Press International, July 25, 1967.
18. *New York Times,* March 3, 1966.
19. Shaw, *The Story of Australia*, p. 91.
20. *Ibid.*, p. 151.
21. *Ibid.*, p. 159.
22. *Ibid.*, p. 160.
23. *Ibid.*, p. 166.
24. *Ibid.*, p. 220.
25. *Ibid.*, p. 222.
26. *Ibid.*, p. 258.
27. *Wall Street Journal,* Letters to the Editor, May 10, 1966.
28. Sulzberger, *New York Times,* March 25, 1966.
29. *New York Times,* May 6, 1966.
30. Sulzberger, *New York Times,* March 25, 1966.

VIII—Frontier Across the Pacific

1. Neumann, *op. cit.*, p. 23.
2. *Ibid.*, p. 30.
3. *Ibid.*, p. 109.
4. *Ibid.*, p. 159.
5. *Ibid.*, p. 127.
6. *Ibid.*, p. 179.
7. *Ibid.*, p. 197.
8. *Ibid.*, p. 196.
9. *Ibid.*, p. 207.
10. *Ibid.*, p. 239.
11. *Ibid.*
12. *Ibid.*, p. 263.
13. *Ibid.*, p. 264.
14. *Ibid.*, p. 267.
15. *Ibid.*, p. 279.
16. *Ibid.*, p. 282.
17. *Ibid.*, p. 292.
18. MacArthur, *op. cit.*, p. 298.
19. Neumann, *op. cit.*, p. 97.
20. Bator, *Vietnam—A Diplomatic Tragedy*, pp. 14–15.

21. *Ibid.*, p. 21.
22. *Ibid.*, p. 20.
23. On the relationship between Chinese culture and Marxism, see Riencourt, *The Soul of China*, pp. 209–213, 260–264.
24. Devillers, *Histoire du Viêt-Nam*, p. 116.
25. *Ibid.*, p. 152.

IX—The Hawaiianization of the Orient

1. Hendrick, *op. cit.*, i, p. 188.
2. Bator, *op. cit.*, p. 145.
3. *Ibid.*, p. 48.
4. *Ibid.*, pp. 163–164.
5. *Ibid.*, p. 166.
6. *Ibid.*, pp. 166–167.
7. *International Herald Tribune*, August 28, 1967.
8. Bator, *op. cit.*, p. 169.
9. *Ibid.*, p. 187.
10. *Ibid.*, p. 188.
11. Shaplen, *The Lost Revolution*, p. 154.
12. Reston, *New York Times*, April 11, 1966.
13. Reuters, March 20, 1967. See also Agence France Presse, February 23, 1968, and *International Herald Tribune*, February 28, 1968, on a motion passed by the territorial assembly of New Caledonia, demanding autonomy.
14. Trumbull, *New York Times*, November 11, 1967.
15. Neumann, *op. cit.*, p. 30.
16. Bishop, *Theodore Roosevelt and His Time*, i, p. 107.
17. *Look*, May 30, 1967.
18. *New York Times*, March 30, 1967.
19. Associated Press, November 29, 1967.
20. Reuters, November 17, 1967.
21. Reuters, June 30, 1967.
22. *New York Times*, November 15, 1967.
23. *New York Times*, September 2, 1965. See also *Peking Review*, September 13, 1965, p. 24, quoted in Kintner, *Peace and the Strategy Conflict*, p. 108.
24. *New York Times*, February 27, 1967.
25. *New York Times*, October 17, 1958.
26. Japan External Trade Organization, *Foreign Trade of Japan, 1966*, pp. 184–185.
27. *New York Times*, April 21, 1967.

X—Latins, Guerillas, and Anarchists

1. Quintanilla, *A Latin American Speaks*, p. 9.
2. *New York Times*, April 27, 1966.

3. *New York Times,* Survey of the Economy of the Americas, February 3, 1966, pp. 4–5.
4. *Ibid.,* pp. 5–6.
5. Olson and Hickman, *Pan American Economics,* p. 50.
6. Sands, *Our Jungle Diplomacy,* p. 154.
7. Nicholson, *The X in Mexico,* p. 126.
8. Reston, *New York Times,* August 3, 1962.
9. Reuters, November 29, 1967.
10. *New York Times,* July 28, 1962.
11. Schlesinger, *op. cit.,* p. 180.
12. *New York Times,* July 9, 1965.
13. Scheer and Zeitlin, *Cuba,* pp. 96–100.
14. *Ibid.,* p. 100.
15. Matthews, *New York Times,* February 8, 1966.
16. Reuters, June 7, 1967. Also United Press International, June 28, 1967.
17. *New York Times,* May 18, 1967.
18. *The Economist,* May 27, 1967.
19. United Press International, July 30, 1967.
20. Reuters, October 25, 1967.
21. Reuters, August 9, 1967. See also *Le Monde,* August 4, 1967, and *New York Times,* August 1, 1967.
22. *New York Times,* October 31, 1967.
23. Brenan, *The Spanish Labyrinth,* p. 133.
24. *Ibid.,* p. 193.
25. Scheer and Zeitlin, *op. cit.,* pp. 60–61.
26. *Ibid.,* p. 118.
27. Larteguy, *Match,* August 26, 1967.
28. Mao Tse-tung and Che Guevara, *Guerilla Warfare,* p. 102.
29. *Ibid.,* p. 111.
30. *Le Monde,* August 4, 1967.
31. Agence France Presse, February 17, 1968.
32. *New York Times,* January 22, 1968.
33. Fulbright, *op. cit.,* p. 95.
34. Schlesinger, *op. cit.,* p. 658.
35. Pflaum, *Arena of Decision,* p. 233.

XI—Race and Africa

1. *New York Times,* March 17, 1968.
2. Reuters, December 27, 1967, and January 1, 1968.
3. Associated Press, December 20, 1967.
4. *New York Times,* November 7, 1967.
5. Myrdal, *An American Dilemma,* p. 807.
6. *Ibid.*
7. *New York Times,* March 26, 1967.
8. Penkovsky, *op. cit.,* p. 236.
9. Associated Press, July 10, 1967.

10. Paton, *South Africa and Her People,* pp. 135–136.
11. Luthuli, *Let My People Go,* p. 206.
12. United Press International, October 29, 1967.
13. *Congressional Record,* Vol. 113, No. 162, October 10, 1967.
14. Luthuli, *op. cit.,* p. 83.
15. Reuters, December 14, 1967.
16. *New York Times,* March 27, 1967.
17. United Press International, December 15, 1967.

XII—Empire and Nation-State

1. Luethy, *France Against Herself,* p. 340.
2. Wighton, *op. cit.,* p. 155.
3. *Ibid.,* p. 157.
4. Furniss, *France, Troubled Ally,* p. 83.
5. Reuters, October 28, 1966.
6. Middleton, *The Supreme Choice,* p. 264.
7. Murphy, *op. cit.,* p. 164.
8. Middleton, *op. cit.,* p. 103.
9. Wilson, *Purpose in Politics,* p. xvii.
10. Reuters, October 28, 1966.
11. Reuters, October 24, 1967.
12. *New York Times,* January 22, 1968.
13. United Press International, March 3, 1968.
14. Agar, *op. cit.,* p. 434.

XIII—Economic Hegemony

1. *New York Times,* July 1, 1966.
2. *New York Times,* July 14, 1966.
3. *New York Times,* October 18, 1966.
4. *Le Monde,* editorial, January 5, 1967.
5. *New York Times,* May 20, 1966.
6. Layton, *Trans-Atlantic Investments,* pp. 11–34.
7. The Chase Manhattan Bank, *Foreign Investments,* September 1966.
8. *New York Times,* November 23, 1966.
9. *New York Times,* December 19, 1967.
10. Layton, *op. cit.,* pp. 28–29.
11. *Ibid.,* pp. 38–39. See also *Le Monde,* January 5, 1967.
12. *New York Times,* October 21, 1966.
13. Layton, *op. cit.,* p. 43.
14. *New York Times,* December 22, 1966.
15. *New York Times,* January 17, 1967.
16. *Sunday Telegraph,* October 22, 1967.
17. *New York Times,* February 7, 1968.
18. *New York Times,* January 29, 1968.

19. *Financial Times* (London), January 25, 1968.
20. *New York Times,* June 26, 1967.
21. Arthur K. Watson, quoted in *New York Times,* June 26, 1967.
22. Layton, *op. cit.,* p. 91. See also *New York Times,* January 15, 1968.
23. Freeman and Young, *The Research and Development Effort,* pp. 11–37.
24. *New York Times,* January 15, 1968.
25. *International Herald Tribune,* May 26, 1967.
26. Freeman and Young, *op. cit.,* p. 12.
27. *Business Week,* April 22, 1967.
28. *International Herald Tribune,* June 28, 1967.
29. *New York Times,* January 15, 1967.
30. *Washington Post,* December 8, 1967.
31. *New York Times,* July 5, 1967.
32. *New York Times,* March 13, 1967.
33. *New York Times,* April 10, 1966.
34. *Ibid.*
35. *New York Times,* April 24, 1967.
36. *New York Times,* April 11, 1967.
37. *New York Times,* July 24, 1966.
38. *Washington Post,* October 10, 1967.
39. *New York Times,* November 16, 1967.
40. *New York Times,* September 15, 1966.
41. *New York Times,* September 9, 1966.
42. *New York Times,* December 12, 1966.
43. *Sunday Telegraph* (London), October 22, 1967.
44. *New York Times,* April 30, 1967.
45. Chalandon, *Le Système Monétaire International,* pp. 14–20, May 25, 1966.
46. *Washington Post,* November 23, 1967.
47. Reuters, September 29, 1967. Also *Washington Post,* August 29, 1967.
48. *New York Times,* May 6, 1967. Also *Fortune,* June 1, 1967.

XIV—The Great Condominium

1. Reuters, October 28, 1966.
2. United Press International, March 16, 1967.
3. *New York Times,* April 13, 1967.
4. Reuters, December 10, 1967.
5. Dean, *The United States and Russia,* p. 7.
6. *Ibid.,* p. 8.
7. *Ibid.,* p. 9.
8. Tocqueville, *Democracy in America,* i, p. 434.
9. Lenin, *Marx, Engels, Marxism,* p. 223.
10. Thompson, *The New Russia,* pp. 159–160.
11. *Ibid.,* pp. 160–161.

12. *Ibid.,* p. 167.
13. Stalin, *Leninism,* p. 85.
14. *New York Times,* August 18, 1967.
15. Desnoes, *Inconsolable Memories,* p. 58.
16. Reuters, July 17, 1967.
17. *New York Times,* October 8, 1967.
18. United Press International, January 24, 1968. Also Reuters, September 13, 1967.
19. Reuters, March 27, 1967.
20. United Press International, August 22, 1967.
21. Schwartz, *New York Times,* March 16, 1967.
22. *New York Times,* March 16, 1967.
23. Austin, *New York Times,* May 15, 1967.
24. Schwartz, *New York Times,* May 7, 1967.
25. Lenin, *op. cit.,* p. 225.
26. *New York Times,* July 24, 1967.
27. *New York Times,* April 13, 1967.
28. Sulzberger, *New York Times,* April 7, 1967.
29. *New York Times,* April 14, 1967.
30. *New York Times,* March 20, 1967.
31. *New York Times,* March 21, 1967.
32. *New York Times,* April 27, 1967.
33. *Washington Post,* December 17, 1967.
34. United Press International, January 24, 1968.
35. *New York Times,* March 11, 1968.
36. Penkovsky, *op. cit.,* p. 256.
37. *Ibid.,* p. 244.

INDEX

Abadan, 120, 121, 124

Aberdeen, Lord, 16, 19

Abyssinian War, 51

Acheson, Dean, 89, 90, 93

Adams, John Quincy, 16, 25

Aden, 133, 156

Adenauer, Konrad, 42, 264, 270

Afghanistan, 115

Africa, 31, 43, 97, 115, 214, 236-37, 238-54, 255, 256, 265, 281

African National Congress, 254

African Nationalist party, 244

Afro-Asian-Latin American Solidarity Conference, 220

Agrarian Reform Law, 219

Alaska, 22, 23, 62, 148

Albania, 84, 323, 335

Alberta, 147

Aleman, Miguel, 211

Alexander II, Czar, 21, 22, 314

Algeria, 128, 132-33, 136, 249

Alliance for Progress, 204-05, 209, 232

"Alsos" (U.S. science/technology intelligence organization), 67-68, 69

American Federation of Labor-Congress of Industrial Organization, 111

American Federation of State, County, and Municipal Employees, 110

American Medical Association, 299-300

American Revolution, 3, 6-9, 11, 82, 87, 139, 141, 151

Amherst, Jeffrey, 6

Amtorg (Soviet Trade Agency), 317

anarchism, 223-32

Andes, 207, 218

Anglo-American Committee of Inquiry, 119

Anglo-Iranian Company, 121

Annam, 175, 190

Anti-Sabotage Act, 244

Anzac Day, 155

ANZUS pact, 92, 156

Arab-Israeli war, 325

Arab nationalism, 81, 133

Argentina, 43, 207, 217, 222, 232

Armas, Castillo, 209

Armed Services Committee, 93

Asia, 31, 162, 163, 169, 214

"Asian Doctrine," xvii

Asian immigrants, 153

Asoka, Emperor, xv

Aswan Dam, 135

Atlantic Alliance, 174, 267, 274, 336

Atlantic Community, 278, 308, 309

Atlantic Pact, 262

atom bomb, 64, 68-69

Atomic Energy Commission, 285
Attlee, Clement, 119
"Austerica," 158
Australia, 31, 43, 70-71, 89, 92, 97, 136, 151-58, 165, 234, 268, 282, 294
Austria, 19, 52, 333
Austrian Succession, War of the, 5
Austro-Hungarian Empire, 30, 33, 40, 258
Azores, 58, 72

Baghdad Pact, 122, 135
Bakunin, Mikhail, 223, 224
Baldwin, Hanson, 100
Baldwin, Stanley, 46
Balkans, 86-87, 89, 92, 161
Banda, Hastings, 246
Bantu Self-Government Act, 247
Bantustans, 245-46, 249, 252-53
Bao Dai, Emperor, 179, 180
Batista, Fulgencio, 218
Bay of Pigs, 219
Belgium, 162, 242-43, 258, 281, 288
Belize, 25
Beneš, Eduard, 45, 260
Benn, Anthony W., 286-87, 300
Berlin Blockade, 79, 88
Berlin Wall, 266, 333
Betancourt, Rómulo, 231
Beveridge, Albert J., 114, 163
Bidault, Georges, 261, 262
"big four," 74
"Big Three," 80
Bismarck, Otto, Fürst von, 21, 33, 333
"Black Chamber," 106
"Black Front," 264
Black Hawk, Chief, 15
Blanca, Florida, 11
Blum, Léon, 260
Boer War, 33
Bogotá, 230
Bohr, Niels, 64, 69

Bolívar, Simón, 222, 225
Bolivia, 209, 214, 221-22
Bonaparte, Louis, 16, 19-21
Boston, 143, 147
Botany Bay, 151
Botha, M. C., 245
Botswana, 245
Bradstreet, Colonel Dudley, 6
Braun, Werner von, 68
Bravo, Douglas, 221
Brazil, 43, 207, 218, 222, 232
Brenan, Gerald, 224
Bretton Woods Agreement, 303-04
Briand, Aristide, 45, 260
Briand Memorandum, 45-46
Briceno, Colonel Gonzalo, 215
British Columbia, 141, 143, 148
British Commonwealth of Nations, 58, 60, 84, 92, 139-60, 256, 263, 268-69, 298
British Conservative Party, 138, 211
British Empire, 4, 32, 55, 100, 106, 112, 115
British Guiana, 111
British Isles, 138, 152
British Labour Party, 49, 79, 120, 138, 264
British Royal Navy, 32-33, 153-55
Broederbond association, 244
Brussels, Treaty of, 87
Bryan, William Jennings, 166
Bryce, James, 193
Buddhists, 188
Bulganin, Nikolai Alexandrovich, 130
Bulgaria, 84
Burma, 69, 81, 115, 159, 191, 194
Burnham, Forbes, 111
Byrd, Harry Flood, 248
Byrnes, James Francis, 69, 75

Caesar, Julius, xiii
Caesarism, xi, 75
California, 15, 17, 23, 148, 162, 164

Camacho, Manuel Ávila, 212
Cambodia, 175, 180, 190, 195
Canada, 4-5, 8, 12-14, 20-24, 44, 57-58, 129, 140-51, 158-59, 165, 198, 202, 207, 209, 266, 268, 281, 282, 288, 294
Canadian Liberal Party, 281
Canning, Bishop, 16, 19
Cao Dai, 186, 188, 190
Cape of Good Hope, 248
Capetown, 251
Caracalla, xvi
Cárdenas, Lázaro, 211
Caribbean, 34, 161, 202, 208, 218, 230-32
Carmichael, Stokely, 241
Cartagena, 5
Casablanca, 105, 118
Castro, Fidel, 218-21, 225-26, 232, 322
Castroism, 222-27, 231, 321
Central America, 161, 202, 208, 218, 231-32
Central American Court of Justice, 29
Central Intelligence Agency (CIA), 106-14, 121, 200, 209, 243
Central Treaty Organization (CENTO), 135
Ceylon, 81, 159
Chaco, 214
Charles III, 11
Chiang Kai-shek, 166, 187
Chicago, 143, 145
Chile, 221, 227
China, 27, 51, 60, 74, 153, 158, 159, 162-81, 184, 187, 191-200, 217, 220-22, 288, 313, 322-25, 329, 333, 337
Chinese civil war, 90
Chinese nationalism, 91, 167, 168, 174, 178
Christian Democrats, 111
Christianity, 163, 166, 325

Chrysler Corp., 281, 286-87, 307
Churchill, Winston, 54, 59, 67, 69, 72-75, 84-86, 105, 170, 262-64
Clay, General Lucius, 100
Clayson Co., 288
Clayton-Bulwer Treaty, 18
Clemenceau, Georges, 42
Cleveland, Grover, 164
Cleveland, Harlan, 330
Coal & Steel Community Co., 265
Cochin China, 189
Cold War, 62, 78-95, 106-07, 116, 276, 337
Colombia, 28, 205, 220, 230
Colonial Conference, 154
Combat Service Support System, 294
Combined Chiefs of Staff, 72
Cominform, 86
Commune of 1871, Paris, 273
Communism, xiii, 81-85, 87, 90, 94-95, 98-99, 108-09, 115-16, 123, 135, 171-73, 176-84, 187, 190, 191, 195, 209-10, 215-23, 226-27, 232, 242, 244, 254, 273, 321-27
Confederación Nacional de Trabajo, 224
Confederate States of America, 19, 20
Conference on Economic Cooperation, 87
Congo, 108, 243-44, 251, 326
Congress of the United States, viii, ix, x, 9, 27, 55, 86, 87, 94, 109, 118, 243
Constitution of the United States, 270
Consular Treaty, 311
Continental Congress, 99
Council of Europe, 264
Council of Foreign Ministers, 261
Council on International Education and Cultural Affairs, 302
Council for South-West Africa, 252

Crimean War, 314
Cromer, Earl of, 301
Cuba, 18, 25-26, 29, 218-23, 227, 230-34, 266, 313, 322-26
Cuban Revolution, 25, 217-21
Cultural Revolution (China), 194, 196
Curtin, Prime Minister, 155
Czechoslovakia, 45, 52, 53, 242, 322, 323, 327

Dai Viet, 178
Dakar, 58, 241
Damascus, 113
Darling River, 70
Davis, Jefferson, 22
Davis, Norman, 168
Dawes Act (1887), 23
Dawes Plan, 47
Deakin, Alfred, 154
Debré, Michel, 288
Declaration of Independence, 9, 26
Democratic party, x, 120
Depression, 43, 46-50, 53
Detroit, 145, 159
Diaz, Porfirio, 211, 212, 213
Diefenbaker, John, 144, 150
Dienbienphu, 136, 174, 180
Dirección General de Inteligencia, 220
Disarmament Conference, 296, 312
Distant Early Warning Line (DEW), 144
Dominican Republic, vii, 29, 230, 232
Dong Minh, 178
Douglas, Stephen Arnold, 18
Douglass, William A., 301
Du Bois, W. E. B., 239
Dulles, Allen W., 106, 107
Dulles, John Foster, 105, 123-26, 129, 131, 173-74, 182-87, 267
Dulles doctrine, 98
Dumbarton Oaks treaty, 80

Dunmore, John Murray, 4th earl of, 7
Du Pont (E. I. du Pont de Nemours & Co.), 291
Dutch East Indies, 60, 61, 69-76, 89, 170-71
Dutch Empire, 162, 323

East Asia Co-Prosperity Sphere, 155, 162, 177, 197
East India Company, 115
Economic Cooperation Administration (ECA), 87
Ecuador, 205
Eden, Anthony, 41, 72-76, 123-26, 129-31, 134, 187, 267
Educational Council for Foreign Medical Graduates, 299
Egypt, 113, 114, 118, 122, 123, 124, 126, 127, 128, 130, 131, 130-35
Einstein, Albert, 64, 65, 66
Eisenhower, Dwight D., ix, 93-94, 98, 101, 103, 105, 125-27, 131, 133, 182, 184-86
Eisenhower Doctrine, vii, xvii, 133-34
Ely, General Paul, 184
Elysée Treaty, 330
Emancipation Proclamation, 22
England, 9, 12, 19-21, 25-31, 32-54, 57-59, 69-76, 79-92, 118-38, 151-54, 162, 167-70, 174, 185-91, 203, 208, 258-78, 281, 283, 284-89, 298-301, 336
Espionage Act, 38
European Atomic Energy Community (Euratom), 265, 295, 296
European Common Market, 258, 263-66, 268-69, 270, 283-86, 290
European Defense Community, 174, 264, 265
European Free Trade Area (EFTA), 264, 268

ELAS, 83-84
Exclusion Acts, 60

Faisal, 134
Far East, 27, 69, 91, 163, 166-69, 173, 183, 192-93, 197-99
Farouk, 122
Fascism, 217, 224
Fedayeen raids, 123
Federación Anarquista Ibérica, 224
Federal Bureau of Investigation (FBI), 107
Fermi, Enrico, 64
Fifth Republic, 265, 272, 274
Firestone Company, 239
Florida, 12, 13, 14
Florida Treaty (1819), 16
Foch, Marshal Ferdinand, 40, 42
Fonseca, Gulf of, 29
Forbes, General John, 36
Fordney-McCumber tariff, 43
Foreign Secretaries' conference, 73
Formosa, ix, 90, 112, 165, 200
Fowler, Henry, 306
"Fourteen Points," 41
Fourth Republic, 111, 265, 272
France, 6, 12, 33-40, 45, 47, 51-56, 73, 74, 87, 88, 111, 115, 124-25, 128-32, 136, 149-50, 169, 203, 213, 259-67, 270-76, 279, 285-88, 290, 305-07, 314, 330, 336
Franco, Francisco, 224
Franco-Prussian War, 271
Franklin, Benjamin, 9
Freemasonry, 212
French Canada, 12-14, 141-42, 146, 149-50
French colonialism, 175-78, 180, 185-89, 192
French Communists, 109, 262
"French and Indian War," 5
French Indochina, 60, 162, 175, 177
French nationalism, 274

French Revolution, 12, 271, 273
French Socialist party, 176
Friends of India Committee, 110
Fulbright, William, x, xvii, 104

Gage, General Thomas, 7
Gallipoli campaign, 155
Garibaldi, Giuseppe, 223
Garvey, Marcus, 235-36
de Gasperi, Alcide, 264
de Gaulle, Charles, 72, 74, 75, 94, 132, 149-50, 259-61, 265-70, 272, 274, 276, 279, 285, 306, 310, 313, 331, 334-35
Gehlen, Reinhard, 112
General Electric, 285
General Motors, 281, 284
Geneva Agreements, 184, 185, 186
George, Lloyd, 42
Gerard, James, 28, 36, 37
Gérin-Lajoie, 149
German Communist party, 332
German Democratic Republic, 89
Germany, 28, 33-56, 61, 64-72, 83, 88, 93, 100-01, 115, 155, 169-70, 258, 260-61, 270-71, 276, 284, 293, 297, 331-35
Ghana, 159, 326
Ghioldi, Rodolfo, 221
Gizenga, Antoine, 243
Goluchowski, Count, 30, 31
Gomulka, Wladyslaw, Premier, 334
Gorchakov, Aleksandr Mikhailovich, Prince, 21, 22
Gordon, Walter, 145
Gordon, William, 288
Goudsmit, Samuel, 64, 68, 69
Graham, Billy, 110
Grant, Ulysses S., 23
Great Barrier Reef, 155
Greece, 80-82, 84-86, 113, 114, 183
Greek Communists, 84, 86
Greek-Turkish Aid Act, 87

Greenland, 57, 62
Grey, Sir Edward, 183
Grivas, Colonel, 83
Group Areas Act, 246
Groves, General Leslie, 69
GRU (Military Intelligence, Soviet Russia), 108, 109
Guadalupe Hidalgo, Treaty of, 17
Guam, 26, 164
Guatemala, 108, 209, 220, 221, 229
guerillas, 220-23, 224, 228
Guevara, Ernesto "Ché," 221, 222, 227
Guizot, François, 16
Gulf of Tonkin Resolution, ix
Guyana, 111, 218
Guzmán, Jacobo Arbenz, 108, 209

Hahn, Otto, 68
Haig, Sir Douglas, 154
Haiti, 29
Hammurabi, xiv
Hanoi, 177, 178, 188, 189, 190
Harrison, Governor, 13
Hart, Liddel, 55
Havana, 222, 231
Hawaii, 24, 26, 148, 158, 164, 168, 192, 234
"Hawaiianization," 192-201
Hay, John, 26, 163
Hawley-Smoot Tariff Act, 43
Healy, Denis, 297
Heine, Heinrich, 332
Heisenberg, Werner, 64, 66, 67, 68, 69
Herriot, Edouard, 45, 260
Hindenburg, Field Marshal Paul von, 39
Hiroshima, 77
Hirsch, Martin, 276
Hispano-American War, 25
Hitler, Adolf, 41, 46-48, 50-55, 62-66, 71
Hitler-Stalin Pact, 272

Ho Chi Minh, 176, 178-80, 184, 187, 191
Hoa Hao, 186, 188, 190
Hokkaido, 77, 92
Hoover, Herbert, 47, 93
Hoover Commission, 106
House of Commons (Great Britain), 137, 138, 275, 286, 300
House Foreign Affairs Committee, 186
House of Representatives, 230
Houtermans, Fritz, 66, 67
Hukbong Magpapalaya sa Bayan, 200
Hughes, Prime Minister, 154
Hull, Cordell, 56, 78, 105, 169
Humphrey, Hubert, xvii, 131
Hungarian Revolution, 127, 129, 322, 334
Hussein, King, 134

IBM (International Business Machines), 301
Iceland, 57, 323
Ickes, Harold, 170
Immigration Act, 165
India, 6, 32, 81, 96, 115, 159, 258, 299
Indians, American, 6, 7, 11, 13, 15, 23
Indian Communist Party, 323, 326
Indian Ocean, 115, 159
Indian Union, 159
Indochina, 177, 185-87
Indonesia, 112, 135, 162, 171, 191, 194-95, 200
Institute of International Labor Research, 110
Inter-American Development Bank, 209
Interest Equalization Tax, 305
International Monetary Fund (IMF), 205, 304, 306, 307

International Transport Federation, 111
Ioannides, Ioannis, 86
Iran, 80, 81, 108, 120, 121, 135
Iraq, 125, 133, 134, 138
Islam, 325
Israel, 96, 113, 118, 120, 122-23, 127-29, 135, 162, 326
Italy, 39, 83, 87, 93, 111, 169, 223, 258, 271-72, 284, 330

Jackson, Andrew, 14-16
Jagan, Cheddi, 111
Jamaica, 159
Japan, 24-27, 51-52, 60-62, 69-72, 77, 81-83, 89-92, 97, 154-56, 162-77, 196-99, 205, 282
Japanese, American, 233
Japanese Diet, 165
Java, 171, 194
Jay, John, 9
Jefferson, Thomas, 7, 12, 13
Johnson, Daniel, 149
Johnson, Lyndon, ix, 94, 191, 220, 229, 288-90, 311
"Johnson Doctrine," xvii
Joint Chiefs of Staff, 90
Joint Defense Board, 57
Joliot-Curie, Frédéric, 64
Jordan, 133, 134
Joseph, Francis, 19

Kanagawa, Treaty of, 24
Kasavubu, Joseph, 243
Kassem, Abdel Karim, 134
Katanga, 243
Kautsky, Karl, xiii
Kennedy, John F., ix, 220, 232, 269, 277, 305, 313
Kennedy-Macmillan meeting, 267
Kennedy-Muñoz Doctrine, 232
Keynes, John Maynard, 47
Keyserling, Hermann, 37, 48

KGB (Soviet Interior Ministry), 108-09
Khmer-Chinese Friendship Association, 195
Khrushchev, Nikita, 220, 319
Kiesinger, Kurt Georg, 330, 331, 336
King, Admiral Ernest Joseph, 79
Knox, Henry, 99, 100
Korea, viii, ix, 90, 172
Korean War, 79, 81, 87, 89, 91, 92, 98, 100, 102, 172, 198, 214, 315
Kosygin, Aleksei, 220
Kuomintang, 90, 170, 177, 178

Laboulaye, Edouard, 21
Laos, 97, 175, 180, 190
Latin America, 58, 92, 97, 116, 182, 202-32, 256, 266, 269, 326
de Lattre, General, 68
Laue, Max von, 68
League of Nations, 41, 45, 50, 78, 251
Lebanon, vii, 125, 133, 134
Lee Kuan Yew, 194
Lend-Lease, 59, 79
Lenin, Vladimir Ilyich, 316, 326
Liberia, Republic of, 239
Liberman, Yevsei, 318, 335
Lie, Trygve, 72
Liliuokalani, Queen, 164
Lin Piao, 196, 255, 279
Lincoln, Abraham, 19, 21, 279
Lloyd, Selywn, 125, 130
Locarno Treaty, 51
Lodge, Henry Cabot, 24, 163
Lothian, Lord, 54, 169
Louisiana, 12, 13, 27, 140
Louisiana Purchase, 16
Ludenburg, Rudolf, 67
Ludendorff, Erich, 40
Lumumba, Patrice, 242-43, 326
Lung, Ch'ien, 18

"Lusitania," 35, 61
Luthuli, Albert, 247, 249

MacArthur, Douglas, 70, 72, 90, 91, 94, 100, 171
McCarthy, Joseph, 39, 105, 108
Machine Bull, 285
Maclay, William, 99
McCloy, John J., 104
McGhee, George C., 281
McKinley, William, 25-26
Macmillan, Harold, 128, 132, 134, 267, 268, 277
MacMurray, John V. A., 168-69
Mahan, Alfred Thayer, 24, 163
Malaya, 61, 69, 83, 115, 155, 194
Malaysia, 136, 159, 191, 194
Malthusian theory, 152-53, 155
Manchu Dynasty, 166
Manchuria, 51, 167
Manhattan Project, 67, 69
"Manifest Destiny," 16, 18, 24, 62, 166
Mansfield, Mike, 186
Mao Tse-tung, xiv, 176, 184, 187, 195, 196, 220, 225, 229, 322
Maritime Provinces, Canada, 141, 143, 147, 148
Marshall, George, 79, 86
Marshall Plan, 86-89, 97, 117, 261, 274, 278
Martí, José, 222
Marx, Karl, 20
Marxism-Leninism, xiii, 41, 82, 135, 183, 222-25, 316-26
Mateos, Adolfo Lopez, 212
Maximilian, Emperor, 21
Meiji Era, 163
Mein Kampf, 54
Mendès-France, Pierre, 187
Menzies, Prime Minister Robert Gordon, 126, 156
Metternich's Holy Alliance, 264
Mexican Americans, 233

Mexican Revolution, 212
Mexican War, 17, 161, 162
Mexico, 16-17, 19-22, 28, 183, 211-13, 216-17
MI 5 (British external Intelligence), 112
MI 6 (British counterespionage), 112
Micronesia, 92, 172, 192
Mid-Canada Warning Line, 144
Middle East, ix, 43, 118, 122, 125, 133, 154, 161, 247, 255, 328
Middle East Treaty Organization, 122
Midway Islands, 24, 70
Military Assistance Program, 98
Military Policy Committee, 67
Mobutu, President, 113, 243
Molotov, Vyacheslav Mikhailovich, 261
Monnet, Jean, 260
Monroe Doctrine, 23, 25, 28, 33, 36, 133, 161
Montreal, 11, 148, 149
Morgenthau, Henry, Jr., 59, 260
Moscoso, Teodoro, 232
Moscow Conference, 78
Mossadegh, Mohammed, 108, 120, 121, 122, 124
Mountbatten, Admiral Louis, 178
Mujica, Hector, 226
Muller, Hilgard, 248
Munich agreement, 155
Muñoz-Marín, Luis, 232
Murphy, Robert, 130
Muslim Brotherhood, 113
Mussolini, Benito, 224
Mutual Security Agency, 87
Myrdal, Gunnar, 238

Nagasaki, 77
Naguib, General, 127
Nahas Pasha, Mustafa, 122

Napoleon Bonaparte, 12, 14, 19, 213, 271, 275
Nasser, Gamal Abdel, 113, 122-28, 132, 134, 135
NASA (National Aeronautics & Space Administration), 292, 296
National Council of Churches, 110
National Security Act, 106, 107
National Socialist regime, 49, 50, 64, 66
Navy, American, 28, 97, 163, 164, 165
Nazism, 118, 217
Ne Win, Premier, 195
Negroes, African, 239, 245, 246, 249
Negroes, American, 158-59, 233-40, 249, 250
Negroes, French, 241
Nenni, Pietro, 330
New Deal, 53
New Democratic Party, 144
New England, 4, 8, 147
New Guinea, 153, 171
New Mexico, 15
New Orleans, 11, 12
New South Wales, 151, 152
New Zealand, 92, 97, 136, 151, 157, 158, 268, 294
Ngo Dinh Diem, 185, 186, 187, 188, 189
Ngo Dinh Nhu, 188, 189
Nixon, Richard, 129
Nkrumah, Kwame, 326
Nomura, Ambassador Yozo, 61
North American Defense Command (NORAD), 143
North Atlantic Confederation, 279, 336
North Atlantic Treaty Organization (NATO), 88, 89, 93, 97, 117, 259, 265-67, 274, 276, 277, 278, 323, 330, 336
North Korea, 91, 323

North Sea, 28, 34
North Vietnam, 177, 187-89, 323
Norway, 323
Nosavan, General Phoumi, 109
Novotny, Antonin, 335

October Revolution, 172, 196, 314, 320
Ogdensburg Agreement, 57
Okinawa, viii, 172, 197
Olney, Richard, 25
"Open Door" policy, 27
"Operation Rat Hole," 87
Opium War, 162
Ordag, Gustavo Díaz, 212
Ordinance of 1787, 10
Organization of American States (OAS), 87, 229-30
Organization of Latin American Solidarity (OLAS), 226
Osborne, John, 137
Osceola, 15
OSS, 106, 177
Ottawa, 142-45, 148-50
Ottoman Empire, 34, 40, 41, 161, 258
Ovamboland, South Africa, 252

Pacific, South, 70, 71
Pacific Fleet, 61
Pacific Ocean, 18, 24, 34, 51
Page, Walter Hines, 31, 37, 183
Pakistan, 81, 135, 142, 159
Palestine, 118-20
Palestine Mandate, 125
Palmerston, Lord, 18, 19, 20, 25
Panama, viii, 28, 205, 214, 221
Panama Canal, 161
Paraguay, 213, 221
Parkinson's Law, 100
Parks, Sir Henry, 153
Partido Nacional Revolucionario (PRI), 212
Partido Socialista Popular, 219
Paton, Alan, 247

Peace of Paris, 4, 10
Pearl Harbor, 27, 57-77, 94, 104-06, 155, 167, 170
Pearson, Lester, 144, 149
Penkovsky, Oleg, 109, 242, 332
Pentagon, 94, 100-03, 106, 150, 190, 216, 229, 238
Perón, Juan Domingo, 210, 217, 218
Perry, Commodore Matthew, 24, 163, 193
Pershing, General John J., 101
Persian Gulf, 80, 115, 118, 132, 136
Peru, 214, 220, 230
Peterson, Rudolph A., 308
Philippine Independence Act, 27
Philippines, 26, 27, 60, 70, 90, 92, 97, 164, 165, 191-94, 200
Plans Division, 107
Poland, 322, 327, 335
Polk, James, 16, 17, 18
Polynesia, 192
Pompidou, Georges, 279
Pope Pius XII, 264
Port Said, 131, 132
Portugal, 58, 72
Potsdam Conference, 119, 177
Pretoria Government, 251
"Proclamation Line," 6
Profumo scandal, 137
"Project Camelot," 150, 216
"Project Mallard," 294
Prussianism, 21, 36, 48, 49
Puerto Rico, 26, 193, 218, 231, 232, 234
Punic War, 46, 115
Punta del Este declaration, 209
Putiatin, Admiral, 163

Quebec, 12, 141, 142, 146-51, 158
Quebec Act, 7
Queensland, 153
Queuille, Henri, 262

Radical Labour movement, 153
Ramadier, Paul, 260
Le Rassemblement du Peuple Français, 265
Reciprocal Assistance, Treaty of, 87
Reiche, Professor, 67
Reichswehr, 48, 49
Remington Rand, 281
Republican party, 120
"R and D" (research and development), 291-92, 296
Reynaud, Paul, 53, 55, 260
Rhenish-Westphalian republic, 42
Rhineland, 41, 51-52, 67
Rhodesia, 244, 246, 248, 254
Richard, James F., 186
Rio Pact, 87
Robinson, Kenneth, 300
Roman Catholic Church, 55, 151, 203, 212, 228, 229, 264
Roman Empire, xiii, xv, 62, 337
Rome, Treaty of, 264
Romier, Lucien, 43-45
Roosevelt, Franklin D., ix, 28, 50, 51, 54-55, 66, 67, 69, 72-76, 80, 167-68, 187
Roosevelt, Theodore, 28, 29, 114, 163, 193, 314
Rootes Motors, 281, 287
Royal Air Force, British, 56, 143
Royal Commission on Bilingualism and Biculturalism, 149
Royal Navy, British, 28, 54, 56
Royal Proclamation, 6
Rueff, Jacques, 291
Rumania, 322, 323, 335
Rusk, Dean, 194
Russell, John, 1st Earl Russell, 20
Russia, xiii, 30, 66, 75, 79-88, 91, 94, 99-102, 109, 110, 122-23, 126-35, 161, 163, 165, 168, 219, 220, 242, 310-38
Russian Revolution, 326

Russo-American Condominium, 310-38
Ryukyu Islands, 90, 92, 172

Sachs, Alexander, 66
es-Said, Premier Nuri, 134
Saigon, 185, 186, 187, 188, 189, 190
Salisbury, Robert Arthur Talbot Gascoyne-Cecil, 3rd marquess of, 25
Salisbury, Rhodesia, 246
San Ildefonso, Treaty of, 12
Saninikone, Premier Phoui, 109
Santa Anna, 16
Santo Domingo, 12, 23, 29, 216
Saudi Arabia, 113, 125, 133
"Schuman Plan," 263
Schuman, Robert, 260, 263, 264
Scottish Nationalists, 138, 258
Second Reich, 33
Sedition Act, 38
Seeckt, General von, 48
Selective Service, 62
Senate of the United States, 22, 25, 104, 311
Senate Foreign Relations Committee, viii, ix, x, xvi, 3, 9, 93
Separatism, 142, 149, 150
Seward, William H., 20, 22
"Seward's Folly," 22
Sharpeville riot, 244
Siam, Gulf of, 175, 185
Siberia, 143, 197, 198, 199
Sihanouk, Prince Norodom, 195
Sik, Ota, 335
Singapore, 115, 132, 136, 155, 156, 191
Sinyavsky, Andrei, 320
Skybolt, 277
Smallwood, Joey, 147
Smelyakov, Nikolai N., 317
Solzhenetsyn, Alexander, 321
"Son of Heaven," xiv, 176

South Africa, Republic of, 234, 241, 245-54
South East Asia Treaty Organization (SEATO), 185
South Korea, 90, 91, 97, 189, 191, 197, 199, 200
South Vietnam, viii, 97, 111, 180, 181, 186-91, 194
Southeast Asia, 116, 136, 172, 184, 190-95, 266, 278, 328
South-West Africa, 253, 254
Spain, 5, 9-14, 18, 26, 111, 213, 222-24, 258
Spanish-American War, 161, 164, 193, 218
Spanish Civil War, 223, 224
SDR (special drawing right), 306, 307
Stalin, Joseph, 75, 76, 261, 317, 319, 324
Standard Fruit & Steamship Company, 208
Stanleyville, 243
State Department, U.S., 104-06, 108, 143, 216, 217
Stephens, Alexander, 279
Stimson, Henry L., 61, 63, 64, 106, 167, 169
Strauss, Franz-Josef, 293, 330
Subic Bay, 200
Sudetenland crisis, 52
Suez, 28, 117-38, 205, 255, 259, 267
Suez Crisis, 73, 120, 128, 136, 156, 315
Sukarno, 112
Sun Yat-sen, 166
Switzerland, 281
Syria, 113, 125, 133, 134, 135
Szilard, Leo, 64, 65, 69

Tactical Fire Detection System (Tacfire), 294

Tactical Operation System (TOS), 294

Taft, Senator Robert A., 87, 93, 94

Taft Administration, 208

Taiwan, 97, 191, 200, 205

Tashkent Agreement, 329

Task Force, 288

Taylor, Maxwell D., 188

Tecumseh's Indian confederacy, 13, 14

Teller, Edward, 64, 65

Teutonic Central Powers, 34

Thailand, viii, 97, 191, 194, 200

Third Reich, 46, 62, 64, 65, 66, 72, 316

Third Republic, 213, 271

Thomas, Norman, 110

Thompson, Dorothy, 316

Thutmose III, Pharaoh, xiv

Tibet, 115

Tito, Josip Broz, 86, 322

de Tocqueville, Alexis, 315, 337

Tojo, Hideki, 60

Tonkin Delta, 175, 178

Torres-Restrepo, Camilo, 229

Trading with the Enemy Act, 145, 287-88

Trafalgar Square, 137

Trans-Appalachian West, 12, 14

Tripartite Declaration, 120

Triple Alliance, 30

"Trizonia," 88

Truman, Harry S., ix, 69, 77, 80, 85, 87, 89, 91-93, 107-08, 112, 119-20, 216

Truman Doctrine, xvii, 85, 86, 89, 90

Tshombe, Moïse, 113

Turkey, 80, 85, 86

Twain, Mark, 26

"Two-Ocean Navy" bill, 63

Ugarteche, Manuel Prado y, 215

Union of South Africa, 251

Unione Anarchica Italiana, 224

Unione Sindacale Italiana, 224

United Arab Republic, 134, 135, 136, 162, 327

United Auto Workers, 111

United Empire Loyalists, 141

United Fruit Company, 208, 209

United Nations, 76, 78, 84, 91, 92, 119-20, 129, 131-32, 252-54

UN General Assembly, 129, 197, 251

UN Security Council, 91, 121, 129, 186, 251, 315

UN Special Fund, 298-99

United States Foreign Office, 121

Universal Military Training, 79

Universal Negro Improvement Association, 235

Universal Suez Maritime Company, 124

Uranium Society, German, 68

Utrecht, Treaty of, 4

Vafiades, Markos, 86

Varentsov, Marshal, 334

Venezuela, 205, 220-22, 226, 231, 232

Vergennes, Charles Gravier, Comte de, 9

Versailles Peace Conference, 155

Versailles, Treaty of, 41, 50, 52

Verwoerd, Hendrik Frensch, 244

Victoria, Queen, of England, 152

Vietminh, 176, 177, 178, 179, 180

Vietnam, 83, 94, 98, 174-76, 179, 180, 184, 186-89, 196, 265

Vietnam War, viii, x, 103, 156, 158, 174, 180, 186, 191-93, 198, 225, 237, 243, 278, 289, 311, 323, 327

Vishinsky, Andrei, 89

Voznesensky, Andrei, 321

Vorster, Prime Minister, South Africa, 246, 252

Wales, 138
Walker, Robert, 162
Wallace, Henry, 87
War Department, 68, 79
War of 1812, 140
War of Independence, *see* American Revolution
Warsaw Pact, 327
Weber, Max, 46
Webster, Daniel, 17
Weissberg, Alexander, 66
Weisskopf, Victor, 64, 65
Weizsacker, Carl Friedrich von, 68
Welles, Sumner, 46
Welsh nationalists, 258
West Indies, Danish, 23
West Indies, French, 58
Westinghouse Electric Corporation, 300
Wheeler, Earle G., 194
Wheeler, Raymond A., 132
White, William Allen, 163
"White Australia" policy, 151, 157
White Paper, 84, 119
Wigner, Eugene, 65
Wilhelm, Kaiser, 34, 36

Wilson, Charles, 103, 104
Wilson, Harold, 136, 269, 273, 300
Wilson, Woodrow, 29, 31, 37, 40, 41, 154, 166
World Bank, 123
World Court, 50
World Economic Conference, 50
World War I, 34, 38, 39, 52, 59-80, 100, 154, 155
World War II, ix, 63, 100, 105, 118, 155-56, 176, 187, 236-39, 260
World Zionist Organization, 118

Yalta Conference, 75, 76, 261
Yemen, 134
Young Plan, 47
Yugoslavia, 83, 84, 86, 114, 313, 323, 335
Yukon, 148

Zahedi, General, 121
Zen Buddhism, 199
Zimbabwe African Peoples Union of Rhodesia, 254
Zuckerman, Sir Solly, 301
Zulu, 246